BOB GIBSON:
I Come For To Sing

BOB GIBSON:
I Come For To Sing

The Stops Along the Way of a Folk Music Legend

BY
BOB GIBSON AND **CAROLE BENDER**

with help from his friends:
PETE SEEGER, JOAN BAEZ, SHEL SILVERSTEIN,
TOM PAXTON, PETER YARROW, NOEL PAUL STOOKEY,
GLENN YARBROUGH, HAMILTON CAMP, GORDON LIGHTFOOT,
ROGER MCGUINN, STUDS TERKEL, GEORGE CARLIN,
ED MCCURDY, JOSH WHITE JR., MICHAEL SMITH, BRYAN BOWERS
SUSAN GIBSON HARTNETT, MERIDIAN GREEN, JIM GIBSON, ROSE GARDEN
And Many More!

PREFACE BY
ALLAN SHAW

EPILOGUE BY
PETER YARROW

PELICAN PUBLISHING COMPANY
Gretna 2001

Copyright © 1999 Carole Bender and The Bob Gibson Trust

All rights reserved. No part of the book may be reproduced or transmitted in any form or by any means, electronic or mechanical, including internet, photocopying, recording, or by any information storage and retrieval system, without written permission from the author.

The author has made every effort to trace the ownership of all copyrighted material and to secure permission from the copyright holders. In the event of any question arising as to the use of any material, we will be pleased to make necessary corrections in future printings. Thanks and credit to all contributors, authors and publications quoted are given in the "Contibutors" section found on page xii.

The author also has made every effort to establish the source of the photos in this book. We will be glad to rectify any error or omission if we are notified of same.

Front cover photos from the Bob Gibson archives. Cover and book design by Carole Bender.

First Edition published September, 1999
by Kingston Korner, Inc./Folk Era Production, Inc., Naperville, Illinois

Revised Edition published July, 2001 by
Pelican Publishing Company, Gretna, Louisiana
Printed in U.S.A.

Library of Congress Cataloging-in-Publication Data

Gibson, Bob, vocalist.
    Bob Gibson : I come for to sing : the stops along the way of a folk music legend / by Bob Gibson and Carole Bender ; with help from his friends, Pete Seeger ... [et al.] ; preface by Allan Shaw ; epilogue by Peter Yarrow.—Rev. ed.
    p. cm.
    Originally published: 1st ed. Naperville, IL : Kingston Korner, c1999.
    Includes discography (p.) and index.
    ISBN 1-56554-908-2 (pbk. : alk. paper)
    1. Gibson, Bob, vocalist. 2. Singers—United States—Biography. I. Title: I come for to sing. II. Bender, Carole. III. Title.

ML420.G415 A3 2001
782.42162'13'0092—dc21
[B]

2001036331

TABLE OF CONTENTS

Preface by Allan Shaw v
Introduction vii
The Contributors xii

Chapter 1 - The Day I Began 1
Chapter 2 - Mommy Likes People Who Make Music 5
Chapter 3 - The Road to Chicago 20
Chapter 4 - The Short Happy Life of the Original
    Gate of Horn 32
Chapter 5 - The Magic of Albert Grossman
    and Gibson & Camp 53
Chapter 6 - The Glory Years 65
Chapter 7 - Bridge to Doom 72
Chapter 8 - "Demons" 89
Chapter 9 - Veiled Comeback 102
Chapter 10 - The Real Beginning 122
Chapter 11 - The Courtship of Carl Sandburg -
    My Theatrical Experience 136
Chapter 12 - Hobson's Choice and the Best of Friends 150
Chapter 13 - Uncle Bob 160
Chapter 14 - One More Time!
    Gibson & Camp at the Gate of Horn 174
Chapter 15 - The Women In My Life 180
Chapter 16 - At Loose Ends 184
Chapter 17 - Stops Along the Way 188
Chapter 18 - Makin' A Mess 200
Chapter 19 - The Illness 211
Chapter 20 - Bob Gibson - The Man 223
Chapter 21 - Farewell Party 238
Chapter 22 - Farewell to Bob 249
Chapter 23 - The Contribution of Bob Gibson 252
Chapter 24 - The Aspects of Genius 271
    Bob Gibson - The Songwriter 271
    Bob Gibson - The Musician 286
    Bob Gibson - The Entertainer 293

    Epilogue by Peter Yarrow 303

APPENDICES

1 - Notes from Pete Seeger's *How to Play the Banjo* 307
2 - The Peekskill Riots 308
3 - Discography 312
4 - Songwriting Manual 338
5 - The Courtship of Carl Sandburg 359
6 - The Chicago Club Scene 390

Index 407

Editor's notes on style: From Chapter one through 24, with the exception of Chapter 23 - The Contributions of Bob Gibson, the different type style is to identify the speakers. Anytime Bob is speaking, the type is in 10 point regular style using the full width of the copy body. When Carole Bender is speaking, it is 10 point italic using the same size margin as Bob's. When anyone else is speaking, it is 9 point non-italic with indented margins.

PREFACE

My memories of my high school years in the Chicago area are pretty dim for the most part, but not entirely. There was a Saturday evening, probably in 1957 or 1958, when a friend and I had dates with a couple of pretty neat chicks that we wanted to impress, so we made arrangements to go to a fairly new club in the city, the Gate of Horn, which was gaining a reputation as one of the hottest spots in town.

Arriving at the already packed club, we were seated along the wall, next to the swinging doors to the back room, where the teen-agers were usually seated and the waitresses were relieved if there was enough money among them to cover the soda tab, let alone leave a decent tip. But there was a pretty good eye-line to the stage, and from the moment the show began, the rest of the evening is but a blur. I remember my date complaining that I wasn't paying enough attention to her, and in retrospect she probably had a valid complaint. I can't even remember her name, let alone what she looked like, but I'll never forget the skinny young singer with the crew-cut and nothing between him and the audience except a long-neck five string banjo. I had discovered Bob Gibson!

It wasn't long after that I learned that Bob had a couple of albums out, and my now well-worn copy of *I Come For To Sing*, with its tattered cover with the $2.98 price tag from Rose Records, is a treasured momento. I was able to see Bob perform a couple of times after that, one of those occasions being a wonderful evening of Gibson & Camp at the Gate of Horn, with a then unknown Judy Collins opening for them. But it was probably close to ten years later that I first met Bob personally when I attended one of his song-writing classes at Chicago's Old Town School of Folk Music, and it would be a few years after that before I got to know him well and we would become good friends.

In the meantime, I started college at Colorado State University in the Fall of 1958, just as the Kingston Trio's recording of *Tom Dooley* was topping the charts. Before Christmas arrived I was learning to play the guitar and during spring break picked up a rudimentary five-string banjo. My talent being limited, progress was slow, but within a year I'd learned enough to be able to finagle free beers at off-campus get-togethers. A friend and I formed a duet, later to become a trio, and a major component of our repertoire was songs I'd learned from Bob Gibson records. But, despite his time in Aspen and his *Ski Songs* album, Bob was not well known on the Colorado State campus, nor among college students generally. That worked to my benefit though as I had a great source of songs (and arrangements) from my Bob Gibson albums and summers spent in Chicago. For awhile I even had some of my friends wondering how I came up with all that great material! Although I always credited Bob and his albums, it wasn't until the Kingston Trio, Limeliters, Chad Mitchell Trio and Peter, Paul & Mary started recording Bob's songs that I began to see some real appreciation of his talent among my friends.

It wasn't just in college that I learned Bob Gibson songs. Although my playing time has greatly diminished with each succeeding year, I recently surprised myself when I realized how many of the songs I'd learned in those subsequent years were Bob Gibson songs. Although I'd always acknowledged my appreciation of Bob and his songs, when I contemplated my repertoire in its entirety, I realized that Bob had meant a great deal more to me than I'd previously known. It was a sobering reminder of how much I miss him.

Over the years I also wrote about Bob. In 1979 I was asked to write a column on folk music for Goldmine Magazine. I called it *The Folk Scene* and, since I had stated my objective to be to write about some of the less well-known but important figures of the folk scene, it was obvious to me that my first column would be about Bob. In that article I described him as having had an influence far greater than the recognition of his name would indicate, and this book illustrates, far more comprehensively and eloquently than I ever could have, the extent to which that is a gross understatement.

I am proud, honored and humbled to have been able to contribute to this book. I am even more proud, honored and humbled to have had Bob Gibson as my friend and to know that he's fulfilling a promise he made to a lot of us — "I'm gonna tell God how you treat me one of these days, Hallelujah!"

Allan Shaw
Folk Era, Wind River Records
27 June, 1999

Introduction

The folk music that emerged in the '50s and '60s reflected social changes and amplified awareness; echoed political and private struggles and sang to our consciences. It had a kind of poetic introspection that drew people to it and then gave itself away to them. Somehow it became the badge of an era associated with many images.

If you talk to some of the people who came onto the scene in the '60s — Gordon Lightfoot, Peter, Paul & Mary — any of the names that we recognize — will all tell you, one of the biggest influences in their career is Bob Gibson — his guitar playing, the 12-string guitar and the banjo playing just was a model for many of the people who came up through the '60s.
(Introduction to a 1986 radio show at the Smithsonian featuring Bob Gibson and Tom Paxton, hosted by Dick Cerri)

In the very middle of the twentieth century there came a beginning; a post-war time of growing prosperity; a time of pride in being American. There was an eagerness to find and appreciate roots.

It was a time when America was trying to find its way, looking for its soul. During the decade of the fifties, while on the surface having the appearance of a Norman Rockwell painting, an undercurrent was rumbling, and we were never to be the same again. The war had changed many things. Many genies were released from their bottles, like the atomic bomb, and women in the workplace. Once the war was over, and the men came home, there were those who tried to shove those genies back into their bottles, but once out, it was impossible to put them away. Once needed to fill the jobs of men who had gone to war, women were being sent back into suburban wastelands, but that didn't last. Once the atomic bomb was used, there was an uneasiness that could not be relieved. The innocence of the American culture had been shattered, and there was no going back. In an instant the world realized the fragility of its very existence, and out of this grew a pall of fear, suspicion and ultimately isolation. Things that before had been blindly accepted, such as religious beliefs and authority, were for the first time being questioned. It was a climate that bred the era of the communist witchhunts of Senator McCarthy and the paralyzing fear of the "red menace."

People like Pete Seeger and the Weavers began to popularize a sound with a comfortable familiarity to it. They spawned an interest that would soon become the folk revival boom by the late fifties.

The blacklisting of the McCarthy era did its best to still the voices, but through the darkness came a young man with a banjo, performing folk songs with an enthusiasm no one had seen before. His name was Bob Gibson, and he carried a fire within his soul which had been ignited by Pete Seeger, prompting him to turn his back on a successful career in business. This fire drove him to travel the countryside, collecting the music of the American people as handed down in an oral tradition through generations; and tour the Caribbean to bring us calypso music. He was not only the bridge which allowed interest in folk music to survive until the explosion of the folk revival in the '60s, but was truly the catalyst for igniting that explosion.

Gibson was a true product of this era and was the first to bring this spirit publicly into his music. While folk music was his passion, at that time it was an art form that lacked the powerful voice he would give it. There were three main schools of folk music then: the academics, such as Carl Sandburg, Mary Olive Eddy and the Lomaxes who studied and preserved; the politicos, such as Woody Guthrie, to whom songs of struggle and workers' history were organizing tools; and the "hillbillies" who played music on the back porch. Folk music was not yet commercial entertainment. Because of Bob Gibson's passion and because he saw these changes in our society so clearly, he was able to create a blend in the music he found, condensing and modernizing lyrics, thereby creating new versions of songs that were pleasant to listen to and at the same time meaningful historically.

Between the beginning of Elvis and the introduction of the Beatles to America, folk music, especially on college campuses, became the voice of a generation and through this became a permanent part of American culture. Bob Gibson spoke to a generation that was dedicated to positive change — a caring, thinking, well-informed generation, and folk music came to symbolize this. It was a simple medium that required only a voice and a guitar or banjo and with that passed on great historic, editorial and prophetic expressions of life. Around this time Bob started writing songs that found lasting expression, writing for his and future generations. As he was so well accepted by performers of the time, they also used his research, his new approach to writing folk songs, new sound and presentation.

In 1957 Bob won on the Arthur Godfrey's Talent Scouts Show and then appeared regularly on the daily *Arthur Godfrey and His Friends*. He helped popularize coffee houses featuring folk music as entertainment in the Village in New York, performed at Carnegie Hall, and then established himself as a local legend in Chicago at the Gate of Horn.

Bob made a hit of the song *Marching to Pretoria* and co-wrote and made a lasting hit of the song *Abilene*. He introduced Hamilton Camp, Joan Baez and Judy Collins and inspired the careers of Glenn Yarbrough, Tom Paxton, Gordon Lightfoot, Roger McGuinn and countless others. Even the Beatles were inspired by listening to the album "Gibson & Camp at the Gate of Horn". His songs have been recorded by Peter, Paul & Mary, Simon & Garfunkel, the Smothers Brothers, Glenn Yarbrough, Tom Paxton, Roger McGuinn, the Byrds, Phil Ochs, Kingston Trio, Brothers Four, Limeliters, The Chad Mitchell Trio, Spinners, Henry Mancini, David Cassidy, John Denver, Judy Collins, Kinsfolk, and Womenfolk, just to name a few.

He brought something so new and fresh to the world of music and performing that his influence reached far beyond the time when he was at his peak. Performers grasped what Bob wrote at that time as well as what he had researched and rearranged. His gift of harmony had an enormous impact on all folk groups to follow. Even though his performing career dwindled because of his personal problems — his "demons" — others built on either what he created or what he researched. Many of those with whom he wrote songs moved on, building on his foundation. Even though he had periods of absence personally from the music scene, his influence lasted. There is almost no popular music being played today that is untouched by Bob Gibson in some way.

Yet this man who did so much to change the course of popular music is strangely overlooked in the history books and the memories of many of today's music lovers. While Bob Gibson fans and professional acquaintances have remained fiercely loyal, dedicated to him and his music, many others give only blank stares when his name comes up, or think he played baseball. How could it be that someone to whom we owe so much could be so little recognized?

In this book, Bob's story is finally told, wherever possible in his own words. For more details, Bob's friends have come together to share their reminiscences. Truly one can see the impact Bob had by the stellar array of friends eager to talk about him including Pete Seeger, Joan Baez, Peter Yarrow, Tom Paxton, Glenn Yarbrough, Hamilton Camp, Gordon Lightfoot, Roger McGuinn, Shel Silverstein and Studs Terkel, to mention just a few. As Gordon Lightfoot said, "Bob Gibson. You know, when I look back, it's him and it's Dylan — and that's about as far as it goes! Truly an amazing person."

As for my own personal involvement with Bob Gibson, I was a latecomer. When I was a young, idealistic folksinger myself, on the campus of Oklahoma State University in the early '70s, my idols were

Tom Paxton and Gordon Lightfoot. Little did I know then that all of their works and performances had their roots in the works and performances of Bob Gibson. Even Simon & Garfunkel owed their beginnings in part to Bob and Hamilton Camp with their hit of *You Can Tell the World,* which appeared on the first Simon & Garfunkel album. Eventually Tom Paxton, Gordon Lightfoot and many others sought me out to share their stories of *their* idol — the one who inspired them.

Once introduced to his music, I became obsessed. I wanted to hear all the Bob Gibson recordings, only to find they were mostly unavailable. I wanted to learn more about this man, only to find there was very little information in print about him other than tributes by fellow performers. Finally I wanted to find him so I could see him perform, only to find to my extreme dismay that he was no longer able to. Still unwilling to give up, I set out on a personal odyssey to meet this giant of folk music and offer to help him tell his story.

Charging ahead, setting shyness and personal doubts aside, I entered a fantasy world approaching an idol and saying, "I want to write your story." Preparing myself to hear, "Thanks, but there's someone else at work on it," I was amazed at his immediate and enthusiastic agreement on the telephone, and his comment, "This is really great of you to want to do this!" I was speechless. How could I *not* want to do this!

As my plane made its final descent into Portland for a series of interviews for this book, a sense of near panic engulfed me for the first time. Was I really up to this challenge? Would I let him down? Still I knew I couldn't live with myself if I didn't try.

His words of gratitude echoed in my mind until I finally found myself at the security check at his apartment where I would contact his son-in-law, Jeff. I went over the instructions in my mind. "Scroll through the screen until you find his name and it will give you his code to punch into the phone. It won't be in alphabetical order, but will start wherever the last person left off."

I started my search and there it was almost immediately — "B. Gibson." I froze. I walked around the courtyard and caught my breath. I wasn't ready for the reality to sink in that this wasn't a dream. It had been a fan's fantasy for so long, that I somehow thought at the end of my journey, I'd find out that it had been a dream. Bob Gibson wasn't really here. He wasn't that easy to reach.

I went back to the monitor. I started the scroll again. "B. Gibson."

There was no escaping it. I entered the numbers and Jeff came down to meet me. All the way up he was saying things like, "He's really out of it this morning. It's like he's taken his medication too early. It's almost like he's not there."

We got to the door and he paused with his hand on the doorknob and said, "You've got your work cut out for you!"

I took a deep breath and waited for the door to open, and there he was — Bob Gibson. In an instant that made decades vanish, I could see that despite Jeff's fears, somehow from deep within a body that was imprisoned by his illness, Bob had used all the strength he had to summon up the spirit that made him Bob Gibson. He looked over at me and smiled as if he was seeing a long lost friend, and at that moment all my doubts vanished. I will never forget that look as long as I live. I was welcomed so openly and without reservation that I could envision no obstacle to completing the project. All that mattered was getting his story told so that people would always know how important Bob Gibson was to folk music and popular music since the late 1950s.

The story of Bob Gibson is complex and not an easy one to tell. There are two distinct sides to the Gibson personality. There is the musical genius and there is the personal side. There is the energetic, enthusiastic young man who chose to set off with his banjo and share his love of music, countered by the performer who turned down virtually every opportunity to become one of folk music's biggest stars. There is the bright, sparkling, charming stage personality contrasted by the man, also known as the "biggest womanizer in folk music," who left a family in the shadows to grow up without him. There is the virtuoso banjo player and 12-string guitarist, countered by the man who sunk to the depths of drug addiction. In putting together the story of Bob Gibson, one is left with almost more questions than answers. His music survives to stir the soul. One day the personal life of Bob Gibson will be told as a fascinating story, perhaps a novel. There was a part of this man that made him great. This is the part of his personality I choose to talk about. Even those who experienced the lowest times with Bob seem to recognize that he was special in some way. The Bob Gibson I first came to know and the one to whom I longed to pay tribute is the one who gave the world a gift of his music. He left us all a wonderful gift. If he had a troubled personal life, it doesn't alter that gift. He presented us with ourselves in song. For that gift I choose to pay him homage.

I come before you with no claims of being the world's foremost authority on either Bob Gibson or folk music history. I come simply as someone who cared enough to assemble the parts of a story that longed to be told.

If you will listen, I'm sure you will hear America singing.

~Carole Bender

The Contributors

Assembling the story of Bob Gibson is a daunting effort three years in the making. The momentum began with Bob's enthusiastic participation to the extent he was able in the last months of his life the summer of 1996. Beyond that it is a story that exists in the memories of friends, fans, fellow performers and a few radio and print interviews. Without the collaborative participation of those who knew and loved Bob over the years it would not have been possible. Every contact I made led to at least one other source or valuable piece of information as yet uncovered. While there is the complication that in dealing with so many memories to relate the story inevitably there will be some conflicting testimonies, omissions or perhaps even errors, as Bob said, "That's folk music!" And so it is. This is a story of a man whose love for his music overcame all the other obstacles he had in his life, and it is a fitting tribute to that man that his story is told by those whose lives he touched in so many ways. In the end the measure of a man is the number of friends who rally behind him. They came from all walks of life, both famous and unknown, but with one thing in common — they saw and were touched by the greatness that existed in Bob Gibson. I owe them all my deepest thanks for helping to complete the picture.

Bob Allen - former Chicago resident who, as a college student taking a photography class in 1960, took pictures one night at the late great Gate of Horn.
Joan Baez - folk singing legend introduced by Bob Gibson in June, 1959 at the Gate of Horn and later that summer to a national audience at the first Newport Folk Festival. She graciously consented to allow use of excerpts from her autobiography *And A Voice to Sing With* (©1987, Summit Books, a division of Simon & Schuster, Inc.)
Jack Bender - longtime political cartoonist, currently the artist of the syndicated comic strip Alley Oop®, and fan of Bob Gibson since the time when, as a student at the Art Institute of Chicago, he saw him play at the Gate of Horn in the summer of 1956.
Bryan Bowers - autoharp virtuoso who became acquainted with Bob when he arrived in Chicago in the mid-'70s.
David Bragman - Bluegrass musician, recording engineer and neighbor of Bob's at his last residence in Chicago.
John E. Brown - musician and former owner of the club called the Centaur in the early days of the coffee houses and clubs in Chicago.
Hamilton Camp - musician, actor and half of the legendary Gibson and Camp duo, then known as Bob Camp.
George Carlin - internationally famous comedian who skyrocketed to stardom after making the rounds of clubs in Chicago during Bob's heyday.

Steve Clayberg - Tulsa writer who was influenced to pursue creative avenues of expression after a visit to his fifth grade class by a young Bob Gibson in 1956.
Anne Colahan - Bob's sister and the first born of the Gibson family. At Bob's farewell party in 1996, she joked with Jim that as a child she had always thought of her brothers as her punishment. Devoted to her brother, she generously donated the use of many priceless early photos.
Judy Collins - folksinging legend who was introduced to Chicago residents in 1960 on the stage of the Gate of Horn by Bob Gibson after he had heard her sing in Aspen.
Diane DeVry - the longest-lasting friendship of Bob's life. They met at the Off-Beat Room in 1955, and it was at her home that he stayed when he went for tests at the Mayo Clinic in Jacksonville in 1994.
Roger Ebert - movie critic of the Chicago Sun-Times and longtime fan of Bob Gibson.
Rose Garden - Bob's first wife who, despite the agony she endured in the dark days of raising three wonderful daughters alone while Bob struggled with his demons, said she was always Bob Gibson's biggest fan. She graciously offered a wonderful supply of family photos and much welcomed editorial help.
Jim Gibson - Bob's brother, the baby of the family, who in the early years got into the music business with Bob and Roy Silver to start a talent agency called New Concepts. Moving on to a career in the oil industry, he recently retired to Florida.
Lou Gottlieb - the "funny one" who played bass and formed the Limeliters in 1959.
Meridian Parsons Green - singer, songwriter and Bob's oldest daughter, born Barbara. Together with her husband, Gene Parsons, formerly of the Byrds, they run a business called StringBender which is both a string bending device for guitars, and a growing music publishing house. Her editorial help and encouragement on this project has been invaluable!
Emmylou Harris - primarily known as a country singer/songwriter, she actually got her start in the folk world influenced by Bob.
Susan Hartnett - Bob's second daughter, who cared for him the last few years of his life in Portland, Oregon, living just two blocks away. Without her generous help during my visit with Bob, this entire endeavor may never have gotten off the ground. Between her and her father I was able to return home with an unbelievable amount of research material, both written and audio.
Richie Havens - folksinger who got his start at the Greenwich Village coffee house scene in the early '60s and was propelled to stardom through his performance at Woodstock in 1969.
Ed Holstein and Fred Holstein - Chicago brothers, both folksingers and songwriters, who owned the club called Holstein's together in the '80s.
Rich Hudson - taught radio and television engineering and production at Columbia College when he met Bob in the late '80s and teamed up with him to write songs during the "Uncle Bob" period.
John Irons - musician and computer analyst who was a guitar student and friend of Bob's for nearly 25 years. He became Bob's manager for a brief time

when Bob recorded *Stops Along the Way* in 1991.
Rod Kennedy - folksinger and founder of the Kerrville Folk Festival in Kerrville, Texas—the longest continuously running folk festival in existence.
Bonnie Koloc - singer, songwriter and artist, Bonnie became a sensation at the Earl of Old Town in Chicago and was touched by Bob's performances.
Leslie Korshak - a fan of Bob's since age 14 in the Gate of Horn days, she went with him to Mendocino at the beginning of his illness.
Lennie Laks - Mendocino guitarist and long time friend of Bob's.
Antonia Lamb - Folksinger, songwriter, astrologer who had a lasting relationship with Bob which began with his giving her banjo lessions and her first good banjo.
Christine Lavin - folksinger and guitarist who came on the scene in the '80s, she is known for her humorous musical commentary on relationships.
Tom Lehrer - currently out of the music business, Lehrer was the original political satire musical performer, giving television's hit show *That Was the Week That Was* its distinctive style. He was on the same lineup during the summer of 1959 in Cape Cod when Bob and Albert Grossman first spotted Joan Baez.
Bruce Levene - Mendocino publisher who interviewed Bob extensively in the mid-'70s.
Gordon Lightfoot - Canadian folksinger and songwriter who owes his original inspiration and decision to turn to the twelve-string guitar to Bob Gibson's performances in Toronto in the early '60s.
Jo Mapes - Chicago folksinger.
George Matson - part-time folksinger/guitar player and close friend of Bob's from Chicago .
Ed McCurdy - folk music legend from the '50s. Currently in Nova Scotia, he is known for his racy and humorous renditions of traditional folk music.
Roger McGuinn - folk legend who as Jim McGuinn got his start as a young high school student exposed to folk music and the banjo by an appearance at his school by Bob Gibson. From that encounter came a career that included being the fourth member on banjo of the Chad Mitchell Trio and then moving on to rock with the formation of the Byrds in the '60s.
Rick Neely - part time folksinger/songwriter from Chicago (as he puts it, folk singing is a cherished avocation) and longtime friend of Bob's.
Odetta - world renowned folksinger.
Tom Paxton - one of the most enduring of the folksinger/songwriters who emerged in the early '60s. He is world renowned for his topical and funny songs.
Marty Peifer - credited on Bob's album *Uptown Saturday Night* for his "snaps".
Gamble Rogers - singer/songwriter and master storyteller from Florida. He died in 1991 in an attempt to save a drowning person.
Dave Samuelson - businessman, radio personality and folk concert promoter from Indiana who interviewed Bob in the early '70s.
Mick Scott - Chicago guitarist.
Shirley Sealy - former Denver Post writer who worked with Bob on *Ski Songs* and was a publicist in Bob's New Concepts booking agency.

Pete Seeger - the greatest folk icon ever produced, Pete Seeger is known as a man of, not only incredible musical gifts, but high ideals, who lives exactly what he preaches. It was a casual meeting with Pete that was responsible for Bob Gibson embarking on his folk music career.
Allan Shaw - Chicago record producer, founder of Folk Era Productions, who maintained a long professional and personal friendship with Bob.
Ian Shaw - son of Allan Shaw and partner in Folk Era.
Shel Silverstein - native Chicagoan and one of the true "Renaissance men" of our time. Shel is known for one reason or another by people from nearly every segment of the population. Getting his start in the late '50s in Chicago as a regular cartoonist for Playboy magazine, a job which he did to the end, he branched out when he met Gibson and Camp at the Gate of Horn in 1960 and began a songwriting collaboration with Bob which lasted until the end of Gibson's career. Shel tried his hand at everything, from more songwriting on his own and with others *(The Unicorn, A Boy Named Sue, Sylvia's Mother* and *The Cover of the Rolling Stone)*, to writing and illustrating a long list of enormously popular children's books *(The Giving Tree, A Light in the Attic, Where the Sidewalk Ends, Falling Up)*, and playwriting. He was Bob's best friend and favorite collaborator.
Michael Smith - Chicago-based songwriter of incredible depth and perception, best known for his song *The Dutchman* and for his score of the Steppenwolf Theater Company's Broadway production of *The Grapes of Wrath*. Spent ten years from '81 to '91 collaborating with and backing Bob.
Noel Paul Stookey - Paul of Peter Paul and Mary. He distinguished himself with his solo performance of his *Wedding Song* in 1970.
Studs Terkel - the Pulitzer prize winning, legendary, incomparable voice of Chicago on radio station WFMT. He was a fan of Bob Gibson's from the early days of the Gate of Horn, interviewed Bob many times on his radio show and wrote the liner notes for his album *Yes I See*.
Art Thieme - known as America's best loved troubadour and greatest punster of all time. He has traveled the country collecting stories and songs from hoboes, children and other musicians. Known for his outrageous stories and his generosity in sharing his music and talent with anyone who will listen.
Ian Tyson - half of the well-known folk duo Ian & Sylvia.
Dave Van Ronk - one of the original Greenwich Village folkies from the '50s who has continued to be an important influence in the world of folk music. He is known for his raw style and his incorporation of jazz, blues and jug-band elements into his music.
Rich Warren - WFMT radio personality who currently does the Midnight Special show and who produced two of Bob's albums.
Josh White Jr. - folksinger and son of the legendary Josh White. Beginning in the '40s and '50s touring and performing with his father, Josh White Jr. has carried on his father's style of music while adding his own flavor as well.
Glenn Yarbrough - folksinger who established himself early on in the Gate of Horn and went on to fame in the Limeliters. Known for his perfect tenor voice, he continued with an enduring solo career.

Holly Yarbrough - Glenn's daughter who, herself, has one of the most beautiful voices in folk music.

Peter Yarrow - Peter of Peter, Paul & Mary. Peter is also known as a devoted organizer of benefits and crusader for causes. He was a lifelong friend of Bob's and was there at the end to organize benefits to help in his medical expenses.

Thanks also go to the following writers and radio interviewers who have provided tremendous archives of information from which I was able to draw: Dick Cerri, Robert Cantwell and his book *When We Were Good - The Folk Revival;* Robert Shelton of the New York Times and his book *No Direction Home: The Life and Times of Bob Dylan* (New York: Beech Tree Books, 1986); William Ruhlman and his article titled *Peter, Paul & Mary: A Song to Sing All Over This Land* (in Goldmine #410, April 12, 1996); Chicago writer G. Gigi Gilmartin; Emily Friedman of *Come For To Sing* magazine, Chicago; Jonathan Abarbanel of the Chicago Express; Ed Kislaitis of the Illinois Entertainer; John Wasserman of the San Francisco Chronicle; Richard Harrington of the *Washington Post;* Nick Schmitz of the Daily Herald; Pete Oppel of the *Dallas Morning News;* Don McLeese of the Chicago Sun-Times; Tricia Fischetti of the Daily Suburban Trib; James E. Harvey of the Flint Journal; Kate O'Neill of the Lansing State Journal; Dave Nicolette of the Grand Rapids Press; Keith Warnack of the Michigan State News; Sharon Schlief of the Towne Crier; Edward Hayman of the Detroit News; Claudia R. Skutar; Garry Cooper of Chicago Singles; Vera Chatz of the Chicago Sun-Times; Bill Dalton; Richard Christiansen of the Chicago Tribune; Reader's Guide to Theatre; Jeff Mintz; Dave Hoekstra of the Chicago Sun-Times; Steve Romanoski; William Carlton of the Fort Wayne News-Sentinel; Julie Cameron of the Chicago Tribune; Howard Reich; Lynn Van Matre of the Chicago Tribune; Steve Aldrich - The All-Music Guide; Transformation; R. Joseph Gelarden of the Indianapolis Star; Jim Murray of Boston Seniority; Asylum Records; Jonathan Takiff of the Philadelphia Daily News; Steve Matteo of New Country; Mordecai J. Hines II of Country Star; Dan Bennet of North County Blade-Citizen; Bill Jarnigan of Times Daily - Alabama Beat; Lisa Grider of Easy Reader; Physician John Rumler; Lawrence Rand and Dan Kening of the Chicago Tribune; and Lawrence I. Golbe, MD.

Special thanks for their help and input go also to Judy Bell of TRO Publishing who gave permission for use of lyrics from the early days by Bob Gibson and Shel Silverstein; the Chicago Public Library; the Fort Wayne, Indiana Library; the Colin Naylor Local History Archives of the Field Library in Peekskill, NY; Marilyn Elie for permission to quote her writing of the Peekskill Riots; WTTW for the loan of a Soundstage video from their archives; Mary Travers; Ron Cohen; Ben Cohen and Michael Dresser for the reference material provided by their Bob Gibson discography located on Roger McGuinn's web page; Alan J. Goldberg who provided Bob's songwriting manual; Hank Knight; and, for their responses, the offices of Yoko Ono, Bill Cosby and Paul Simon.

For Bob,
who's singing
still...

Some come to dance,
Some come to play,
Some merely come
To pass time away,
Some come to laugh,
Their voices do ring,
But as for me,
I come for to sing.

Some folks enjoy me,
Others do not.
Some love to extoll
On what I ain't got.
But I don't mind,
It don't mean a thing.
I'll keep on comin',
Comin' to sing.

Some come to dance,
Some come to play,
Some merely come
To pass time away,
Some come to laugh,
Their voices do ring,
But as for me,
I come for to sing.
But as for me,
I come for to sing.

~ Bob Gibson
(©TRO Publishing)

1

THE DAY I BEGAN

I never got to know Pete Seeger well, but he had a profound influence on my life. It was 1953, and the day I met him was really the day I began.

I had been syndicating little articles written from around the world by my friend, Dick Miller. We had 40 newspapers on a list, and eight or nine would buy his columns every time at $15 apiece. That was a lot of money to us. We were rolling.

Dick was what was known in those days as "spiv", which came from an English expression. They lived by their wits, mostly in the Soho region. Later they became "beatniks". Prior to that they would have been "Bohemian". Anyway, Dick was an early "spiv", going to the Sorbonne on his GI bill. He wrote a great column about Big Bill Broonzy, the blues singer, whom he met in Paris. During the interview, Big Bill talked about Pete Seeger. So one of the first things Dick wanted to do when he got back to the United States was to meet this guy Seeger.

I had heard of Pete Seeger, especially because of the Peekskill Riots in August, 1949. That happened about seven miles outside of Peekskill on Hollow Brook Road. I was nearly 18 and the Gibson family was living in Tompkins Corners at the time, which wasn't far from there. A lot of people went up there to hear people like Pete Seeger and Paul Robeson — listen to the music and hear the political speakers and stuff. The locals, who were the people I lived around, started to picket this group of people. A lot of rock throwing began. It got real ugly. Maybe not by today's standards, but by the standards of those days, it was awful. A car would be overturned and the roads would back up. Actually, there was basically only one narrow road getting out, so then no one could get out. There they were, in the cars, being stoned and harassed and beaten up.

So with those memories in mind, we hitchhiked from New York up to Beacon, with our friend John Revis, who had a camera, to meet Pete Seeger. We didn't know what we were doing, but usually on most of our "things" there was a good deal of beer involved, so no day was a loss. If we didn't arrive at our destination, at least we had a good time.

We got to a little post office. A sweet lady there told us to find the mailbox and go up the hill. And so we trudged up this dirt road and came around a curve and there was a log cabin on a little knoll, overlooking the Hudson River — very small, very primitive.

I later learned that Pete had an obsession of building his own house with his own hands of materials from his own land. Pete had built this wonderful log house with just a few things. There were a few nails and some glass, but he even used the mud from the brook on his property for the caulking.

Now he was building a fieldstone addition to it and he was working on the chimney as we came up. He was up on this homemade, Mickey Mouse scaffolding, and when we announced ourselves, he said something about he had to go on the road in two days and couldn't take any time out to talk, much as he'd like to.

(At that time Pete wasn't performing much, except in union halls, in some schools and a few Quaker churches. It was the era of the UnAmerican Activities Committee, and he wasn't too popular then. There wasn't a commercial outfit that would have him, but he occasionally would appear for a group, like a union, that just didn't care. They loved the confrontation of it.)

But he "Tom Sawyered" us. He got us to help with the chimney. I think he said, "Would you hand me that rock?" We got to talking, and the next thing, we were making mortar. I knew a little bit about breaking rocks; I'd done a little bit of masonry in my youth.

Pretty soon, we were talking to Pete a mile a minute, and he was asking us a lot of questions. He's just a wonderful man. We had a great afternoon drinking some beer and building a chimney with a fascinating man, who began to tell Dick stories of Big Bill and Woody Guthrie and others, all of whom Dick was familiar with. I wasn't, but I wasn't bored, either, because Pete was warm and articulate and told a good story. I loved the stuff he was talking about.

From that same home in Beacon, New York, in August, 1996, Pete Seeger remembered Bob's visit on that fateful Saturday:

I remember him visiting my house when I was building it. I'm not sure, but I don't think I even had plumbing in it yet when he was there. I was just delighted to see his youth and energy being thrown into reaching people all around and I so envied him his ability to ski.

Around sundown, Toshi, Pete's wife, called us all to the other side of the cabin where they had a little rock patio and a view of the Hudson River north of the Bear Mountain Bridge. They call it the "Rhine of America". It is absolutely beautiful.

She had made us this wonderful wok full of mostly vegetables and rice. That was very special. Her father had grown most of it in a garden they had. They'd cut out some steps — terraces — so there was cultivation going down the side of the mountain.

After the meal, it was very quiet, very nice and very . . . kind of holy. I don't use that word lightly. Pete stepped inside the house, took this long necked banjo off the log wall and played it. He played *Leather Winged Bat* and some other songs. By the time the evening was over, I knew I was going to get a banjo.

I was already captivated by the whole setting and the man. But when he played the banjo, it blew me away. It changed my life. ***IT CHANGED MY LIFE!*** Here was a committed man. I knew that he lived the life he talked and sang about. He didn't just talk the talk. I really had that feeling. His songs are more than just the way he makes his living. They are part of his tools he's trying to build something with. He's really trying to change the world. He's a very passionate guy. I thought that was very noble and wonderful. Pete was different than a lot of guys. He never dazzled you with his footwork. I saw an incredibly charismatic man who was not only entertaining and interesting and vital and incredible and eccentric, but he also leaves you with the feeling, "Hey, you could do this too. Grab up your old banjo and pluck away!"

It was just simply an incredibly influential afternoon. Because of this incident I got exposed to the fact that there was a body of music that was folk music. Now I kind of was exposed to that before but I had no idea of what was out there. I'd heard a little Burl Ives and a little Marais and Miranda. I was brought up with that. That was good stuff — Rachmaninoff's 2nd, Beethoven's 5th, Marais and Miranda, Burl Ives and that completed your musical education. So I got a glimpse, just the barest glimmer that there was a lot of great and sophisticated music. As I said, he sang *Leather-Winged Bat* that afternoon. It was incredibly sophisticated. I don't even think it was traditional. I don't know where it came from, but you can't convince me that it's traditional. It's a really hip, hip song, but it sure is of the roots — in the milieu.

I loved the music that I heard. That was on a Saturday, and being totally compulsive, the very first opportunity I had, which was Monday when the hock shops were open, I took the money I had set aside for rent, and I got whatever records were available and I bought a banjo. My wife was appalled. I said, "We can always find somewhere to live, but I've got to get a banjo today." She never understood my compulsion. That first banjo I got was a big, heavy dog of a thing.

Pete Seeger in Beacon 1953

It had a huge, overly large drum head and a special kind of resonator ring inside. It was just fascinating. It was custom made and somebody had played it professionally. Good banjo, good banjo!

I had had ukeleles, and I had taken a few lessons on piano, trombone, violin, voice lessons. Music already was around in my life, but that banjo eluded me for awhile — for damn near a year. The only way to learn the banjo at that time was either from a banjo player or from this five- or six-page mimeographed thing by Pete Seeger called "How to Play the Banjo." *(See appendix)* For awhile I picked up the 10-string ukelele instead because I was having so much trouble with the banjo.

About a year later in the spring I went out to one of the few folk festivals in existence at that time. It was the American Folk Festival in Philadelphia, sponsored by the Saint Louis Post Dispatch. They'd bring people out of the Ozarks and out of sections of Missouri and they had a lot of ethnic groups and that was it. I mean, they had the REAL THING! The people then who were interested were not interested in the entertainment value or the music. The interest was in the literature — the American literature.

I went with this lady, Ann Grimes, who later became a fabulous collector, and her husband Jim, who was the head of the English Department at Ohio State in Columbus at the time. I brought my banjo and guitar and I even did a couple of songs on the guitar from the stage, but driving back was a long, long trip after a long, long day. Anyway, driving back, I just spent the entire trip strumming that banjo and reading that book and trying to figure it out. A few things began to come, so I had a couple of licks down and I started pickin' it.

It was shortly after that that I ran into Erik Darling and Frank Hamilton and they were all pickin'. We began to swap who knew what lick — you know — "How do you do that? How do you move your fingers?" It was all Pete Seeger - a lot of it with variations we'd individually evolved. Once I saw how you move your fingers and how Pete wrote about it, then the rest of the manual was easy. I went right through it.

I saw Pete perform 25 years later. That man does have the magic. I had the distinct feeling that if I hadn't dropped everything and taken up the banjo and become a performer at age 22, I would have been inspired even then, at age 47, to do the same thing. Only it's easier when you're 22.

This seemed like a radical departure for me. I mean, nothing in my childhood, my experiences growing up, had prepared me for what I was about to do.

Or had it?

(For more information about Pete Seeger's banjo instruction manual and the Peekskill Riots, including what Pete Seeger had to say, see the appendix.)

2

MOMMY LIKES PEOPLE WHO MAKE MUSIC

I was born Samuel Robert Gibson on November 16, 1931 in Brooklyn, New York. My parents, Sam and Annabelle, lived on Jane St. in the Village at the time. I think my mother was visiting her aunt, which is why I happened to be born in Brooklyn. There were three kids — me, my older sister Anne, and younger brother Jim.

My dad was from Boston. We go back on his side very directly to the first governor of Massachusetts. In Cambridge there is a Gibson Street and the old Gibson house is there. My mom's side is from Brooklyn, New York, and they came over when the potatoes gave out. Both parents were mostly Irish and maybe some other stuff, but they never left the islands. It was either Scottish, Irish or English.

At weddings and funerals there was always an event. You'd bring the families together and they ended up at war. Every time! You know, a few glasses of sherry, which was the accepted social thing to do, at a funeral particularly; you'd view the body, you'd sip some sherry and begin to talk about or commiserate, and of course it always ended up with, "Well, he never liked you anyway." And the war was on.

My family wasn't dysfunctional. After years of therapy, I've concluded that my parents were just as fucked up as anyone's were. We just didn't know what to call it then.

My dad was very musical and had a dear friend who was one of the big mucky mucks in Decca records. Just prior to getting married, my dad had the option of going to work for

Bob at just over a year - 1932

1947- Annabelle & Samuel Gibson - parents of Anne, Bob & Jim Gibson

1933

I COME FOR TO SING - 5

Arthur D. Little Co. in Boston in the early days of radio, with a 15-minute show. That was shortly after WWI, when Dad had gone over there and done his number. For whatever reasons, and I'm sure family pressure had a lot to do with it, he opted for the career as a chemical engineer. Working in that direction and as his lot improved, as he made more money, they moved out of the city; first to Tuckahoe, then to Yorktown Heights and eventually on up into Putnam County in a little town called Tompkins Corners. Through a series of houses, we moved further and further out with my father still working in the city all the time. So I was raised in an ex-urban community because it was pretty far out to be considered suburb. That was the world I was raised in — very middle class; all those kind of values.

Age 2 at Green Garden Apts., Greenwich Village

At Fire Island 1933

My childhood memories are spotty and scattered, but very vivid, and probably say more about me than I would care to admit.

My first memories were on Bella Vista Street in Tuckahoe, New York. It was a gorgeous corner lot with a lawn that sloped down to the street. I remember Richie Kessler was my best friend. My first memory was of sitting by our drop-leaf breakfast table and waiting for the toast to finish. The toaster was electric, the old kind of flip down side toaster. It had one heating element in the center of the toaster and two holders for the toast when it was done. It was very modern and hip, I thought, to own a toaster like that and only have to watch it to turn the sides so the toast wouldn't burn. Why I have that memory, I don't know, but that is a very, very early one. It's funny that my first recollection of my life had to do with food. I've been struggling with that issue for the

Bob at the tender age of 3

last few years and I'm sure that I picked up my fascination with food at an early age.

Bob's daughter, Susan Hartnett:
I think my dad had a hole that he never found a way to fill, and to the end of his life he kept trying to fill that hole. He was doing it in his last years by eating everything that he could put his hands on.

I have other early memories from the house on Lincoln Avenue where I spent a lot of time. The house was about a quarter of a mile from an old abandoned quarry. That quarry had a great fascination for me as a kid and of course just scared the shit out of my parents. But I remember that huge hole in the earth. Boy that was fascinating. There was a big fence around and everything. To me the height of thrill and danger would have been to get near the edge and look down in that sucker. Of course the fence was far enough back so that you could only look across the opening, but I saw it as just an opening to the middle of the world. That was wonderful to me.

Mom warned me repeatedly about going too close to the quarry. She once put me in a dog harness tied to the washer in the back yard because I had been running off. I remember the agony and frustration at being tied to the pipe in the back yard and not being able to unfasten the harness because the hooks were in the back.

I remember my dad and mom having a real doozy of a fight. Dad was a member of the War Mobilization Board and had to do some traveling. I think he'd either met someone or took his secretary with him on this trip—I don't remember— but it was some fight. I awoke during it and I remember Dad at the foot of the stairs shouting something at my mom, who stood at the top of the stairs hurling imprecations at him.

1938

I also vividly remember the fire truck I was given one Christmas by my mom and dad. I was ecstatic. I was the only kid in the block to own a pedal-driven fire truck. I was in ecstasy. That afternoon, Christmas day, I was at the window when I saw my Uncle Ed and Aunt Sadie drive up to the front of the house. Uncle Ed got out of their car, and what to my wondering eyes should appear, but another fire truck, just the same as the one I had received as a gift that morning. I was elated. I swelled with pride, for I was going to be the first kid on the block to own TWO fire trucks.

Then my dad dashed my hopes. He said, "Let's get the other one" (the one I'd been playing with all day) "down to the cellar and pretend you didn't receive it." I should have known something was up then, for not only did the other fire truck go down to the basement, but it never came up. I was appalled. Still am! Why did I have to get only one fire truck for Christmas? Don't Mom and Dad still owe me one Christmas gift for the truck I had to permanently move to the basement?

I remember living on Marbledale Road and trying to float to the earth from the top of the garage with my parachute which was an umbrella. Instead I knocked the wind out of my system and wasn't able to breathe. It was scary and awful, that not-being-able-to-breathe feeling.

I remember being taken to the orphanage when I had misbehaved again. My folks threatened to leave me there if I ever did *"it"* again. I don't even remember what *"it"* was, but I sure can remember the orphanage; stark, brick-made, with the gates locked — it was Sunday I recall — and a winding driveway up the hill to the front door. A right scary place that I didn't want to be left in. I don't think it had any effect at all on my behavior, though. It was just an empty P.R. scam to "teach me a lesson".

I remember living on Baptist Church Road in Yorktown Heights, New York and playing with a lighter I'd purloined from somewhere and setting a tent on fire. Fire trucks and firemen came to put it out. The tent was a total loss by then. I was terrified they'd find out who the miscreant was. My dad pronounced that the cause of the fire was "spontaneous combustion", a phrase I cherish to this day.

I remember the afternoon that we had seen *Wizard of Oz* and going immediately after the Saturday matinee to Dr. Bishop's office and then to the hospital. Rheumatic fever! I was 10. It was a devastating thing. It was pre-penicillin. It was tough stuff, you know, and very scary. They didn't know much what to do about it but bed rest. It was an internalized stomach infection, and they didn't know how to deal with that stuff. Interestingly enough, my dad's friend was very involved in the making of penicillin, one of the two wonder drugs that came out of the second world war, the other, of course, being amphetamine.

For a long time I was real sick with rheumatic fever and you were very restricted with that in those days. There were a lot of things you couldn't do, so your mother would be in a position to have to say "no" all the time. There were a lot of "no"s coming down. I ended up feeling really deprived and resentful, and I was an angry kid. I got pissed off and stayed that way for a number of years.

I never felt very bad. So much for Dr. Bishop, my folks or the nurses trying to keep me in bed. I did enjoy the months I spent in the hospital. Dad would bring me comic books and some toy cannons that had springs in the barrel. I loved to shoot broken-off kitchen matches at my folks or the long-suffering nurses. It was my only display of anger. Was I stifled even then?

1941 L-R: Bob, Anne & Jim Gibson - One of a series of photographs taken for a story that appeared in Woman's Day *magazine in 1941. (The dog was called Tony and was Bob's dog)*

Then I was home in the house where I recuperated. I read and read. By the time I was permitted back in school, about a year later, I had read all the adult books that were available to me, the entire *Hornblower* series, a lot of Hemingway, etc. I never had to read another book; just write reports on the ones I had read.

I went to Peekskill Academy for another year, just attending in the mornings. I was always "out of the mainstream" — a real oddball. I mean, boy, I had missed it all. I didn't know how to do the basics. I didn't know how to play baseball. I didn't know how to run. I didn't know how to curse. You have to know that shit when you're 11, 12 years old, so I was the butt of a lot of bullying. Of course the bottom line was I couldn't take gym. I couldn't do a lot of things. I couldn't go out at recesses. I was never permitted to run and jump like the other kids, just to practice my skills manipulating adults and writing book reports for the teachers' favor. I really became a hostile and angry kid.

I didn't get along with my father for years. I didn't know him. He devoted a lot of time to being on that train. Two hours going and two hours coming out, which meant that a great deal of our life was his getting up before us kids getting up to go to school, and we went to school 15 miles from where we lived, so we got up pretty early. During most of the winter months he'd get home well after dark. We just didn't know him real well. Weekends were usually devoted to his passion. He loved building stuff and carpentry, and we were always in old houses that my mom and dad were remaking. The last one we did had no plumbing, or electricity when they started. He did it from the ground up. It was wonderful. A lot of the weekend was spent either with my brother and me having to help dad, or he'd take out his belt and hand out the retribution for whatever we'd done during the week. So even the weekends weren't too hot.

He finally developed high blood pressure and took a year off from work just prior to when he died, and he was home all the time. I got to know him really well in that year, and that was pretty neat. It took us a while to do our dance, but we finally got it together, and it was really nice. I was very pissed off when he died. I mean I really resented that. Still do. I just got to know him and then he took off. I mean it was like he was always taking off. So that was another resentment to an already resentful kid.

I was never very close to my mother. Actually I was very distant from my mother. She was a weird woman. She was an alcoholic. She was only impressed with what I'd do when I was on the Arthur Godfrey Show.

Bob's daughter Susan talked about his mother:
I think to this very day he's seeking the approval and love from his mother that he didn't get. I don't know that grandmother at all. I think the last time I saw her I was 11 years old. I never saw her again after that, and she's dead now. Both of my sisters had actually seen her within five or 10 years of her death, which was in about 1990. I could have sought her out if I'd wanted to, but I frankly didn't have any real desire to.

She was a martini-drinking, under-control alcoholic for as far back as I remember. When she came to visit us in upstate New York the last time I saw her, she brought martini-making paraphernalia with her. I remember my dad describing that she wouldn't let herself drink before 4 or 5 o'clock, but the last hour before that she was real fidgety.

When my grandmother died and my dad went through some of her stuff that was for him from her, what I found real interesting was that he sent me an envelope of pictures that apparently she had of us. I think he sent some to Meridian and to Pati as well, and he said in his letter to me that he kept some because he could tell from the fact that my grandmother had pictures of us, that she had loved us, and that he wanted to keep pictures of us because he loved us, too.

Up until the time Dad moved into my house in 1993, I had not talked to him for five years. The few communications that we had in those five years were very strange. One of them was this package of pictures that he had sent when his mother died, and I just felt like, "you haven't talked to me in five years, and you're going to tell me that some crumpled black & white picture of me as a child tells me that you love me?" It's like that has very little to do with who I am right now. To me he was repeating his mother's behavior. He indicated that his mother loved him and us because she had pictures of us as children, and that this was a meaningful way of showing love. He was always so critical of how she had shown her love and yet he did the same thing himself.

    Music had always been a big deal to me. When I was in school, I had no particular idea of becoming a performer or desire to sing songs. I didn't think in those terms, but I was involved in everything musical in school, mostly choruses — mixed chorus, a cappella chorus, men's chorus — and also marching band. I was in one of those schools that had a lot of vocal stuff to do. I was lucky, but I wasn't satisfied with just what the school had to offer. I formed an octet and we sang at different businessmen's luncheons and civic stuff. I knew I would rather do chorus than football. I took a little violin, and when I was a kid I took piano. I never could get past them wanting me to learn technique, though. They wanted me to learn the basics and I wanted to play. So on the piano it was easier for me to pick out a couple of tunes by ear and I'd sit there and play them endlessly rather than practice. There was that obstacle between me and being able to make music that was too severe. But that's okay. It really worked out well, because I know a lot of people who really can read music well and play a lot of stuff, but they really can't play in the sense of "play" with their soul, and that's too bad.

    I mentioned earlier that my dad had the option to be a professional singer. He had a radio show offered. How serious or how big a decision it was, I don't know, but in later life it was one of those things that you heard about, "Oh, your dad had the option..." You know, that was real important.

    It was pretty standard, at parties at the Gibson house, that after enough martinis, they would begin to encourage Sam "Gibby" Gibson to play the piano and sing songs like *Mother MacRee* in his truly beautiful high, lilting Irish tenor.

    I know that I got a clear message early, "Mommy likes people who make music. You get mommy's attention. You get mommy's strokes. You get everyone's strokes." There was always music around.

    I've talked to a number of performers at some time in their lives. They all got a clear message, "Mommy likes people who make music. If you want Mommy to like you, make music!" An extension of that is that EVERYONE likes people who make music, but there is a real "mommy" connection there.

    I got into community theatre productions of things like *Down in the Valley,* where I sang the lead. I got very exposed to all of that kind of folk music without ever realizing that there was a whole other world of it out there beyond that. I thought, "That's cute," but it didn't touch me.

I grew up at the edge of ex-urbia and it was a two-hour commute in those days into the city. They sent me down to a parochial school in the city. I commuted every day with my dad, the idea being that I was deemed incorrigible by the school board, and they figured a year at the Irish-Christian Brothers would straighten me out. I went to school for a year in the city, and it was crazy. I learned that when you lived that far out, they didn't bother to call and find out where you were if you didn't show up. I'd get off the train at 125th Street, and I was supposed to take a subway up to the Bronx to this Catholic high school, and I'd get on the express right down to Times Square where 42nd Street was nothing but movies. The movies went on day and night. I loved it there. It was wonderful. That's probably the source of most of my education. I realized that everything that I've come to know about all of it — American history, relationships — all the fundamental things in life, I learned at the movies! At the end of the year I had set some sort of a record for cutting school. I mean it wasn't even a question of truancy. It was a question of not being there for weeks on end. I really had it covered. I would just lay in, not excuses of a day

Bob & brother Jim Gibson on Confirmation Day

BOB GIBSON - 12

sick, but long bouts of illness and stuff.

The upshot of that was, of course, that I was totally divorced from Catholicism, the religion that I was raised with. That was it. Having come from a fairly small town, the only thing was catechism training and inferences that you get when you're around your family, going to church, the higher holidays and stuff. From that I went to classes in religion which were just graduated catechism, a lot of stuff by rote and a lot of really hard-to-swallow stuff to deal with as a kid. Pragmatism of a kid, reality. You know, they wanted me to get into all this mystical stuff. Well, okay, but help me a little, and they couldn't and they wouldn't, and to ask was to challenge, and to challenge was to put them in a defensive posture. It just didn't work. I'm amazed at that, at how much I'm still drawn to trying to solve all those, not the questions, but to solve that whole. I think the things that are unresolved in our past, we still set ourselves up to try to go back and resolve, at least I know I do. One of the unresolved things for me was the fact that I was not a religious kid, but I was sure accepting because that's what I was raised with, but I wanted to know more. I had the access to know more. These guys wore funny clothes and they dedicated their lives to know about this shit, and yet they wouldn't tell me. On top of that I was pissed off going in, anyway. I mean, I did not like any authority figure. So they not only were preaching the gospel of Christ, but they also had relay sticks from the track team which they would whack you on the ass with. "Hey, wait a minute! Just a minute! What's going on here?" I thought. I got mixed messages. "You preach the gospel of Christ and you're gonna hit me? You're gonna hit me if I ask about the gospel of peace and love??? What's all that about?"

The first song I ever wrote was an anti-Catholic diatribe. I was a real young kid. It was about a thing that they have in the Catholic Church called plenary indulgences, which are ways in which you can do novenas and certain ritualistic prayer and religious things now and gain yourself green stamps so you'll pass through purgatory. Purgatory is an intermediary stage between this world and heaven. You can't get straight to heaven no matter how good you are. You have to go through purgatory and burn awhile. Isn't that wonderful? Who created this shit? Plenary indulgences got you through the most corrupt thing and then, of course, they would pass out plenary indulgences if you gave extra contributions to the missions in Africa or wherever they asked you for. Even as a kid I knew it was corrupt when

Prom, 1947

PHOTO COURTESY ANNE COLAHAN

I COME FOR TO SING - 13

I saw it, or it seemed that way to me. I guess the Brothers were doing the best they knew how to. They not only were supposed to have the answers to the mystery, but they had all these rotten kids to get to. It was a hard life for everyone.

I had a mentor at that time, a guy named Don Rock, who was the organist at the Catholic church. I also sang there. We had a very, very involved big congregation there. People came from miles around to go to that church. We had, among other things, one chorus that was made up of boy sopranos, boy altos and men singing bass for high mass and high holidays. It was fabulous. Fabulous music. Don was a very far out kind of guy. He was definitely a Bohemian. He had us do beautiful masses far above what normal church choirs would take on. But Rock was inspirational and had tremendous enthusiasm and would just come in and say we would do it, and we would. I loved Don. I really did. He was a wonderful guy. He would do things like, during the consecration at high mass, when the organist is basically called upon to do sort of church-like doodlings on the organ in the background, he'd slip in themes like *Heart and Soul* and just crack me up. If he'd do it in a minor key, the priest wouldn't turn around from the altar and glare. This kind of stuff really appealed to him.

I pretty much lost any interest in religion per se, but now I was involved with the Guardian Catholic Church, because they had a real good music program.

Since I was so hostile and angry as a kid, I guess I really have a lot to be grateful for that I didn't get any more messed up. There were times there when for whatever reasons — lack of the occasion, lack of courage or something — I could have gotten in trouble. I could have really gotten in trouble. The idea of being destructive, being vandalistic, of being wantonly destructive was appealing to me. I did enough kid vandalism. I remember there was a time after I'd left home, I was trucking around New York a lot, and I was running in some seamy circles. I was fascinated by people who were street hip; fascinated by street cunning. I always had been. There was a time when I was 17, I was running around carrying a gun regularly, which shows you a certain amount of hostility and paranoia. I was travelling in rough circles, and I was doing some stuff that could have gotten me in trouble. I could have gotten in trouble with the bad guys, but I always felt totally inadequate around them. They could have beaten me up and really hurt me. I never considered myself street wise.

Nobody messed with me, though. I think they probably thought I was a crazy little bastard. For whatever reasons, I mean, I'm sure that if a guy's walking around as crazy and mixed up as I was, I think a lot of people pick that up, you know, and think, "That guy's nuts!" And they just stayed away from me.

That was an interesting period of my life, which I've never really come to terms with or dealt with, but it's exciting. A lot of adrenaline.

From the time I was 11 or 12 I had a hard time just hanging in there and relating. I chose to have a hard time with it and I didn't get a handle on how to do any of it, so eventually I ran away from home. A good deal of the problem was my inability to relate effectively, to my parents, to the school, to the whole thing. I was very uncomfortable within myself. I didn't recognize it as such. I was looking for the reasons outside of me that were the cause of the bad feelings inside of me and a change of scene seemed called for.

I took as much school as I had to and I left during my senior year twice. I was well into the year when I said, "That's it!" I packed it in and took off. It was too hard for me to deal with being who I was, or figure out what that was all about. The idea of learning a bunch of academic stuff was very unimportant. I was really good at history, and English was okay, but sciences and math courses were terrible to deal with.

When I took off the first time, I guess I left for a lot of general reasons. There was a great feeling of being misunderstood at home. It was not easy for me and my parents.

It was also creative adventure. Don Rock was going out to the University of Colorado to teach. I thought that was great, and I said, "I want to ride out with you." He said, "Sure," knowing full well what the implication was — leaving home and everything. So I did, and we set off in an old Dodge and drove out. I didn't tell my parents I was leaving. I just ran away from home, which was part of the deal. I think I had to punish them, but I got in touch with them in short order and let them know that I was okay. That was part of it, too. You have to let them know that you're able to exist very well without them, thank you. I don't have too many real answers. Mostly I can tell you what happened, but I can't really tell you a lot of stuff about the whys.

My first trip was out to Denver and Colorado Springs. I got out to Colorado and did some auditioning at the music school, and I found I lacked a lot. I lacked my last year high school credits, but they still were willing to work up a deal with me. They'd give me a scholarship deal, but I'd have to finish my high school credits pretty soon. Not first, but pretty soon. They really wanted me. I was a good musician. I sang well, and I was a boon to any chorus because I sang in first tenor well enough to help, and that was a hard one to crack. All the guys' voices were changing, and to have anybody who could hit the notes and read, somehow seemed to be rare everywhere I was. My voice hadn't changed, but it had done whatever it was going to do and remained pretty much the same.

As soon as I got past that initial, "Let me in your music school", though, I realized what was really involved. I had to major in piano — piano again! That was the basic, and everything was related to that. All those hours of practice! I had already passed on that, so then I decided I had to go back and try to finish school back home.

I went back, got back in senior class again and tried that for four or five months, I guess, and that's all. That time I took off again and went out to California, Arizona, New Mexico, Oklahoma . . . . this time alone.

I started hitchhiking all around the country. You could really travel and kind of bum around in a sense in those days. You'd pick up enough odd jobs now and then and you'd stay at the Salvation Army, and of course you got to meet all those wonderful people who pick up hitchhikers. You'd get all these great hitchhiking stories. It was wonderful. There was a lot to absorb, a lot to see, just seeing the country. The immensity of it. We all know it's a big country, but every time I drive across, wow . . . I forget how big it is and how many textures there are to it.

There were always jobs and stuff to do, but there was no success in the jobs like that. I didn't do any of them very well, but that was what you did.

I was a lobster fisherman for a while up in Maine. I had a lobster license and spent a summer doing that.

I worked with a guy on his truck for awhile. I'd help him unload or load and stuff like that in return for rides or money or whatever. Get a guy with a load of melons and, boy, all he wanted was a young strong back to load melons.

At work in Maine, August, 1949

I had a job in Santa Fe, New Mexico as a short order cook, that only lasted two weeks because I never remembered to put water in the chili. The guy was a fanatic about his chili making. You'd cut it up in big frozen chunks, throw it in the steam table thing and you had to keep putting water in it. Every time anybody would order chili when I was working, it would look like the desert. It was all full of cracks, because I had forgotten to put water in the chili. I did everything else well, but I didn't put water in the chili. So finally he fired me one day. That was it! He looked in it, and it looked like the desert. It looked like sun-baked clay — you know clay with all these cracks in it. It really looked terrible, and you couldn't really offer that to people — not in a restaurant, and if you tried to put the water in and stir it up real quick, they'd catch you, and they'd pass on the chili.

I can remember going down to the packing houses at Phoenix. I'd heard about this great job packing lettuce, and you got something incredible, like 10¢ for a case of lettuce, for every case you packed! They were these flat lettuce cases, and a case held, I don't know, probably a dozen heads of lettuce or something.

I thought, "Jesus, you stuff a dozen heads in there and you nail them shut and you get 10¢!"

It was a ways to get to this place and wait and all, and you had to do quite a number to get a job of that kind. The guy asked me if I'd ever packed lettuce? And of course, I had to say "Yeah," you know. Of course I'd packed lettuce! I'd eaten lettuce, I'd seen lettuce . . . but I had not, in truth, packed lettuce.

Well, then I learned why you got 10¢ a crate. I mean, it's not that good a job, because the things come from the field, and they're the size of medicine balls, and they've got a whole bunch of leaves on the outside that are real shaggy looking, and you have to cut them off. Then there's a root that's got the consistency of plastic. I mean, it's really tough. You wear a specially curved knife thing on your palm. You strap it across your hand, and it sticks out of your thumb like a rooster's hook there. You have to tear off the leaves, cut off that root, and you have to make the head a certain size, and pack them all into the case, and then you pick up your hammer, without getting your blade stuck in it, and don't forget the blade or you'll cut your leg off, and then you hammer these little nails in.

The guys who come across the border and do this line of work were awfully good at it, and it was beautiful to watch. It was a ballet with them. They could make a dollar an hour. The guy in charge let me fumble around for an hour there, laughing all the time. I guess at the end of an hour I got two crates done, and they weren't done right, at that. He gave me enough for a cup of coffee and sent me on my way.

There were a lot of experiences like that. They were really good years, between the end of the World War II and 1950 or so. There was a certain openness about them. Maybe it was because we were that age.

When I came back from the time I spent hitchhiking, I had to make some decisions based on the draft. That was a big consideration. There was a deal where if you got into the Merchant Marine and you sailed out for six years on merchant duty, you didn't have to go in the Army. I thought that made a lot of sense, because I had the instinct then — and I know I was right — that I would not do well in the Army. It was a real definite conviction on my part that, at all costs, I had to stay out of the Army because I would have ended up in some kind of trouble. I know that. I was just too messed up in my life to deal with that kind of authority!

So I sailed out for about eight months on Merchant Marine duty. The proviso was that you couldn't spend more than 30 consecutive days on the beach. You had to keep sailing. You could spend 28 days on the beach and then sail for a quick coast-wise trip for two weeks and spend 28 more on the beach, but you couldn't spend 30 consecutive days on the beach. I got a variance the first 30 days I spent on the beach because I kept going into New Orleans on the coast-wise tankers and kept forgetting to get back on the ship. By the time I got back to New York and lined up another ship, it wasn't just overnight. It would take a couple of weeks, and that would be more than 30 days. The second time I did that, I got my final draft notice. I went up and found out I was 4-F. Of course, there had always been that possibility because of the heart murmur from the rheumatic fever and all, but I was so desperate to stay out of the Army that I didn't want to take any chances on anything or even getting restricted duty, because they were handing them out then.

After all that I quit sailing out. By that time I was involved with Rose, the lady I eventually married. We got married and I got a job in New York. I worked in a photostat division. I don't remember the name of the outfit, but they did a lot of atomic energy stuff and I had to get all kinds of clearance. That was interesting that I got clearance, because I wasn't sure I could. I'd been real involved with American Youth for Democracy in 1948, (actual-

1952 wedding picture L-R: Jim, Bob & Rose Gibson, unidentified friend

PHOTO COURTESY JIM GIBSON

BOB GIBSON - 18

ly, to tell the truth, I went there to be with this girl I was interested in at the time), and they were very, very liberal. AYD was the direct offshoot of the Young Communist League which was Young Progressives for Henry Wallace.

I only worked there a few months, and then I met two guys who had the concept for a business built around teaching speed reading. One had worked with the guy who developed all these perception training techniques and stuff, so he knew what he was talking about. It was a whole new thing — speed reading. We packaged it for business and sold it to a lot of companies. The one who knew about speed reading was the training director. The other one knew how to run a business and motivate people. I knew how to sell. I mean, I didn't know how to sell, but they said, "We need somebody to sell," so I said, "Sure, me, man." So in that way I became a partner in the firm and sold a lot of speed reading for a couple of years. It was very successful. I did all the public relations for the firms. It was a tremendous education those two years.

That was my first taste of stardom, too. I was a young punk — 21 years old — with my little gray flannel suit. Wailing — I was wailing! I got written up in a lot of stuff because I was selling a lot of speed reading. I was bringing in one hundred, two hundred thousand dollar contracts. It was a really unheard of service.

From the book When We Were Good - The Folk Revival *by Robert Cantwell:*
>...to anyone familiar with the history of the folksong movement, even more incongruous — was the appearance of Bob Gibson, introduced in the program notes [of the 1959 Newport Folk Festival] as follows: "A phenomenally successful New York businessman at the precocious age of 22 (his brilliant innovations in the management consulting field were acclaimed by the August *Harvard Business Review*)..."

Even with all this, though, I didn't have any well-directed ambitions when I was a young man. Not many folks I knew did. When I was asked, "Well, what do you want to do?" I didn't know.

And that was when I met Pete Seeger, and my life changed for good.

Bob on right with his brother Jim and sister Anne Colahan, circa 1991

PHOTO COURTESY JIM GIBSON

3

THE ROAD TO CHICAGO

After I met Pete, I spent a few months still working for the reading laboratory, but more and more taking longer and longer periods of time off studying folk music - long weekends and eventually four or five days at a time, until finally, the owners were concerned because, I mean, I sold the friggin' program and there was no cash flow of business happening down the line if I wasn't out there doing my work. So they said, "How about tightening up?" I said, "Well, I really want to do it the other way — I really want to take more time off. How about if — well, I'm just going to take off — let me out of here."

So, it was decided I would take a leave of absence, because they really wanted me to come back. As a matter of fact, they wanted me to not just take a leave of absence, but, while traveling around the country, making a few stops in a few cities, I should try to sell reading training — which I never did. The hats were too different. I didn't want to do that. I was more interested in the folk music thing, so I just finally took off.

I started hanging out at Washington Square. There was a good scene there, a conclave. Once I even got to see Woody Guthrie there, being led around drunkenly on a weekend when he'd left the hospital and gone out on a bender. I resented that son of a bitch who was dragging him around like he was a trick dog. I'll always remember that.

Folk music had really gotten hold of me. It was fascinating that it was music that had a reason to be sung. I loved the idea that this was the way cultures told their stories. Few could read and write a long time ago, so the way information was passed was through song. The people who could sing folk songs told about heroes — some real and some mythical — but the whole idea was that the song writers were really the historians. They reflected what was

Bob in Washington Square 1953

going on in society at a certain time, and as things changed and we moved into modern times, folk singers were still reflecting society.

I went to Ohio because I had friends there and they had a very active folklore society. I knew Dick Miller was from Cleveland and he knew all about folk music, but all I really knew about Ohio and Folklore was a couple of things I'd read. One was a book by Mary Olive Eddy that was wonderful and full of great songs. Then there was the Ohio Folklore Quarterly that was for the whole Ohio Valley Region — including Indiana and Kentucky. It was one of the more active folklore societies and they gathered a couple of times a year. So I knew there was some active work going on out there.

I never have been carried away by the Lomax legend. As far as I was concerned, the great unsung hero in folksong research was Carl Sandburg, and one of my discoveries was Carl Sandburg's *American Songbag*. Without his work, the Lomaxes wouldn't have existed. Sandburg's 1927 anthology, *The American Songbag,* collected the 19th century heartland music that he grew up with. Because of his standing in the literary community, and by saying, "This stuff is valid literature — the voice of the people — and warrants appreciation," folksongs gained a permanent stature. Sandburg tended to build up his favorite version of a song from several different sources. He'd lump them all together under the tune he liked the best. The man really was the trigger. He loved the everyday language, the real way people talked and the stories they told through their music.

Mary Olive Eddy was an Ohio school teacher and folk song collector. I learned *Lily of the West* from her marvelous book that was published in the 1930s. It also appears in a Lomax book with credits to her.

A great many of Lomax's books were done that way. He was more of an anthologizer than an actual field collector. And by the time he was doing his work, he and others were able to get grants from the Carnegie Foundation.

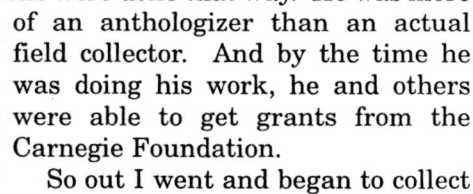

So out I went and began to collect — began to seek sources, and none of it would have happened if I hadn't met Pete Seeger. In those days — '53 or '54 — you could find the music out there really easily. I would go to a small, rural town and talk to the lady behind the counter in a general store, just to start chatting. Usually she was the postmaster. I would tell

Bob in Cleveland 1954

PHOTO BY RICHARD MILLER - USED WITH PERMISSION

her that I wanted to contact people interested in the old songs.

Generally speaking, you just kept pressing the hand until you met somebody who knew a few of the old songs. If it wasn't what I wanted, I would say, "That was wonderful...I want a couple from the same period..." then I would say, "You know what I'm REALLY looking for..."

I always had one or two that I could pull out and they'd say, "Oh, yeah...I know who sings those kind of songs..." and send you to the next person. Or sometimes they'd say, "Oh, I know that song! You don't sing it right. Let me sing it..." or "Here's how my mother sings it..." or "Here's how my grandmother sang it."

Then I got involved in a wonderful project, trying to track down a number of people still alive in one family — three different generations — who still sang several songs that they'd learned from their grandmother. The whole point of that was to try to tell whether changes in the song were done consciously or accidentally. Sometimes someone will bobble the storyline somehow and fix those words so it comes out right. It is incredible what folks'll do. They'll sit there and sing the different version. You've already heard their grandmother sing it and have it on tape, but they'll sit there and tell you that the way they're singing it is exactly how grandma sang it. It's wonderful! They mean it! To the best of their ability, it's exactly how grandma sang it as far as they know it. So generally speaking, out there in folklore land the changes are not conscious.

At that time the interest everywhere was in traditional music, and I had immense respect for the tradition — for the music. I wasn't a purist, though, because those ballads go on and on. What I found was that a lot of the traditional songs came out of a culture that consisted of the grandmother teaching it to the grandchildren while they dried the dishes, or sat around the front porch of a cabin swapping songs. There was no time limitation on them. When you're singing in a saloon and people are coming in, paying a couple of bucks to forget their lives of quiet desperation, then you don't have the same kind of freedoms. They're not family and friends, and you've got to communicate something to them. They were very unfamiliar with the kind of stuff I was doing, so the more I could communicate, the more cogent my message, I thought, the better. I immediately began to find fault with traditional and began to rewrite and make it work better for the audience I was singing for.

So I was already fixing songs. I started deleting material or taking two lines from one verse and two lines from another and just sticking them together and deleting extraneous stuff that didn't move the story line. I would "do stuff to songs," but you never said, "I rewrote this or changed anything." You just didn't say that. It was not the thing then to write your own songs. I was adding words or fixing them, or adding a last verse. That was the period when John Jacob Niles, when asked about a song called *Black is the Colour of My True Love's Hair,* said it was something he collected in the Appalachian Mountains. When he found out that it had been recorded a number of times and that it had earned quite a bit, then Niles said, "No, I didn't collect it, I wrote it." And write it he did, and prove it he did.

I love traditional — the elements of it. I love the songs, but sometimes for the audience, and as an entertainer, I felt I could make them work a little better. There were historical references and words and phrases that didn't have any meaning to a contemporary audience. They didn't know what they meant. There were those who said, "That ain't the way you do it. You have a pure artifact here and you gotta leave it." One could be a purist and sing those songs, and some chose to do that, but I needed to communicate with an audience. I was taking a lot of liberties with the music because I was looking to introduce people to folk music as an entertainment medium. The bottom line was that I wasn't trying to fix the tradition of America, but rather I was performing for groups of people, and I needed to capture their attention. It seemed to work.

Of course, this upset the true folkies of that time, but the thing was, I was working and they weren't! The *Little Sandy Review* devoted three pages of an issue to a condemnation of one of my albums, and the briefest of paragraphs to an album that they approved of. I think that epitomizes folk music and the people in the field. A lot of the literature is just misfocused.

Musically, when I got into it, I didn't want to have to master a lot of technique — I just wanted to make music. That's probably why I'm a banjo and guitar player. I wanted an instrument where I could make music as soon as possible. I never thought I was going to be a singer. I was interested in the music. It's like collecting antiques — when you get them, you don't want to put them in the garage. You want to have them in the living room to show to people. When I collected a good song, I wanted to share it with people. I didn't expect to be paid for it. I played at parties and gatherings, whenever it was appropriate.

When I had gotten into collecting folk music, I really didn't have in mind ending up as an entertainer. I didn't consider myself cut out to be that. But the first time I got paid to perform it, I thought, "God, this will underwrite the search for more and more of these songs." It wasn't until I was in the Gate of Horn for about a year that I realized that I loved it, that being an entertainer was what I liked to do better than anything.

The Weavers had come and gone, and only the left wing seemed interested in folk music, and then only the left-wing content. There were all the books — Mary Olive Eddy, the Lomaxes, Cecil Sharp, all this good stuff — but at that time, the only people performing in the clubs were Susan Reed, Josh White and Richard Dyer-Bennett. When I began to work in clubs and found that there was a woman working the Tin Angel in San Francisco named Odetta who sang folk songs, I said, "Oh, my God, another kindred spirit." By the time I was working the Blue Angel, Josh wasn't working clubs. He'd made some scenes. He didn't work that tight little circuit of clubs anymore.

To support myself then I was scufflin' in Cleveland. The Shaker Heights Women's Club decided to pay me $50 to sing some songs in between two sections of, I think, a dramatic program or a variety show they were doing. God! I thought it was wonderful! *$50!* It was a substantial sum then, but, more important, I would have been delighted to sing — just to be asked to sing, because I was, at that time, busy looking for an audience. I just loved to share what I was doing. I was the person who took the banjo out at the beginning of the party and was oblivious to everyone getting bored with the whole thing and if they all drifted out to the kitchen or the bathroom, that was okay with me. I was unaware. I was there pickin'. If I knew any more songs, I'd continue to pick. And usually the last person there was me packing up my banjo getting ready to go. Later I identified that type and said "Aha — I was one of those, wasn't I?" But I carried on with incredible, boundless — just boundless — enthusiasm.

During my travels in the Merchant Marine, I had gotten interested in calypso I was hearing, so I decided I wanted to go in search of some of that kind of music, too. I went down to the islands and spent some time learning a whole bunch of songs. I went on one of those cruise ships as an entertainer — ten days, I guess it was — stopping in Nassau, Kingston, Havana. Going down to the islands was very important..

Then I made a deal to go to Nassau and lay over until the next ship came around, so I had six or seven days. Brian Blake was still alive and playing then in Nassau. That was his stomping ground — the Royal Palms — or something — Hotel. Also on the ship, I met a young guy named Roy Model. Lord Composer was his working name. He had a six-piece calypso band from Kingston. I spent about two weeks right in Kingston, staying at his house, going to church with him and his mother to hear music the likes of which I've never heard since — in black churches, going up in the Cameroons which were the mountains in central Jamaica, where Roy's cousin was the leader of a digging gang.

None of the roadwork was done by machines. It was all done by hand labor, and the guy who led the singing was held in such high regard that he was employed by the guys on the crew. He was paid standard wages by the boss because he dug, too, but he was also paid a bonus, so it was very competitive. I don't know how much the fee was, but he was making something like double salary to sing these work songs. For the money, anyone would have done it, but you had to be good at it. Roy's cousin was one of the best guys, so I learned a lot of work songs.

When I came back I started singing some calypso stuff. That was a big influence then. I was really excited about that music — work songs from Jamaica, plus, you know, "git along little doggie." Traditional stuff. I would sing "The banks are made of marble" occasionally — not because of its content, but because I liked the song. Sing songs like "hush little baby, don't you cry, you know your mama's going to die" — in a night club? "Mommy, 'out the light and give me what you give my daddy last night." That was great night club lyrics. I had trouble sometimes because there was lot of bawdy kind of calypso sung for tourists, and it translated real well into clubs. I mean, it worked too well. It's always tempting to take the cheap shot. It's easy and works so well. There's no content and bull shit, but, oh boy, when you're struggling along and you can't get anybody's attention . . .

When I came back to the states and talked to the Tarriers, I sang them the banana loading song. I told them they should sing it, so they recorded it, but it wasn't the first recording released of it. Belafonte had it on an album, but it wasn't doing anything. It was the Tarriers who broke the hit. It was after their record was taking off that RCA re-released Belafonte's, which became the bigger seller. It was on his *Calypso* album. The Tarrier's version starts off with, "Hil un galy rider, hil un galy . . ." which is a digging song from the Cameroons. I taught them that and the banana boat song, which Belafonte called *Day-O*, but I didn't learn that from anybody. I was there in Kingston when they were walking with these bunches of bananas on their heads to load the ship. It was cheaper to hire labor than it was to get a conveyor belt.

Those early albums had wonderful songs like *All My Trials Lord* and *Michael, Row the Boat Ashore!* They were the first recordings of those songs, the first time they saw the light of day. They saw the light of day by me. Then people began to sing them, and they became part of the literature of the time. That always pleased me. That was part of the purpose of it. When I was starting out, people wanted to hear things like *Blue Tail Fly*. I wanted to show them there was a lot more to folk music than that.

On all of my earlier albums, I usually attributed who I got the songs from, whether they were as I got them, whether I rewrote them, whether they were changed in any way. There was no real attempt to put my name on them — or adapted and arranged by ... that kind of thing. I might have been better off if I had put my name on them. I didn't at the time. The emphasis was to gather this stuff and be the conduit and the entertainer who brought it, shared it. It was nice. It was a good thing to do.

ఌ ఌ ఌ ఌ ఌ ఌ

In Cleveland I gave a lot of thought to my future plans. What I wanted to do was find a place where I could get paid somewhat to sing my songs because that would then underwrite my continuing to look at the music and find out more. I thought it out carefully and decided Florida — Miami — would be a great place — it's very seasonal. I knew that, therefore, because it's seasonal, in the winter they'd need more musicians, more entertainers and there'd be lots of openings — it'd be real easy!

So after collecting in the Bahamas, I went and spent a month or two in New York. I started out working clubs like the Village Vanguard, which was a famous old club and the avant-garde clubs like the Blue Angel, which was on the upper eastside of Manhattan. I worked with a lot of great cabaret performers — the Lenny Bruces, you know. The people I got to work with were incredible because you could learn so much. It's where a lot of folk music acts got their start. People who were working there prior to my working the Vanguard were people like the Weavers, Josh White, Susan Reed and Richard Dyer-Bennett.

Ed McCurdy, famous in the early '50s as folksinger/songwriter, recalls his first meeting with Bob:

I met Bob in New York in 1954. I was living there and he was living, I think, on the Island. He had been down in the West Indies, I think, prior to my meeting him. His sister came to see my wife and me and asked if we thought it would be advisable for him to get into show business. Interestingly enough, I said I didn't think so. I wouldn't advise anybody to get into show business. Later I ran across him in Chicago. I don't think I really had anything to do with his getting into the business, but she certainly asked me. Sisters have a way of being like that.

After that I headed on down to Florida. I wanted to get down there early enough to get the pick of the jobs, so I arrived in late October, early November. It took me a couple of weeks to realize that every musician in the country wants to work down there so it's very hard to get work. I, fortunately, was naive enough that I wasn't discouraged at all and got some jobs in spite of myself because I didn't know it was "impossible". I just kept trying.

For $175, seven days a week, four and five sets a night, I played bars and lounges in Miami. One was upstairs above one of the most notorious strip joints in Miami. The mobsters who were friends of the owner would go upstairs for the class acts, while the strippers worked the main floor. It was a place where the customers pounded the tables with little wooden mallets instead of applauding. I shared a dressing room with 20 naked women.

There was a guy in Florida, Wolfie Cohen, who started all the "Wolfies" restaurants. He was a helluva restauranteur—a high roller — made fortunes. He'd start the restaurants, get them going himself and go gamble all the money away. He was my first employer and a wonderful guy. He became very dear to me. The headliner was Adriana Caselotti. She was the voice of Snow White in the movie, and that was her claim to fame. It was that kind of place. There were three or four acts, but I just remember her. She looked like Snow White should have looked in real life and sang that way, too.

Wolfie was the kind of guy who would come in, and, as he walked through the long room, ask me to sing *Get Along Little Doggies*. He loved it. Every time he'd ask me to sing it, he'd send a $20 bill up. Tipping was big in those days. As a matter of fact, some jobs you took at scale because there were tips. At some jobs, you did real well in tips. But those were different days than now. In those days, the customer was right and if the customer was a good, big tipper and wanted to hear, for example, *Stardust,* brother you better fake it, no matter how bad you do. You'd better try it, because you don't offend the customer. You would literally lose your job!

Anyway, Wolfie would always request that song and always send up a twenty dollar bill. One night he walked in with a couple of friends or clients, and he asked for *Get Along Little Doggies,* and I said, "Oh I just finished that. I don't want to do it again." That week, when I got my $175 paycheck, there was $20 deducted from it. I thought that was wonderful! He was a classy gent, of the real high roller type.

The second job I ever had in the business was in a place in Miami on Biscayne called the Vagabonds Club. They were a comedy quartet and played instruments — guitar, accordion, bass. One guy looked funny, another guy acted funny and one guy sang good. They were very, very famous by way of many appearances on the Arthur Godfrey show. They had their own club — a lounge — that seated 300 people. It was a pre-Vegas type, big bus stop kind of club.

I had one experience that was very meaningful to me. There was a guy named Charlie Farrell — same name as the actor, but not the actor. Charlie Farrell sang in New York and in Miami — Miami in the winter and New York in the summer. He had an INCREDIBLE following of devoted fans who packed the lounge every night. They loved him. Charlie was their boy. He sang *As Time Goes By,* and he was just great. He was a wonderful, charming man and he shared something with the people that was really an experience. He just sat down by himself at the piano and sang old standards and told stories and just "shared Charlie Farrell" with the audience. They would pack it for the first show and damn near fill it for the second. He did a lot of business!

I was hired as the act to open his show and, for a couple of nights, I did twenty minutes. That was standard. You did ten minutes, you did twelve minutes. In those days you went to an agent and he would ask, "What do you do?" You didn't say, "I play the banjo." You'd say "I do twelve minutes of banjo — I do six minutes of comedy — I do eighteen minutes of dance." It was down to that, because that's how it was sold and that's what you did.

There was still a great awareness of vaudeville style. As a matter of fact, there were still some houses open in New York, and the bookers were real conscious. They had an hour or an hour and a half to fill, and they had to put together so many minutes of stuff.

For two nights I opened for Charlie. It was hard and oppressive because there were 300 people waiting to hear Charlie Farrell. When I walked out there, there was not one diminuendo in the decibel level! What was this kid doing up there with a banjo?! They didn't even know what a banjo was, and they didn't care. They were there to see Charlie!

Well, I guess Charlie heard the show the second night and must have heard something because he came backstage to the little dressing area and said, "Hey, you're all right. Say, listen, how about tomorrow night — would you follow me?" to which I said, "Sure!" I mean, he was the star — he did an hour — or an hour and ten — and it was a killer. I used to just sit and watch him because he was just that good.

The following night, I got there. Charlie went on first and did his hour and ten minutes to this incredible applause. He was brought back for the second encore and before he went into his second encore, he said, "Listen, I want you to do me a favor. There's a young fellow that plays with me. He would be my opening act ordinarily, but I've asked him to go on after me. I want you all to really listen to him. I like his work. I think you may like it."

Even if they'd never heard him before, after the hour and ten minutes Charlie had just done, they would have to do anything he wanted. And they sat. I can't say that they understood what I was doing or even liked what I was doing, but for Charlie Farrell, there was not a peep. I was singing calypso songs and weird stuff on a five-string banjo, but they listened! I don't even remember whether the applause was sincere, polite, enthusiastic or what, but I do remember that it was my first experience at playing in a real saloon to a real saloon audience with rapt attention. I can't remember any other lessons I learned during those couple of weeks. I'm sure there were plenty, but I'll never forget Charlie. I certainly learned a lot from him, but that's what you did. I do not remember ever asking anybody who played anything, "How do you do that?", without getting an answer. There was a lot of sharing going on, and what Charlie did for me was the same thing.

I was among the first to start to sing folk music in clubs where people had to pay money to come in and listen. You take it for granted today. There are listening clubs where you know you're going to go in and hear a performer, but it wasn't that way in the '50s. I don't even know how I got the jobs to begin with. I think I was a novelty act. Here was this guy with a real high tenor voice, playing banjo and singing calypso songs in amongst *My Funny Valentine* and the dirty comic. I look back on it now and I don't know how I got the jobs.

I just kept learning, and when it finally came around to the coffee house circuit and clubs like the Gate of Horn in Chicago, The Bitter End in New York, the Cellar Door in Washington DC, and later on the Banducci's place, the hungry i in San Francisco, I was ready for them.

After Miami I bounced around from Cleveland to New York and many places in between. I travelled to Chicago with a comedian I knew who stopped at the Green Door in Michigan City. I sang there. He did a set and I did one too. I was hired and that was how I ended up in Chicago.

I went to Chicago in 1955 to see the agents. I went to a talent agency and I got into Helman Rowe's office. He booked me immediately into the Rathskeller on Randolph Street. It was a German restaurant that was in a basement on Randolph in the Loop. The act I followed was a guy who had been working there for 14 years. He sang German songs for the German American furniture-makers Wisconsin who were in town on buying trips.

Here I was, a guy with a banjo and a crew cut, singing calypso and Appalachian Mountain ballads, and they didn't care for me at all. I worked the Rathskeller for one night. I went up to the owner after the show and said, "I think I'm wrong for this place."

He said "Let me hear your next show." He heard it and he agreed. He said, "You *are* wrong for this place."

I found work with the National Barn Dance on WLS radio and appeared with Big Bill Broonzy at the College of Complexes on North

State Street, which offered a mix of poetry reading, debates, soapbox orators, blues and folk sings. It was there I met Ken Nordine, the great radio voice, who was opening his Off-Beat Room on Granville and Kenmore. It was a place where he could perform his word jazz, and he did a very important thing there, a very revolutionary thing, in fact. There had been no such thing as a listening room up to that time. Nordine changed that. He made a rule that the audience had to pay attention or leave. He'd say, "Anybody talks, gets out." He didn't need the money. He wanted to make money for the place to be successful, but it had to be on his terms. Most of the places in town then were owned by "the boys", and the crowds were noisy.

The Off-Beat Room was open about six months, but Nordine was only there about six weeks because he came down with pneumonia, so it was just me and the Fred Kaz Trio.

Dave Samuelson, midwest folk concert promoter:
To put things in perspective, especially in the club scene in Chicago in the '50s when Bob was thriving at the Gate of Horn, the Offbeat Club and places like that, a lot of these places were not necessarily mob-owned, but you had to deal with a lot of mob organizations to get the napkins and the equipment for your club so you could remain operating. That goes back to the '20s when the Capone mob controlled all the speakeasies. The underworld got a foothold in the night life in Chicago and many other major cities, and that lingered on throughout the '50s and '60s. The consequence was that Bob knew a lot of underworld figures. It was just that kind of undercurrent of small time drug pushers and burglars. It was an underworld kind of environment, and that was just inherent in it. The consequence was the clubs were not idealized coffee houses like you might think but basically organizations with direct or indirect ties with the mob. With folk and jazz which had specialized types of audiences, that's what you dealt with. Bob was never a concert performer. He was always a club performer, so in order to make a living at what he was doing, which was basically performing in a lot of folk and jazz clubs, that was the world Bob operated in. Bob's mindset was pretty much like a small time vaudevillian in some ways. You had to do what you had to do to survive and thrive in that kind of environment. Bob, with all of his talent and all of his charisma, thrived.

If "the boys" came in and 15 of them were sitting around a table with their bimbos and they wanted to mess up your show, or get in your show, or in your face, that was it. There were a lot of wise guys in the audience, and they would heckle and interrupt performers. And whether they were "the boys" or just customers, they were right. You just smiled and carried on.

Bob in 1954

4
THE SHORT HAPPY LIFE OF
THE ORIGINAL GATE OF HORN

*There are two Gates of Dreams,
that of ivory and that of horn.
Dreams which delude pass through the Ivory Gate.
Those which pass through the Gate of Horn come true.*
~Penelope - Homer's Odyssey

Bob Gibson's personal fame as a performer, as well as his influence on other folk musicians, closely paralleled the life of Chicago's Gate of Horn nightclub under the ownership of Albert Grossman.

These were the years of being the first to re-write, arrange and record modernized versions of traditional folk songs, of co-writing Abilene *and* Well, Well, Well *and many others, of performing solo at Carnegie Hall recital hall, of 17 appearances on the enormously popular Arthur Godfrey TV and radio shows, of bringing Joan Baez to her first national acclaim.

In the latter half of the decade of the 1950's, Chicago still was the nation's Second City. It may have had laughable boss politics, but it seemed to be run pretty well. Its police always seemed to be on the scene of a traffic infraction but usually were invisible if crime were in the air. But you still felt safe enough on the streets there. And the skyline, especially at night, when you drove along the Outer Drive, was magnificent.

As for entertainment, on any given day, Chicago visitors could find West Side Story or The Music Man on stage at the Shubert, Rosemary Clooney or Frankie Laine in between movies at the Chicago Theatre, Count Basie at the Blue Note, Nichols and May in a benefit show. Even Frank Sinatra might be there at some place like the Empire Room in the Palmer House Hotel. There also were the Cubs.

The Korean War was over. Communism was feared, as was the House Un-American Activities Committee, but the real impact of Blacklisting was yet to be understood. People had money, jobs were available and Vietnam and the Domino Theory were yet to be introduced.

People in their 20's considered themselves too old for Elvis and too young for Sinatra. The Beatles were not yet a glint in John Lennon's eye.

In Chicago, the young intellectuals (and pseudo-intellectuals) frequented the Near North—Old Town—the area just north of the Chicago River that was just beginning to blossom with antique shops and basement clubs. There many of them lived or often would come to visit friends who were living in stark little loft apartments while attending classes at The Art Institute or The Goodman Theatre, to talk about Gide, Sartre and Camus, and — soon — Bob Gibson, the hot new folk singer.

Gibson was in his mid-20's then. Young adults could identify with him. They had found THEIR voice, THEIR music, at The Gate of Horn.

By the time I was at the Offbeat Room, I knew a few folk singers from the University of Chicago, a guy from Detroit, and so on. I got them all together for a 12-hour program of folk singing. It was well attended even though the room only held 125. One of the people who came in to hear it was Albert Grossman. He was working for the Chicago Housing Authority at the time, and he had brought a friend with him, Les Brown, who became his partner.

Albert came and talked to me afterward. He had an idea for an intimate little place, near the Rush Street area that sold charcoal broiled bratwurst and beer and had a little entertainment. He had seen a club like it in Paris that featured these two American guys who used to get up on a stepladder and sing French songs like those of Jacques Brel. It was all very intimate and very basementy. It was one of the places the Americans went and said, "Ah hah, we've been to Paris." Albert thought a similar club would go well in Chicago.

It turns out that he had also seen me at Ken Nordine's Offbeat Room. Albert saw that Ken's approach, this respect for the performers, would work and planned to use the same idea. He said, "This is interesting; a place like this could work downtown." It wasn't the folk music, because Albert knew nothing about folk music and could have cared less when he opened the Gate of Horn; he knew that a listening room would work. He told me about his idea, and he asked me if I'd like to work there sometime and I said, "Sure." It sounded great. That idea became the Gate of Horn.

A lot had been happening for two or three years. When I was in New York, I helped to get coffee houses started in the Village, most of them operated by people who couldn't get a cabaret license. Then there were a lot of changes happening in the night club business. The Gate of Horn idea was something quite different in Chicago, as contrasted to the Black Orchid over on Rush Street, the more or less avant-garde type place, where Don Rickles or Frank Sinatra or Johnny Mathis played. But pretty soon after that, there were a lot of peripheral places, like the Hungry i in San Francisco and they would spawn their own imitations.

In 1956, with Albert Grossman and partners Les Brown and later Allen Ribback, the Gate opened at the corner of Chicago and Dearborn right across the street from the YMCA, but I hadn't just been sitting around waiting for the club to open, and I wasn't available right away. So at the start, Grossman had a female folk singer and a man and guitar player who were friends of Genevieve, who was very big at the Empire Room at the Palmer House then. They did a lot of French stuff, all very affected.

In those days, the club schedule was five nights a week for headliners and they opened later in the week and had Monday off. But everyone kept their club open all the time. That's why you had a trio or some little band that played the other two nights. At that time there were three acts in a show — a two hour show, and the show was divided up so there were the first two acts and the third act did an hour and 10 minutes.

I worked there for the first time with Katie Lee. I was hired to cover for a couple days. Albert hired me for the one night and I worked for eleven months nonstop. That's how it used to be, though. You worked a place two weeks minimum. It was nothing to work some places four weeks. Now it's one nighters. It's crazy. In those early days in Cleveland, I'd go to Cleveland and start working in a joint for two weeks. The first night nobody would be there. The second morning I'd be on the phone calling up the television stations and the newspaper reporters and saying, "Come down," or "Do you want to have lunch?" or "Let me tell you my story," trying to get some press. I tell you, by the end of two weeks, there were lots of people coming to see me. You can't do that on a one-nighter. It just isn't there. If you don't have an audience, it's nearly impossible to build one.

So there I was at the Gate of Horn the third week it was open. The crowd rapidly increased from the usual forty chairs to eighty and eventually to 100 and, boy, that was all the place could hold. Many acts came and went and I was still there, pickin' my banjo and doing my thing. By the end of the eleven months I was, as often as not, headlining or splitting bills. I started out opening for everyone and ended up at the Gate of Horn closing for everyone. Everyone — even Big Bill Broonzy. But those years as an opening act and then as an intermediate act — those were the learning experiences. That's when I got to study great performers and see how it was done.

Studs Terkel recalled Bob at the Gate of Horn:
A memory comes to me at once. People say memories deceive — memories don't! Memories italicize — are indelible. And to me the

memory is 1956, 40 years ago. Al Grossman opened the Gate of Horn in the basement of the Rice Hotel, across the street from the YMCA. It didn't work those first two weeks. Two good artists were there, but it didn't work. In the third week appears a young guy with crew cut blond hair, an infectious grin, a banjo on his chest.

When the kid with the blond crew-cut first appeared on stage, plunking at his banjo, I thought, "Another one!" It was no more than a passing glance I tossed, there had been so many kids of like build and appearance cloning Pete or Woody. But when he began to sing out — that's what he did — I knew he was special. It was a desultory night at the Gate of Horn, yet Bob sprang it to life. I forgot the song, but it caught the scattering of listeners that was there that night. Suddenly the place was electricity. From that moment on, the electricity of Bob Gibson caught on. It was the excitement of Bob's performance that spread the word and the scatterings had become sold houses. It was Bob, the house artist who, more than any other performer, established the Gate of Horn and Chicago as a citadel of folk music in the country, and Bob's role was that of a troubadour of ancient days, but of now.

John Brown, performer, songwriter, and former Chicago club owner adds:
I remember the first night I saw Bob Gibson. I walked into the Old Gate of Horn and there was this guy in a checkered shirt with a banjo, singing *This Little Light of Mine,* and I said, 'I want to do that!' I remember the first time I heard him do his *Sweet Betsy From Pike* arrangement. A bunch of us sitting around said, 'Listen to what Gibson's doing now!' because we were still trying to figure out *Betty and DuPree,* y'know!

Jack Bender, artist of Alley Oop™, who became a Gibson fan when he first saw him in July, 1956 says:
Gibson's style was something new to folk-singing. It was upbeat and vigorous. And while out-of-towners might routinely seek out Duke Ellington or Muggsy Spanier, native Chicagoans were lining up outside a new basement club in the Near North, The Gate of Horn, where Gibson held court nightly.

The place, charitably described as 'intimate', seemed rather stark in between shows, and seated only about 100 at tables and at the bar, but when the spotlights illuminated Gibson on the little stage, the atmosphere became magical. His blondish crewcut hair glowed under the light. His handsome, cherubic face added to the illusion (but he definitely was not an angel). He wore a checkered shirt. He was stocky and of average height. He looked like Everyman, but he performed like no other. He strained his tenor voice to hoarseness. He alternately played his banjo with delicate fingering and powerful strokes. He had great energy and his enthusiastic showmanship turned that basement club into a palace.

Before Gibson, folk music was either akin to a dirge, or was entirely frivolous. He introduced a new approach—a brighter outlook and shorter presentations—and Chicago loved it. Folk singing COULD also be entertaining, he showed. And the art never would be the same again.

The Gate of Horn was the very first place where folk music as such was the draw. It had a greater effect upon a number of people than did all the clubs put together in those days. People would come up to me and say, "We don't go to clubs usually, but we go to the Gate of Horn all the time."

I started something there early on and it became some sort of a tradition. When I was in town I would put on a finale number with the other people in the show, people like Paul Clayton and Odetta. Whatever the three acts were, we'd end up working out something. There was always some common ground, musically, and we'd do two or three numbers after the headline show. I'd call them back out and then we'd do something together. This was in the very early years of the Gate of Horn.

Glenn Yarbrough, known now by the whole world for his singing career, remembers those days of following Bob:

It was about '56. I'd just come out from the Korean War, and I went down to Mexico first and spent about a year and a half, two years. The only reason I happened to end up there in Chicago was that I sang a song at Cynthia Gooding's house in New York one night and Al Grossman was there. He came up to me and he said, "How'd you like to work in my club?" I said, "Sure!" So nobody knew who the hell I was. I was hired to follow Bob when he finished his run at the Gate. The first time I met Bob was when I arrived to do the Gate of Horn.

It was very difficult following Bob. I was going to start the next night, and I thought I'd go over and see what his show was like. He had been there several months, and the lines were just around the block. Then I watched him perform, and I thought he was one of the finest performers I'd ever seen. In the beginning he was really quite a showman. Frankly, I liked him better the way he was in the beginning. I felt that what he did later on in life was tinged with a little bit of sadness because he'd never really achieved what he should have achieved as a performer or as a writer. But I remember that Saturday night I went into that place and watched him perform, and I thought I'll never be able to do this. Nobody knew I was there. Nobody knew me.

It was very different the night after I took over from Bob. It took awhile. I was there about the same length of time Bob was, and although I didn't have the same kind of verve that he had, they seemed to like me. We eventually had lines around the block, too.

For the next few years, I came to the Gate of Horn every June. Albert and I shared an apartment in Chicago on Superior Street at that time. He was now beginning management in the sense that I was his first act. He said, "Let me manage you." He saw that I really didn't know what I was doing as far as getting bookings. He had been making the rounds and felt he understood the situation very thoroughly and knew what he was doing.

It was May, 1959 and I was working in Boston, on the Cape. Tom Lehrer and I did a couple of gigs together. In June I was due back at the Gate.

Tom Lehrer remembers the summer also:
I was on the same bill with Bob for a week at Storyville Cape Cod (a night club in Harwich, MA) in the summer of 1959. That was the only time our paths crossed. We were never on stage at the same time, and I don't recall having any actual conversations with him, but I enjoyed his performances very much.

Albert said he had heard of a girl named Joan Baez singing at a small club in Boston named Club 47 and said 'Let's go over and hear her.' So in between sets one evening, we ran over there and listened. She was fantastic. Albert brought her to the Gate of Horn the next month because that was when I would be playing the club. That was her first time coming out of Boston - June, 1959.

Joan Baez sang with me for that month of June in 1959 in the Gate of Horn and it was very, very exciting. It was also prom month and people would come in in the crinoline and the white jackets. Kids come up to me now and they say "My mom and dad got engaged watching you at the Gate of Horn." And there were many who didn't get engaged, but those are other stories.

Then there was the Newport Folk Festival!

I was scheduled to be in the show, and the co-producer of the Newport Festival, George Wein, had told me and everyone else who was on the bill not to add anyone else to their performance because if 'everyone did that, it would ruin the show.' But after singing a few songs, I brought Joan onstage. I knew I could get away with it. It was magical.

People have tended to make a big deal of this, but I never have really known why. If I hadn't 'introduced' Joan Baez, someone else would have. It was like 'discovering' the Grand Canyon. I may have introduced her to her first large audience, but what does that mean? Do you think that girl was going to stay unknown in Cambridge? It wasn't my saying, 'Look what Albert and I discovered', it was 'Hey, you want to hear something GREAT?!' That's all it is. You don't discover anyone. They're going to become known. I'm just glad that for a few people, I was the lucky one who got to say, 'Hey, you want to hear something GREAT?!'

To appreciate the impact of the legendary "introduction" by Bob Gibson of Joan Baez at the Newport Folk Festival in 1959, one must understand where and who Ms. Baez was (or wasn't) at that time.

In the winter of 1958, she had made her professional debut, at $10 an evening, at Club 47, a jazz club in Boston. Its owner was attempting to convert it into a twice-a-week (Tuesdays and Fridays) folk club to take advantage of the changing times.

Her first performance there was for a total of eight people — her father, her mother, her sister, two friends, a friend of her parents, the owner of the club and her partner. "It was a ridiculous situation, friends and family all trying to look like an audience, trying not to peer hopefully over at the door every time they heard footsteps," she recalls.

"A few stragglers wandered in for the second set," she adds. "When I returned the following Tuesday, word had gotten around and we had a half-filled house."

She began building an audience in the Boston area, appearing at Club 47 and others, giving a concert, making a record in a friend's cellar. She also managed to flunk out of the Boston University School of Drama.

By spring, she still was living at home and had a day job teaching people how to drive a motorcycle and then taking them to get their license. But her reputation as a singer had grown enough to attract the interest of Albert Grossman, who owned the Gate of Horn nightclub in Chicago and was Bob Gibson's manager. He offered her $200 a week, which was a lot of money to Ms. Baez, considering her salary at Club 47 had remained $10 for her weekly performance.

This account is from Joan Baez's autobiography, And A Voice To Sing With, A Memoir, *©1987, Summit Books, and is used with permission. Bracketed quotes are from the booklet included in her Vanguard collection,* Joan Baez: Rare, Live & Classic.

Joan Baez:
    I was frightened of flying alone, of staying alone, of a club where people drank and might not listen...
    Albert's club was one of the finest in the country, the Gate of Horn, and featured Bob Gibson, at that time a very popular singer

who played 12-string guitar and banjo. I got a crush on Bob, of course, and was terrified of him because he was at home in a den of sin called a nightclub, was marvelously sarcastic and funny, drank too much, sang both serious and silly songs, and cracked jokes in between them; he actually 'entertained' people. I lived at the YWCA. ...The time left over was spent sitting in the metal stairwell of the Y where the acoustics were positively liquid, practicing the songs I'd learned from Bob.

I spent two weeks at The Gate of Horn baffled, flattered and terrified by what appeared to be dazzling success just within reach. Within me the demons engaged in a riotous dance, coaxing me with the soft light, the maleness around me, the overt sexuality that erupted as inhibitions were anesthetized by alcohol. I knew only that at age 18, I was not cut out for the cocktail crowd. I needed my academic, rebellious, coffee-drinking admirers who listened single-mindedly to their madonna, and dared not touch her.

Bob Gibson invited me to appear as his guest at the first Newport Folk Festival. I have only patches of memories of that historic occasion. It was August [album says July 11, 1959] I went to Newport with Odetta [whom she had met at the Gate of Horn] and her husband [Danny Gordon] ... It rained every day. Bob Gibson had a very rich girlfriend named Penny, who was nice to me. There were tents full of folksingers, banjo pickers, fiddle players and gospel groups, and streets full of hitchhikers. The kids who flocked to the festival were trim and had short hair: the '60s had not begun yet. Pete Seeger was there, my second living idol. (Martin Luther King Jr., was the first.) There were black blues singers with broken down guitars, and white kids trying to sound like them. There were big dinners where fiddle bands played long into the night. People put dishes of food into my lap and then asked me to sing. I was like a tiny star in the middle of an as yet unnamed firmament.

On the second night there were 13,000 people sitting out in the Rhode Island mist. After other performers...Bob went on to delight the audience with his ballads and jokes while I stood in gladiator sandals down in the mud, stage left, gripping the handrail that led upstairs to the stage...My other sweaty hand was clutching a guitar.

Finally, I heard Bob Gibson announce a guest and say a few words about me.

I have no idea what they were, but I knew that in a minute I would be singing before what seemed to me to be the biggest crowd ever assembled in the history of the world. [I was petrified. There were more people there than I had ever seen in one place.] In that moment there was only the speeding of my heart; all movement was a silent film, and all sound was surface noise. There were nods of encouragement and thumbs up all around. It is my style when I am let out of the chute to walk swiftly and steadily, and I did so up the soggy stairs to my doom or glory. Bob was giving me a bright and cheery smile, and his cocky look which meant that life was only one big joke anyway, so not to worry. We sang, *Virgin Mary Had One Son*. He played the 12-string, and with 18 strings and two voices we sounded pretty impressive...We made it to the end and there was tumultuous applause. So we sang our "other" song, an upbeat number (thanks to Bob) called *We Are Crossing Jordan River*. [It turned out to be a big thing.]

An exorbitant amount of fuss was made over me when we descended from the stage. Into one tent and out of another. Newspapers, student press, foreign correspondents and, of course, Time magazine. [Naturally I reveled in it. It was like a dream to me.]

I realized in the back of my mind and the center of my heart that in the book of my destiny the first page had been turned, and that this book could no longer be exchanged for any other.

In August of 1963, I went out on tour and invited Bobby (Dylan) to sing in my concerts, following the example set for me by Bob Gibson four years before. I was getting audiences of up to 10,000 at that time and dragging my little vagabond out onto the stage was an experiment and a gamble...

Joan Baez at the time was just like a bundle of energy. We would come off the stage, and she would say, "Bob, I love the rhythm of these songs so much that I can hardly stand it!"

Looking back at the first Newport Folk Festival in 1959 I have very sketchy memories. I remember a hotel room with Odetta, Theo Bikel, Joan and myself and other folk singers making music. It was magic. I remember Joan at that time when she was 19 as puritanical, not knowing whether she should sing for money or for fun.

Some years later, I commented to Joan, "I've been going to festivals for years looking to reproduce that moment, but it's like chasing that will-o-the-wisp."

I had been living in Aspen, Colorado, writing and performing in clubs there. While there met a young singer named Judy Collins. The next summer, 1960, I brought Judy from Denver to Chicago to perform with me for a month at the club. That was quite a formative period there for folk music. I called Albert and just told him that "this woman has to sing with me for the month of June."

Bob Allen, at that time a student and a regular customer of the Gate, remembers the first time he saw Judy Collins:

We saw Judy Collins at the Gate in 1960 when she was a warm-up act for Bob. She was just starting out when we saw her. She was congruent to a toothpick. She had blond short hair, and she was really good.

I came back to Chicago from Aspen, and I walked into the apartment a week before that job began, and here was a guy who says, "Hi, I'm Bobby Camp. Al Grossman sent me." I said, 'Well, what am I supposed to do?'

And he said, "Albert thought we should sing together."

Albert had heard him singing with Jimmy Gavin in a club in New York in the Village and said, "I'll give you a ticket to Chicago." He also gave him the key to my apartment.

He hadn't told me about it at all. I called Albert, and said, 'What the fuck is going on?'

Albert answered, "This guy's great, he sings great, try him out."

Tom Paxton:
I'm fascinated to hear about his meeting up with Camp, because I can offer a little perspective about that. I had just come in on a weekend from the Army, and I was at a coffeehouse in New York. Camp was singing there and sang a song with Jimmy Gavin, and it was announced from the stage that he was leaving for Chicago to sing with Bob Gibson. So I knew before Bob did, and I never knew 'til years later that he didn't know.

It really hit me hard. I thought Albert was losing confidence in me. Of course, at that time I was using a lot of speed, so I probably had some reason to wonder about Albert's motives. In retrospect, I think I was probably doing my best performing ever. I used to do ten minutes or so of standup comedy in the middle of my act. I'd put down the instrument and just talk, because I couldn't sing. (Albert later was to comment that I was having trouble with my voice at that time in my career.) That was what the act was.

Bob's longtime friend John Irons offers this information about Bob's style in performance:
Bob talked a lot in his performances. He just didn't get up there and sing his ten songs, but he told little jokes and stories while he was doing it. One of the reasons was that he always suffered from bronchitis. He found out that if he talked a little bit that he wouldn't stress the voice as much and he could get more mileage. That was another reason I think he liked a lot of people to come up and sing with him because he didn't have to push the voice.

Camp and I didn't sing together for several days. We just looked each other over like two stray dogs. Finally, he came to the club and after the show, probably about four in the morning (the show stopped around one), we were sitting at that little bar there drinking some beers. We started to sing and it was great. Once we started, we never stopped. I was hooked on singing with the guy. I think he's got one of the greatest musical ears and a very exciting voice. I love his voice.

Probably the next night, I called him up on stage to do a couple of numbers. So I called Albert and said, "Okay, you're right. I'm wrong." By the end of the month, we were doing a segment. We went to Newport '60 later that summer. I did my show and then called him up, just as I'd done with Joan the year before.

Hamilton Camp recalls the beginnings of their time together:
We appeared for about a month together at the Gate of Horn when I first met him. He'd call me up on stage for the last 15-20 minutes which grew longer and longer.

In April of 1961 we recorded *Gibson & Camp at the Gate of Horn* and did a couple more takes that summer to finish the album.

Allan Shaw of Folk Era Productions comments on this album:
In December of 1961 the landmark record *Gibson & Camp at the Gate of Horn* was released. Critics rate it with *The Weavers at Carnegie Hall* and the Kingston Trio's first album, and it is included in almost every discography of folk music. It was everything one could hope for. It became a benchmark by which other folk records of the era were measured.

That was the end of the club. The original Gate closed that fall. It closed because Albert sold it, but it really only was being relocated. In a few weeks they made a whole new place up at Elm and State. The new owner moved it because he had a lot of business up north and he thought he'd start all over at the new location. It did well, but I only played there once.

But I'll never forget those days at the old Gate of Horn. It was incredible the people who hung out there, like Studs Terkel, Shel Silverstein, and the Bunnies from the Playboy Club up the way would hang out there. They'd work the Playboy Club all night, being hit on all the time, and then they'd come over to the Gate because nobody would hit on them there. It was a wonderful place. There was a lot of creative energy around there. After the show there was a lot of sitting around singing at the bar. Shel started hanging out there in 1958. He was living over at the Playboy mansion then. At that time he was exclusively doing cartoons. The first thing he ever wrote was with Bobby Camp, a song called *The First Batallion.* After that we started to write songs together there. He became one of the most important people in my life.

One of the earliest songs I ever wrote, which also became my biggest money-making song, was written at the Gate of Horn. Les Brown and I were sitting at the bar there one afternoon. (This was not the band leader! Les was part owner of the Gate of Horn and he later became the television critic for the New York Times.) We had nothing to do, so we were talking about this movie that I'd seen the night before. It was *Abilene,* and it starred Randolph Scott. Like all good Americans, I got most of my ideas from the movies, and then later from television. Anyway, we started singing, "Abilene, Abilene, prettiest town I've ever seen, people there don't treat you mean . . ." (Actually, what I originally wrote was, "women there don't treat you mean," but that was many years ago, and my consciousness has been raised a little bit since then. *As Bob said in his introduction to the song in the 1980 concert filmed for Ohio public television:* I got my act together, let me tell you. See, I attended meetings of N.O.W. — that's the National Organization for Women. Their meetings are open. Men can go, too. Some of you fellas probably oughta go. You learn a lot — change a lot of your basic attitudes. You meet some great broads there, too, I'll tell you! *Then he threw his head back with that huge Gibson smile, said "Oh, Bob!" and broke into the chorus of* Abilene.) John Loudermilk's name is on the song, too, and it belongs there, but that's another story.

Life was pretty wild there at the Gate of Horn, too. It was incredible. I think about the night that Judy Collins came over to my apartment that I was sharing with Camp. She was staying at the hotel a few blocks away. When she left she said, "I'm worried about going there late."

I said "Don't let it bother you. I'll loan you my gun, but it has a hair trigger on it, so be careful."

She ended up shooting the ceiling. She called me from the hotel. "Oh God, the gun went off!"

I said "Don't touch it. Where is it now?"

She said "It's on the bed."

I said "Don't touch it." So I went right over and fixed it.

John Irons recalls a story told to him:

Sam Freifeld was a lawyer who used to be an attorney for the old Gate of Horn. One story that Sam told me was that they'd always have these parties after the show and Sam never got invited. One day Sam asked Allan Ribback, "How come I never get invited?" Allan said, "Well, we always figured if we ever got busted, it's best to have our lawyer on the outside."

There were lots of really great people I got to work with there like Big Bill Broonzy and Josh White. Josh White was a great stylist, and when people would hear Josh, whether they were named Joan Baez or Judy Collins, they would be very affected by the liberties, the style that Josh put into everything. It gave us a lot more freedom. I think he's one of the great unsung heroes.

Comedian George Carlin:
There's a friend of mine named Herb O'Brien who used to be a bartender at the old Gate of Horn and he said that Bob Zimmerman, who we now know as Bob Dylan, used to come in there. Allan Ribback told all the bartenders to give Dylan free drinks while he copied down Bob Gibson's chord changes.

Those were good days. It was fun to hang out there at the bar at the Gate of Horn because it was a good place. It was really THE place to be. There's never been another place like it. There were many clubs at the time — Mother Blues, Rising Moon – but none had that impact. It was unique. The people who went there identified with it. It was their place.

A lot had changed by the time it closed. I was already a disaster area. I had discovered liquid methadrene. By the next summer I was a crazy man.

Success was, unfortunately, the Horn's own undoing. Outgrowing its old space, the club closed in 1961, and then reopened in larger and plusher quarters on Rush Street. To the regulars, though, it just wasn't the same.

Significantly, the most notorious incident in the club's history occurred at the new location, when three Chicago detectives, backed up by eight squad car units, interrupted a performance by comedian Lenny Bruce and arrested him, charging that the show was obscene.

George Carlin vividly remembers the events of that performance:
I was there that night. I was one of those that thought Lenny Bruce was terrific. I was working at the Playboy, and during that run of Lenny's, which was probably two weeks, or intended for two weeks, I would be in the audience a lot of nights after my last show. I was sitting there that particular night with Bob Kerry of the Tarriers. We were fairly loaded and proceeding to drink more beer and listen to Lenny. That's when the policeman stood up and said, "All right, the show's over!" And, you know, it's one of the few times when they get to say that that it was literal, that the show is over! The police were really more interested in closing the club and getting its license revoked, so after they stopped the show, they made everyone leave one at a time showing their ID to prove they were legally

there. Along the line in checking everyone's ID, which was a slow process, they found a couple of girls who were under age, and that became the basis of a problem for the management. Bob Kerry and I maneuvered so that we were among the last few people to go out and we were pretty loaded by then, so when the policeman asked me for my identification, I said, "I don't believe in identification!" I guess they were pretty frustrated by this time and he kind of grabbed me by the neck and the seat of the pants and hustled me down the stairs. I remember going past the bar area and saying to someone, "Tell my wife I'm going to jail." I went into the paddy wagon and Lenny was in there, and he said, "Well, what are you here for?" I said what I did, and we laughed about how stupid that was. There was also a writer there from *Swank* magazine, which was one of the Playboy knock-offs. I was just held overnight with him and released in the morning. There were never any charges against me, and then Lenny's legal thing proceeded against him the way it did.

Despite testimony in court by novelist Nelson Algren and popular disc jockey Dan Sorkin, defending Bruce's performance, the club's liquor license was suspended for 15 days. It was a blow from which the Horn never fully recovered, and the club finally shut down in the mid 1960s. A third Gate of Horn opened later at another location, but it had absolutely no connection with the original club.

At Bob's farewell party in Chicago, 20 September, 1996, John E. Brown offered this:

Elaine "Spanky" McFarlane and I started writing this song in a hotel room one day. We got about three verses done, and we were anticipating the benefit that was two years ago this month, but we never got it together. Well, she called me about three weeks ago, and she dictated what we had on paper and I wrote three more verses. The lyrics are just a little sort of historical account of Bob at the Gate of Horn about 1959.

Excerpts from   Sweet Bobby From "Chi"
(Sung to the tune of "Sweet Betsy from Pike")
Lyrics by John Brown & Elaine McFarlane

Oh, don't you remember sweet Bobby from Chi?
He sang in a cellar, a folk-singin' guy.
He picked on a banjo and a twelve-string guitar,
The old Gate of Horn was a wonderful bar.

Down in that cellar, all smokey and damp,
He sang of Old Blue with young Bobby Camp.
The crowd was ecstatic, my God, what a scene,
With liner notes written by Shel Silverstein.

*They gave the old folk songs a twist that was new.
Camp hollered, "I'm sorry your mother turned blue"!
In three-button suits they were polished and lean.
They kept off the weight with that pure methadrene.*

*Now all us young folkies thought Bob was the rage.
We'd sneak in the "Gate", and we'd sit near the stage.
But we didn't go there a-lookin' for chicks.
We'd check out his changes and copy his licks!*

Excerpted from
Gate of Horn
by Roger McGuinn *(included on his CD* Live From Mars*)*

*I'm goin' to the Gate of Horn
In my memory
Red light flickerin' on a tablecloth
Big, dark beer in front of me
How I wish that I was there
Standin' at the bar
Listenin' to Bob Gibson play
On his fine guitar*

*There was Judy and Peter and Josh and Odetta
The Clancies and Mary and Paul made it better
Grossman and Tommy and Dicky and Lou
When no one was lookin' McGuinn was there too*

*Well then they came and tore it down
Song birds scattered
They all left town
Gate of Horn meant everything to me
Gate of Horn - Gate of Horn
I'm glad I was Chicago born
Gate of Horn meant everything to me*

by Roger McGuinn / Jacques Levy ©EMI-Blackwood / Patian Jackelope-BMI

Following are the famous liner notes written by Shel Silverstein for the Gibson & Camp at the Gate of Horn *album, 1961. They provide the most vivid description imaginable of the club, and as Bob said, "*The liner notes outsold the album two to one. They were wonderful!*"*

I'll tell you a little bit about the old Gate of Horn. It was in the basement. I don't mean a basement club, I mean it was a basement. Chicago is full of places like that. Leroy Neiman the artist was living around the corner in another basement and it wasn't a basement apartment - he was just living in a basement. The Gate of Horn was sort of the same. It was just sort of chiseled out. It was on North Dearborn Street and there was a door that said "Gate of Horn" and some steps that led downstairs and then when you got down there it had a sign on the door that said "use other door." So you had to climb up and go around the other side and there was another door that went down and you were in this crowded little ante room, or whatever the hell it was.

The bar was off to the right. That's where you would find everybody mostly between sets. Either there or in the back room - it was really more like backrooms plural and it was all like carved out of rock with bricks showing through and ashcans sitting around and the further in you got the more like the catacombs it was. And any minute you expected to trip over the dusty bones of some medieval folk singer and there was one bright light and you had to sit on the ashcans or lean against the icebox and that is where you would see Gibson and Camp tuning up to go on stage or combing their hair or going over some arrangement or complaining about some chick who didn't show up the night before. Herb Brown was back there too, doing something great with his bass but I never heard him say anything. Oh - there was a combination office-rehearsal hall-dressing room that was about three feet square and occasionally they would rehearse in there when they wanted real privacy-until Marilyn or one of the other waitresses had to go in there and change so they would come out and play on the coca cola cases and Marilyn would go inside and change until Alan Ribback had to go in and check some books then Marilyn would come out and Alan would go in and fool around with some papers until maybe Cynthia had to go in there to change or the cook had to go in there to get some hamburger-anyway, it went on like that. There wasn't much room and there was an awful lot of confusion.

The waitresses used those catacombs as a short cut from the bar to the main room. There it was in the dark and hot and crowded and great. They would come in from the back of the club - that's where the entertainers came on too. Gibson would come out of the back with Brown and they would do a few numbers and then he would introduce Camp and when Camp came on the whole thing would start to jell and swing and Brown's bass would be going like hell and Gibson would be up there cool and cocky, playing that 12-string and singing and Camp would be like a little rooster with his head back screaming and bouncing up and down and it was really something. After the show we would all be out front, Gibson, Camp and Joel something, and the bartender with the mustache and Ira and Inman and Camp's chick Ginger or Camp's chick Margaret or Gibson's chick Gloria or Gibson's chick Patty or Gibson's chick whatever the hell their names were I don't even remember their names and there was a lot of booze being sopped up between sets and a hell of a lot of musical chairs being played with the girls around there.

There was a great-looking tall colored girl there sitting at the bar. I never met her and I don't think she ever said anything, but she comes to mind. There was a girl named June who used to work at the Playboy Club and a goofy little blonde stripper and God knows what the hell she was doing in there but she got me to draw something on her navel when I was half-crocked and always a few girls from the University and one beautiful little eighteen-year-old who never ever said two words to anybody but was always there, smiling and somebody said she was a little off her rocker, and some tall blonde who was the ex-wife of somebody, and Barbara who was doing the publicity for the Gate, and some of the Second City crowd and a girl with long black hair and white white skin who wore Chinese dresses. And that is where we would sit and booze and talk about the new songs we were going to collaborate on and plan the party that would start about 3 o'clock in the morning-maybe at Gibson's room, at the whore hotel he was staying in or in Camp's apartment which was some girl's apartment or at somebody else's house, sometimes the waitresses. That bar was really the social center for the hip crowd. Gibson and Camp were the social directors. And they would sit there and whisper and work up wild scenes that couldn't possibly turn out as great as they sounded.

After a while I think Gibson and Camp even started to look alike. They must have weighed about 45 pounds together and they sat and they whispered and they looked like two crooked English jockeys fixing a race. And they wore those thin grey suits that look like they've been made by a shoemaker for an elf, and they each had the cowlick falling onto their forehead just so, and those skinny ties—but there wasn't anything little about their singing when they did stuff like Betty and Dupree or Daddy Roll 'Em or - anyway I am not going to tell you how good the stuff is. Mostly the liner notes you read tell you how good the stuff is before you even hear it and they say "notice the fantastic guitar work on 'Tisket a Tasket'" or "this rendition of 'Roll Me Over in the Clover' will rank as the greatest" etc., etc. That's all a lot of crap. You can't explain music. These songs by Gibson, Camp, and Brown will speak for themselves. If you dig it, fine, if you don't, well, it's too bad. I happen to dig it but I am not going to start telling you how good it is. I'll tell you some more about the Old Gate of Horn, though. The final night there was really a blast. Everybody was wearing carnations, and there were more people high than I would care to mention and it was a full house and that English comedian Charles, whatever his name is, was better than ever which is really saying something because he is even great when he is lousy and Del Close did one of the wildest, funniest bits I have ever seen and closed with a bit that would have got him put in jail for five years if there had been any police around there and I am not going to tell you what it was.

Gibson, Camp and Brown they were up there singing, shouting and playing and stomping and wailing and yelping and barking and dropping raw eggs on the floor and yelling at Ray about the lighting and wearing straw hats and drinking beer and joking with the audience and doing encore after encore and we did a set together on Betty and Dupree and we must have done fifty-five choruses and everybody in the club was screaming and it was great and if the walls had collapsed right then and there it would have been very poetic. But they didn't.

And finally it broke up and everybody went away wherever the hell they were going.

They left their carnations laying around on the floor with the raw eggs and that was the end of the old Gate of Horn and I told myself I would come back the next day and do a painting of it, but I never did.

I don't know what they do with it now. Maybe they filled it up with sand, maybe there is somebody storing canned salmon there, I don't know - maybe somebody turned it into a rumpus room, but it is gone and if you missed it you missed something.

Ribback has a new Gate of Horn now over on Rush Street and it is very fancy and there are carpets and velvet ropes at the door and everybody wears dark suits and ties and there are two floors with a bar downstairs and a beautiful showroom upstairs and they say the acoustics are great. They have costumes and they say it is greater and better, more beautiful than ever. They say it is better to work in, better to run and everything and maybe they're right.

But you should have seen the old Gate of Horn.

SHEL SILVERSTEIN
Hudson Street, New York City, September, 1961

And what I owe Bob, I will tell you, what he did for me was he set the time for us and I know that at the time of the *Earl* and the *Gate* and John Brown's club — to be where Bob was, was to be the best place in the world. To be where we were at that time — I've never had anything better — I've never known anything better. I think it's important for us to know that we were at the best place at the best time.

SHEL SILVERSTEIN
Chicago,
September 20, 1996

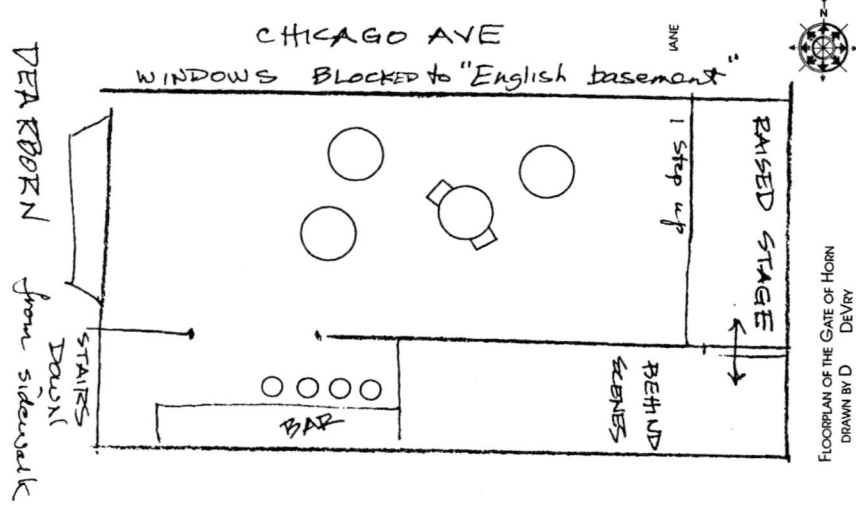

BOB GIBSON - 50

Left to Right: Herb Brown on bass, Bob *(later Hamilton)* Camp and Bob Gibson

I Come For To Sing - 51

Left to Right: Herb Brown on bass. Bob *(later Hamilton)* Camp and Bob Gibson

All photos by Bob Allen

Very special thanks go to Bob Allen, currently of Colorado, who generously contributed the rare photos of Bob Gibson at the Gate of Horn. I have found no one else who has pictures of the place!

Bob Allen:

I was basically in a situation where I had an interest in photography, and I was taking a course in it there in Chicago in college. I thought I'd just shoot up a roll of film there at the Gate of Horn. I asked them at the club if it would be okay, and they said as long as I wasn't making a lot of noise and didn't use a flash, "go ahead and help yourself!" So I did, and thank God they let me do it. I liked the way they turned out, because they really gave the feel of the place. It was really a small place with little tables that you could just barely fit two people around, and the only light was a spotlight on the stage.

5
THE MAGIC OF ALBERT GROSSMAN AND GIBSON & CAMP

Just as Bob Gibson was on the cutting edge, or ahead of it, in the '50s with his performing, arranging and writing, so was his manager, Albert Grossman, equally ahead of his time. Grossman, who created the Gate of Horn in Chicago, which became the first true new citadel of folk music, had an ear for a sound and packaging that the public would soon embrace.

His early "finds", whom he booked into his Gate of Horn in addition to Gibson, included Glenn Yarbrough, Odetta, Joan Baez, Bob (later to become Hamilton) Camp and Judy Collins. Peter Yarrow and Bob Dylan were to follow when Grossman sold the Gate of Horn and moved his base of operations to New York City. When folk music interest passed its peak, he added rock 'n' roller Janis Joplin to his management stable.

Grossman was born in Chicago in 1926 and majored in economics in college. As noted in the previous chapter, he was working for the city of Chicago when he had the idea for the Gate of Horn and when he "scouted" Bob Gibson as one of its earliest performers. He and his college friend, Les Brown, came up with the money to start the folk club. Alan Ribback and John Court were later partners.

It became a pattern that those whose careers Grossman touched were almost magically transformed even if they were not personally managed by him. In 1957, Grossman heard Glenn Yarbrough singing at a party. He offered Yarbrough $150 a week to sing at the Gate of Horn, to succeed Gibson who now was moving on to other gigs but who would return for at least a month each year through 1961.

In 1959, another chance meeting turned to gold for Yarbrough. He was at the Cosmo Alley folk club in Los Angeles and was introduced to Lou Gottlieb and Alex Hassilev. After several tentative rehearsals together, Glenn invited Lou and Alex to join him at his newly purchased club in Aspen, Colorado, called the Limelite. The group's great new sound attracted the ski crowd in Aspen to the club, making it the hangout of choice for the entire town and launching the legend of the Limeliters.

While spending a good deal of time in Greenwich Village looking for talent, Grossman joined forces with George Wein in 1959. Wein was a jazz musician and club owner from Boston who had been pro-

ducing the Newport Jazz Festival in Rhode Island since 1955. Sensing that interest was growing rapidly, the two put together the first Newport Folk Festival in the summer of 1959. Additionally, Grossman and Wein established Personal Artist Management Associates, based in New York City. When Albert moved to New York permanently, he started Albert B. Grossman Management.

In her 1987 autobiography, And A Voice To Sing With: A Memoir, Joan Baez described Albert Grossman as:

> ...a sly, furtive, nervous, soft-spoken, funny, generous and bizarre man with a round form, round face, round eyes and round glasses. Above his round eyes arched black eyebrows, like smudges of charcoal, (that) rose in an expression of surprise. He terrified me by saying things like, 'You can have anything you want. You can have anybody you want.' Before the end of the '60s, he would be managing Bob Dylan, Peter, Paul and Mary, Janis Joplin and Jimi Hendrix, to name just a few. Albert was the best.

By the late 1950s, with the baby boom generation emerging from pre-adolescence, the American college population was exploding. In fact, about a quarter of all Americans were between 21 and 24. This created an affluent, literate audience that did not identify with either Frank Sinatra's older sophistication on the one end of the musical spectrum, or with Elvis Presley's rocking fervor on the other end. As the new decade would confirm, they were also interested in politics. Grossman's influence clearly was already shaping the new form of music, but he had even bigger things in mind, that would truly revolutionize the sound of popular folk music and impact everything else that followed. It all began with his pairing of the two Bobs — Gibson and Camp.

Of course, it was Albert who put me together with Camp. Camp used to sing with Jimmy Gavin in the Village, who I thought a lot of, but I really fought being teamed up with Camp at first. As I said in the previous chapter, we circled each other like two stray dogs for a couple of days, kind of looking, until we finally gave it a try.

So I called Albert and said, "Okay, you're right. I'm wrong. I'll sing with him."

Albert said, "Well, OK, good, I knew you would, but listen — I want you guys to get together with this woman and form a trio." He said, "Neither one of you are going to like it because she's taller than both of you."

I said, "No way!"

He was looking then to form a "Peter, Paul and Mary" type group. He knew that it was a very viable format, and it would prove to be, but we refused him. We didn't need that!

Since Grossman had been in the folk music business, groups had been some of its most successful performers. From 1950 to 1952, the Weavers — Pete Seeger, Lee Hays, Ronnie Gilbert and Fred Hellerman — had scored a series of major hits with harmonized pop arrangements of traditional and contemporary folk songs before they were forced to disband due to the anti-Communist witch hunts of the era. They later returned with some success, although they were still banned by radio and television well into the 1960s.

In 1958, the Kingston Trio — Dave Guard, Bob Shane and Nick Reynolds — released their version of Tom Dooley, *which became a #1 hit and launched their career. The Kingstons then became a model for other folk trios such as the Limeliters, who formed in 1959.*

Grossman's idea was to combine the successful elements of these earlier folk groups. From the Weavers, he took the idea of featuring a woman, and from the Limeliters, the idea of having one member provide a comic element. In the Limeliters, that character had been Lou Gottlieb.

Robert Shelton, a music critic for The New York Times, watched Grossman try out different "components" for the trio and later wrote about it in his book No Direction Home: The Life and Times of Bob Dylan *(New York: Beech Tree Books, 1986). Grossman "briefly considered Molly Scott and Logan English," Shelton wrote:*

> Next, having long admired Bob Gibson, he thought he would use the former Chicagoan as a keystone. For some months, Grossman worked informally with Gibson, Carolyn [Hester] and Ray Boguslav, a commercial artist and highly schooled musician. But the group didn't jell either. Gibson had periodic losses of voice and was befouled with problems...Carolyn Hester later commented, "We ended up with little semblance of a 'blend' or 'sound.' The trio also lacked the dedicated toughness Albert ultimately found with Peter, Mary (Travers) and Paul (Stookey).

In the same book, the author quotes Dave Van Ronk as saying:

> Grossman had lined up musical director Milt Okun and a contract with Warner Bros. Records before forming the trio. It was after Bob, Carolyn and Ray didn't pan out, Grossman turned to Peter Yarrow.

Peter Yarrow corrects this account saying:

> Neither an arrangement with a music director, nor any record contract was in place for Peter, Paul & Mary prior to our getting together. The trio arranged its first few songs alone including *This Train* and *The Cruel War*. We realized that none of us had the musi-

cal knowledgability to shepherd the arrangement process for a full repertoire of songs, so a search was made by Albert for a music director to work with us as a fourth creative partner. First asked was Robert deCormier, our present music director and the former director of the Belafonte Singers, of which Milt Okun had been a member. Bob was involved in a multitude of projects and couldn't make the commitment. I believe he recommended Milt Okun, who did become our music director for the first decade of our association.

As to our record contract, after we had rehearsed for about seven months, finding our personal muse and chemistry, we began performing. Shortly thereafter we started to audition for record companies. The main competitors that were interested in Peter, Paul & Mary were Atlantic Records, Columbia and Warner Bros. But that's another story.

Interestingly, Bob Gibson did not mention the Bob-Carolyn-Ray attempts in any interviews of record, and his extensive personal collection of tapes does not include any of the demos of this trio. It seems likely that the recording contract Grossman negotiated was on behalf of Gibson-Camp and a woman whose name Gibson always claimed he never knew. That trio, proposed by Grossman, never got started because Gibson rejected the concept, as detailed earlier in this chapter.

Albert didn't tell us who the woman was, but it was NOT Mary Travers — it was NOT Judy Henske. As a matter of fact, years later I was visiting with Al Grossman in Woodstock and said "Who was the woman? Camp and I are very, very curious." He was really, really right about the idea, of course, but we never did find out who the woman was.

Rich Warren of WFMT's Midnight Special adds what he had heard about this proposed trio and who the woman might have been:
I can't resist adding to this folklore. WFMT was around (although I personally was not) in the good ol' Gate of Horn days in Chicago. Albert Grossman ran the Gate of Horn. However, having personally taped and co-produced two of Bob Gibson's CDs, we talked extensively about those days. Grossman matched Gibson with Bob Camp (now Hamilton Camp). Jo Mapes, a popular (blonde) female Chicago singer was to complete the trio. The whole purpose was to popularize Bob Dylan's songs since Grossman had signed Dylan, but he wasn't going anywhere at the time. Needless to say, neither Gibson, nor Camp was enthused about the idea.

Once again Peter Yarrow corrects the rumors that circulated about the establishment of Peter, Paul & Mary:

Bob Dylan was signed by Albert sometime after Peter, Paul & Mary were already performing, so it's not the case at all that "the purpose" was, or could have been, to popularize Dylan's songs. In fact, Peter, Paul & Mary had our first album's repertoire together long before Albert managed Bobby. It was not until our third album, *In the Wind*, that we recorded any of his songs.

Hamilton Camp has a revelation that neither Bob nor anyone else, for that matter, ever knew:

When I first met Bob and Al Grossman, I sat in a room while they sat staring at the floor and, you know, I'm sitting there crying. It was the first time I met Bob and I barely knew Grossman. He paid my way out to Chicago to be a partner with Bobby Gibson and some woman. He was already looking for a trio which later became Peter, Paul and Mary. He didn't tell us who the woman was, because we turned him down, but I looked on Grossman's desk when I was there and saw Marilyn Child's name on a contract! Grossman had already gotten a contract together with Bob Gibson, Marilyn Child and Bob Camp. I'd barely met Gibson, I never met Marilyn, and he'd already booked us! Well, you know, knowing Marilyn was an old hand, and he knew that I was quick, he figured, rightly so, that within a week we could have a set together.

Everytime I hear Peter, Paul & Mary, I think, "Oh, yeah, that would have been me." Oh, well, I guess I've never been known for the wisdom of the choices I made.

The insecurity that Bob felt over this episode prematurely ended his relationship with Grossman as his manager. Despite the fact that Albert's first choice turned him down, he remained undeterred in his vision of a trio.

Grossman first heard Yarrow early in 1960 when Yarrow was performing at the Cafe Wha? in Greenwich Village. That spring, Grossman saw Yarrow again when he was auditioning for a CBS folk music special, Folk Sound USA. At that time he became Yarrow's manager. That summer, due to Grossman's sponsorship, Yarrow was included in the second Newport Folk Festival, at which Gibson introduced Camp.

With Grossman booking him, Yarrow began to appear in the major folk clubs around the country: The Gate of Horn, the Ash Grove in Los Angeles and Folk City in New York.

"I worked with Grossman for about a year," Yarrow recalled, "at which point he suggested that I form a group."

One night in the spring of 1961, Noel Paul Stookey, who was singing at the Gaslight, was approached by Grossman, who told Stookey he was putting together a new act, a folk trio, and asked if he would be interested in joining it.

Peter, Paul and Mary finally were assembled and rehearsed for many months before they were ready for their first performance. In the fall of 1961, Yarrow was booked for a two-week engagement at Folk City. Grossman contacted Mike Porco, the owner, to book the trio. Porco said he wouldn't want to pay any more than he was paying for Yarrow. Grossman agreed to add $20 to the fee himself.

Three years later, in 1964, Peter, Paul and Mary placed first in the Billboard ranking of most popular folk groups on campus. (The most popular group in general was The Beatles, who had just taken the country by storm.)

On June 19, 1961, Stookey read an article in the NY Herald Tribune about a Father's Day boat cruise up the Hudson River to Bear Mountain that had gone awry due to counterfeit tickets and overcrowding, and showed it to a recent acquaintance, a 20-year-old singer named Bobby Dylan, who had arrived in New York from Minnesota the previous winter. "He brought back a song the next day. It was astounding," Stookey said. The song was Talkin' Bear Mountain Picnic Blues, which Dylan wrote in the style of his idol, Woody Guthrie. Dylan was not, at that point, known as a songwriter, which made the composition all the more surprising. Stookey told Albert Grossman that Dylan was somebody worth watching.

Early in 1962 Grossman took over as manager of Bob Dylan. In taking over Dylan's management, Grossman had the strong support of Peter, Paul and Mary and not long thereafter, Dylan's Blowing in the Wind became a big hit for the trio.

In 1972, Peter, Paul and Mary made their solo debuts. None were as successful as their group albums had been. Some blamed it on the fact that Grossman didn't mastermind their music on these.

"He was dealing with his own travail," Yarrow said (in Peter, Paul & Mary: A Song to Sing All Over This Land by William Ruhlman in Goldmine #410, April 12, 1996). "There was trouble in the country and there was trouble in that world of his. It was after Janis Joplin had died and I don't think he was really able to give me the kind of guidance that he might have at another time. I think his heart was broken in some ways by her tragic passing."

Grossman died early in 1986.

"Albert Grossman had a vision of a more accessible form of folk entertainment," said Stookey in the same Goldmine article. "He understood and valued the tradition of folk music, but he saw no reason at all why it couldn't be available to more people. He was wise beyond his years."

He wanted to sign his artists to major labels. He had signed Odetta to RCA and his falling-out with Baez had occurred when he *tried to take her to Columbia. She wound up on Vanguard.*

🌿 🌿 🌿 🌿 🌿 🌿 🌿

What remains the greatest legacy of Albert Grossman, though, as far as it relates to Bob Gibson, is the legend of Gibson and Camp. In the early '60s at the Gate of Horn, Bob Gibson and Bob (later Hamilton) Camp were revolutionizing folk music in the same way, and at the same time, that Second City was revolutionizing theater.

When you talk about the "good old days" in Chicago, many assume you're referring to Gibson & Camp at the Gate of Horn. Their mood, their harmonies, their energy and their constant improvisations made them something original and unique. They were a profound influence on many duets that followed them, including Simon & Garfunkel.

How do you describe Hamilton Camp? He's short and he's got incredible energy. He is a genius and he has the best musical ear I have ever known. I got hooked on singing with the guy.

I don't know, it was very intense singing with him, and I think there was a competitive thing which always existed between us. We were singing parallel solos for awhile, and then we got a gig when the Playboy Club opened the Penthouse. It was the big room upstairs and we were the one of the first acts in there. It was Camp and me and Herb Brown playing the bass and 300 people out front, and again, like working with Charlie Farrell, not a drop in the decibel level. They were all looking at the bunnies. It was just incredible. The show was not what was going on that night. They were there to be at the Playboy Club. We were there for 21 days, the longest 21-day gig I've ever had in my life, but it turned out real good because we began to listen to each other since nobody else was listening. We suddenly hooked up to a thing where we began to do variations of what we were doing to each other. We'd just fool around and make Herb Brown grin behind us because he heard it to a point where he knew it all really well, and we'd make each other smile.

Ed Holstein remembers those days:
Bob was on the *Playboy Penthouse* which was a show Hugh Heffner had in 1959. He had a studio made to look like his living room with couches. Cy Coleman did the theme music. There was a picture of an elevator going up and it opened up to a party at Hugh's. Heffner had on a smoking jacket and pipe and he had all these very interesting people sitting around. He was able to get people who couldn't get on TV like Pete Seeger. Pete couldn't get on national TV but he could be on affiliate TV. It was funny to see Pete Seeger

singing *Wimmaweh* with bunnies all around him. Heffner had Lenny Bruce and Norman Mailer, and people you didn't see on other shows. Heffner liked Gibson and he was on the show a couple of times. He'd just recorded that record of ski songs and he was doing that in a tuxedo.

Gibson & Camp performed at the Playboy club when it first opened but I don't think they liked them much. It was basically a bunch of loud guys looking to chase bunnies.

There's a certain kind of sound Camp and I developed together. Either of us was likely to have the high or low harmony at any given moment. Then there were times when we'd cross over and even kind of pound away with no melody. We'd actually get the melody out in two or three passes of a chorus. Then we'd both sing harmony. The melody was still evident because people were still hearing it in a shadowy kind of way in their minds. That's why it sounded larger than life — because we almost were getting three-part harmony, with the third part in your head.

I sincerely believe that Bobby Camp was a great improviser because he had a hell of an ear for music. We went down to the Archway Lounge one night which was a south side jazz joint. We heard Coltrane play and he ended up this great set by taking about eight bars after the rest of the group stopped and he just went wild. Well, Camp said, "Wow, did you hear that?!" And then he proceeded to sing every note back imitating what he'd played. I couldn't believe it. I said, "Okay, that means this guy can improvise." So I was always pushing him to do that. I learned later, though, that maybe improvisation in music may not have been his forte, but he could sing anything — ANYTHING!! He could find weird intervals, and I'd know that they were mistakes, but then he'd start singing the song that way everytime because he really liked it. But I could see that he had a hell of an ear, one of the best musical ears I've run across, and a great sense of pitch and stuff and we'd do improvisation that was pretty far out. There were a couple of songs we'd do, *Skillet Good & Greasy* and *That's What You Get For Lovin' Me,* where everytime we'd do them we did not know what we were going to do. We explored pretty much all the possibilities. Therefore, we were not going to do anything totally brand new to either one of us, but on the other hand, we'd explored enough possibilities so that we had a lot of options, and some of the options would end up doubling a note. That's not what we meant to do. Other times it was uncanny how we were in tandem, and no matter how outrageous I'd try and reach for a part, he was doing something right or how outrageous he was, I'd be there. . . . Sometimes it works and it's just magic. So it was really exciting working with him. I think both of us would have done more of it if we could. We were always kind of limited. He had a big family and made his living as an actor. We were never at a place in our lives like young guys who'd say, "Okay, let's devote a year of our lives and make it happen." It had to meet us half way or we couldn't do it.

In 1961 we made our debut album, *Gibson & Camp at the Gate of Horn,* recorded on Elektra records. That album was a benchmark — a watershed for a lot of the singers. Everyone from John Lennon to Gordon Lightfoot to John Denver say that album influenced them.

Hamilton Camp remembers those days:
I might not be your best witness on that era, as Haldeman once said, 'cause we were pretty wacked out when we were together and I really never got to know Bob that well over the years. He's a pretty close man. Other than what we were gonna sing next or rehearsing, we never really exchanged much in any way. It was all on stage and that seemed to be enough. There wasn't much to say off. It was a sporadic association. We appeared for about a month together at the Gate of Horn when I first met him. He'd call me up on stage for the last 15-20 minutes which grew longer and longer. That was the first gig and the second gig was after we went from there to Newport. We came back and did two or three weeks at the old Gate and then the new Gate and it's already getting fuzzy. We went on the road briefly and did some bad ass concerts at various venues with the Brothers Four and people like that. That was very short. We ended up in New York. Right after Newport and the second gig I went to Second City and that was about it except for a few reunions over the years. We didn't see too much of each other in between. He was in Chicago usually and I was always living in L.A. because I was an actor then.

It was fun. On stage we were the best of friends, and in that way I never felt closer to anybody, but off, you know, there wasn't that much going on. Communication together was never a strong point. Bob had problems communicating with everybody.

When we'd sing, what I always loved to do was to sing the arpeggio of the chord or as much of it as you can get hold of. Sam Cook and Ray Charles were great practitioners of that art. It's fascinating when it gets really complicated because nobody would be left singing the tune. When you sing something like *For Lovin' Me,* all you really need to do is say first time out in the first verse, "Here's the tune. Remember this tune?" Remind everyone. Get their tapes going so they've got the tune going. It was as if we'd say to the audience, "Okay, now here's the tune in harmony. That's what we do with the second verse. Here's what we do with the harmony. He's gonna go high, and here's what it sounds like that way. Okay, now he's gonna go low and I'm gonna go high. Okay, you all got the tune and the harmonies in mind? Now keep them in mind, because you're going to sing them in your head. We're gonna sing something else! Neither of us is now responsible for the melody. You are!" And it works! The audience will then know the melody. It's there and then we're singing three-part harmony, but the audience has got the melody in their head.

Chicago writer G. Gigi Gilmartin wrote this about the legendary duo of Gibson and Camp:
Some performers generate electricity and excitement, charging the very air with their talent. Gibson and Camp went beyond mere electricity to megaton atomic explosions. Gibson on guitar or banjo laying down riffs so easily, so casually, you never realized how complex they were until you heard someone else trying to imitate him. And Camp's voice soaring, sliding, hitting notes not yet written and creating harmonies not yet conceived. But beyond the music, there was plain good fun. Camp bouncing one-liners off anyone and anything. Prepared shtick that veered on into wild improvisation. Satiric bits and songs on local celebs, the Chicago cops, sacred institutions - even satire on folk music itself.

They were only together for one year. Yet anyone who has ever heard *Gibson and Camp at the Gate of Horn,* anyone who has ever seen them perform together, will never forget the experience.

Long years. Good times, bad, times, hard times. Marriages, kids, money, no money. The Gate died. Two reincarnations of the Gate died. Albert still wanted a trio and went off to put together Peter, Paul & Mary. Gibson dropped out of music and went to New England to make cabinets and kill the monkey. Camp divided his talents between acting and music and barely survived. Then Camp dropped out and went to Skymont, Virginia, where he hooked up with Lewis Ross, Lew Arquette, Rusdi Lane and Jakub Ander, the Skymonters. The Skymonters had more in common than their show business backgrounds. They were all members of the same spiritual brotherhood, Subud. Camp doesn't fool with drugs anymore and he's been married to the same woman for 15 years *[1978 - now it's 36 years!].* He credits Subud for the stability of his life in a business not noted for stability.

Their talent, honesty, humanity, sense of humor - these know no borders or generation gaps. The ethnic purists who once criticized, now laud Gibson and Camp as one of the last bastions of "real" folk music. They're wrong. Folk music isn't sociology, it isn't acoustic instruments versus electric instruments; it isn't moldy ballads or wishy-washy songs of feeble protest. Folk music is nothing more than simple human honesty, a genuine expression of things we've all known and felt and experienced. As long as we can feel, there will always be Gibson and Camp.

When you leave Earl's and go home to your families and problems, so will they. Gibson and Camp are what we are and what we might have been if we had talent. The legend doesn't have to be reborn because it never died. Those in Subud believe that through their spiritual brotherhood, they have established eternal links with those who share their beliefs. Gibson isn't a member of Subud, but his link with Camp, the brotherhood the two have established for themselves, is eternal. They couldn't break the bond if they tried (and they've probably tried many times!). Camp was writing about his wife when he composed *Partners,* but one line in the song applies as much to Gibson as it does to Camp's lady. "It's two for one and partners all the way."

Camp settled in Los Angeles and claims a wealth of show business credits that include motion picture, television and stage. He recorded several solo albums in addition to the three he did with Gibson. Hamilton Camp has had supporting roles in the movies Heaven Can Wait, Eating Raoul, Nickelodeon, Rabbit Test, *and* American Hot Wax, *to name a few. His best remembered television roles include Andrew the maintenance man on* He and She, Lorenzo & Henrietta Music Variety Show *(with Gibson),* The Smothers Brothers Show, The Glen Campbell Show, Love American Style, Starsky and Hutch, McMillan and Wife, Forever Fernwood, Flip Wilson Show, Big John Little John, Feather and Father, M.A.S.H., WKRP, Cheers, The Mary Tyler Moore Show, Hill Street Blues, *and, most recently,* Lois and Clark. *He has done commercial work and his voice is heard in* The Smurfs *animated cartoons. He has a strong background in improvisational theater and was one of the early members of Chicago's Second City at the same time that he was performing with Gibson at the Gate of Horn. He also co-wrote and starred with Paul Sills in* Story Theatre *on Broadway and its sequel,* More Story Theatre.

Gibson & Camp

L-R: Camp, Gibson 1961 at Gate of Horn

Gibson & Camp, 1978 from the *Homemade Music* album

L-R: Camp, Gibson 1972 at Earl of Old Town

L-R: Camp, Gibson 1971

L-R: Gibson, Camp 1986

6

THE GLORY YEARS

As big a deal as the Gate of Horn was, amazingly enough that was far from being the only thing going on in my career at that time. All of a sudden everything was happening for me.

Allan Shaw:
Back then Bob Gibson OWNED Chicago!
The first recording effort of Gibson was a 45 and/or 78 rpm release on Decca during 1956 of two traditional folk songs, *Marching to Pretoria* and *I'm Never to Marry*. These two songs, which first introduced the public to Gibson's smooth and velvety voice as well as his ability to convey a feeling of good times and fun through his singing, were his first recorded hits. They later were re-released on two *All-Time Hootenanny Favorites* albums.

My first released album was called *Offbeat Folksongs*. It got that name because the songs were a little off-beat and I was working a lot in Chicago at the Off-Beat Room. It was just intended to be an audition tape but later it was made into a record.

It gets complicated saying what my first record was, though. *Offbeat Folksongs* wasn't actually my first recording. As far as places putting out folk music in those days, there were Folkways and Stinsons and that was about it. I went to the guy who owned Stinson and played him a tune. He said he'd have to think about it and that I should go across the river to Jersey to a little studio he had in his house and make an audition tape. "We'll see what you sound like," he said. I put down a good 22 minutes of recorded music — two or three takes of everything. I heard from him a few days later, and he said he didn't think there was a record there. I went on to meet Ken Goldstein who was working with Riverside, and, in his living room, recorded *Offbeat Folksongs*.

That became my first album which was released on Riverside. *Offbeat Folksongs* got to be successful, and my next album was released, which was *BOB GIBSON: Carnegie Concert* and then — Bang! — Stinson put out an album of my music on his label. The album was called *Folksongs of Ohio*. He did it without a contract and without my permission. At first he released 22 minutes of music on a 10" LP with big bands between the tracks. Later, when everything

I COME FOR TO SING - 65

went to a 12" format, he re-released it. Then the bands between the songs were bigger than the songs! It was appalling, but it was also of interest to me to hear where I was at that time. I had a very high voice then. I had always been told and convinced that I was a tenor, so I was always trying to sing high. It was frustrating because 25 years later, when none of my other albums were available, *that* record was still in catalogues. I never got a cent from it, and I never talked to the man since that day!

> *Shaw adds these comments on Bob's first album:*
> Gibson's first "commercial" album, *Offbeat Folksongs* on the Riverside label, was recorded in April, 1956, by Kenneth S. Goldstein, a noted folk musicologist, who commented in the liner notes, "These selections are 'offbeat' folksongs in a quite literal sense, being for the most part far off the beaten path followed by most current entertainers in the folksong field... A further 'offbeat' aspect of the Gibson approach is the very wide scope of his repertoire. He ranges from the intricacies and subtle nuances of Flamenco dance (as played, uniquely, on banjo rather than guitar) to the hard-driving banjo-picking style of Southern mountaineers; from the tender lyrical beauty of Irish love songs to the rocking rhythms of a Calypso...(The selections) suggest the open-mindedness of Gibson's song-collecting habits. He has recognized that a college student can be as valuable a source as a venerable mountaineer! In travel throughout the United States and in the West Indies, he has collected from traditional singers, other club performers, students—from "folk" in every walk of life. Nor has he been afraid to delve into the numerous books and recordings of folksongs, from which comes some of his best material. As a combination scholar, collector and performer, Bob Gibson has thus been able to recreate—and create—the essence of the best of folk music, to the great satisfaction of audiences, reviewers and even the severest of all critics—those people from whom he has learned much of the material he presents."

I performed at Carnegie Hall February 11, 1957. That was an incredible experience. Two albums were produced from that concert. One was *BOB GIBSON: Carnegie Concert* and the other was *Bob Gibson Hootenanny at Carnegie*. Both were put out by Riverside and both had basically the same material.

> *Roger McGuinn remembers being blown away by this recording:*
> Listen to his early works like his Carnegie Hall concert. Here he was in his early twenties and his instrumental abilities were just mind-boggling — the way he played the banjo and sang, and he could talk while he was playing. He'd be introducing a song and playing this intricate arpeggio on the banjo, like on *Alberta*. Amazing work!

And his vocals are spot on tune. I really can't sing that well now!

The Hootenanny at Carnegie *liner notes do a wonderful job describing the evening's performance:*
Few musical experiences can be as stimulating and as satisfying as those in which strong, direct contact between the performer and his audience is clearly in evidence. For this reason, few studio recordings - no matter how high the degree of technical excellence - can approach the excitement of a first-rate live performance by an artist whose personality reaches out to spark his listeners.

BOB GIBSON is just such an artist; and the evening on which he captured his audience at New York's Carnegie Recital Hall was one of those excitingly *live* occasions. Side one in particular is filled to overflowing with the feeling of communication between Gibson and his audience, as they respond to Bob's invitation and become performers themselves, joining in on these half-dozen numbers and turning them into zestful examples of the let's-all-sing-together *hootenanny* tradition. Gibson as a leader and impromptu teacher is a wonderfully warm individual: you can immediately sense and hear the enthusiasm and good spirits he generates. In addition, the Gibson comments on the audience's doings and shortcomings are, as the saying goes, worth the price of admission all by themselves.

Thus it should be clear that this album offers considerably more than just the songs listed in the next column. Not only is there the *hootenanny* fun, but also Bob's running introductory commentary on the various selections, his remarks to the audience, and their spontaneous reactions to his comments and his songs.

The material is Gibson's usual adept combination of the unhackneyed and fresh treatment of the familiar. He can breathe new life into as standard an item as *The Erie Canal,* can restore a full folk feeling to *Day-O,* can convey the rich beauty of *John Riley* and the sheer nonsense of *There Once Was a Poor Young Man,* as well as the rousing power of the gospel-imbued songs that open and close Side 1. As a result, everyone always has an extraordinary good time at a concert by Bob Gibson and his banjo. This time, "everyone" can include record-buyers, too.

These additional comments appear in the liner notes from BOB GIBSON: Carnegie Concert:
The second side of the album is entirely devoted to what might be called group singing — but don't let that put you off. As an old scorner of "community sings" (where no one really seems to know the words and half don't particularly care), I was notably surprised at this concert. Particularly noteworthy is the segment that opens this side of the album, in which Bob sets forth his views on group singing.

The Arthur Godfrey Show was a real biggie for me. That also

happened in 1957. I competed in the Arthur Godfrey Talent Scouts show. I sang in this really high tenor voice I had, and I played a banjo tune that I had put together simply because everyone kept saying, "Would you play *The World is Waiting for a Sunrise?*" and all that other good Eddie Peabody banjo stuff. This was a five-string banjo I was playing, and it had nothing to do with that! They either wanted to hear *The World is Waiting for a Sunrise,* or *The Blue Tail Fly,* the way Burl Ives did it. I was just trying to let them know there was a little more to it than that. I won the competition, and because of that I became a regular on his show. We'd play together on the show. I had the banjo and he played the baritone ukelele, so it was perfect. Whenever he would come out to Chicago and do a stock show from the International Amphitheater, he'd put me on, and I would go to New York and work at the Blue Angel at night and work his show in the morning. It was big time.

But I would be dead at the end of two weeks. It was ridiculous. Jonathan Winters would always end up at the Blue Angel at the end of whatever running around New York that he had been doing that night. The crew there then would go have breakfast and stay up until five or six in the morning, which was the time I had to go to the Godfrey show.

One day I fell asleep on the Godfrey show. I'm sitting there asleep and Godfrey went right through a commercial and then jabbed me in the ribs. He thought it was funny—thank God! He could be a funny guy.

I never got to know him offstage, though. I never talked to him away from the program — not one word — in the 17 weeks I was on the program. Whatever it was that he had, it worked. He could be corny and friendly on stage, but he kept it there. He never got to know his guests.

Sometimes you got messages by way of the producer. If Godfrey was on a tirade, it would filter down. Everyone would be uptight. But by 11 in the morning, after he'd drunk two or three cups of tea, or whatever it was, he was okay.

The show was simulcast — radio and television — and was incredibly long. The first part was just radio, part was both radio and television and the last part was television. The pay during the simulcast was network radio pay plus network television. It was like $800, as opposed to $200 and something for radio or television only. There were a lot more radio stations that carried the program than television.

A lot of times I would take out a segment, singing *Marching to Pretoria,* or one of those songs, with the audience. Whoever was in the cast, plus Arthur would play, then he would say, "Well, I see we're running short. Bobby Gibson, would you give us a tune?", so I'd grab my banjo and get up there and begin to strum.

It was only a couple of minutes to station break, commercial, and the simulcast, so I began telling them where the song came from and by the station break, he cut me. We went into the station break, then came out of commercials and then into my song. The second time I did that, the producer said to me, "I know what you're doing. Don't do it again. I'll give you the second song of the simulcast, but when I say sing, SING, don't talk about the song for two minutes."

There were a lot of songs that I came up with at that time in my career that became very important in the folk music thing. Even on the *Offbeat Folksongs,* there was *All My Trials, Lord, Soon Be Over,* which later was recorded by many others. At that time I didn't attempt to copyright any of the songs I found. I didn't feel that my arrangements were copyrightable. You don't really copyright arrangements, but you can copyright orchestrations. But these really weren't orchestrations, they were just chord changes and differences in quality, style or character, which weren't protectable. But a lot of people sang them the way I did, and I'm real pleased about it.

I had the first recording of *Michael, Row the Boat Ashore* by a year or two. The album liner said "Gibson learned it from Pete Seeger," which was wrong. Pete and I both learned it from a guy named Tony Saletan. Three years after I recorded it, it supposedly was written by one of the Highwaymen — but that's the folk music business!

On the other hand, there's *John Riley,* that Ricky Neff and I wrote, which is based on one of the oldest stories in folklore. It's the story of the unrecognized lover who returns and puts his lover to the test. It's in song in almost every country in the world, but the version that Joan Baez, Odetta and Judy Collins recorded is our version. It is based on a traditional song, but is not the traditional song, and we collect royalties on it.

The liner notes written by Kenneth S. Goldstein about the song, *Abilene,* on the early album, *I Come for to Sing,* are not very accurate. The album says, "Little is known about the origin of this song. In any case, the version of the song performed here is a typical example of modern tradition in practice. To the original stanzas have been added several written by various big city writers, including Les Brown of Chicago and others." All there was to begin with, was "Abilene, Abilene, prettiest town I've ever seen," to which I added the verses as they are now, with Les Brown, a Chicago writer. By that time, my shift from searching and rearranging to writing was already starting. I was already adding verses and making changes, fixing stuff up and completing. That was the case with *Abilene.* It was incomplete. I just put some words to it and completed it so it could be sung.

Allan Shaw continues his comments:
Less than a year after recording *Offbeat Folksongs,* Gibson followed with *I Come for the Sing* in January 1957 and the recorded *Carnegie Concert* in February 1957. Both of these albums clearly demonstrated Gibson's emerging prowess as a performer and his ability to present material that would not only please his own audiences (both live and via recordings), but would impress later performers as material with strong audience appeal. Perhaps it is this as much as anything that demonstrates Gibson's amazing feel not only for the music but for its appeal to audiences.

Michael Smith, who at this point had not met Bob, remembers the atmosphere of those early days when Bob was on top:
I'd heard of Bob for years because I'd worked in a lot of coffeehouses in the early '60s all around Chicago, working in a new act with John Mellencamp. Gibson was certainly in the air. I traveled throughout the midwest during that time, and Gibson pretty much dominated the folk music scene in the '60s in the midwest. At the time there was a gentleman whose whole act was he "did" Gibson. He was very serious about it. It must have taken a lot of work because Gibson to us was very sophisticated. There was no comparing Bob with anybody else. We thought of him as jazz because he seemed that removed. Even his songs were sophisticated. He was so advanced! At the same time he had a kind of an "infant terrible" reputation.

I had worked in Miami with a group called Just 4. There were three guys and a girl. The girl was the sister of Lydia Wood, who wrote *Anathea,* a great song recorded by Judy Collins. To me, immediately, that was a big deal because *Anathea* was a heavy tune around the coffeehouses. The Just 4 was a quartet that did nothing but Gibson material, and they are the folks on the cover of *Where I'm Bound.* They were very good and worked for a long time at a coffeehouse that I was at home in called the House of Pegasus.

I also had a friend named Bob Ingraham, who was in a group called Les Baxter's Balladeers with David Crosby for a few years, and they did Gibson songs. Through all these connections, I got to feel really familiar with Bob's songs. I loved *Fog Horn* and the *New Frankie and Johnny.* There was a recording of that which got to be fairly popular by a group called the Steel Town Two in 1962 or '63.

Everybody was imitating him in 1963! I remember the Smothers Brothers in 1962 came down to St. Pete. I was in a junior college there, and playing in a folk group. The Smothers Brothers were doing a concert and they wanted to borrow our bass. Afterwards we hung out with them a little bit, and I said, "Where'd you get..." and I named a couple of songs. They said, "Gibson!" They did *Stella's Got a New Dress,* and I was blown away.

Bob Gibson & Joan Baez at the 1959 Newport Folk Festival

Postcard that was sent to fans who purchased the 45 of *Marching to Pretoria*

I COME FOR TO SING - 71

7

BRIDGE TO DOOM

The world, it seemed, was at Gibson's feet — at least in the world of folk music. He was at the very center of its universe, influencing everyone around him. Yet at the same time, the edges of his fame were showing signs of crumbling. His personal battles with drugs and his difficulties in handling relationships began to overlap onto his career advancement. The astounding successes were still to occur and the "glory years" still seemed to be going on even as Bob, himself, was disintegrating. The absolute peak of his fame, the recording of Gibson & Camp At the Gate of Horn, *with Bob Camp, in retrospect, came at the beginning of the decline.*

Repeatedly, Bob was offered the chance of soaring to the top where, not only would he be known to all in the folk music world, but his fame would have been of the magnitude of those he inspired and introduced. Every time opportunity knocked, Bob turned the other way. He would either turn it down directly, as in the case of the trio offer from Albert Grossman, or the drugs would talk for him. The eternal question asked by all who love Bob's work is, "Why did this always happen?" Was he afraid to reach the top? Was he consumed with self doubts? Was he satisfied with where he was so on a subconscious level he did something to ensure he wouldn't have to move on?

The answers don't come easily, and perhaps no one, including Bob, will ever know for sure why things happened the way they did, but there are several theories.

As Bob, himself, said in an introduction to his video Ramblin': Bob Gibson In Concert, *filmed in 1980 in Athens, Ohio for PBS:*

I had a couple of good years in the early '60s — matter of fact, I think I had a pretty good shot at the brass ring. But it's also evident to me that I couldn't handle it . . . I'm really a saloon singer. I sing for small audiences well. I get a little lost when they're larger . . .

John Irons offers perhaps the best perspective on what happened to Bob.

I don't think there was anything that scared him. He had all the natural talents and was very musical and technically proficient and the voice was always there for him. All that opened doors for him. He could meet people and people fell in love with him. Depending on what his needs were at different periods of time, he would sometimes abuse those situations. But basically, he just kind of rolled with the punches and tried to keep his own house in order. It was only when the house was out of control that he got in trouble. Generally when somebody is ready to make that leap from doing very well to stardom — I mean major stardom — if they're doing very well, they've got more than a casual amount of money, and it brings the same type problems as with the rock stars today. They're people that don't have to practice a lot, they've got a lot of money, got groupies, whatever they want following them around all over, they've got all this money and all this time and there's always some shithead in the wings saying, 'This will alleviate the boredom.' Usually those people don't come around unless you've got the money, so when Bob would move up to a point where he had a lot of excess cash, then somebody would come along with a remedy and the remedy would knock him down again.

In the recording studio there had been a long dry spell. After the flurry of activity with the early Riverside albums released one after another, it had been nearly two years since he had a record out. Finally, there was a new release, **There's A Meeting Here Tonight,** *on Riverside.*

Allan Shaw:
Despite the fact that the Kingston Trio had by then started the world on its folk music binge with *Tom Dooley,* Gibson showed the good sense to stay off the bandwagon and not commercialize himself by overly polishing himself and his material. This album presented what I call the "old" or "traditional" at its finest. Due to the timing of this album, it would be hard to say that other performers took songs from it, even though many of the songs were later recorded by others. The arrangements, too, although very typical of Gibson, were not that unusual compared to what was coming from others, but this was not a sign that Gibson was slipping. Rather, it was a sign that the folk era and those who were to become its superstars were catching up to him and more particularly, copying from him. This album of Gibson's, more than any other, ushered in the popular folk era, and did it in style.

Also at this point Bob was showing his influence in developing a concept that had a profound impact on the public, commercial entertainment value of folk music.
I started what we called a "hootenanny" at a place called The Bitter End. I was very involved with that club. As a matter of fact, it was a coffee shop having poetry readings and bongo drum players when I said, "Hey, let's put some folk music in here," to the owner, Fred Weintraub. He went on to be a big movie producer, did a lot of

Kung Fu flicks, but we started with folk music, and then I said, "Let me do a hootenanny." Weintraub said, "Everybody's got a hootenanny. Mike Porco's got one at Folk City and there are another couple of coffee houses with them." I said, "Stick with me, Fred. I haven't steered you wrong so far. I'll put a hootenanny in here. It's going to go somewhere." I started it, and I asked Ed McCurdy to be the host. Ed was well respected, but not in any particular genre. He wasn't a blues singer, a ballad singer or a banjo picker, he was just something else. He worked real well — real erudite guy. That way the host didn't put any particular stamp on the occasion, like it was going to be this kind or that kind of show.

Then I would go around and say to all the artists things like, "We had a hoot Tuesday night at the Bitter End but you probably wouldn't like it. I know you wouldn't because there are a lot of agents and managers all looking for new acts. They're a real pain in the ass." Then I'd tell the publishers, "Aw, you wouldn't have liked it, man. Nothing but new writers, nobody you guys would know. They're all a bunch of kids just got off the bus with their guitars." Tell the agents and managers the same thing. Well, it became a meat market, everybody went there, everybody was there. It was where it was happening. You know, the Theo Bikels and Pete Seegers and Jean Ritchies coming in to do their acts.

Finally Fred got the guys from Ashley Famous Artists, which was an agency that was beginning to produce television, to come down and I put together a one-hour hootenanny for them. It was a Tuesday night hootenanny, but a very special one. They saw it and said, "This would be a great television show. We'll do it with a live audience, just this way." The program debuted on April 6, 1963, so, of course, I appeared a number of times on Hootenanny. Never really liked it. I was at great odds with the management and the producers all the time because they blew the most important concept of all. They didn't get the idea that they should book an artist and turn over to him and say, "Do whatever you want in your slot." Rather they'd ask a guy, "Why don't you do that song?" The producer — the person who was creating the show — was working with a known palette. It wasn't ever, "We'll give him seven minutes. I don't know what he's going to do. After that we'll do that. I don't know what's going to happen next, maybe we'll have a commercial." Instead it was a case of, "Let's ask the artist to duplicate moments that we know about." No spontaneity.

For instance, once in Ann Arbor, Michigan, Josh White was there along with the musical director, Fred Weintraub and Josh's musical director. They were all trying to decide what songs Josh was going to do. He did a little bit of *Strange Fruit*. If you've ever heard Josh

White, you know he would absolutely put an audience away with that song. His voice wavered a little bit, and it was a very difficult song for him to sing because he'd been drinking and smoking a lot of cigarettes over the years. Nevertheless, the song was mesmerizing, but all they could hear was that his voice wavered. It wasn't a pure clean tone. They said, "Well, that won't do." The impact of that song from Josh on an audience, almost invariably, was something you could really work with. They said, "No, let's not do that one, let's do something else," and they listened to a song called *Scarlet Ribbons*, which Josh used to do — the same one Harry Belafonte recorded and made famous. It's a ballad. It starts here, develops completely and ends there. The producer said, "That's wonderful, it's exactly what we want. Could you cut a little bit out?" I couldn't believe the guy asked him to do that! He obviously hadn't heard what the hell Josh was singing. Those guys used to make me nuts!

I evolved this "Let's all get together and we'll do a 'come all ye' type of song" to do at the end of hootenannies. It's a nice thing when there are several different artists who can get together to try something different. It's great when artists are willing to try and make music together. They instituted the singalong as a standard with the show. They were doing *Kumbaya* one time, and they had it in a terrible key and doing it too fast. They would shoot somebody doing a verse and then they'd back off and show a whole shot of the assembled cast singing it. They'd roll the credits over it, then they'd zoom back in again. I got to my verse and I didn't think they were zoomed in, so I sang, "Somebody's kidding, Lord, Kumbaya." I was just pissed off with the whole issue. Well, don't you know, that's what made the final cut. The producer saw it and I didn't work there again.

Clearly, no matter what turmoil existed, Bob could still deliver. As long as he could make it out in front of an audience, he could find himself, but it became increasingly more difficult to carry on. Probably the earliest signs that Bob was slipping personally came in Aspen. Still at his peak when he would return at least every June to the Gate of Horn, and yet to meet Bob Camp, Bob was already letting the destruction of his drug use and the womanizing for which he became famous affect his performance and career decisions.

Ed Holstein:
Bob was hot! Woody Allen, Bill Cosby and Shelley Berman would open up for him. He was on the Mike Douglas show, the Hootenanny show and the Guy Mitchell show. (Guy Mitchell was a popular singer in the early '50s who did all the songs that Frank Sinatra didn't want to do during Frank's bad time. Later on he tried

to be a country singer, and he sold 8 million records. He was big. He did songs that were almost like folksongs, but Sinatra said he didn't want to have anything to do with those songs. We called them novelty songs. Mitchell recorded all of them. He had a show on ABC Monday nights from '57 to '58— a big show.) Bob was supposed to be on the show *Route 66*. As a kid I always thought they must have wanted Bob for that show, because Martin Milner looked like Bob Gibson. Bob was up for that role, and I guess he walked in stoned. The show went on the air in 1960 but without Bob!

Glenn Yarbrough:
Bob was a different guy in those days in Aspen. He damn near destroyed my life before it started, when I got the Limelite club there. We had done such a good job together the year before when I was leasing the club that when I bought it I went to him and I said, 'Bob, I'll give you a piece of this just to work with me, and we'll work together and we'll make it go.' For some reason — I could never understand why, because I was *giving* him an equal share with me — he went over to the Durham Hotel nearby and made a deal there that I didn't know about. Suddenly I was stuck with it. I'd put a lot of money into the bar and everything. I'd done all kinds of things, very loose with money, intensive things, and I had nobody to work with. Luckily, Marilyn Child, who is probably the nicest person in the world to work with, came out to help me. She was understudying in New York on Broadway, and she was so sweet. I said, 'Look, I'm in terrible trouble here, and I'm gonna lose my ass if somebody doesn't help me.' Turns out Bob screwed somebody's wife at the Durham Hotel and got fired, so it didn't make a hell of a lot of difference.

But still even after that I loved his work, and I loved to work with him. He was a wonderful guy to work with. I approached him in 1958, and I said, "Look, let's just go into the Purple Onion or the hungry i in San Francisco. We'll take Marilyn Child, you and I, and we'll start our own group. We were all set to go, and then at the last minute again for some reason he changed his mind. *I had the gig all set!*

That's when they hired the Kingston Trio at the Purple Onion. Instead of us making a success there, the Kingston Trio did. I really don't know what the problem was. Maybe he was already doing drugs. I don't know.

I lived in Aspen from about '57 to '61. I loved to ski, and I would spend all day long skiing on the slopes and then sing every night to support myself and my family in ski lodges. I was skiing there all the spare time I had, but I was also travelling a lot. I'd go to Dallas and Chicago and New York to work, but I'd always be real happy to get home to Aspen. When it was ski time and the snow was good it was real hard to get me out of that town. You had to pay me more than when there was no snow.

Bob's oldest daughter, Meridian Green, remembers those days in Aspen just a little differently:
I have some pretty clear memories of Aspen, living with my mother, my sisters Susan and Pati, in a tiny one bedroom shack with asphalt shingles. There was a partially deconstructed old house that Bob had started to remodel on the property. There were lilac bushes in the spring and rhubarb leaves we pretended were umbrellas and in the winter it was a world of snow. I remember eating whip cream and cadging martini olives at the Crystal Palace where Rose was a cocktail waitress. I remember Kathleen, who also worked at the Palace, lived with us and helped out financially by baby-sitting, and she taught me how to give back-rubs. I remember Sharon and her kids and the nursery school she ran with my mother at our house. I remember the inexperienced baby-sitter who I conned into believing that I was indeed allowed to cook and melting cream cheese and butter in a sauce pan. I remember seeing Bob play at the Red Onion and having a really good time clapping as loud as I could.

I remember a lot, and how I remember Bob is kind of like this guy, Daddy, who'd come and visit from time to time, often around Christmas. I remember being five and being profoundly enraged because he said I had to take a nap, and I was certainly too grown up for a nap. It was the first of many battles. It was probably around then that I started keeping track of my father's sins and failures in order to have ammunition in our fights. I was pretty well armed by the time the bank foreclosed on the house in Aspen.

I met Jac Holzman from Elektra Records before I went to work for Elektra. There was a parallel, in a way, between what was going on in the late '50s and what happened the end of the '70s — a lot of similarities. We were in the second four years of a Republican president, and there was a terrible recession that the country went through. A lot of major record companies went under. Dot and Decca completely ceased to exist. Some very small offbeat labels like Atlantic, which was a jazz label, and Elektra, which was a really esoteric folk label, began to do well. Riverside came and went. Jac was doing folk music with Theo Bikel and a couple of people like that. He asked me if I would do an album for him. He wanted to use me and Hamilton Camp. Gibson and Camp was like a meteoric thing — a shooting star. We burned ourselves out just about that quickly, as well. The record with Camp was to come later, though. The first record I did for Elektra was *Ski Songs* in 1959. By this time I had been living in Aspen a couple of years.

Writing had become the next major and logical step in my career, and I started to write some songs with a couple of gals who were writers for the Denver Post. I decided to write a musical about skiing. It was fun to do, and it produced entirely new songs rather than being rewrites or new arrangements. Out of it came songs like *In This White World* and *What'll We Do?* and *Ski Patrol*. I also rewrote a couple of traditional things and put ski lyrics to them. Some of the songs in the album are not folk songs, but you can hear my roots. *In This White World* was a big hit for Glenn Yarbrough and also was recorded by Vaughn Monroe. *Super Skier* was a hit single for the Chad Mitchell Trio.

I don't know why nothing ever happened with the ski play. It was a good play, but it was never produced. As it turned out, all that was ever produced was the album, *Ski Songs*. It was the biggest selling album I ever cut. It seems a little isolated subjectwise, but there are a lot of skiers and I made a lot of money from that album. I recorded it backed with an electric guitar, a bass, a banjo, plus background singers. This was happening stuff. It may have been a major change, but it was the next logical step. *Ski Songs* was a major album for Elektra. It sold real well.

Former Denver Post Writer, Shirley Sealy:
I was one of the "Denver Post writers" who worked with Bob on the ski songs. I had met him after reviewing his performance at the Jerome Hotel. Then he came to Denver a lot, and we got to be friends. Actually, doing the musical was my idea, and I wrote most of the words to *This White World*. My friends Gail Pitts and Blanche Hardin (not Nardin as on the album credits) and I lived in Bob's shack behind the Jerome in Aspen while we wrote the musical and worked with him on lyrics. (Once an angry husband of one of Bob's ladies stood in front of the house shouting for Bob and shooting a gun in the air.) Unfortunately we refused permission for Bob to record the show's best song, which was entirely his inspiration, and mostly his lyrics. Bob sat down one day with his 12-string and said "This is how I feel when I ski," then played this really jazzy number which turned into *"Down, Down, Down."*

Allan Shaw:
Ski Songs, Bob's first album on Elektra, had come out practically on top of *There's A Meeting Here Tonight,* his last on Riverside. Not classifying *Ski Songs* as a folk album, Gibson thus had only one folk album in the nearly four-year period during which the folk boom was really coming into its own. Milton Okun, musical director for Peter, Paul and Mary and The Chad Mitchell Trio, later commented that Gibson's erratic performances became almost legendary and that during this period Gibson's star flickered. Perhaps the *Ski Songs* album, good that it was in its own right, was both a consequence of and partially responsible for this.

Whatever the reason, whether it was, again, sleeping with the wrong woman, or drugs or both, Bob was run out of Aspen, having burned his bridges there. Yet, at nearly the same time, contrasting that tremendous blow, the greatest achievement of his career hit the record shelves — **Gibson & Camp at the Gate of Horn!**

Meridian Green:
We moved to Tremont Place in the Bronx, into a studio apartment in the building where my mother's foster parents, my Oma, Opa and Tante Bette, lived. Bob was living in the Village, and a few months later we all moved into a fifth floor walkup on Broom Street between 6th and 7th Avenues. Before long Bob had a studio over on Hudson with Shel and he was still spending lots of time on the road, but he was home enough for me to remember lots of trips up and down the stairs carrying his banjo or guitar. There was music in the living room. Greenwich Village was vibrant. It was a really big party, and my Daddy was the king, which made me a princess, and that was okay with me!

In 1961, Roy Silver, my brother, Jim, and I started an agency called New Concepts in New York City. Our office was at 237 Sullivan Street in the Village. We formed the agency to book me and some other folkies in some of the places available. These were artists who prior to that were trying to book themselves very unsuccessfully. We had an incredible roster of people, Freddie Neil, David Crosby, Bobby Dylan, Richie Havens, and several others, nearly all of whom went on to do great work. The gigs we could get them were like $125 a week. That's all there was. We'd book up in Canada and a lot of other places in the United States as well.

Jim Gibson:
I was living in Seattle, Washington in 1961, and Bob was living in New York in the Village. He wrote me a letter saying, "Hey, I'm thinking of putting a folk music booking and management agency together. Why don't you come join me?" A couple of months later I did. I'm really not sure if that's when he left Al Grossman. I'm not sure who was booking Bob at that point. I think he was handling himself but I'm not positive. I'd been living in Seattle and hadn't seen him for years prior to that.

Roy Silver represented Bill Cosby at that point. When he took on Cosby he concentrated on Bill and didn't do much at the agency himself. I can remember getting Davie Crosby a job over at a club in the Village called Gerde's Folk City run by Mike Porco, a really nice guy who was willing to take on new talent.

Then Bob and I made a trip to Chicago, and I came down quite ill. I had jaundice, and it appeared as if I had hepatitis, or that's what everybody thought. When I got out of hospital I went to some friends in Chicago and laid up for about a month, and then I went to sea on the Great Lakes in June or July of 1962. In August, I went back to Chicago and got offered the job of managing the Gate of Horn by Allan Ribback. I did that for two weeks and got sick again. I went to the Vet's hospital in Chicago where they discovered I had a liver parasite which was probably picked up in the Far East when I was in Korea from '51 to '52. They treated me, I was out in about a week, and I've never had a problem with it since. Unfortunately during all this the agency just sort of floundered and disappeared.

Shirley Sealy:
  Ski Songs was not my only connection to Bob, for I was the fourth "partner" in New Concepts. He asked me to come from Denver, which I did. I worked as the publicist, and I manned the office on Sullivan Street on a daily basis. The whole thing fell apart for me after about six months...very little money coming in, so I rarely got paid, and there was just too much drinking!

  Bob Dylan went on to be managed by Albert Grossman after that. Grossman took over Dylan in 1962, buying out Roy Silver, for a reported $10,000. We had some gigs after that, and some of the clubs up in Canada said, "Can you get us Dylan?" We said, "We'll give it a try." So we called Grossman. I then went back to Grossman's office myself as an artist probably from '62 to '64 and that was the end of New Concepts. But we got some really great artists out there for a brief time.

  The next album I did was *Yes I See* for Elektra. Jac Holzman couldn't believe it because we spent **$1,600** to produce it. He told me he was outraged! "I spent **$1,600** on this album!!" And I thought, "Well, that's not so very much. You got all the instruments and all those voices and everything." We had five of the hottest gospel singers in LA, Bessie Smith and the Gospel Pearls, along with their band, which included a piano player and a bongo player. I had guitar players, guys like Tommy Tedesco, who played on that album. I mean, the playing was hot. I love that album and it was one of the first times where a white guy sang with black women. It was great. Everything in those days went right to two tracks. I was really the producer of that album. I had all the conceptual stuff and all. Somebody wrote some sheets for the girls and the other musicians. Half the album was them. Half of it wasn't. Some of the songs were written by me, some by Shel Silverstein, and I also wrote with Fred Neil. There's stuff on this album that people weren't doing until much later. It wasn't until the early '70s that this was a common format, but I did it ten years earlier.

In keeping with the precedent set by the Gibson & Camp at the Gate of Horn *album, the liner notes for* Yes I See *were written by another well-known Chicago writer and Gibson fan Studs Terkel. His words reflect not only the spirit of the time but also Bob's importance in it:*

"Spirit is movin' all over this land...."

Perhaps it is. Perhaps the long sleep is over.

We've been told this is the time of the sleepwalkers. Dehumanization has set in. The cult of the impersonal has become the order of the day. The generation that "felt" has been supplanted by the careful young men who "couldn't care less." And status has been achieved with a key to the *Playboy Club.* Yes, we've been told this is the time Billie Holiday sang about: When loveless love leads to soulless souls.

I believed it and still do — to some extent. And yet... The Peace Corps is winning enthusiastic volunteers — all among the young.

And in a tangential, yet altogether related way, the young are seeking a meaning in folk music. Never in all the history of our popular arts has there been evinced such interest in our native music. Throughout the land, young people, with or without followings, are singing these songs. Ranging from excellent to indifferent, they are participating. And that perhaps is the most important aspect: they are *doing something.*

And from the young have come excellent professionals. Among the best of these is Bob Gibson. Aside from his clear, strong tenor voice and his deftness with guitar or banjo, it is his impact upon the young that is so salutary.

On the night before I wrote these notes, I visited Chicago's Gate of Horn where Bob was performing with his ebullient colleague, Bob Camp. (A forthcoming Elektra album will feature this infectiously alive duo.) The place was jam packed. This came as no surprise. Ever since he opened at the Gate, Gibson has been a phenomenal drawing card. At a nearby table was seated a newspaper woman of my acquaintance. I was watching her sixteen-year-old nephew, just arrived from Tulsa. He had heard of Bob, but had never seen him perform. The kid was instantly caught by the high spirits of the performance, and as of that night, he was a Gibson aficionado.

"How come this appeal, this hold?" I asked Bob. "I'm not sure," he mused. "Perhaps kids can't articulate their feelings about many things these days. But when it comes to a folk tune, they understand. Things they feel, but cannot say, are said for them in this music." It may also be their tendency to identify with Bob, who sings and speaks a language they understand; irreverence toward pomposity and phoniness, and a healthy respect for the genuine.

It's been an incredibly short seven years since Gibson took up the banjo and then the guitar. "As a kid I had no idea what I wanted to do. Messed around with the piano, then the violin. And even my horsing around with the banjo had no real meaning at first. Before I knew it, though, I was involved."

That is probably the key to Bob's big score. As a result, his listeners become engaged. It is American music, wholly, that intrigues him. "I don't go for labels. You will find some people much too serious about one aspect of folk song, at the expense of another. The fact that more young people than ever are hearing these songs is great." Certainly Bob is one of the major influences in this direction. Kids, who might otherwise have been restricted to the music of Irving Berlin and company, have now had new avenues opened for them. Gibson's value then is twofold: as performer and as ground-breaker. As Bob says, "If in some way I can lead a few of them back toward the roots of this music, to recognizing the work of Big Bill, Woody Guthrie and Leadbelly, I'll feel a mission accomplished."

Rick Neely remembers the beginning of the darker stories:
My cousin saw Bob in a concert at Illinois Institute of Technology in 1964. He said that Bob came out on the stage and struck a sour chord — something was out of tune. So he commenced to tuning it, and he tuned and tuned and tuned some more. He must have tuned for 15 minutes, and finally he got it right and played a good strong chord. Some jerk in the audience applauded, and Bob took a nice bow and left — went home or wherever he went. So he must have done some strange stuff in those days.

There was a very big gap then before I recorded my next album, *Where I'm Bound,* in 1964. By then I was getting very nuts. I mean, I was real self-destructive. That album had tons of my own songs. By then I was writing and I wasn't interested in doing traditional too much, or the traditional I was doing was so grossly arranged that it was hardly related to the traditional form anymore. On *Where I'm Bound,* there's a version of *Nora's Dove,* and the credits on it are me and the Lomaxes. Because it was such a distinctive arrangement, the Lomaxes said, "For this arrangement you can put your name on it — for the arrangement only." That was a hard estate to crack. You could make a lot of changes on their songs without them getting upset. You could go ahead and make them, but they'd still take all the royalties.

In this case, however, they were very cooperative.

Allan Shaw:
   Where I'm Bound was, like *Yes I See,* a new direction for Gibson after the two-year layoff. *Where I'm Bound* was an outstanding album. Gone was the large contingent of electric instruments. Other than a good solid bass accompaniment, this was just Gibson accompanying himself on the 12-string guitar. And what a sound! If anything, Gibson's voice had improved over the years and certainly his presentation of his material had matured and become more sophisticated. The guitar accompaniment in particular stood out. Although Gibson's earlier work on the 12-string was well worth listening to, *Where I'm Bound* demonstrated fully the promise that had been previously indicated but never delivered. From a musical standpoint, the album was another of the greats of the folk era.
   Where I'm Bound also indicated a new direction in that almost all of the songs were written by Gibson himself, in several cases with Shel Silverstein. Although Gibson had previously shown himself to be a master arranger (or re-arranger) of traditional songs, he now demonstrated his writing prowess as well. Without exception, the songs were outstanding and most have been subsequently recorded by other artists. For those of his fans who had stuck with him during the preceding lean years, this album rewarded them with the best of Gibson for which they had been waiting and then some. The liner notes from the album well summed up both Gibson's career and many of his major achievements, as well as the album itself in saying: "The music of Bob Gibson is unlike the music of any other folk artist. For throughout the 'folksong revival,' there have been the originators and the imitators. Bob Gibson could be nothing else but an originator, a creator, a prime mover...Not only is Bob a magnificent instrumentalist and showman, extraordinary composer and arranger, but he has an uncanny eye for discovering new talent. He was the first to introduce such highly respected artists as Joan Baez, Mike Settle, Bob Camp and Judy Collins. Except for Pete Seeger, no single figure in recent years has influenced the folk field in as many diverse ways as Bob Gibson...Every album that Bob has made has provided material and musical ideas for other folksingers. Indeed, it is difficult to find a folk group album which does not contain at least one Gibson creation..."

Ed Holstein remembers a Gibson introduction:
   The first time I saw Judy Collins, Bob brought her on stage at Orchestra Hall and introduced her. I went to see him in concert and he said, "I want to bring somebody onstage that I think is the greatest singer, bar none!" It was Judy Collins, who was real nervous! That was 1964, and then his career started to go downhill. I think he was on drugs that day during that show. He was real hoarse.

Roger McGuinn offers his perspective on why, perhaps, Bob didn't become better known:
    It's hard to say why Bob didn't go farther. You know, it's a tough business. Of all the people who have made it, there are probably hundreds for each one who haven't. He did pretty well if you think about the whole thing and especially as far as influence goes. He played the big festivals like Newport, and he was nationally known, not just in Chicago, but he was a national artist. He did the Hootenanny show, and I think he could have ridden that crest of folk music a little higher, but I think it was basically his drug problem. If he'd been more together as far as his that had gone, he probably would have done better. He was doing pretty well in the Village, and then about '62 he was starting to sink off. *Gibson & Camp at the Gate of Horn* had been out for awhile, then the folk music thing was dying out, and he didn't want to go rock & roll.

    Everything had moved so fast for a few years. The Newport Folk Festival in the summer of 1959 was the first convention of folkies. It put a big commercial stamp on folk singing. It put guys in the larger cities in touch with what was going on in Chicago and the Village. It was the coming together of a lot of things that were going on. A lot more people became convinced they could successfully operate a folk singing club, at least for three or four years, until interest peaked and audiences went on to something else. By the end of that period, owners figured they had had every act that should have been working Holiday Inns. Everyone was picking up a guitar and singing. It was just ghastly. But that's how it goes. At that point, folk singing had had it. Musical tastes were changing. That's the one thing you can always count on. They come and they go. The Cha-Cha, the Twist, Disco — something's going on all the time, but, just as soon as it arrives, it's gone.

    But some people really got their roots there. A lot of the '60s rock 'n' roll people came out of the folk music movement. The groups that went on to be the Byrds, Buffalo Springfield, lots and lots of groups originally were folkies.

    Once folk singing moved out of the coffee houses and got up on a big stage with a large audience, they started to experiment, through the festivals, with larger sound systems to try to re-create a different type of experience. It became loud enough so you had to feel it. The experience of being in a concert hall with some of them meant that the music would be literally in your bones.

Rick Neely reminisces about his introduction to Bob's music and the profound effect it had on his life:
    My dad died in 1961, and the following summer a junior high school English teacher came to my house with a stack of folk music

records. This was a guy who had been into it from the early '50s up until then and he brought me this bunch of records which had Pete Seeger and Bob Gibson and the Kingston Trio and all those early people. He said, "Here, these might make you feel better, lift you up." And the ones I honed into were Bob's. His were so musical and his voice and my voice were in similar range and the music was sophisticated but it didn't seem so complicated that you couldn't figure it out. So I've spent my whole life figuring out this stuff, figuring out what he was doing musically.

When I was 16 in 1965, it was the summer of the New York World's Fair and my family went to New York for the fair and I went immediately to Greenwich Village and cruised around. I can't believe that times were so different or maybe just ignorance is bliss but I cruised all over the Village looking into all kinds of stuff, and Bob was playing at a place called the Cafe A-Go-Go. There were pictures outside. I remember this promotional picture he had. It was real cute. He was leaning on the end of his banjo. He was wearing the standard uniform of the day which was a turtleneck. And I said, "Oh, God, I gotta do this." Some of the older people that I knew who were playing in my town of Moline which was about 150 miles west of Chicago, they would go to Chicago and go to the Gate of Horn, or probably Mother Blues at that point and see him and then come home and say, "Oh, God, Gibson is playing this stuff and using these strange chords and what's going on?" They were trying to figure it out, and I was trying to figure it out, and we'd sit around for hours holding these basement symposiums on what Gibson was doing.

When I got the chance to see him in New York I was under age to be in a place that sold liquor. I was only 16. So I dressed up. I wore a sport coat and tried to be more mature and when I went to pay and they said, "Where's your ID?" I went, "Oh, oh, man I left my wallet at home and I just have money," and I told them I was in college. They let me in. I was trying to be low profile. I walked in and a guy standing on the stage setting up stuff says, "Hey, you, come up here." I said, "Me?" And they made me stand on the stage because we were about the same height - Bob was a little bit taller - so they could adjust the microphone, because in those days the show business thing was the performer stayed out of view until the show began. There wasn't this informal kind of thing there is today where people kind of mingle around. It was very formal, even for a nightclub kind of place.

I sat and I had my Coca-Cola™ and I watched the show which was very short. It was only about 35 minutes - seven or eight songs and it was over. I thought that was kind of a rip for the money, but I think in that time period that was about all he was doing because I think the drugs were in pretty full swing, and the Beatles had taken over.

I think his whole career was in sand and it was shifting around then, and I think shortly thereafter he kind of faded out of the scene.

But I came home and I played this stuff and I've played it all my life. The albums would come out and I would learn all the songs just as fast as I could. My favorite is still the *Where I'm Bound,* album which is from that time period, 1964.

Michael Smith details what he heard about Bob in those days:
I lived down in Coconut Grove near Miami in the late '60s, and there was a club called the Gaslight down there, run by Sam Hood. It was a lovely club and people like Ian and Sylvia and Odetta performed there. Gibson played there, too, and that was the first time I'd heard about him in awhile. I started hearing scary things, like that he was high all the time. Of course everybody was high all the time at then, but it seemed that he was more extreme. The story I heard was that he fell off the stage, so I began to get a picture of him as being a decadent individual.

Allan Shaw recalls:
Gibson had pursued music with a renewed vigor. He introduced electric guitars into his concerts and he hit the college circuit. He says one of the most satisfying moments of his career came in 1964, when he was the feature act of the Red Rocks Theatre in Denver. The Smothers Brothers were the warm-up act. "That might have been my peak," Bob recalled.

It would have appeared to the record buying public that Bob Gibson was at the top. Bob had been everywhere there was folk music. Coupled with the album, Where I'm Bound, *TRO, his publishing company, put out a guitar songbook of the songs on the album. He had influenced everyone at that time, and yet, at the same time, he, himself, had hit the bottom. Rick Neely must have seen one of his last appearances that summer of 1965, because it was soon after that Bob finally decided he had to do something to change the direction of his downward spiral with drugs and disappeared for three years.*

It was really an incredible time for me from the '50s and into the mid-'60s. I think for a while there I had a real shot at making it to the top, but I had never set out to make it big. That is not to say that I didn't want to make it big. I didn't perceive it as big or little. To make it big was for all the people to applaud. But what is "all the people"? All the people at the Gate of Horn? All the people in the studio at the Arthur Godfrey Show? All the people listening to the Arthur Godfrey Show? All the people listening to the Hootenanny TV show? All the people who bought my records?

My goal was to arrive. The whole thing was for approval, but not for my work but for ME. If I'm approvable as a human being in your for my work but for ME. If I'm approvable as a human being in your eyes, you stand up and applaud.

But what does it mean at 2 a.m. and I'm alone in my motel? I still have that nagging fear that I'm not approvable. I'm not loveable. I am less than I should be and that's the trap you set. You get the approval for the work, but you're actually looking for approval as a human being.

The problem is if it's 40 people this year, next year it's 400 I need. When 400 of them applaud like crazy, buy the record and stand on the chairs, I say, that was great, but is that all there is?

I see it constantly in show business. You get more approval and bigger approval and still more approval and you work even harder, but you never get satisfied because you're looking for approval as a person. Some of those people who are out there in the stellar reaches who are so devoted to their work and have no personal life, find that there is no person. They are the act. Who is Bobby Dylan anyway? When does he get a chance not to be Bobby Dylan? People don't look at him as a human being. They look at him as Bobby Dylan.

Dollars? Fame? None of those things had any meaning to me. One of the things that seems to have meaning to me is that I'm able to do a lot of stuff if I really choose to. But I have a terrible tendency to want to prove myself.

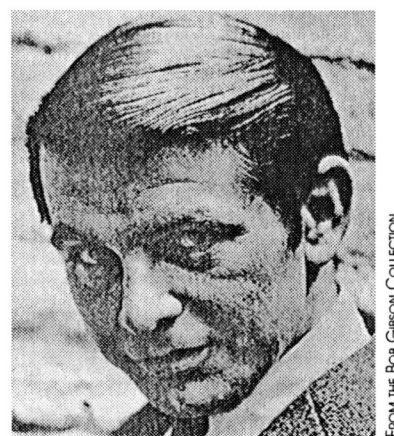

Haunting photo that was used in *The Bob Gibson Songbook* published by TRO in 1964

Bob being hauled off to Narcotics Court, Chicago, 1970

I COME FOR TO SING - 87

Rose & Bob looking like the perfect couple in 1954

The Gibson Girls on Broom Street 1962
L-R: Pati, Susan, Meridian

(Above) Christmas in Aspen 1961
L-R: Meridian, Susan, Pati

(Right) Meridian says, "My mother is still proud of having put together this vacation on Fire Island in 1964."

Back L-R: Bob & Jim Gibson; Front L-R: Meridian, Susan, Pati

I Come For To Sing - 88

SING FOR THE SONG

Sometimes you sing for the money.
Sometimes you sing for the show.
Sometimes you sing for those dewey-eyed darlins —
Still makes 'em cry, don't you know?
One time you sang for the glory,
But the glory didn't last very long.
Through the haze of the stage,
You look back to the days
When you used to sing for the song.

But you really don't make too much money,
And you don't put on much of a show,
And those dewey-eyed darlins next week will be cryin'
For somebody else, don't you know?
And the tune is becoming your burden,
And the words all sound twisted and wrong,
And the song that you sell
It don't taste quite as well
As when you used to sing for the song.

Sing for the song, boy,
Just like you did when you did
When you stood on that corner
And didn't even feel the cold
Sing for the song, boy,
Just like you did before all of the cocaine
And flashbulbs and bright painted ladies
Got ahold of your soul

~ Shel Silverstein
(©Evil Eye Music, BMI)

8

"DEMONS"

Drugs were all over the place. The business I was in condoned it. But I had no sooner gotten in than I wanted out. I spent from 1960 to 1978 trying to get out, quitting for two or three years at a time, but I always went back. I remember looking at my arm and saying, "Why'd I do that? Why?"

Drugs were my bane. Adjusting reality. And I kept trying to do it. I have a lot of real strong attitudes about it all, but I'm not against drinking. I'm not against anything. But I sure am against it when it doesn't work anymore. That's when I had to stop. It didn't work anymore.

Sometimes it would be wonderful, but sometimes it led me to funny places. And I don't like those funny places.

I know a lot of people who know how to drink. But the difference between most of them and me is, a lot of people say, "No thanks, I've had enough. No thanks, I'm feeling the last three."

Not me, man. Feeling the last three, I say now let's get down to some serious drinking. You know, "Let's get messed up, you can be somebody."

I've seen people step over that invisible line when the addiction itself takes over, and suddenly it becomes horrendous.

I started to use drugs when I was a teen. It was rare for people to use them then. I was 22 before I began to make music, and it was well before that that I got started with drugs. Drugs were never recreational for me. My use of them from the beginning was abusive because I felt they were going to help me get through my life.

The first time I really drank, other than sipping one around the house, which we were almost encouraged to do, was when I was about 15 maybe. I was with a couple of my buddies and we each went to a lot of trouble to win half pints of wine at a firemen's fair. It was for the local volunteer firemen and there was a penny toss. If you tossed enough pennies, you got a half pint of wine. It was an acceptable way for us to get what we wanted without going to the liquor store. Anyway, there was no question about it, we were getting the wine to chug-a-lug it and get messed up. There was no experimentation about it.

Very soon after that, I got into the dexedrine and dexamyl in the medicine cabinet. As I mentioned before, my father worked for a chemical firm and had been involved in those miracles of the second world war, penicillin and amphetamines. Those were the new wonder drugs then. Cure all the housewives' ills — give them some dexedrine.

Of course, it all happened really fast after that, because if you kept taking from the medicine cabinet, someone would miss their pills. Then we got into the benzedrine inhalers. You'd tear them open and get ripped. I learned very early on that drugs were to be used and abused. Inherent in the use of drugs was to abuse them. It wasn't recreational. Using stuff was never to enhance the party — it was to keep the party going and to include the next day. I didn't like drinking though. I'd drink socially, but after a couple, I thought I could handle it. The truth was I never really knew where I was going to end with that.

Drug use was special at first, though — not a regular thing. Drugs were not necessarily accessible. For long periods of time, there would be no drugs involved. But by the time I was 22, before I began to make music I had really gotten into it.

All during the late '50s, I would get stuff to use on long driving trips for gigs. There also would be the late hours, working around the clock. There was a certain amount of social drinking that would tend to get you fuzzy. Then I'd drop something to get over feeling fuzzy and that would make me edgy. Then I would smoke some grass to take the edge off. That was terrible pharmacology, trying to get feeling okay. But that was the reason I felt different from most people using drugs. I told myself I was just trying to get feeling okay.

Then there were store drugs that began to arrive on the scene, the libriums, etc. You didn't even need to get street drugs. I got bogged down in it all. My use began to accelerate and I really got into the heavyweight ones. I used heroin for about two years in what I thought was a sensible, discriminating manner. It gave me control of my emotions, I thought. I ceased to deal with any kind of emotional factors in my life. I tried to handle them chemically instead.

I didn't want to deal with the fact that my marriage had fallen apart. Like all marriages and everything else, there are ups and downs. But I was trying to escape, rather than deal. The more I tried to avoid the problems, the larger the problems became. They never went away, which required more pharmaceutical help to get by. It was the only thing, I thought, that was getting me through.

I remember telling a therapist that if he could help me find the root of my problems, then I could quit using drugs. But he always responded, "Quit using drugs, then ask me what your problems are." I didn't think much of that at the time, but when I finally did quit using drugs, I realized that I really didn't have any significant problems.

Allan Shaw:
By the end of 1959, alcohol and drugs almost ruined him. His behavior became unpredictable, and he often missed engagements or performed far below his potential. The big halls wouldn't book him. His productivity in the recording studio suffered as well; during a period of four years, he cut only one folk album, *Yes, I See*.

My drug use escalated again when I discovered heroin. I took to it like a duck to water. I thought it was wonderful. There had been too much free time and a lot of anxiety. I had just cut loose from Grossman. He'd been really active in the management of my career until then, but I also felt very threatened. He took on other people too, and I felt threatened. I was too immature and crazy. I was incapable of dealing with it. I did not deal with it. An anti-anxiety agent came into my life. I'd heard all the horror stories about heroin, but none of that would happen to me because I was smarter than that and I would know when not to use it.

Anyhow, from about 1960 on, drugs really began to affect what my priorities were in life. There were periods of as much as two or three years in there when I would be clean. But that wasn't long enough.

In the '60s there was a lot of money coming in, seventy, eighty thousand dollars a year. That was a lot in those days. There was always enough. I had a wonderful career and the possibility of making all kinds of money.

They were handing me money for stuff that I never even knew you could make money from. They'd say, "Here, sign this and we'll give you this." You know, $5,000 advance from a publisher and stuff, just when I shouldn't have had it.

With a home and kids and all of that and still using drugs outrageously, we still never wanted—until the work began to suffer.

Meridian Green:
We moved up to Houston Street, to a larger three bedroom apartment in a building with an elevator. There were a lot of financial ups and downs. It was roller coaster ride of feast to famine and back around. My mother is a paragon of frugality. Any money that comes her way, she puts aside for a rainy day of which there were many. My father's imperative seemed to be, "Quick! Spend it 'til it's gone!" I tried my mother's way for a while when I

was eight. I opened a Lemonade and Art Show stand on the corner and stashed away a five dollar bill. My plan was that the next time there wasn't a dollar in the house and my mother was getting frantic, I would save the day. But my five dollars disappeared. I concluded my Dad's imperative had merit. Bob was having a really good time rolling in it! He bought a red velvet couch, antiques, brass collectables and extravagant gifts for everybody.

When he had money in his pocket he wanted to buy a round for the house, eat lobster, drink champagne, and buy another round! Until it was gone. He spent it as fast as he made it, or faster. He was frantically generous trying to buy his way out of broken promises. And to keep the party going. His addictions to everything grew enormous, bigger than life, faster than a speeding train, higher than a kite. When he ran out of party he'd flatten out like popped balloon, hole up in the bedroom and self-prescribe chemically induced R & R until he was ready to soar again. When he had his chemistry working he was so wickedly beguiling, so charismaticly intoxicating that people became addicted to him. When I was nine or ten Bob disappeared for awhile and my mother wouldn't tell me what was up until I found a letter in her purse written by my Dad from a Toronto prison and demanded an explanation. The letter was about what she should do to raise the money for his bail so that he'd be home in time for Christmas. That was when I first understood that my father's "medicine" was illegal. It was also, I think, when the fast slide really began. A year later we were evicted from our apartment, sold the couch and moved upstate to Wassaic.

Of course I was in and out of jails all over the place; Chicago, Canada, Cleveland . . . My brother Jim had gotten involved in the music business, and we made a trip to Cleveland together in 1964 because I had an interest in a club there called La Cave. I knew this doctor in New York who worked with terminal cancer patients and so through this he worked with a lot of addicts, and he decided he could cure addicts. He'd make up this syrup of chemicals that you'd inject and it would keep you from getting too sick. It didn't get you high — it just kept you from getting too sick. I was several days into using this when we got to Cleveland.

Jim Gibson:
We had gotten a concoction of various drugs and methadone, which was a drug they give to withdrawing heroin addicts. We had flown to Chicago, and the methadone was packed in Bob's suitcase. Unfortunately the suitcase did not arrive, and Bob was going through a rough time in withdrawal. We went on to Cleveland. The brutal reality of it is I suppose we could have gone out to a section of town where drugs are prevalent and try to make a connec-

tion on the street, but that's a good way to get your head bashed in or worse, so I didn't consider that an option. Bob had a problem and there was no way I could desert him, so I was part of it. Not having any contacts or anything there, I started to call around to hospitals. It was all very straightforward, and everything was divulged. I said, "Look, here is the situation. Is there anything you can do for my brother?" Actually one doctor agreed. He prescribed a small amount of morphine to get him through the gig only. Bob was not able to get out and around so I went to pick it up. If memory serves me right, there was a doctor who actually sent some to the hotel we were staying in. I didn't know that, though, because I was on my way to the hospital where they said they could help, and when I arrived they had already contacted the police who were waiting there to scoop me up. When I arrived they popped me, and on that basis they popped Bob, too. There was discussion with the police of me taking the fall for it if they'd cut Bob loose because his career didn't need that, but it makes much better headlines if, "Bob Gibson, International Folk Singer...blah, blah, blah..." went to jail instead of his brother. So we spent 30 days in jail. Yes, there was drug use, but there was no scam involved because someone has to write a prescription. All you could do is ask them. To give them their due, they came in and checked the situation and found the morphine there. The methadone did eventually get found, and they verified that it wasn't there when I made the calls, which is why we only got 30 days. The judge decided that was enough. He could have made it a lot more severe.

Bob continues:

Out of this experience comes one of my favorite stories, though. My dear mother had, up until this time, managed to ignore the fact that I was a dope addict. She had to know, though. All the evidence was there. You can't be around someone who's going through all those incredible personality changes and not notice it. Anyway, with my brother and I both being in jail, this was something she couldn't ignore, so she flew out to see us. We were in the day room and a guard yelled our name and told us to come on, we've got a visitor, which we figured must be our lawyer, because we didn't know our mom was at the jail. We walked into the visiting room and a minute later the door opened and in she comes and says, "How could you do this to me?" Just wonderful! Classic! I, of course, went ape shit and started to yell at her. The guard kept saying, "It's your mother!" I said, "Get her out of here. I'll kill her!" I left and my brother stayed and visited with her. This episode did later become the seed for one of my songs, *How Could You Do This To Me?*

By the mid '60s, my life really became untenable. I simply had to leave the business. A lot of times my work had no longer been a priority. I couldn't work unless I was "well". I did not feel capable. I was ill. Everything became secondary to, first, getting well. And 'getting well' meant mainline injection every six hours. It became expensive and you can't just go to a store for it. My whole life just became enmeshed in that thing. If you don't have drugs, you really can't function. But you don't realize that all you're doing is trying to catch up - you're not functioning. It seemed to me that I had to keep enough drugs in my system so that I wasn't sick, so I could function.

There were a few times I couldn't get on stage. Once in Cleveland, where I was a partner in a club, I couldn't get out of my chair backstage.

I didn't want anyone to tell me about my problems. I became very isolated. I went through a lot of friends.

When getting a drug was my highest priority, I felt I had to have whatever drug it was before I could live. If I was not using drugs—on a day-to-day basis—then all of my consciousness was taken up with the thought of not taking drugs. You know you can't use them anymore, but you've got nothing to replace them with and they were the thing, I thought, that was getting me through.

Then there were the horrors of trying to maintain a heroin habit on the road, on tour. I'd try to figure how much I'd need for a month and take that with me, and then it would be gone in two weeks. Then I'd be stuck out in the boonies and I'd have to involve other people in getting more stuff to me.

Roger McGuinn recalls being asked to be involved:
You know, Bob was my idol when I was a teenager and he actually influenced me to get into drugs, too. I have to tell you the negative side. Because he was taking amphetamines and smoking pot, I wanted to try those things, and I did, and I stayed with them for a long time. I don't think that's a very good thing, but it's something that happened. One time I was pretty upset. He called me when I was living in Los Angeles. It was pretty late at night. And he asked me to get him some heroin. I had never done heroin and I wouldn't know where to find it. It was really upsetting. You know, here he was, my idol, calling me to get him some heroin. I thought, "Oh man!"

I had been coasting for about seven years and hadn't played some clubs for about three years. I wanted to be an entertainer again and I liked the idea of being recognized again. But there was a lot of anxiety involved in going back to work. I felt I was capable of anything when I was on heroin. The thought of failure was terrifying.

So in 1966, I left the business. It seemed to me that it probably was working in clubs and being on the road and being in show business and around musicians that allowed me to always use the drugs. I thought if I got away from that, everything would be fine. I had decided to try the "geographic cure." I moved out of New York City to upstate New York. I spent almost three years up in the country with the wife and the kids, trying to be the father and husband I had never been; trying to completely quit drugs. I had always liked working with wood, so I set up a wood shop there. I collected antique wood working tools.

It didn't work. I'd just go into the city on the weekends to get high or I'd write my own prescriptions for speed and stuff.

The marriage broke up during that time. It was very painful. I was trying very hard. Of course, that was the solution Rose and I had to all our problems - to try harder. And we truly did. Sometimes I would be madly in love with some other woman, but then I would think, Rose is the woman I chose. We've come along this far. We've got kids and all. We've just got to try harder, which we both would. But it just got worse.

At this point, out in the country, I must have been really odious to be around, because now I was going to be the gung ho father and husband I'd never been during all those dope years. So I was around. But who was around? I was out to lunch all the time.

It was a classic syndrome. When there's one alcoholic or drug addicted partner, the other person generally gets a lot stronger. They have to. She ran the whole family. Our unspoken contract was, I'll go out and make enough money that everything is taken care of and I'll take what's left over from the realities. Of course, in very short order, that became, I'll spend my money my way and whatever's left over, you can run the house with.

Meridian Green:
Wassaic was hell. We moved there in '66 so Bob could "get well", by living in country. What a doomed idea! I was metamorphisizing from a confused child into a toxically angry adolescent. I already suspected that my father was monumentally stupid in certain areas and as far as I was concerned his pathetic attempts at living in the country and being a parent were irrefutable proof. I was really incensed about the very idea of taking instruction about anything from a man who had made, and was still making, such a mess of own life. Bob was at the very bottom and he was still digging himself in deeper. At first I was out for blood, armed to the teeth with my arsenal of his sins. By the time he moved his mistress into the living room I just wanted him gone.

He did try, he just didn't have a clue, and he was totally crazed. He tried real hard in his own peculiar way to make a go of this family life in the country show. He got a couple of cats. We had 28 kittens within a year. He got a goat named Spinky who ate herself death a week later. He got a cute pair of puppies, both male, who fought all the time. He became obsessed with the idea having a tame raccoon. First, he needed to capture a pair of raccoons to breed so he spent long, sleepless nights driving around with a flashlight and a trap. He stayed awake, around the clock for weeks, trying to catch raccoons. We'd wake up in the morning to the find the family patriarch passed out in his cereal bowl at the table. We stopped using the front door so the pair of feral raccoons he finally caught could spend months in the glassed-in front porch glaring at each other in a totally non-reproductive way. When Bob left we let the raccoons go and we never saw them again. Bob also disappeared in the spring of 1968, without a word, for almost a year.

"Wassaic was hell." 1967
L-R: Meridian (then Barbara), Rose, Bob, Pati

By the time Bob showed up again a year and half later we'd moved from Wassaic, New York to Sharon, Connecticut. Rose was emerging from a scary spell of depression and illness that had seen her hospitalized twice. Pati was returning from living with Uncle Jim and his family for a lonely while. Susan and I were careening into our teens, pedal to the metal, racing towards adulthood as fast as we could go with Pati trying as hard as she could to catch up. Bob was playing Sam Hood's club, the Elephant, in Woodstock and hanging at Tim Hardin's. Rose was having a personal Renaissance scored by B.B. King's "The Thrill Is Gone." Spring before the Summer of Love, the Gibson girls, mother and daughters, were making the rounds in Woodstock, psychedelic debutantes taking the season by storm. Bob finally had his raccoon. He'd spotted a dead mama raccoon by the side the road and searched until he found her babies. He named the sole surviving orphan Rocky. When Bob went back out on the road, Rocky stayed with us. He got to be good buddies with our new puppy Oopie. They made a nest together in the box spring of Susan's bed. Rocky's befriending dogs was his undoing. Not long after Bob's road trip, Rocky died playing with Tim Hardin's German Shepherd. The family disbanded that summer. Rose and Pati moved to Florida. Susan went to went to live with Bob, first in Chicago and then California. A few months shy of fifteen, I struck out on my own, back to Greenwich Village. A year later both Susan and Pati were living with Bob in California. Rose persuaded me to drive to California with her. She painted "L.A. or Bust!" on the hood of the same 1960 Dodge that had gotten her to Florida, loaded up Oopie, and came to fetch me in the Village. Oopie was still searching for Rocky and thoroughly and feloniously tore up the box spring of every bed in every motel in which we stayed along the way. Rose and I drove through the Mojave desert on a boiling July day and found our way through East L.A. to arrive, weary and wilted, at the Troubadour, in Santa Monica, where Bob was playing and the girls were waiting. I knew that night I wanted to go back to the Village but it took me three months, living on Beechwood Drive in a one bedroom apartment with Rose, Susan and Pati, and working at the House of Pies on Hollywood Boulevard before I could leave.

Susan Hartnett recalls Bob as a father in those days of drug use:
He travelled a lot and we didn't even live in the same place until I was about six that I can remember. My parents lived in Chicago — I don't even know how long — not very long. I was born in Chicago. My older sister was born in New York. And up until the time we moved from Chicago to Aspen, Colorado, where my younger sister was born, my parents pretty much lived together. My father took off again to pursue his career, and we lived in Aspen until I was five, but he didn't really live there, so I have no clear recollection of him prior to my being six when we moved to New York City. Then when we lived in New York, he travelled a lot. I can remember he'd be gone months at a time, and he was not into being a father at all, because he was also into doing a lot of drugs. That would cut into physical ties, because he wasn't around — physically was not around, and frankly when he was around, he was high a lot. I have very few recollections of my father as an active participant. My recollections tend to be more on the outside edges.

Let me give you my armchair psychology. I think my sisters to some degree, and myself to some degree are of the generation where recognizing the impact of their family of origin is a lot more encouraged and the legacy of dysfunction in your family once you open your eyes to it is pretty easy to see, and it's there on both sides. Dad doesn't hold any patent on this one. I would have to be in a complete state of denial, having a father who was a heroin addict and a mother who allowed that to occur for as long as she did, to say that I do not come from a dysfunctional family, but more than anything else I try and find some empathy.

I came to Chicago clean one time. The Sunday Chicago Sun-Times ran a big story referring to my drug experiences as a thing of the past. And only a few days after the story ran, I was stoned and picked up. The club owner bailed me out. It made all of the papers. I went to work that night and crowds came to the club to see me, like in '60. But my work must have been terrible.

A short time after that I tried to do serious work on the problem. For periods of time it was helpful to me to stay in a rigid kind of environment. But if I ventured out into the real world, I was gone again. I was afraid to be around people, because everyone was starting to use drugs. It was around 1969. People knew I was a doper. They'd offer me grass. They knew I'd want all the drugs I could get. But I didn't; therefore I was afraid to be around. I felt I just couldn't be around drugs.

I eventually did come out, but I don't think I ever wanted to be cured. I guess I really just wanted to go back to the time when drugs worked for me and I could say, "I want to use this drug and feel this way" rather than "I must have that drug." But you never can go back. When you take it up again, you take up exactly where you left off.

Drug withdrawal is not the worst thing that happens to you. The physical side is not that bad. But you're in a terrible state emotionally. You're sick physically and you know the solution—an injection of the stuff. You have no character left. You already have traded that in.

I had learned in 1969 that I needed some kind of a structure. I knew I needed something regular. I had a few friends who were going to AA meetings and doing very well. But I had been turned off by the 'God' aspect. I felt I didn't need any holy rollers.

Then about 1976 a friend from Cleveland called and said she needed help. I called the director of a clinic and she spent time in a detox ward and got a big taste of AA. For a couple of years she continued to tell me about her progress, during which she was still attending AA. Finally in 1978 I went to Cleveland and attended an AA meeting. By then I was an expert on "cures," but there still was a part of me that was curious.

But immediately I was right at home. They offered no cure. Rather they were talking about their situation, for which there was no fixing. On a daily basis, they had to change it. It stayed a tremendous support system to me.

In just a few months, I began to see that you have to live life, rather than retreating. I realized that retreat had engaged me totally. Once I stopped running, nothing caught up with me that I wasn't been able to cope with. Up until that time it had seemed to me that if I ever stopped running, it would do me in. I thought it was beyond my ability to cope. Absolutely nothing changed, just my attitude about everything. AA taught me how to live a life without drugs.

Ed McCurdy comments on Bob's later views on drugs:
I felt a certain kinship with Bob because he was an alcoholic at one time and also on drugs. It would not be a full story of him without that. He was on heroin which is just about as bad as you can get. I was in Chicago working and he and another fellow who was also an addict happened to drop around that evening to the club where I was working and they came back and told me that they had quit that week. I don't think it took at that time, but I saw him in Chicago a couple of times, and once I had mentioned something about having smoked some pot, and he was very upset. He said, "You're not using that shit are you?" I said, "No, I've had it twice in my life!" I didn't have any appetite for any mind altering substance other than booze. I was an alcoholic. I still am. I haven't had a drink in 30 years. I couldn't safely drink. Nobody really has tested that. Most people who think it's true are scared to experiment. It's a miserable life for yourself and everybody else.

Unfortunately by the time Bob cleaned up for good, the big money from the public interest in folk music had peaked and passed him by. But he made a living at it until his voice was stilled by illness in 1994 which led to his death two years later.

In a deeply profound self-analysis, Bob has several times commented on why he may have turned his back on probable fame and public acclaim similar to that heaped on Bob Dylan and others, turning instead to uncontrollable drug use.

From his introduction to the video Ramblin', *filmed in 1980 in Athens, Ohio for PBS, just two years after he cleaned up for good:*

I had a couple of good years in the early '60s. Matter of fact, I think I had a pretty good shot at the brass ring. But it's also evident to me that I couldn't handle it, because by 1966, I left the business and I didn't sing for the next three years. I was hiding out in the country thinking that staying out there and away from show business would take care of all the problems that I was inflicting on myself. It's a good place I'm in right now. I think I'm in the place I oughta be. I'm really a saloon singer. I sing for small audiences well. I get a little lost when they're larger, and I'm real happy, able to do what I like to do right now with good balance in my life. I'm able to travel enough but not too much. I write a few songs, but I've never written too many of those. I'm in a good place. I'm in a happy place right now.

PILGRIM

Deep in the darkness I have known,
I stumbled aimless and alone.
At last too weary of the pain
I choose to find my way again.
I journey step by step along
This healing path that makes me whole.
I am a pilgrim of my mind.
I am a seeker of my soul.

Yesterday is history.
Tomorrow is a mystery.
I know the past is dead,
The future's blind.
By looking to this moment
For the light I need to find my way,
I will make it one day at a time.

And though this journey is my own,
I need not travel it alone.
By sharing faith with broken friends,
A broken pilgrim slowly mends.
We journey step by step along
This healing path that make us whole.
We are the pilgrims of our minds.
We are the seekers of our souls.

~ Bob Gibson - 1984
by Bob Gibson / Marv David ©1984 Robert Josiah Music, Inc.

9

A VEILED COMEBACK

In 1968 Bob was lured out of his self-imposed isolation and retirement by Richard Harding, owner of the Chicago club, Quiet Knight. Sadly for the world of music, by the time Bob came out for his triumphant return, the musical tide had turned and the interest in folk music had gone on to other forms. The Beatles had made their invasion, which overnight changed the focus in popular music to rock & roll. While folk music was still around and remained a strong influence for many more years in the music of performers like Peter, Paul & Mary, Tom Paxton, Gordon Lightfoot, Simon & Garfunkel, James Taylor and Carole King, the emphasis had definitely shifted more in the direction of folk rock or country, and Bob had been passed by in his absence. Three years is an entire generation in audience terms, and although many remembered him, he was never again to capture the mass public attention that his early career had promised.

In addition, when he came back, he unfortunately still hadn't conquered his demons, and his battles with drug addiction continued to haunt him for ten more years. Sometimes clean for periods of a year or two, he managed to come out with some very important records, but contrasting that, he still was to face some of his lowest points before cleaning up.

Rick Neely looks back on the valleys of Bob's life:

There are some spaces in Bob's life that I'm not 100% sure of where he is or what he's doing. I'm pretty sure that he did some jail time. There was a rather celebrated episode where, in Bob's really lowest points, he got caught breaking into apartments in Marina City in Chicago. On another occasion in 1969 Bob had come out, performed a great concert and then right away had been arrested for possession. He was clean and he came back in the environment. They say in recovery circles, if you don't want to slip, don't go to slippery places. Well, all of the places that Bob went to ply his trade — small clubs and bars, that kind of scene — were slippery places. He said he came back and he wasn't ready and they were waiting for him and got him first thing. He fell right back into it.

Ed Holstein, singer/songwriter, recalls the same times:

I got to know Bob in 1968. He came back and the word was he was cleaned up but he wasn't. He was involved in a publishing company and he published my song *Jazzman*. It was exciting to get to know Bob Gibson, who was a hero of mine, but at the same time he was going through that stuff and winding up on Armitage and Fremont with the other junkies there eating sweet rolls. I think he got arrested for something to do with some Marina City stuff, burglaries or something. He was going through a bad period at that time.

In an article titled Bob Gibson Looked Trouble in the Eye — And Smiled, *published in the Chicago Tribune on Oct. 7, 1996, Bob Greene remembered his assignment to cover Bob Gibson's trouble in "the Marina City incident."*

I met Bob Gibson only once, when I was a very young reporter, and that meeting has always stayed with me because of what it taught me about several things: about a person showing grace under unpleasant circumstances, about the conventions and follies of the news business, and about the way one should behave when faced with troubles.

A bulletin had moved across the City News Bureau wire saying that Gibson had gotten in a nonstop-the-presses scrape with the law—as I recall, it was a marijuana-possession arrest which would later be dismissed. Things like that frequently happened to musicians in the late 1960s. The bulletin said that Gibson was living in an apartment in the Marina City highrise.

The bulletin identified Gibson as the writer of the song *Abilene*. *Abilene* had been a moderate hit in 1963, an amiable and endearing song, and that mention in the bulletin was enough to persuade the editor on the city desk at the paper where I was working that we must run a story. If the person who wrote *Abilene* was in trouble, then that qualified as news. The editor handed me the wire copy and told me to go over to Marina City and knock on Gibson's door.

So I did, feeling rather stupid. The unspoken message is the same on all such visits — "Hi, you have no idea who I am, but you're famous and you're in trouble, so I've been sent here"— and I knocked on his door and when he answered I stammered out some marginally more polite version of that sentiment.

A lot of people might have said, "Talk to my lawyer about this," or "I have no comment," or "You must be very proud of yourself, showing up here to bother me at a time like this." Gibson asked to see the City News copy I was carrying: he read it, smiled at what he saw, and invited me in.

We sat and talked. He told me the details of the trouble in which he found himself—the specifics of it escape me now, but it was nothing he was evasive about, he was forthright and wry—and he didn't just stick to that, he told me about his life and music, and I think he had as many questions for me as I had for him. He wasn't nervous or defensive; he seemed amused by the absurdities of life, a life in which, because he had written a somewhat successful song and then found himself in trouble, and because I had been given a job at a newspaper, we found ourselves sitting many floors above the Chicago River, both of us talking but only one of us writing things down.

He showed me his guitars; he answered everything I asked him, although he certainly didn't have to. He struck me as a man so confident about the path he had chosen in the world, so unfearful of life, that something like this— a beginning reporter knocking on his door with the assignment to write a story that would almost certainly place him in an unpleasant light — not only didn't offend him, but clearly struck him as one more humorous quirk in a world that will always make you laugh, if you let it.

I trudged back to the city room and wrote the story the editor wanted, about the trouble in which Gibson found himself. I recall that the next day, the headline above the story identified him as "Bob 'Abilene' Gibson" — hey, if the paper was going to trade upon the fact that a well-known person was having some problems, it had better make sure that the readers knew who the person was. They might not know Gibson's name, but they probably had heard the song, *Abilene*. So "Bob 'Abilene' Gibson" it was, right there in the headline.

I sometimes ask myself why some people seem always so afraid and distrusting of life, and others welcome it in. Maybe it's all in the eyes of the beholder — how those eyes choose to look at life. If you remember the words to *Abilene*, you'll recall a line: "People there don't treat you mean. . . ."

Rick Neely:
There are another two or three years when he was out in California where things are kind of vague and then about 1970 he came back in a big way. He was working hard and singing really well, and I think he was for the lion's share of the time, trying to stay pretty clean of drugs. We were all still drinking a little bit and smoking then. He used to chain smoke Pall Mall cigarettes like they were going out of style.

Unsure of what he wanted his musical future to be, Bob settled in Los Angeles for a while at the end of the '60s. Singer/songwriter and astrologer Antonia Lamb recalls:
I'd known of Bob when I was living on the lower East side, but everybody always warned me about him because he was a womanizing junkie. By 1969 I was living in the Hollywood hills as was Roger McGuinn who had been a good friend of mine since the early '60s in New York, when he Roger gave me my first banjo lesson. Roger had learned from Bob to play the banjo back when he was a teenager in Chicago. One day I was visiting Roger's house, and there was a nice pleasant sort of round man playing the banjo. He didn't look at all like the Bob Gibson that I knew of so I didn't recognize him. I

thought, "Man, that guy can play banjo!" Roger had given me that one banjo lesson the night that John Kennedy was shot, and then I had played on my own, and I had the Pete Seeger book. I had started playing the banjo within three weeks of the time I became an astrologer. At the time I saw Bob I was doing an astrology column in a local paper, so I said, "I'll do your horoscope and analyze it for you for a couple of banjo lessons." He said, "Sure!" So I said, "Okay, fine, what's your name?" He said, "Bob Gibson." I was terribly embarrassed, because I should have known just from the banjo playing. It turned out we lived about half a block from each other. I went to his place for the lesson and then during the second lesson, I played him some songs I wrote. I had this horrible banjo that had been owned by somebody who died, and I think they died because they could never tune the fuckin' banjo! It would go out of tune in the middle of the first note you played. When I finished playing my songs, Bob said, "You are a great songwriter, and you ought have a great banjo." So he went in the other room and he got his other banjo, and he gave it to me. His generosity and perceptiveness, and the banjo, changed my life. It was a Vega longneck that used to be owned by Johnny Horton, the great banjo player who did that song, "In 1814 we took a little trip..." It had been in the plane crash with him when he died, and Bob had inherited it.

When I met Bob, I knew he was somebody who was going to be in my life forever. You meet certain people and you just know. I had no idea at that moment of the depth and complexity of the connection and how it would involve us all, but I'm damn grateful for it!

In 1970 I started playing clubs again. By 1971 I was out in LA making an album for Capitol called *Bob Gibson*. That was a great reunion. I hadn't seen any of those folks in ages....you know, David Crosby and Roger McGuinn and Spanky McFarlane, that whole gang. They were all beginning when I was already established in the early '60s, so it was great to see them. They had all gone on to do amazing things.

Roger McGuinn spoke in 1997 about working on the album:
I worked on the album *Bob Gibson* with Bob and Chris Hillman. We played electric guitars on it, so it wasn't that he wouldn't go rock. We were kind of doing a little bit of rock & roll on that record, but his heart wasn't in it, and it was kind of a hodge-podge. It wasn't really like his former albums where it had a sense of continuity and direction — integrity. It was almost like the company was making him do something he didn't want to do. We were definitely pulling for him and trying to help him out to get a hit or get something — get going. I don't know, it's just a tough business. I performed on that album because we were friends. He called me up and asked me to do it, and I was more than happy to.

Roger had no knowledge of the comments Bob, himself, had made about this album 20 years earlier. Amazingly, both used almost exactly the same words to describe it. Here are Bob's thoughts:

This album was sort of a hodge-podge. There was no place I was coming from, except back out of being out of it. This was my first exposure to multi-track recording. There are a couple of cuts I do here with Camp, but we did not record our voices at the same time, and there was a different feeling to the resulting sound.

A review appeared in the Chicago Tribune in 1971:
Bob Gibson Revisited, by Lew Harris

The best record news of all, Bob Gibson, the 12-stringing ski bum, has a new album out, *Bob Gibson* (Capitol), which brings back more memories than all the other new releases put together.

Gibson, in the early days, was to commercialized folk [as opposed to pure ethnic folk] what, say, Johnny Cash has been to country rock; a gap bridger. He sang old mining songs, but he wasn't an old miner; so he made the songs he sang show his empathy. His 12-string honky-tonk version of *Frankie and Johnny* is probably better known than the original.

After half a decade or so of being quite down, Gibson reappeared here last year at the Quiet Knight. More recently he showed up on the Flying Burrito Brothers' latest album. Now he has one of his own, at last!

My first thought was, "How does he sound?" Well, you almost don't have to play the album to find that out. The first song is *Fog Horn*—one he wrote with Shel Silverstein for his last album with Elektra, *Where I'm Bound*, released in 1964.

He sounds just the same. Even when backed by people like Roger McGuinn, Chris Hillman, David Crosby and Sneeky Pete.

And even when singing something as pure Dylan as *Just Like a Woman*, it's Gibson all the way. On the original version, when Dylan says she "breaks just like a little girl," you feel he's the one breaking her; with Gibson, you feel he's merely noticing a more tender side to her nature.

(Parenthetically, Bob recalled this about Dylan: Other than being involved in New Concepts which managed him in the very beginning, I met Dylan only a couple of times and passed up my opportunity to know him. He came one time with an entourage to my place at Los Angeles. He came knocking, unannounced. I already had plans with a 6'2" blonde who had a Corvette. I had a choice and I chose the girl with the Corvette. I said, 'I'll see you guys later.')

The review continues:

The album includes some Gibson-penned tunes: *Leaving for the Last Time, Easy Now*, the bitterly sarcastic *Ballad of Fred and Mark* [Fred Hampton and Mark Clark], as well as one by John

Prine *[Sam Stone]* and one by Hamilton Camp *[About Time]*.

Which brings me to the best part of the album, Gordon Lightfoot's *For Lovin' Me,* when you hear this voice harmonizing with Gibson — you realize it's Camp singing along, just like he did in those old days.

By the time their second duet, *A Hard Rain's Gonna Fall,* was done I found myself very grateful that Gibson had returned, and that he had returned not as a washed-up folk singer making a comeback singing old Beatles ballads but as one of the most creative forces in commercialized folk music continuing his work.

My old former partner from New Concepts, Roy Silver, was the manager who put the whole album together, and I picked Jim Dickson to produce it. He was also Camp's producer. I'd known him out on the West Coast. I'd been working out there for a long time at places like the Troubadour and the Ash Grove. I met him first in the early '60s. I started in the Ash Grove about 1958 and the Troubadour in 1960.

I had a John Prine demo tape when I went out to LA. Through Roy Silver, we had a deal going with A&M and John Prine, in which I was going to put the song on my album. John knew I was doing *Sam Stone,* and my album eventually came out two weeks before his. We were getting a lot of airplay on the album. Then Jerry Wexler enjoined the album in court, which took the roll off it entirely. Prine's version was so different. Prine himself, always said he was sorry that happened because he knew I was recording the song. He knew the whole thing and Jerry Wexler said, "Oh, my God, we can't have this copy going out before John's original sung version." John was the only singer on his version. I had all these people singing on it and it was a great version. The FM stations were playing it like crazy, but .... a moment of nearness to it, but it didn't happen.

They pressed 17,500 copies of my record, they went, and that was it for the Capitol album. That was not successful from their point of view, and they didn't want to go any further with me.

There's no pressure from record companies to *be* commercial. They only *want* commercial. If you have a national firm with offices of promotion people, and a staff, and telephones and overhead, you've got the capability of handling so many albums a month. Therefore, you can't handle albums that only sell 5,000 because you can't make any money. The first 5,000 cost $12,000 just to produce.

The record people have never been in *music,* and it's crazy to think they have been. They sell flat, black plastic things. When *we* say good, we're talking about artistic and musical taste. When *they* say good, they're talking about if it sells.

There were quite a few songs on that album that I co-wrote with Shel Silverstein. We'd spend some time together every so often. He was, by that time, living in the Playboy mansion on the West Coast. By then, he was concentrating on songwriting and would go to Nashville a lot. We'd get together and write a few songs. He had made a couple of albums by this stage. His first one was on Atlantic. But his albums were like novelty records. It was shortly after that that he constructed Dr. Hook, because he was writing all that great stuff and had nowhere to go with it. Nobody in Nashville was recording that kind of stuff. For instance, the story about how Johnny Cash happened to record *A Boy Named Sue* is like off the wall. Johnny loved the song and wanted to record it. His producer and his manager had a meeting about what songs they were going to record for his next album. John said, "Well, there's this song..." They loved it and they laughed but said, "You can't record it." He said, "Why?" and they said, "John, you're a country artist. You'll lose your country following. You can't do that. It's a cute song, it's a novelty song, but with your kind of image - *Ring of Fire* and all - you can't do that, no matter how funny it is. You just can't, John. Anyway, nobody has ever heard of this writer." John said, "Well, he's the guy who wrote *The Unicorn*. That song had been a big hit for the Irish Rovers." They said, "Oh, he wrote that song?" Well, that song was a novelty item. It came off an album of theirs that was totally Irish, just like the Clancy Brothers. The one song that wasn't Irish was *The Unicorn,* and it became a hit. Then they said, "Well, maybe you could do that song on an album. Maybe *A Boy Named Sue* would work on an album." He put it out and it was the one that really took off. It opened all the right doors then for Shel. For instance, Bobby Bare records whole albums of his songs. Every major country artist has done his songs, from Willie Nelson to Dolly Parton.

Rick Neely was finally about to meet the man who had been so important in his life. He recalls the occasion:
    I was in the service 1969-71 and when I got out, my wife and I, at the time, were living in a little apartment in Rogers Park in Chicago. There was some program that had a little interview with Bob and someone said, "Where are you living now and what are you doing?" He talked a little bit about trying to get back into playing and stuff and said that he was living in West Hollywood. So I said to my wife, "Let's see if there's a listing." We called directory assistance, and there was a listing for a Bob Gibson in West Hollywood. So we thought, "What the heck, let's call it up." So we called up on his birthday and we said, "Is this Bob Gibson?" He said, "Yes." "Is this Bob Gibson, the folk singer?" "Yes." My wife and I sang *Happy Birthday*. He thought that was a big kick, because who on earth would have remembered that it was his birthday? He said he was going to be in Chicago and "let's get together." He was going to be at

the Earl's and "come backstage. I'd like to meet you." Then I just followed him around everywhere for the next five or six years. He'd break strings and I was the guy who ran up with the package of strings and the pliers so he could make the repairs. I just followed him and talked and learned and just absorbed the whole thing.

During that time, I was also a music student and I annotated music. In those days when you wrote a song, you had to submit a printed lead sheet in order to apply for a copyright. Now you can submit a cassette tape or whatever, but in those days you had to have a printed lead sheet, so I would transcribe his songs and write lead sheets for him.

Ed Holstein:

He started playing at the Earl's in about '70 and started becoming a part of our group a little bit, as much as he could given the situation with the drugs because he was in and out of it.

But 1972 was when it all came together again, just like the old days. Del Close and George Carlin were the moderators when Gibson & Camp sang together for the first time in 11 years. Gibson & Camp had not sung together in 11 years and Earl Pionke booked them at the Earl of Old Town 1972. They had a show at WTTW. George Carlin, Del Close and Shel Silverstein and they're all doing this Gate of Horn reunion with a live audience and Camp came in and they started singing *Skillet Good & Greasy* and it was, like, unbelievable. They honestly did not rehearse! It was unreal! I never saw anything like it in my life. Then they started working at the Earl of Old Town.

The phenomenal show from WTTW was written up in great detail by Jonathan Abarbanel in the Chicago Express.

They Brought Back the Good Times at a Gathering for the Gate

Sunday morning at 10 am is not a good time for aging night clubbers. And a television studio is virtually an impossible place to reproduce the kind of warmth and spontaneity generated in a good old Chicago folk club.

Yet that is what happened last weekend, when WTTW brought together a reunion of performers from the well-remembered, but now gone days of the Gate of Horn.

Singers Ginni Clemmens and John Prine (representing the current club scene) are here. So are writer Shel Silverstein and humorists Del Close and George Carlin. And soon there will be Bob Gibson and Hamid Hamilton Camp (once known as Bob Camp), who both were featured performers in the years 1956 to 1964, when the Gate, first in a basement at 753 N. Dearborn and then in its own building at 1036 N. State, was the mainstay of the Chicago folk scene.

The Gate didn't produce these people; they produced the Gate—

and Mother Blue's and Second City and many another North Side club. Now the same electro-chemistry of personality begins its good vibes work on everyone.

We file into Studio A, the big one at WTTW, for a taping of the station's Sunday evening Open Air program. A peanut gallery of high bleachers is filled with an audience of young people, none of them looking old enough to remember the old Gate, or Lenny Bruce's bust there in 1962, or Severn Darden, or Josh White, or Lord Buckley—names that keep popping up, for they were all part of that scene.

Down below, on the studio floor, are five little nightclub tables with red-and-white tablecloths, where we privileged friends and guests of the performers sit. There is a head table, too, where the on-camera conversations take place.

Little red lights flash. Gibson opens with *Cindy*. Gibson, a Santa Claus in hippie drag, seems to be healthier than he has looked in years. The voice is still the same husky baritone. Later, there is a clip of Gibson 10 or 12 years ago: clean-shaven, square-jawed, crew-cut, Ivy-Leagued. But the same voice.

The program format mixes conversation with songs, stories, comedy bits and film clips. Shel, Del, George, Bob and Ginni realize they can say and do almost anything, and quickly take over the show from host Jerry Bishop, who lets them play fast and loose.

Those who don't know soon learn about the Gate.

Carlin describes his years as a closet freak; how the bar in the old basement Gate was the first place he found other freaks. Silverstein says that there you find insanity. We hear about Mother Blue's backporch, where you could turn on (Mother Blue herself sits in the "privileged" section of the audience). There's a clip of one of Lenny Bruce's more innocuous routines. Carlin tells about his obscenity bust in Milwaukee.

In between, we see a kinescope from the old WGN Folkfest program of Will Holt singing his *Lemon Tree*. Later, we see a clip of Peter, Paul and Mary doing the same song on the same show.

Close does some of his old stand-up comic routine about the philosophy of resistentialism, based on resistance to inanimate objects which are "out to get us." (At the old Gate, Del was billed as the "incredible thinking man.")

Prine does his *Sam Stone*.

He doesn't know the old Gate from borscht. He'd rather just watch the "old-timers" do their stuff. He gets off on it, like we all do.

The only one to keep John company is that beautiful lady, Ginni Clemmens. But wait. She was at the old Gate, too! And here's a film clip of her singing there, 10 years ago. She's the living continuity, the Chicago constant between then and now.

There's more. Stories of Lord Richard Buckley, whose marvelous comic madness must be heard. Prine does another song. Carlin does some material. Then Shel Silverstein is up, the ring leader. He has been subtly, funnily animating everyone all morning. Now his incredible fog horn voice

BOB GIBSON - 110

bellows forth with *Sausalito Witch* and *Sarah Cynthia Sylvia Stout*. He has such a good time forgetting the words that everyone breaks up.

Silverstein finishes fast. He sees that Ham Camp has arrived. Silverstein introduces what we are all waiting for: together again for the first time in 10 years, Gibson and Camp.

Gibson and Camp! Legends! Newport Folk Festival, 1960. Bob Gibson, already a star, introduced Bob Camp. I still have the record. They tore the festival apart. They're about to do it again at Channel 11.

Camp sets up, a little pixie joking, mugging, making music. Gibson strums. For the first time in a decade, out comes *Old Dog Blue,* soaring into perfectly recalled high harmonies. A good show becomes a great one. The missing fraternity brother has arrived, the last atom in the electro-chemical good vibes molecule.

When the song ends, cheers. Right into *That's What You Get For Loving Me.* Everyone rapt. Prine digging it. Close, Carlin, Silverstein, Clemmens, Mother Blue looking at long lost siblings.

But TV is TV. Ninety minutes are up. Open Air is over. Flash the final credits. Someone goes up to give Gibson and Camp a "cut" sign. He never makes it. No way. A half-dozen hands hold him back. Song over, a standing ovation. No one would dare stop them now, so it's into *Drunk and Goosey.* Finally, someone at the station gets a bright idea: they start taping again. Forget the 90-minute limit. There's magic here.

When the song ends, mayhem. People are shouting, jumping, running. Gibson and Camp do one last song, *Betty and Dupree,* with Del, Shel, Ginni and George joining the final chorus. A whole TV studio is high!

It has been a functional reunion, not a remembrance of things past. After all, these "old" men are just rounding 40. From 1959 to 1963, they were Chicago's cultural revolution. And some of them are part of the current one, too. Ginni Clemmens has always been here. Del Close returned to work in Story Theater, found the Chicago Extension Improv. Group and direct at Second City.

The stories a decade old are funny and sweet. But there is agreement that today in Chicago is just as good. In fact, better because it's bigger. As Del or Shel or George remarked as the Studio "A" door closed behind us, "The good old days are now."

G. Gigi Gilmartin wrote of this time of reunion for the two:
December, 1972. Chicago is still the folk music capital of the world. But now its White House is the Earl of Old Town, the tawdry bar that spawned the likes of Steve Goodman, Bonnie Koloc and the Holstein brothers. The word went out Gibson and Camp are back and Earl's got 'em. Two rough beasts slouching toward Chicago to be reborn - to re-create a legend that was good when it was happening, but had grown even bigger in the memories of those who had waited for more than ten years. Could they really re-create those good ole

days? No. And Camp didn't even want to try. He had a new band and he agreed to the gig with Gibson only because it was the best way to ensure a good crowd to introduce the Skymonters. But talent can't be denied. The songs may not have sounded the same, but the excitement, the thrill, the fun, the humor — these had grown with the years.

Antonia Lamb:
    Bob and I had a lot of friends in the music industry who moved to the hills of northern California. Gene Clark, who I'd met after Roger, Gene and David Crosby had founded the Byrds, also lived in the Hollywood hills. He had fallen in love with his future wife Carlie and moved to Mendocino where Ramblin' Jack Elliott had a place. Gene called one day and said I should come up there. I went up to visit them. I had a powerful vision that my children's lives would be damaged if I stayed in Hollywood, so I moved to Mendocino. Bob and I were still friends and I kept sort of leaning on him saying, "You really ought to check this out. It's really pretty darn great!" Eventually, between me and Jack Elliott, we got him to come up and visit, and it was a done deal by that point. Once he got here he understood. Bob moved into my house. It was great. We'd have dinners and Bob and Jack and I and a lot of other musicians would sing and play.

    During the time I was in Hollywood, Rose *(Bob's ex-wife)*, Pati, Meridian and Susan *(his daughters)* moved right down the road, and I got friendly with her and the kids. Then, when Pati was having a hard time when she was 13, she came up here and lived with me and my family for a while. By that time Bob had his own place up the road. Later on Meridian moved here, too. At the time, it just seemed like the right thing to do, and it all created a kind of a web of life-long love between us all.

Bob & Pati in 1972

PHOTO BY ANTONIA LAMB

    I moved up to Mendocino in late 1971 or early 1972 and spent a couple of years there. As before, I'd go out and work in Chicago and LA and other cities. I'd go back there and spend a lot of time just hanging out because I like the area. During that period there weren't many jobs for me other than in clubs in the Old Town of Chicago. I was just hanging in. I'd been doing the same set of songs for several years, and I wasn't writing or learning. Shel Silverstein was very helpful in jarring me out of this. Shel would come up there and we'd write songs. It was up in the redwoods on the ocean. It was very colorful and very nice.

Antonia Lamb:
    That time in Mendocino was so wonderful, so incredibly great

and Bob was happy there. Shel came out for a little bitty while, but it was more than Shel. When Bob came to Mendocino what happened was we had this incredible musical community here and everyone embraced him with open arms. We had outdoor boogies. We had music twice, three times, four times a week. Everybody had music parties in their yards. There was music everywhere. It was just an incredibly fertile time in the '71 to '74 period, and Bob started writing again. He wrote not just with Shel, but with a couple of other people up here. There was an atmosphere in Mendocino at the time that reminded me of the early Greenwich Village days. That's what was happening here. Unfortunately, the same thing happened of course — the greed. The artists and musicians created a scene that was then taken over by real estate greed, and they basically made it so that right now it's too expensive for anybody to live here anymore, so it's like a ghost town filled with shops. But it was a vital creative community and it inspired everyone who was here. There was an enormous amount of creative partying and I'd say that that was very important. We'd sit around and do round robins where each one of us would make up the line of a song. We had a lot of fun.

Bob's dear, dear friend Victor Biondo came to live here and that was a big deal, too. The two of them were very old friends from the mid '50s. Victor and Bob were a success story together at quitting heroin. Victor became a very powerful therapist and worked with people in various forms of addictive distress. Victor decided to come to Mendocino and I can remember the first night he was here we put him up at my house and he decided to live there that morning. He and Bob ended up living next door to each other for a while. Victor became one of the most beloved figures in this town and Bob was too when he was here. That's the nice thing about a small town. We're all big fish in a small pond.

I remember when Bob and Biff Rose and I went down to LA to play at the Ice House in Pasadena in '72 or '73. We drove down in Biff's Volkswagen bus that had a little 1/4 size piano in the back, so we played piano while we drove, and we all wrote songs on that trip. At that time Bob had gone in and out of the whole musical community and record community and fame and fortune community. When he came to Mendocino he really was uncertain about whether he ever wanted to do that again. Actually I think it confirmed for him that he indeed did want to do that again, but when we went out to LA, as he was seeing a lot of record people, it seemed clear to me that Bob was a complete innocent in that area of his life, and that he didn't really have that canny savvy to sort of push himself in the right direction. It was a kind of a bittersweet experience in a way because audiences loved him

1972 L-R back: Bob, Antonia, Biff; front: Biff's son Eben, Antonia's children Joanna & Jim (behind), Biff's son Andrew

PHOTO COURTESY ANTONIA LAMB

so much, and whatever the wonderful presence that he had was, in the '70s, folk music was quickly losing it, and no one understood either how to market it or how to deal with it. As a result, Bob was in between a rock and a hard place in a way during that whole period between the mid '70s and early '80s. It was a dark time in some ways for acoustic music. I think there's been a resurgence in recent years, but I feel sad for Bob, because I could see even then that timing-wise, part of what he did to himself with his alcohol and drug abuse was that he sort of cut his career off short right when it should have been growing. It's like a plant. If a plant doesn't get nurtured at a certain point it never grows as big, and I feel like that's what happened to him in terms of the realities of his career. But this is a classic pattern with abused children. That's the other story. Many people who have early histories of really difficult childhoods, often shoot themselves in the foot. Of course we didn't know about "inner child" stuff like that then.

Ed Holstein:
I think he had a pretty good period around '73, '74. He lost some weight, he looked great, he got involved in the Old Town School of Folk Music with Ray Tate for awhile. We did some gigs together in downstate Illinois and played a concert at a place called the Red Herring.

It wasn't 'til I made the decision to move back to Chicago, because I needed an audience again, that I did an album titled *Funky in the Country (1974),* which I produced. It was a live performance album which was distributed by Mountain Railroad. The album was really on the Legend label.

It was at about this time that John Irons first became acquainted with Bob. Years later, he would briefly become Bob's manager, but he recalls this as Bob's best work:
I think the best album he ever made was *Funky in the Country.* That was recorded on a Crown recorder. A friend of mine, Dan Tucker, met a boyhood friend named Dwane Lundeen, who had a place called Multi Media Sound. One of his employees was a fan of Bob's. Bob was playing at Amazingrace, and he asked if he could take the Crown decks out to just record it. It was a good show and recorded very cleanly, so it became *Funky in the Country.* I thought that was, because of the material, his best album.

The album *Funky in the Country* all came about backwards. I was playing at Amazingrace, a coffeehouse in Evanston, Illinois, with John Guth, a terrific guitarist. The ambience was very special there, and we knew it would be really high energy performing. We decided to try and make a recording of the performance. So on April 9, 1974, we borrowed some equipment from friends and got Jim Cunningham, who is sort of a sound engineer's sound engineer, to mix it down to four tracks. Right there they've broken all the laws in the recording business!

We got lucky. When you realize that what you're saying is being immortalized on tape, you tend to blow it all. We didn't think we were going to have a tape. The mikes were so poor, we just forgot about the whole deal. But someone borrowed some great mikes unbeknownst to me, and while I was up there singing, over being self-conscious and free of worries about making an impression on the machine or the audience, the people at the controls were getting a great tape.

I knew I'd never record with another major label. It would just be the same old situation and that wouldn't suffice. You read about $75,000 to $100,000 to do it right and everything is deductible from the artist until the company starts showing a profit. Then the album has a short shelf life. You can't get them to reprint small batches to keep the stores stocked. The pressing just disappears even though you need to have your name and albums out there.

Anyway, I took the recording we'd made and I was going to try to drum up some support for producing it in Nashville. I dropped by Ray Tate's office at the Old Town School of Folk Music to play the tape for him, just to check it out before I split with it. Ray's recorder was on the blink, so we both went over to John McGuire's. It was a lucky thing, because both of them were so enthusiastic about it that they decided on the spot to back the record themselves. That was the beginning of Legend Enterprises.

Meridian Green:

My sister Susan came to visit Mendocino in the summer of '74. I was ready to set out from Mendocino on my quest for a nest egg to buy a country cabin of my own. Chicago sounded like a good place to seek my fortune and so Susan and I drove off across the country. I was also intrigued by Susan and what she was up to. Susan, from early on, and even more so these days, has always had a unique kind of visionary pragmatism. To this day I'm totally mystified by how Susan, in the midst of the maelstrom that was our childhood, first figured out that what she needed was a college education, and second, managed to live with one parent or the other most of the time until she graduated. Susan and I rented a comfortable flat with Bob and his girlfriend Debbie. It was an odd but rather pleasant little household with both Susan and Debbie (who was in law school) studying and going off to school bright and early. It was a little pungent as Bob had given up Pall Malls for Cuban cigars. He was also getting enormous pleasure out his domestic innovations like adding cinnamon to the coffee and having family bagel and lox brunches. I was working as a waitress, intending to return to Mendocino with means to buy a cabin and a car, when I found myself entranced by an even bigger dream, Bob's dream of Legend Enterprises.

It was brilliant and way before its time. Today just about anybody who's ever made a record, and for sure anyone who's ever had to deal with a record label, big or small, has at least thought about having their own label. But in 1974 it was a relatively novel idea born, I think, out of his frustration with how the Capitol deal had gone down. Bob's idea was to make Legend Enterprises a little homemade label that could profitably sell 5,000 to 10,000 records. He knew he could sell that many albums directly to his audience at concerts and clubs in the mid-West. It made perfect sense to me and I was thrilled to be involved in the launching of Legend Enterprises.

Bob had the support lined up for the pressing costs. He was working on designing the record cover and the company look. He decided that pumpkin paper with purple ink would give the company an eye catching edge. My job was to do the publicity. First I had to write a bio and a press release, not an easy task for I'd completely skipped high school and had never written promotional material or anything else before. Bob seemed quite comfortable leaving it to me, and I was fortunate to have mentors at the Old Town School explaining how to do it. Camp helped too, giving me an earful one day at the café under the El tracks, when I showed him my first draft of the bio. He jumped up out of the booth, so frustrated that he was hopping up and down and hollering, "You just don't get it! Your father was not an influence! He invented folk music!" So I got a little less tentative in my writing. I sent out hand calligraphed cover letters, in purple ink on brilliant pumpkin paper, with the press kits and albums to the reviewers and radio. When *Funky In The Country* got a great review in Billboard magazine I thought we were unstoppable.

I lined up a series of shows for the summer, each one a record release party, and I was counting chickens like crazy. I figured we'd sell tons of records at each show and wondered how soon we'd need to press more. The premiere record release party, at the Earl, was a big an event. The Earl of Old Town, both the man and the club, were great. Earl grumbled a bit at first about having to work with Bob's kid on the event but he was, in fact, gracious, if a little gruff to work with. The night of the show, in addition to a great Gibson performance and the usual kind of quack that attends a premiere event, we raffled off a Gibson concert to benefit Quetico, an organization providing wilderness canoe trips for inner city kids that Bob supported. I swear it wasn't rigged. I put the thousand or so ticket stubs in the fishbowl. I blindfolded the kid, whom I selected at random from the audience, to pull the winning stub out of the fishbowl. The Earl won, fair and square. Gus, the doorman at the Earl, who always ushered the audience to their seats, in the manner of an impeccably dignified butler, in order to pack them in like sardines, gave me a somewhat suspicious look and loudly inquired across the club to Earl, "Does this mean you're not paying Gibson tonight?" Earl answered, "Hell, no! I'm giving the show to Jimmy. Jimmy, where you gonna have Gibson play?" Jimmy, the beatific bartender paused for a moment, smiled, and announced, " We'll have Gibson play over at Cabrini Green." I don't know if it ever happened. When we sold over a hundred records that night I thought we were unstoppable.

    The next day Bob confided in me that we'd need to postpone a bunch of those record release shows because he was in a Methadone program and couldn't leave town until he kicked again. We were stopped and we never got started again. Bob spent most of the summer in a live-in rehab program. I waited tables at The Earl until I could afford to travel. *Funky In The Country* was licensed to Mountain Railroad later that year. We had such a powerful dream in Legend Enterprises and I loved it so much that it took me years to get over my disappointment.

In an article called The Cheerful Bear Comes Out of Hibernation, *writer Ed Kislaitis reviewed the album in the* Illinois Entertainer:

What's different about his album and the dozen or so preceding efforts? *Everything.*

    Bob Gibson lives in a modest walk-up in a mid-north side Latin Community. The place is filled with overstuffed couches and chairs which are comfortable if a little faded. The surroundings reflect the man. Bob is comfortable, and overstuffed in a cheerful bearlike way. His large full beard and his sense of presence complete the image of something a little out of place when it's not in the woods. In fact, Gibson's laid back aura can only be described as "funky." No put-ons, no bull-shit. It's almost sad how the people who sang the songs ten years ago have grown into the people they were singing about.

    The special quality that Gibson brings to the Silverstein cuts on side one has to come from long years of mutual experience. Bob reports that the last time he sang *Living Legend,* three women in the audience started crying, and not just because of his technique. When Bob sings *Cindy Dreams,* or *Funky in the Country,* you can hear the happy memories of Mendocino in his voice. The days when Kristofferson, Jack Elliot, and people like himself were doing a different and easier lifestyle out in the forests. You can also hear his longing to return. Where years ago he might have flashed his collection of instruments on an impressed guest, today he just smiles and says, "You can only play one at a time."

When Shel first wrote *Living Legend* and brought it to me, I said I couldn't sing it, it was just too close to my life. He insisted. "Go on, sing it," he said. I had a tape of it and listened to it a few times. I tried it once and that was it. It felt good.

As always, no matter what problems Bob may have had, he was always ready to welcome talented new performers, and was never too down to help them along. Just such a rising star came to town in 1974, and nobody was more eager than Bob Gibson. Autoharpist Bryan Bowers remembers the obstacles of his arrival in Chicago and finally meeting Bob Gibson:

I met Bob in Chicago. I came to Chicago because the Dillards told me about the Earl of Old Town and that I'd be perfect there,. When I finally got to play for Earl, he said, "Wow, you're really good! I'm gonna book you for two weeks, and we'll figure the price and everything."

Then he said, "Come on, I want to take you around to meet some people." He took me to Orphan's, and that's where I met Bob. I heard Earl take Bob aside and say, "Get this kid up to play." Bob was on the bill so he got up, and he said something like, "Earl said this guy who plays the autoharp is worth hearing. I don't know what he does, but his name's Bryan Bowers." I got up and played, and Gibson came up to me afterwards and said, "You're great!" He was just a big supporter of mine! He told people about me, and he helped me out a lot.

A major highlight for Bob in this shadowy time was a performance on June 9, 1974, with a group of fellow singers at Charlotte's Webb in Rockford, Illinois. They called themselves "Sparrow," and the group consisted of Bob, Claudia Schmidt, John Bassette and Bryan Bowers.

The evening, while a bit rough and obviously still tinged with an "edgy" quality at times, was full of excitement and wonderful harmonies, so characteristic of Gibson collaborations.

Bryan Bowers:

We had fun as Sparrow. Claudia could sing harmony with a post and Gibber could sing harmony with a post, Bassette could — I was the weak link harmony-wise. They'd always make me sing lead because I couldn't sing harmony worth a shit. I'd go along pretty good and then all of a sudden I'd get to where the harmony's supposed to bend or something, and I didn't get it in those days about how to do that. I'd just squawk through some terrible note and they'd all be giving me a horrible look.

Unfortunately, Bob's continuing drug and personal problems kicked in to ruin yet another opportunity. Bryan continues:

Gibber was such a notorious latenik — I don't know whether it was the drugs or not — but he'd always show up late. The three of us got to feeling like it was just a power play on his part because he was the old pro and we were rookies. We got sick of it so we blew it off. We figured, "Hey, if we're all putting in equal energy, equal time, equal effort, okay," but he was always late. He always had excuses why he couldn't come or why he had to leave early. We rehearsed a bunch of times, and we actually did a whole show up at a festival in Rockford. It was the only time we played on stage. Actually, that's wrong! We played Charlotte's Webb.

*In the one recorded performance of Sparrow at Charlotte's Webb, it was evident that the performers had fun from the beginning to the end. Through a series of mishaps, Bryan Bowers was late to the gig. Having been at a muddy bluegrass festival in Kansas that day, he was delayed in his arrival at Rockford. One of the great bright spots in that evening's performance was when Bryan stepped up to the microphone with his autoharp and spent the next **20 minutes** performing a hilarious narrative song recanting one catastrophic event after another beginning with the previous evening when he gassed up his truck to the moment when he tried to sneak in unnoticed, caked in dried mud, only to be caught by his friends on stage who greeted him with a chorus of* For He's a Jolly Good Fellow. *As Bryan says, "That song I did there was definitely improvised on the spot. I never wrote those kind of things down." The audience and the other performers fell apart at the end of the song. It was Claudia who had to speak next and it took her at least half a minute to be able to get anything other than laughter out. When she finally regained enough composure to make a sound, the first words out of her mouth were, "Sing it again."*

The whole evening was a delight, and it was obvious they all were having a great time. What a shame that it didn't work out, but how wonderful for that audience to be part of a once-in-a-lifetime moment!

The members went their separate ways. Bryan lives in the state of Washington and tours the country, renowned for his phenomenal autoharp technique. He comments on the other members:

> Bassette I lost touch with, actually. He was in Cleveland and I saw him a couple of times there. I knew Bassette before I knew Gibson — before I knew Claudia. John Bassette showed me my first G chord — he showed me a G and a D chord. He showed me how to play *I'm on My Way to Canaan Land* — first song I ever learned! I'd have done anything for him, but now I've lost touch with him.
>
> Claudia has a bed and breakfast up in Michigan with her new husband Bill, who used to be on the radio up in Minneapolis. She's cooking now more than she's playing, but she goes out and does gigs on the road occasionally and still gets a nice draw. The critic from the Los Angeles Times once called her one of the great voices of the

century!

Would the group have had a chance to last if Gibson had been clean at the time? Who knows, but it was fun while it lasted.

In the meantime, the lure of another singing partner just would not disappear, and once again they would work their magic. G. Gigi Gilmartin continues her story of Gibson & Camp:

Now it's 1975. The Skymonters became Camp's True Brothers and are now disbanded. Camp has gone back to Hollywood to play actor again. But the pull of music is strong. Earl Pionke asked him to come back and do a gig with Gibson. Camp agreed. He'll tell you he agreed only because of the money Earl offered. Maybe so. But once he gets on that stage, once Gibson's twelve-string starts sweetly singing, Camp is there because he has to be. No, man, it's not nostalgia. Sure they do some of the old songs, but there's new material as well. New songs by Gibson with Camp's additional harmonies. New arrangements of Camp's new songs. They are artists and as such are continually growing, creating, changing and coming on strong.

Michael Smith remembers how he connected with Bob's music again:

After the late '60s, I just really didn't hear about him until I moved to Chicago from Detroit in about 1976. Lance Brown, who now is booked by my booking agent, at the time was living out in LA, and had learned a song of mine and had taught it to Gibson. So Gibson was doing a song of mine called *Twelve Golden Strings,* and now I see, "Oh, yeah, it sounds just like a Gibson song." At the time, I thought, "Well, that's nice that he's doing it, but it didn't occur to me that, of course it was written under Gibson's influence, because when you thought of 12-string guitar — HE WAS THE GUY! Either him or Leadbelly, and Leadbelly was kind of far removed from what we knew. When I first moved to Chicago, he was doing, on occasion, a song of mine, and that was a thrill to me — really a BIG deal!

My wife and I were working as a duet in '75, and we were at the Earl one time. Gibson came to one of the shows. Afterwards he sat down, and the first thing he did was sing a little bit of my song. He actually gave me about two measures of my own tune. We talked a little bit and then about ten years went by, in the course of which I lived in Chicago and he lived in Chicago, but we didn't cross paths.

Not much happened with Bob for awhile after that. It was another dry period as far as recordings go and another unexplained absence from the scene. No matter how hard he tried, he couldn't find the formula for kicking his habits for good. On Friday, April 1, 1977 a review by John L Wasserman of a Bob Gibson performance appeared in the San Francisco Chronicle:

Bob Gibson, who opened Tuesday night at the Boarding House, is today's living legend. Although his career as a name folksinger spans more than two decades, he has never before played a regular gig in San Francisco. He did one audition set many years ago at the hungry i, at which point he says, "Enrico Banducci and I agreed to disagree" — some say blows were exchanged. He played only once in the Bay Area, at the Lion's Share several years ago.

Now, he says, "after a long dry spell," he is busily churning out the tunes again and has hit the road to lay his handiwork in front of the folks.

Gibson's first set on Tuesday was a delight. He is a buoyant, personable, humorous presence on stage, and his songs — which included *The Last Reunion* (high school graduating class variety), *It's Just a Thing I Do* (a wonderful song about a woman who uses men for one-night stands) and an untitled song ("Let's call it the *Mendocino Shuffle*") which has more local references than the phone book — are likewise. He is an excellent singer and good guitarist.

Clearly the gift Bob Gibson had, was still there. He could still mesmerize an audience. The power of his guitar playing, his beautiful lyrics — none of it had left him — that is, as long as he wanted it to be there. The key to controlling the inner Bob, though, had still eluded him. Sometimes he was on track; sometimes he was lost again. People who loved his music eagerly awaited that magical moment when he would, at last pull it all together, but some must have wondered if it could ever happen.

Rick Neely, who had been so close to Bob, recalls the heartbreaking incident that ended their relationship, but, more importantly, perhaps, finally turned Bob's life around:

I dropped out of Bob's life in 1977 when he was with a woman who was a waitress at Earl's or Troubles. That was where he met a lot of women. They were waitresses, and they'd hang out in the afternoon when there wasn't a lot to do. During the time Bob was seeing her, he was struggling with his demons and she caught him with some stuff. In his attempt to cover himself up, he said he was out with Rick, and he got the stuff from him. I was totally unaware that this had happened, of course.

They used to do a Sunday matinee kind of thing at the Earl. The gig at the Earl of Old Town ran a week and they did shows Wednesday, Thursday, three shows on Friday night, three shows on Saturday night, and two shows on Sunday, one of which was an all ages matinee at 3:00 in the afternoon, and then they did an early evening show on Sunday and then that was it. I had come boppin' in to the Earl on Sunday afternoon, minding my own business, saw Bob's lady there and said something like, "Hi, how are you?" She just was all over me, and, of course, I didn't know what was going on. So after she accused me and harangued me, I went in the back room and I said, "What's going on?" Bob said, "Well, you know, I got caught with some stuff and I told her that I got it from you."

I was devastated, because of the irony of the whole thing. I think more than anything else in those times when people were dabbling with all kinds of drugs, somehow my knowledge of Bob had always kept me away from that, because I recognized that that stuff caused his deterioration throughout his early adult life. You can hear it in recordings. One recording he had a beautiful clear voice, and the next one it'd be raspy and almost in a different range. It was the drugs and the lifestyle that went along with it. I had always managed to stay away from it because I saw what it did.

We had a confrontation there in the back room of the Earl which was a horrible dank place with a cooler and junk and thousands of sheets of receipts and paper stuck in everywhere piled up to the ceiling. It was really a hole. I said, "This is the cruelest thing you could have possibly done. I don't know how you could have done that to me, of all people. This is IT! "

And then I left. I lived maybe eight blocks away from there. I didn't have a car so I was walking, and I probably cried on the way home. It hurt so bad. After that I didn't have a lot to do with him. We would pass in performing things. I had changed my playing to be less like Bob at that point and went off on a similar but divergent path.

Margie, Bob's second wife, says, "You never know. Maybe you were one of those pivotal instances where it suddenly dawned on Bob that his behavior was affecting things much wider than he suspected, and it maybe urged him to get a grip on whatever was going on."

He really worked hard at it. I know earlier than that, in 1976, he'd go places and he'd slip out the back and smoke a joint with somebody and come back, and I would say to him, "Don't you think that's kind of chancy?" He'd say, "No, I'm not doing much, it's just a little." But just a little is too much for somebody for whom the line needs to be clearly black or white. You can't do ANY! As soon as you start to dabble, you delude yourself.

I'm so grateful to his shining bad example, that I never got started because I'm an addictive personality. I can fall into that stuff real quick. I was fascinated because I was fascinated by him, so I'd think, "This guy's involved in this stuff," and I'd go off to learn about what the fascination was.

The truth is, getting in is exciting and attractive, but the getting out and getting well is ugly. To think of anybody trying to kick a habit tears your heart out, but especially him because he was basically a really sweet, wonderful person suddenly caught up in something that was out of control.

10

THE REAL BEGINNING

When Bob finally discovered a new way of life in AA., he, at last, was able to emerge victorious with a new perspective and outlook on his career. Thus in 1978, Bob Gibson quietly embarked on what was to be, undoubtedly, the best and most productive time of his life. The tragedy is that few outside of Chicago got to know about the work he did then, but the record of what he accomplished is there. He attacked music with a renewed, if mellowed, enthusiasm and explored a wide variety of new avenues of expression which allowed him to reach much broader audiences.

He approached life with the cheerfully shrugging attitude of "I don't worry anymore. I've tried it before, and it didn't do any good."

Roger McGuinn commented on the change he saw in Bob:
After he cleaned up, I found a softness in Bob that I hadn't seen before. Before he had a kind of cutting hard edge, and I thought that was kind of honed off. Maybe he wasn't as ambitious anymore. Maybe he'd kind of resigned himself to the fact that he wasn't going to be a celebrity.

At long last in 1978 I felt ready to do some real work. I've had a lot of gifts, I've done a lot of stuff, and a lot of times I wasn't comfortable with it. A lot of that came together, and the gift was still there, and audiences still noticed. For the first time I felt comfortable about a lot of it, and it was like a whole new beginning. It was wonderful. For me there was a whole lot involved in my earlier problems. It was wanting to do it, and then as I did it, that either wasn't enough or I wanted something from it that you can't get from your work. I'd also used it and abused it, and I'd used and abused my audiences, and it was all okay. We all got this far and they didn't turn me out. I had a lot to be grateful for and a lot to pay back.

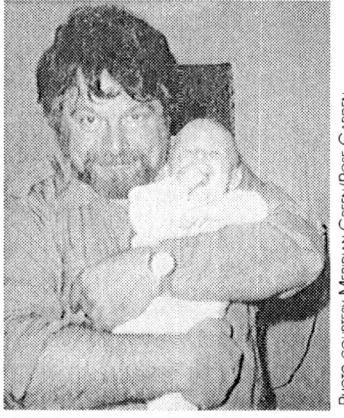

1978 - A time of birth & rebirth. Bob with his first grandchild, Meridian's son Terra

Somebody said to me, "It ain't how good you are, it's how long you've been around." That may sound like a cute, facetious line, but I really felt that way. To me the most important thing was that I lasted this long. I just felt like, at long last, I'd lasted long enough to integrate a whole lot of that stuff, and it became pure joy to do it. I didn't have any more goals. I wasn't doing it for anything. I was doing it because I liked doing it. It's a great joy to be happy in your work. I was writing again and really considering my show — not just doing what seemed right or what felt right — I really was giving it some thought. I wanted to try to reach out and stretch out and do some stuff. I had gotten to the point where I was ready take a chance. I'm very slow to change, I'm really scared to death of change, but change was all I felt I'd accomplished. Through no good grace of my own, I was still around and whatever I had to work with wasn't gone, either, so that was a major accomplishment.

Almost as if to celebrate his new life, Bob kicked off this era with a series of reunions. Tom Paxton remembers that monumental year in Bob's life:

I hadn't seen a lot of Bob for several years, so we hadn't become friends yet. Then after Bob got sober in 1978 I met him again in San Francisco, and we became real good friends. Right away we started writing together. We became tight buddies.

The Washington Post on Monday, July 17, 1978 carried news about the reunion of Bob and Tom in an article titled Gibson & Paxton *by Richard Harrington:*

Bob Gibson and Tom Paxton reaffirmed the participatory quality of folk music in a delightful program at the Cellar Door last night.

Both songwriters must be counted among the survivors from the early '60s folk revival. Paxton in particular has maintained his songwriting skills, alternating between sharp wit and poignancy to bring subjects home.

Bob Gibson has not been very visible over the past decade, and his charm and considerable talent make one wonder why. His 12-string guitar work was a major influence on musicians in the early '60s, and his return to performance is a much more important event than the reunion of Peter, Paul and Mary. That trio probably conjures up more images of the folk days than Paxton and Gibson combined, but, as so often happens, the real vitality and talent emanate from songwriters and performers like these, who quietly ply their trade.

After repeated requests, Camp and I cut another record, *Homemade Music,* in 1978. At the time I said, "If it does as well as the last one, we may make it a habit to record a new one every 18 years." It not only reunited me with Camp, but with an old friend of mine, Dick Rosmini. Dick is an engineer and a musician. He can do just about everything. He played on all the tracks besides Camp and me — bass, mandolin, synthesizer and everything. You name it, he played it, and he recorded the album. I mean, it was definitely just him and me and Camp, that was all. It was literally made in his home, too. The picture on the cover was taken by Dick on his front porch. That was one of the reasons we named the album *Homemade Music*.

There's a song on that album called *Billy Come Home* that's about always looking for greener pastures and they're not really there. You've got to stay where you are. To go somewhere else is an illusion. Sort of a poetic treatment about the young man who goes off looking for "it", and "it" was there where he had been in the first place.

Josh White Jr. comments on the importance of this song to him:
Gibson & Camp had not been together for a long time and Gibson had gained the weight and then they came back and did this album. When I heard *Billy Come Home* I was just — some songs compel you to learn them, and that was one of them!

To herald the release of the record we performed at Park West in Chicago September of 1978, with Tom Paxton as the opening act.

Allan Shaw:
After *Funky in the Country*, Gibson had disappeared again from records for four years until late in 1978, when the album *Homemade Music* appeared on the Mountain Railroad label and Gibson and Camp were back together for an entire album. Even after 18 years and only occasional sporadic appearances together, their voices still blended together and complemented each other in a way that is little short of amazing. Four of the 11 songs are Gibson compositions, and, while they don't seem to have the quality of some of Gibson's earlier works, the combination of Gibson and Camp singing together again more than makes up for whatever shortcomings the songs may have.

The album was reviewed by Nick Schmitz on Friday, Sept. 29, 1978 in The Daily Herald in an article called Gibson and Camp back with album:

Gibson and Camp at the Gate of Horn was one of the first to show the commercial potential of American folk music to a non-esoteric American album-buying public. And it helped Gibson to sell a generation of folkies on the virtues of the 12-string guitar—its big, mellow and resonant sound.

Gibson and Camp are back. For the first time in 18 years, Chicago folksinger Bob Gibson and Hamilton Camp have come out with an album.

Homemade Music on Mountain Railroad Records is a worthy followup to *Gibson and Camp at the Gate of Horn*, the album that established their national reputation during the folk music revival of the early '60s.

Gibson and Camp both were in their early 20s then. They were both mischievous and cocky, and their music, *Chicago Cops* and *Skillet Good and Greasy*, showed it.

On stage, Gibson and Camp would cook and sizzle — the big 12-string, harmonic vocals that just seemed to take off out of sight and humorous one-liners aimed at each other and the audience.

They were good, destined for stardom, and they knew it. But they did not know what stardom would hold for them, how long it would last, or that Gibson would take a fall.

Homemade Music is a thoughtful and perceptive album that does not hide the fun and enjoyment that is the basis of whatever Gibson and Camp do together. Yet it is an album that is, in a sense, biographical — for Gibson, Camp and writer Shel Silverstein, their long-time friend and songwriting collaborator.

Gibson no longer is the cocky kid singing *All My Trials* without ever having had any. *Homemade Music* provides insight into just how hard and long the road to personal maturity was for Gibson.

Gibson and Camp were together for only one year. Camp, who had attended Hollywood High and was a child star in the "Our Gang" comedies, was bitten again by the acting bug. He left Gibson for Second City and other acting companies.

And while Camp became more interested in acting, Gibson was getting hooked on drugs. Gibson is very happy he has since recovered from that "detour" in his life.

Camp is still basically an actor who has a part-time musical career with Gibson. During the 18-year interim between their albums, Gibson and Camp sang together only occasionally. But the sound they always have had is still there.

The material for the new album began to come together last year in California, where Camp was directing a TV show. Gibson and Camp soon realized they had enough material for a new album, so they said, "Why not?" to suggestions they put out a second album.

In addition to including several Shel Silverstein songs, *Homemade Music* also features the producing and musical virtuosity of Dick Rosmini who backed up Gibson on guitar when he first introduced Camp to the folk music world at the 1960 Newport Folk Festival.

In fact, the entire album is homemade. It was recorded in Rosmini's home.

"Work for us comes effortlessly," Gibson said about his collaboration with Camp and Rosmini. "We are dealing with 75 years of experience in this business. The effort already has gone in."

Songs on the album range from the traditionally oriented songs like *Dogies* and *Jimmie Rogers* to the perceptive, introspective and biographical new *Self-Satisfaction, Billy Come Home* and *Fancy Ladies.*

The sound Gibson and Camp always have had is still there. And Gibson has no difficulty in explaining the essence of what he does with Camp: "Either of us is likely to have the high or low harmony at any given moment. Then there are times when we cross over and even kind of pound away with no melody. We actually get the melody out in two or three passes of a chorus. Then we both sing harmony. The melody is still evident because people are still hearing it in a shadowy kind of way in their mind. We almost are getting three-part harmony, with the third part in your head."

At this same time, in 1978, Bob began a tradition that became very important to him. He started going down to Kerrville, Texas to take part in Rod Kennedy's Kerrville Folk Festival, which now has become the longest running folk festival in existence. To this day, for two weeks around Memorial Day, folk artists from all over come together to make music. Not only did Bob love to play there, but it was at Kerrville that he began his equally important occupation — teaching songwriting.

I love Texas. I always have. I used to work there a lot. From Aspen I got exposed to a lot of Dallas and Houston people who were avid skiers and were up there. They saw to it that I came to Dallas to work. It had nice places with lots of money and lots of nice people. A very gung ho bunch. They like it that I wrote *Abilene.*

Also there's a festival down there that I'm very fond of, the Kerrville Folk Festival. It's the best thing for folk music that was happening. I started a songwriting seminar there and then got more and more involved in songwriting teaching. I loved it.

Rod Kennedy comments on the importance of Bob's joining the Kerrville family:
Bob had been one of my heroes forever and I don't really remember how I got in touch with him, but I asked him to come and play, and he talked to me about starting a songwriting school. He started the school in 1979 and he ran it until 1991.

We toured and we took him to Abilene the first time. I can't remember when all that happened but it was in the late '70s. He'd never seen Abilene at that time. He wrote *Abilene* because it rhymed, not because he'd seen Abilene. He never said whether it was Abilene, Kansas or Abilene, Texas, but it rhymed with prettiest town you've

KERRVILLE FOLK FESTIVAL

Photo courtesy Rod Kennedy

1981

Photo by James R. Willis

Photo courtesy Rod Kennedy

1985

Photo by Brian Kanof

Photo courtesy Rod Kennedy

Bob & Allen Damron

Photo courtesy Tom Paxton

1985 with Tom Paxton

BOB GIBSON - 128

ever seen. He couldn't think of any other town that rhymed with it, which kind of takes the romance out of it, but . . .

I wrote the song, *Abilene,* in 1957. People had always asked me, "Bob, did you write that song about Abilene, Kansas or Abilene, Texas?" I'd always have to say, "I don't know." I didn't know! Like all good Americans, I learned all my history from the movies, and I knew that Abilene was this great railhead. I started going down to Kerrville for the folk festival there in 1978, and the first time I got on that stage at Kerrville and sang *Abilene,* and 5,000 Texans stood up and put their hands over their hearts, I knew right away I'd written it about Abilene, Texas!

Kennedy adds:

He also went on the first bus tours with us, and, in fact, I think he was kind of the chairman of the rolling poker game on the bus. Bob and I were really close and I really loved him. He was one of my favorite performers.

Peter Yarrow said of his involvement at the Kerrville Folk Festival:

The New Folks Concert at Kerrville is one of my proudest co-achievements with Rod Kennedy. We worked hard to design a contest for new singer-songwriters. We hoped to help strengthen their resolve and confirm that others thought their work was valuable. Those who are chosen to participate turn out to be very supportive of one another rather than competitive. In the following year's festival some are invited to perform on the main stage. Fully half the performers, like Lyle Lovett, Nanci Griffith and Tish Hinahosa, have participated in the New Folks program.

Yarrow spoke further about his projects at Kerrville and Newport that closely parallel those ideals that Bob cherished throughout his career:

There are certain philosophies of encouragement that Bob and I shared. I became one of the founding members of the Newport Folk Festival Board of Directors, and in that capacity I was very involved in the encouragement of new artists in a particular part of the festival that I conceived of, called the "New Folk Concert." That concert recognized new singer/songwriters, in contrast to the evening performances which focused on traditional performers. My passions about the importance of acknowledging the new generation of performers matched those of Bob Gibson. Bobby was an extraordinary writer. There's no question that he was a seminal writer who sparked future generations of songwriters.

On an ongoing basis, the New Folks Concert helps to establish the egalitarian spirit among performers which continues to make Kerrville a place that is non-hierarchical and non-competitive. In that same spirit Bob founded the songwriting school at Kerrville. He loved to nurture songwriters by working with them to encourage the evolution of their craft..

On April Fool's Day, 1979, Bob Gibson reunited with a couple of friends to perform at the Old Town School of Folk Music to play a benefit for Alternatives, Inc., a north-side youth services agency. He was together again with former Sparrow partners, Bryan Bowers and Claudia Schmidt. Now with the shadow of drugs behind him, Bob had a new conviction in his performance with them.

Alternatives was started in Chicago in 1971 by north-side parents concerned about teenagers hurting themselves with drugs. From the beginning their attitude was nonpreachy and understanding.

Bob said of this program:

The idea really was to offer kids 'alternatives' to drugs. Kids are going to try new things — and I don't just mean drugs. Whatever their friends are doing, they think that's the place to be. But when they find out there are other things to do with their time, things that are important and fun, drugs don't seem so great.

I knew some of the folks who started Alternatives, and saw some of the good things that happened to the early Alternatives kids. They were into radio projects and other meaningful stuff. Really, the weight was always on them to make something happen. Alternatives offered them a chance to do something with their lives, and a lot of them took it.

Bob also took advantage of time in the recording studio to get his new drug free message across even if the humor involved wasn't universally approved by radio stations.

I did the album *Perfect High* in 1980. I put a message on the back cover that two of the songs shouldn't be played on the radio. The songs referred to were *Box of Candy and a Piece of Fruit,* and Shel's poem, *Perfect High.* You know what happens if you put "motherfucker" or "shit" in a song. Of course, to put a disclaimer like that on the back, all the kids that play records or college radio stations would just run out and play it right away. But I really didn't want to rattle anybody's cage who wanted the opportunity to avoid that. Since I didn't normally do that kind of thing on an album, I just wanted to warn people in case they just blindly played all my songs. But, that poem, *The Perfect High,* was picked up by the Archdiocese of Chicago and played in all kinds of Catholic schools for the kids and all. They thought it had a great message. I stand behind it and I think it's wonderful. If anybody's going to be offended by it, I certainly am not trying to change anybody's opinions.

All sorts of new opportunities opened up for Bob now that he was clean.
Ed Holstein:
    Bob went out to LA in 1981. Lorenzo Music was a big Bob Gibson fan. He wanted to <u>BE</u> Bob Gibson as a kid. Mary Tyler Moore gave him a show and he had this idea. He was gonna have Bob Gibson and Erik Darling as the musicians. It was the Lorenzo & Henrietta Music Show and it was syndicated. So he had those two guys come out and this woman — it was a Peter, Paul & Mary kind of thing. The show bombed, but Gibson decided to stay out there and try to do some commercials because he liked to do that kind of work. He got a call and when he got there, there were, like, 5,000 people there, and he was sitting next to E.G. Marshall! So he decided to come back to Chicago. He said, "If *THIS* guy is sitting here trying to get a job, where am I gonna go?!" He did commercial work in Chicago. With his banjo he did the Gingiss Brothers commercials. He did a lot of voice-over stuff.

One of the most significant meetings for Bob during this period was with Michael Smith, of The Dutchman *fame, who was well on his way to becoming the legendary songwriter he is today. Michael became a very important musical partner and collaborator for nearly ten years. He was someone for whom Bob had tremendous respect. After following the various twists and turns of Bob's career, Michael recalls how he and Bob finally became linked:*
    It was 20 years after I first heard him that we first played together. Past about '65, I was listening to Dylan and the Beatles and stuff, so I hadn't really focused on Bob for some time, and yet when when I went to play with him, he was so easy. It was osmosis.
    We first got together when we did a show in 1982 called *Chicago: Living Along the Banks of the Green River.* It was a musical play with Bob, me, Ginni Clemmens, Thom Bishop and David Hernandez.

The Chicago Sun-Times carried a review of the show on March 31, 1982, written by Don McLeese:
FIVE FOLK SINGERS EXPLORE CHICAGO'S SWEET AND SOUR NOTES

    Monday night, March 29, 1982, the Goodman Theater presented, as part of its "Chicago Writers in Performance" series, a program devoted to "Chicago Songwriters: An Oral Tradition." Brought together were five Chicago folk singers: Thom Bishop, Ginni Clemmens, Bob Gibson, David Hernandez and Michael Smith.
    It was a fine and noble con-

cept. And when it worked, it worked so well, that one only wished that the performers had been able to sustain such peaks of inspiration throughout. Reaching far, the performance hit a lot more often than it missed.

The easy thing would have been to have each do four or five of his (her) best-known numbers and then make way for the next. Instead, these representatives of very different styles decided to collaborate on a series of very different styles for the event, with life in Chicago providing the theme.

More often than not, three, four, or even all five were performing together. The material ranged from Gibson's folksy traditionalism to Hernandez' street-wise raps to Smith's carefully crafted vignettes—with all sorts of combinations of those elements and more, since so many of the numbers were collaborations. The songs were mostly stories, and many of the stories were of love—how impossible, how inevitable.

Representative of the evening at its most exuberant was *Everybody On,* kind of a secularly contemporary reworking of *This Train* that had Hernandez shouting verses with the others chorusing behind him. Everybody clapped along.

Gibson provided one of the evening's highlights with his *Uptown Saturday Night,* the story of a guy who's down on his luck and looking for trouble. "We're in pretty good shape for the shape we're in," went the classic drunkard's self-assessment.

The best of a more contemporary style was provided by Smith, perhaps the best known through Steve Goodman's recording of his *The Dutchman.* In *Who's Your Best Friend?* (all lyrics taken directly from a Sun-Times PhotOpinion) and the "Ballad of Parker Roberts" (based on the college trustee who used state funds on B-girls), his material was as fresh as the day's newspaper. At the other extreme was *Adios Ciudad* (written by Smith with Hernandez), one of those "the city woman" tunes.

In tribute to the Blues Bishop contributed *Four Foot Record of the Blues,* a roll-call celebration of the Blues greats, and later Clemmens did *Jane Byrne Don't Get the Blues.*

Odd man out, but a surprise delight, was Hernandez, a Puerto Rican-born poet whose material was the least folk-oriented, at least in the traditional sense of the term. More spoken than sung, Hernandez' lines were more than lively enough to be great fun.

Through the collaboration of the five emerged the celebration of a city—in all its glory; for all its flaws. The program demonstrated that there's still plenty of vitality in the folk tradition. And in Chicago itself.

The show began very quietly with a soft lyrical piano playing as Bob Gibson read a letter to his mother:
Dear Mom,
   Real glad to get your letter. Glad to hear you're well in Florida. Life goes on pretty much as usual here along the Green River.

Weather's gettin' warmer. Spring is finally here after a long hard winter. I heard we had a great spring last year in Chicago, but I missed it. I was in the washroom at the time. That's all for now, Mom. Gotta rush — catch the train. More later.

From that point on, the entire show became a letter of love — love on a romantic level, love of family, and, above all, intertwined through it all, love for the city of Chicago in all its layers, personalities and textures. Whether in subtle references or direct tributes, the city was woven into everything that was spoken and sung that night. The styles and tones were as varied as the performers themselves, and they all blended to form a totally electric atmosphere.

From the end of the first song, about the L, one exciting enough to have been a closing number, the five performers OWNED the audience.

There was Bob's new song, Uptown Saturday Night; *Thom Bishop's tribute to Chicago as the home of the Blues in his* Four Foot Record of the Blues; *Ginni Clemmens' fabulously electric Blues piece called* Jane Byrne Don't Get the Blues!; *and the various poems of David Hernandez full of images of the city, (especially his hilarious account of why he didn't take the next door neighbor's 25¢ Chicago Sun-Times one day). There was the highlight of bringing Bob and Michael Smith together in* The Bells of St. Michael *and a new song from Bob, never recorded, built around his love for songwriting and his new found love for life itself. There was Michael Smith's clever song,* Who's Your Best Friend, *using the actual letters sent to the Chicago Sun-Times as lyrics to the song.*

Besides the music, one of the great delights of the show was the commentary about Chicago provided by the individual performers, and in Bob's continued letter to his mother:

Anyway, Mom, in answer to your question, I don't know if Jane Byrne still lives in Cabrini Green or not. You say you heard about it all the way in Florida? That's not such a bad place to live, Mom. I always wanted to live in the John Hancock Building. I think it's the most beautiful building in the world. Then I realized one day that if I lived in the John Hancock Building, I'd never get to see the most beautiful building in the world. So I'd rather live in Cabrini Green. That way, when I look out my window in the morning, there it is, the most beautiful building in the world. And to the south—the Sears tower, rising against the sky, looking like it was purchased from Montgomery Ward. Cabrini Green got fixed up a lot when Jane moved there, and all us folks around here have got our fingers crossed that she might start riding the subways now.

There was the Thom Bishop tribute to Chicago business empires, and his song Old Ray Kroc Had a Big Idea, *Michael Smith's wonderfully hilarious song about the educator who was caught in a sex scandal in Chicago; ("It wasn't news that he paid for love. It wasn't news that he paid for knowledge. What was news was he paid from a bank account of the state supported college!"); Thom Bishop's* The Hawk Has Flown Away, *a celebration of the end of winter, referring to the infamous Chicago wind as "the hawk"; the teaming of Michael Smith and David Hernandez in the beautiful bilingual* Adios, Ciudad.

Finally, a piano played softly, much as in the beginning of the play, bringing the evening full circle. all sang:
    We all go 'round together
    On a wheel that spins and spins
    We've all been here forever
    And we'll all be here again

Far too soon for the crowd the play came to an end. They roared their approval. What began as a musical play with the theme of Chicago writers creating songs about Chicago, through all the varied styles of the different performers, became a gift of love to the people of Chicago. Bob sang the perfect tribute to all those things that breathe life into Chicago:
  Would you like to walk with me beside the lake?
   It's a lovely stroll that you and I could take
Amid the bathers and the waders and the joggers and the skaters
 The lovers and the daters and the mellow frisbee players
    It's a circus for your eyes for goodness sake
  Would you like to walk with me beside the lake?

    Would you like to go to Shedd Aquarium
    And later to the planetarium
    There'll be starfish on the ceiling
    They will send our senses reeling
    Like the flowers at the arboretium

   Would you like to walk with me to Navy Pier
   When they have Chicagofest again this year
    We will dance 'til we are loony
    Then buy flowers from a Moony
   And then we'll drink about a case of beer

    Or we could go to see Venetian Night
   With all the floats and boats a festive sight
And a fireworks display that looks like Armageddon day
    With all Chicago lit up by the light

And if city livin' makes your noggin ache
I advise you that it's time to take a break
And come to a decision
Turn off your television
Come and take a walk beside the lake.

(by Gibson/Bishop — ©Robert Josiah Music, Inc.)

It was a truly special evening and a very important event in Bob's continuing career for three reasons. First of all, Bob and Michael Smith finally sang together for the first time that night in a monumental occasion which heralded a long association to come. Secondly, it gave Bob a chance to voice his deep feelings of affection for his adopted city and the people who loved him and had stuck by him through the bad times. Most significantly, though, this production opened up new avenues of thought for Bob, providing direction for what he would do next.

L-R: David Hernandez, Ginni Clemmens, Michael Smith, Bob Gibson, Thom Bishop
1981 - *Chicago: Living Along the Banks of The Green River* at the Goodman Theatre

I COME FOR TO SING - 135

11

THE COURTSHIP OF CARL SANDBURG
My Theatrical Experience

I've had a firm belief as a songwriter and a creative person interested in a kind of story-song, music and songs that have content, that it was only a small transfer to really move out of saloons into small theaters. It's a natural development for a songwriter to become a playwright. A play is a sort of an expanded song. Organically, they're alike. Both have a beginning, a middle and an end. Both have characters and a point of view. Both state a problem, or ask a question, or capture a feeling. But the song is self-contained, and especially when you sing your own, you don't have to depend on anyone else. Theater makes a lot of sense. There are fewer and fewer saloons and a lot of the songs I write are just mini-theatrical experiences. I love a theatrical experience, so why not try and work in a longer and broader medium? My good friend Shel Silverstein told me it was easy to write a play. You put down a character's name on a piece of paper. Then you list underneath everything he has to say. Then you put down another character's name and write what he has to say. If the play's too short, you add more; if it's too long, you take some out.

I didn't set out, though, to write a theater piece. I've always been fascinated with Carl Sandburg. In 1927 he published *The American Songbag,* the first compilation of American folk music. When I began with folk music, the *Songbag* was one of the main sources.

Then I actually met Sandburg because I was part of a project to read and record some of Sandburg's poetry and also provide a banjo accompaniment. It was in the '50s and here I was, a young folksinger most people hadn't heard of. And there he was, poet Carl Sandburg, an imposing, white-shocked chunk of Americana. I cautiously said, "I was wondering if you have a few moments to spare?" His response was, "I'm at an age when I don't have any moments to spare." I immediately decided I liked the guy!

Throughout all the ups and downs in my life and the business, I always kept in mind doing something in tribute to Carl Sandburg. I always felt we should honor him. I hoped that someday we could have an annual summer festival of folk singing in Chicago that would always include a section devoted to Sandburg. When that idea fell through, I still wanted to do something about Sandburg, but there was just too much to say in one song.

I Come For To Sing - 137

In 1981 I received a small grant from the Illinois Arts Council and began collaborating on a musical about Sandburg's early years. I started working with Ray Tate, providing a musical background for an actor's reading of Sandburg's works. The project was enlarged and had a successful run at Evanston's Northlight Repertory Theatre. It was called *An Evening with Carl Sandburg.*

On May 7, 1982, the Daily Suburban Trib carried a review of Bob's An Evening with Carl Sandburg *written by Tricia Fischetti:*
SINGER-COMPOSER BOB GIBSON BRINGS LIFE OF AMERICA'S POET OF THE PLAINS TO STAGE

We're not trying to bring you Sandburg's poetry tonight. We're trying to bring you Carl Sandburg.

Before his performance in Park Forest last week, Bob Gibson reflected on the purpose he had in mind when he wrote, *An Evening with Carl Sandburg of Illinois.*

"This show tries to be entertainment, but it also tries to get your juices flowing about Carl Sandburg."

Saturday night's performance in Freedom Hall succeeded on both counts.

On one level, the show was pure entertainment, Gibson and Ray Tate, executive director of Chicago's Old Town School of Folk Music, which sponsored the show, teamed to provide a smooth blend of vocal and string harmonies to many of the selections from Sandburg's 1927 collection of folksongs, *American Songbag.*

Gibson and Tate appeared to be having such a good time that it was fun just to watch them play and sing. And the more than 200 persons in the audience loved them, many of them tapping, singing or humming along to old favorites.

Secondly, Saturday's performance did indeed "get the juices flowing" about Carl Sandburg. John Starrs, a professional freelance actor from Chicago, portrayed the famous midwesterner, giving a sensitive, powerful performance in this almost disarmingly personal study of a man who was much more than a poet and biographer.

The three performers were on stage together throughout the show and worked as a unit. Gibson and Tate sang and played guitar, banjo, fiddle and mandolin just to the left of center stage, while Starrs portrayed Sandburg to the right of center. As Starrs performed at and around his office desk, Gibson and Tate sat in semidarkness and watched, listened and laughed along with the audience.

Lighting shifted as the musicians played, and Starrs as Sandburg busied himself at his desk, frequently nodding his head in time with the music. With this intimate staging and subtle lighting, the two performances were woven together.

The material for *An Evening with Carl Sandburg* was drawn from only a few years in the Galesburg native's life — from the courtship of his wife, Lillian, to the birth of his two daughters. Sources for the script, written by Gibson and Starrs, included Sandburg's autobiography, *Always the Young Strangers,* and music from *American Songbag.* Combining Sandburg's letters, some of his writing and the music he loved, the production achieved a delicate balance between drama and music that helped define the man.

Gibson and Tate's music mirrored the highs and lows in Sandburg's life. For example, between Sandburg's reading of love letters to his future wife, the musicians sang the romantic *Somebody* and *Dream Girl.* After we learned of Lillian's acceptance, we heard the lively *I Got a Gal.*

We discovered Sandburg's delight in fatherhood dramatically through letters and phone calls to his friend, George, and musically with the gentle lullaby, *Go to Sleep,* sung with a beautiful, dreamy quality. Later, Sandburg's preoccupation with death is apparent, as Gibson and Tate recite a passage from his autobiography about the death of his two brothers. The somber folksong *Tell Old Bill,* deepens this mood.

Before his performance Saturday, Starrs commented that he did not try to imitate Sandburg, opting instead to suggest his presence. The actor wore a small bow tie, a familiar Sandburg trademark, and combed his hair into the distinctive straight white mane of the Illinois writer.

But the most commanding suggestion of Sandburg was Starrs' voice. His deep baritone glided over words, transforming prose into poetry.

The most memorable sequence of the evening was Starrs' portrayal of Sandburg telling the delightful children's tale, *Five Marvelous Pretzels.* The story is of the nonsensical variety children of all ages can lose themselves in and Starrs made the most of it.

He commanded the stage, using full body motion and piercing facial expression. Starrs' phrasing and timing were flawless, and his audience exploded into applause after the story.

An Evening With Carl Sandburg was the brainchild of Gibson, who claims, "Sandburg has always been a big hero of mine." Gibson said he had long been familiar with Sandburg's *American Songbag,* having drawn from it for some of his early albums. But he had to delve into other sources to learn more about Sandburg's personal side.

Gibson, who serves as director of special events of the Old Town School, presented the idea to Starrs, and the two worked on gathering and writing material for the show for about a year. They applied for and received a partial grant from the Illinois Art Council to fund the show.

Tate described the whole production as a "true labor of love" and "a lot of fun." He would like to see the show tour colleges throughout the state. He also sees the show as a good piece for local and high school theater groups.

Gibson, Tate, Starrs and others involved with *An Evening With Carl Sandburg* share an obvious pride and excitement in the show. Their exuberance spilled over into the performance.

As it grew, the whole piece began to draw the musicians into it. It was performed in several places as a work in progress until the final, polished version opened in 1984 as *The Courtship of Carl Sandburg.* As things developed and became more refined, I had come up with the idea for the play. One day in Chicago, I ran into an actor I knew and I said, "If I write a piece about Sandburg, will you be in it?" And he said, "Sure!" It was like an Andy Hardy movie: "Hey, let's get all the kids together and put on a show!"

It was a two-act play that was kind of like a scrapbook, based on Carl Sandburg's life, his papers and letters he wrote. Sandburg was an intensely private man. He never revealed himself in his poetry or even in his autobiography, but in his letters, he couldn't hide out that much. He wrote great, poetic letters. Letter writing was such a wonderful thing at the time. Now nobody ends up with a pile of love letters tied up with a ribbon. All you end up with is a bunch of phone bills.

Sandburg was an early media product. After he became famous, he was careful that what he did worked for the Sandburg image. Big Fourth of July spreads for the *Saturday Evening Post.* That sort of thing. He knew he was a star. Well, at this point in his life (his early 20s, the period covered by the play), he was a real hustler. He wasn't sure exactly what he wanted to do, but he wanted passionately to succeed. He was star-bound.

He was wildly enthusiastic about Lillian Steichen, whom he did marry. She was the sister of the famous photographer Edward Steichen. She's never in the play but she's very much in evidence throughout.

We got the play ready for production, and it opened the first time in Lansing, Michigan. The cast was Carl Sandburg and two musicians. Carl Sandburg was played by Eric Tull in the Lansing, Michigan run. Tom Amandes played the part later in Chicago. Anne Hills and I played the musicians. We sang to each other in the junction and stuff. It was really good and very pretty. We were like the Greek chorus. We would come back to Sandburg and sing around him, doing stuff around him. If anything, I'm not sure if the spoken part is continuity for the music or the music is continuity for the spoken part.

The time period the play covers was a time in Sandburg's life when he was holding a succession of temporary jobs — painting houses, selling stereoscopic photographs, writing ads for a Milwaukee department store, organizing for the socialists in Wisconsin — and traveling — riding the rails and making speeches in small towns about the poetry of Walt Whitman.

It was a time when he flunked his entrance exam to West Point –

a turning point — and when he courted and married Lillian Steichen, a teacher in Princeton, Illinois, and they began raising their family. We cover a period in Sandburg's life that ends about 1911. That's the time I find of real interest, when a person is coming to terms with himself. He was a young man of fascinating contradictions — ambitious and yet with these rigid standards and high-blown principles. He was trying all these different things, yet we always knew he was a writer, even if he didn't. He was working out the reality of how his principles and values work in life. He believed in family and home, and he had a love of the land and the common man. And all along, he was writing, writing. He wrote some of his best and most energetic poetry and essays during these early years. Later he became harder to reach because success always changes us and isolates us. When people told him he was a great poet, he became a bore because it's very hard to write great poetry when you're told you're a great poet. I've seen the same thing happen to songwriters.

The play was successful as evidenced by the numerous reviews carried in papers from all surrounding areas. Following are excerpts from these reviews:

Grand Rapids Press, 12/18/83:

Eric Tull, an actor with BoarsHead Theater in the 1976-77 season, returns to play the role of Carl Sandburg in the original production of Bob Gibson's *The Courtship of Carl Sandburg*.

Also joining Gibson on the stage will be Anne Hills, a folksinger who recently released her own album, *The Panic Is On*, with Jan Burda.

BoarsHead also announced that Nancy-Elizabeth Kammer has replaced Tom Gruenewald as director of the production which originally had been titled *Sandburg County Fair*.

Gibson, nationally known folk singer and composer, wrote *The Courtship of Carl Sandburg* based on love letters from poet Sandburg to Lillian Steichen, whom he ultimately married.

Tull most recently appeared at the New Jersey Shakespeare Festival in the fall, doing *Beyond the Fringe* by Peter Cook and Dudley Moore. He has appeared Off-Broadway in *Say Goodnight, Gracie, The Show-Off* and as an understudy in *Table Settings*. He also has worked at the Long Wharf Theater, the American Shakespeare Theater and the Hedgerow Theater in Boston.

Hills, a native of St. Joseph, is a member of the folk trio, The Best of Friends, with Gibson and Tom Paxton, and is featured vocalist on Gibson's album, *The Perfect High*. She also appeared on five Tom Paxton albums and has done back-up vocal work for Si Kahn, Cindy Mangsen and Ginni Clemmens.

James E. Harvey, The Flint Journal, Friday, 1/6/84:

Carl Sandburg once defined poetry as a synthesis of hyacinths and biscuits, and so is the charming program of music and monologue about him that opened Thursday night at BoarsHead: Michigan Public Theater here.

The homespun and the lyrical get along comfortably in this portrait of the multi-faceted American writer by Bob Gibson. Gibson, with deep roots in the folksong revival of the 1950s and '60s, also appears in the production with fellow singer Anne Hills and actor Eric Tull, who plays Sandburg.

Gibson has chosen the period when the poet was struggling to find himself, in order to illuminate one man's development in the heart of the country as it takes him to the love of his life, Lillian Steichen. Thus the play is quaintly called, *The Courtship of Carl Sandburg*.

Letters that Sandburg wrote to his future wife form some of the most moving passages in the program. Carrying the action past the wedding and into the early family life of the couple is a risk that comes off because of the powerful material to be found there, especially that involving the discovery that one of the Sandburgs' daughters had epilepsy.

As a first-time playwright, Gibson emphasizes his strengths — songwriting and performing. With his delicate banjo accompaniments and caressing baritone voice, Gibson sang frequently throughout the show with the sympathetic partnership of Hills, who also played guitar and autoharp.

Perhaps it is to Nancy-Elizabeth Kammer's credit as director that the show works so well as a piece of theater, continuing to engage the attention as more than just an excuse for some nifty harmonizing. Tull, who returns to BoarsHead for this engagement after an absence of about seven years, reflects this concern for dramatic projection of Sandburg's story with his alert, sensitive portrayal.

Thus the audience is presented with vivid evocations of the patent-medicine salesmen of Sandburg's youth in Galesburg, Illinois, and the young man's stint in such capacities as a lecturer, a socialist organizer, and an advertising copy writer.

One of the most delightful segments occurs in the second act, when the two musicians plus Tull enact Sandburg's nonsense tale of "the five marvelous pretzels." This extended comic relief is well-timed because, although the mood of the program is mostly light, the story leads up to the somber news of the daughter's lifelong illness near the play's end.

Without sentimentalizing, Tim Stapleton's set design of large panels arranged to look somewhat like leaves from a scrapbook manages to recall an era and a special relationship. It is unambiguous in its significance for the play, yet understated as well.

Kate O'Neill, Lansing State Journal, 1/6/84:

Hardly a conventional play or even a biographical narrative, it is instead — as Tim Stapleton's imaginative set suggests — a scrapbook of first-hand memories of a man who was to become an eloquent spokesman for the "American common man." And it is most effective in those moments which crystallize Carl Sandburg's youthful dreams and joys and sorrows.

Sandburg, born in 1878, came to be revered as a poet, historian, humorist and folklorist before he died in the late 1960s. But *Courtship,* compiled by folk musician Bob Gibson, focuses on the young Sandburg — by turns hobo, a salesman, a radical organizer, a lecturer and a writer — as he discovers his voice and his life's purpose.

More important (to this theatrical account at least), he was also discovering the woman with whom he would spend the rest of his life, Lillian Steichen Sandburg. The final portions of the play contain some warm recollections of their family life with their young daughters.

And the folk music Sandburg loved and collected adds an emotional intensity to our understanding of the man.

Courtship allows many glimpses of young Sandburg's inner life, but leaves the viewer somewhat frustrated for lack of narrative . . .but narrative biography is not Gibson's goal. Rather, he is conjuring up young Sandburg's emotional life as expressed in his letters and reflected in the folk songs he cherished.

Eric Tull gives a remarkable portrayal of Sandburg, slipping easily from one mood to another and bringing vivid color to his long descriptive monologues.

Gibson and Anne Hills, singing off on one side of the stage, set the mood for these fragmented scenes from Sandburg's life, provided commentary and sometimes entered into the action.

Dave Nicolette, Grand Rapids Press, 1/6/84:

Another new stage work, teetering between a play and a folk concert has been brought to life by the BoarsHead Theater.

With beautifully paced, silkily gentle direction by Nancy-Elizabeth Kammer, the BoarsHead gives Bob Gibson's *Courtship of Carl Sandburg* the appearance of a wonderfully successful production.

What Gibson, the beloved composer-performer of hundreds of folk songs, has wrought is a wonderful framework around which he and Anne Hills weave beautiful music. Some of the songs are revived from the old American tales set to music (*Hallelujah, I'm a Bum, Down in the Valley,* among others) that Sandburg collected in his wanderings around the country which he so graphically describes in his poetry. Others are newly created by Gibson, who also assembled the words of the play part.

The production has a handsome simplicity about it, the tone set by the two singers and the handsome setting by Tim Stapleton created of platforms designed in the form of large desk blotters.

Keith Warnack, Michigan State News, 1/9/84:

Carl Sandburg was a poet of the American people, a historian, novelist, journalist and an organizer of the Radical Democratic Party — he was also a hopeless romantic.

Evidence of Sandburg's malady of enamor is beautifully shown in the BoarsHead's latest theatrical venture, *The Courtship of Carl Sandburg,* which began its month-long run on the stage of the Michigan Public Theater.

This creation of 1950s folksinger and lyricist Bob Gibson does not attempt to recount the entire life of Sandburg (1878 to 1967) or to dramatize his political career, rather, *Sandburg* is a musical sweep through a lover's scrapbook, taking the letters he wrote to his wife, Lillian, and weaving them around a number of tender, sad and sometimes humorous folksongs.

Starring as Sandburg is Eric Tull. His slight stature and wide-eyed, innocent appearance allows Tull to easily slip into character as the young, starry-eyed Sandburg, as well as convincingly portraying a more mature, less naive man towards the play's end. Tull has obviously researched the character, demonstrated by familiar Sandburg postures he takes and the emotion heard in his voice when reading a famous speech or writing a letter describing the joys of fatherhood.

Providing narration and song are Gibson and Anne Hills. Hills, a folksinger who has recently released her first solo album, *The Panic is On,* occasionally takes on the persona of Lillian as Sandburg composes his love letters. But her major contribution to the play is her tender, lilting voice, which surprisingly, harmonizes with Gibson's coarser, campy style of singing. These two are also allowed to step in as characters - the most memorable being their portrayal as two of the *Five Amazing Pretzels,* characters in a Sandburg children's story. As pretzels, Hills and Gibson are fine.

To highlight all the flaws . . . may be misleading. This is a new play, about a month old, and director Nancy-Elizabeth Kammer admits that each performance is another step toward defining what the play will look like at the end of January.

But theater enthusiasts might want to see the play before all the bugs are exterminated. What Kammer, Gibson, Tull and Hill have is a fresh, touchingly sentimental play, which, in many ways, is enhanced by its rough edges. Following each performance, the audience is allowed a few moments of discussion with the actors and crew, which provoked praise of the play's strong points and a few criticisms of minor flaws. At least one of the critical comments prompted Kammer to take a thoughtful drag on her cigarette and chide the three performers, telling them, "it better be fixed by tomorrow night." This talk-back seemed a rare, memorable moment for the audience, who were allowed to criticize and contribute to a play all seemed to enjoy.

Keep working on it Nancy, Eric, Bob and Anne — but not too much.

Sharon Schlief, Towne Courier, 1/12/84:

There you sit, engrossed in the biography of Carl Sandburg unfolding on stage. Suddenly the trio on stage bursts into a flurry of activity. From their calm reflection of Sandburg they twirl into an amazing rendition of *The Five Marvelous Pretzels!*

"Pretzels??" Pretzels. From a story Sandburg wrote for one of his children, singers Anne Hills and Bob Gibson and actor Eric Tull twirl into a fast-paced fairytale of five (marvelous) pretzels who dream of joining the circus.

The segment comes as a delightful surprise. Hill's expressions of glee, surprise and dismay were perfect. For me it was the highlight of the evening.

Edward Hayman, Detroit News, 1/10/84:

As one might expect, Gibson and Ms. Hills produce a sound that is honey smooth, a stream of the folk songs Sandburg cherished, the 19th century heartland music he grew up with and collected in his 1927 anthology, *The American Songbag*. The songs all have been reworked by Gibson, with four of his own compositions added, including the theme, a pretty love song, *He Really Said a Lot to Her*.

Gibson switches among a short-necked and two long-necked instruments, depending on tuning requirements, and plays in an old-timey, frailing style. Ms. Hills, too, plays with velvety precision. Their harmony takes us back to the Weavers.

Gibson's play is a sweet study of a gifted young man's process of self-definition. The young Sandburg is fueled by love for his intended. He writes to her of his success in retailing as a writer of effective advertising. A glorious future beckons. "I know I can be anything," he writes. Later, when the Sandburgs have two small daughters, he rejoices in his new role. "I'm very comfortable as a father," he says proudly, and shares with the audience *The Rutabaga Kids* and *The Five Pretzels,* stories he wrote for the girls.

Director Nancy-Elizabeth Kammer has staged all this with the flavor of a Pete Seeger sing-along, on an imaginative set by Tim Stapleton that has the players strolling around on the pages of a Sandburg family album.

It's a visually attractive production, but *The Courtship of Carl Sandburg* is designed primarily to be listened to — a lovely valentine for those who appreciate folk music.

Claudia R. Skutar, theater critic:

There is more to the new BoarsHead production, *The Courtship of Carl Sandburg,* than immediately meets the ear. On the surface it appears to be a slow-paced musical, or as the play's author and folksinger Bob Gibson remarks more accurately, "a play with music in it." Underneath this, however, is a collection of stories, poems and letters strung together with music designed to tell the story of Carl Sandburg's life; not the famous life of the poet, but the life of the inner man virtually unknown to the public.

The format around which the play is structured is a solid one. Gibson and fellow folksinger Anne Hills provide the musical backdrop for BoarsHead alumnus Eric Tull in his characterization of Sandburg. This creates a sound triangle of characters, the apex being actor Tull as Sandburg.

The absence of characters other than the musicians (Sandburg's wife Lillian, for instance) gives the play a unique and unconventional abstractness, abstract in the sense, as Director Kammer noted, that it frees the production from having to portray reality through a lot of details. And because those details aren't necessary with this structure, more is left to the audience's own imagination, something rare in a visually-lazy age.

On the whole, this interaction between the musicians and Tull is very smooth. Each has a well-defined role and stays clearly within his or her boundaries; except for one scene. This occurs when Anne Hills is temporarily projected into the role of Lillian in a scene meant to introduce the courtship between Sandburg and his future wife. The bridge between Lillian and Sandburg at this point is music. They sing, they dance and then Hills resumes her role as a musician on the sideline.

The songs in the production are a mixture of those written for the play by Gibson and selections from Sandburg's favorites which were collected and published in 1927 in *The American Songbag*. They fit somewhat loosely with the characterizations of Sandburg but at the same time provide a cohesive transition between scenes. Gibson's skill as a folk musician seems essential in his writing of the play, because, without the music, the play would be merely a collection of images.

Tull does an excellent job of showing Sandburg as a man of very strong and simple values. With everything laid out firmly in his mind, Sandburg embarks on each life adventure full of hope. He never deviates from those values, even when life lets him down. And it is in the portrayal of each unfolding part of Sandburg's life that the play succeeds in revealing the inner man, the plans and fears and emotions he had which people can identify with and can understand.

The Courtship of Carl Sandburg is the sort of treasure which, like the living scrapbook it is, gives a rare glimpse into the little known human college that was Carl Sandburg.

From Chicago Singles - Bob Gibson: The Quiet Voice *by Garry Cooper 1984:*

Writing *The Courtship of Carl Sandburg* puts Bob in touch with one of the great voices of the Midwest. The play, even though his first, carries all the trademarks of Gibson, from his performing to his personality. The play has no artifice, no subtlety, no pyrotechnics. Instead, you find yourself lulled by its simplicity, and through its quiet quality, the power builds. At the end of the play, when Gibson invites the audience to sing along with *Down in the Valley,* you find yourself re-experiencing the quality and power of simpler times and emotions.

The resounding success of the play in Lansing, Michigan demanded that it move on to Chicago. The Courtship of Carl Sandburg *opened first at the North Light in Evanston and then at the Apollo Theater in August, 1984. As Bob said earlier, the only cast change was the character of Carl Sandburg, played by Tom Amandes. Following are the reviews of this run:*

August, 1984 - Chicago Sun Times
THE SANDBURGS: 'A GREAT AND GLORIOUS ROMANCE' BY VERA CHATZ:

When she was a child, Helga Sandburg, daughter of Illinois poet Carl Sandburg, would read the love letters her father and mother had written to each other. In Evanston, Helga Sandburg heard those letters recited, along with original music by folk singer Bob Gibson in his play, *The Courtship of Carl Sandburg* at the North Light Repertory Theater.

"I think this man's production is wonderful," Sandburg said. "Gibson is looking at the man behind the words, the man who caused the words to come. I've always been wary about people trying to make my mother into a heroine because she insisted that my father have the dominant role in their life together."

"It's not as though my father deprived my mother," Sandburg said. "She was exactly what she wanted to be."

Every piece of paper on which her father wrote has been kept by Sandburg and her two sisters, Margaret and Janet.

"I always knew what my parents were; I always knew they were unique," Sandburg said. "They had a magnificent marriage, and I would record their conversations."

Carl Sandburg, a vagabond since his youth, continued to travel extensively during his marriage to Lilian, who was the sister of photographer Edward Steichen. Sandburg was organizing laborers, lecturing and serving in World War I. Consequently he was often separated from his family. The separations produced letters in an unending flow of language.

"My attic, my home are loaded with memorabilia — my father's hat, his visor," Helga Sandburg said. "I'm thinking now of editing my daughter's letters. If she had telephoned me to tell me her child was gathering autumn leaves, rather than putting it into writing, that thought would have been lost. I look at her letters, and I weep."

Of herself as a child, she said, "Life in our house revolved around my father, like a great wheel spinning around the center."

August 10, 1984 - Reader's Guide to Theater:

Twelve crucial years in the life of an American laureate. Bob Gibson, the well-known folkie, put together this show, directed by James O'Reilly. *Courtship* is a collage of songs Sandburg collected for his *American Songbag,* his letters to his wife, memoirs, poetry, a children's story, and five songs written for the production by Gibson. He and singer Anne Hills play guitars, banjos and townspeople as actor Tom Amandes portrays Sandburg from 1908, when he was a restless young spirit just turned 30, to 1920, by which time he'd acquired a wife, daughters, a writing career, and a family tragedy that seems to have focused his energy and determination to succeed.

What *Courtship* does very well is convey the sense of expansive, fantastical enthusiasm that the young Sandburg fairly glowed with. The way that energy tugged against, but never pulled loose from Sandburg's intelligent, unaffected midwestern skepticism created a classic American voice.

Bill Dalton, Chicago critic:

In a time when so many people seem to be striving to be in, cool, with it, fab, or just on the front edge of the latest fad or craze, the play *The Courtship of Carl Sandburg* seems woefully out of place. Here is a play that is simply witty, gentle and endearing, and, though at the Apollo Theatre, about as far away from the sexual perversity in Chicago as one can get. The play is written by Bob Gibson, folksinger, songwriter and now playwright.

Weaving the music and singing of Gibson (who many consider the founding father of the folk music revival of the late 1950s) and Chicago singer, Anne Hills, with the dramatic passages acted by Tom Amandes as young Carl Sandburg, the play tells the story of the life of the poet from 1908 until 1920.

The courtship of the play is not merely that of Sandburg and Lillian Steichen whom he eventually married, but also the courtship of a young man and the world around him. At one time or another, Sandburg was a dishwasher, sign painter, brick maker, stereoptical salesman, hobo, soldier, journalist and lecturer as well as poet.

In his first published work, *Reckless Ecstasy*, Sandburg wrote, "I glory in this world of men and women, torn with troubles and lost in sorrow, yet living on to love and laugh and play through it all." In *The Courtship of Carl Sandburg*, both audience and actors alike are loving and laughing and playing through it all.

Chicago Tribune - 9/13/84
COURTSHIP EVEN SWEETER AT APOLLO - BY RICHARD CHRISTIANSEN:

Sometimes shows really do get better as they go along. When *The Courtship of Carl Sandburg* opened its summer engagement at the Northlight Repertory Theatre in Evanston last July, it was a loveable and slightly fashioned collection of songs and stories based on the early years of "The Poet of the Prairie."

In its move to the city, to the thrust stage of the Apollo Theater, the *Courtship* is still immensely loveable, but in addition, it has picked up noticeably in performance and plotting.

Bob Gibson, who conceived, wrote and produced the show, has edited out some scenes and added others in a successful attempt to keep the story more focused on Sandburg's courtship and marriage with Lillian Steichen.

At the same time, Tom Amandes, as the young Sandburg, has grown in assurance and strength, charmingly leading the audience through the sketchy narrative and closing with an impressive reading of Sandburg's poetry.

Even with its better construction, *Courtship* is never going to be a complex work of theater. But it has heart to burn, which is more than enough to make up for its narrative limitations. And when Gibson [still cherubic after all these years] and the dark-haired Anne Hills pick up guitar and banjo to sing *Who Will Kiss Your Ruby Lips*, the evening soars above technical matters.

James O'Reilly's direction on a relatively uncluttered stage keeps matters straight and intimate, letting Sandburg's writings and the songs, so sweetly sung, gracefully interact.

It's a simple but mysterious alchemy of sentiment, music and story that adds up to much more than the sum of its small parts.

❧ ❧ ❧ ❧ ❧ ❧ ❧ ❧ ❧

The play ran for eight weeks in BoarsHead Theatre in Lansing, Michigan, and 11 weeks downtown in Chicago at the Apollo. It was good. But I walked out one evening and I said, "What am I doing?" There I was bringing up the overture piece and counting the house and I said, "I can't do all this. I gotta be able to care about one or the other. I can't care about everything." My main flaw was being in it and producing the same thing. I liked acting. The theatre audience, I thought, was very interesting. There weren't many of the people who were involved in music as such — they were all theatre people and they're a different audience, but a good audience. They came over to see what I had to offer, which was good.

I put the play on a couple of times since then; at the University of Cincinnati once. It was their summer opening — the riverboat show. They increased the Greek chorus to 12 or 15. It was too much. The audience just wouldn't bear that.

I was pleased that a lot of stuff that seemed like incompletions, blind alleys, or cul-de-sacs in my life — or even things that I may not have skills in, but possessed a real interest in — came together in *The Courtship of Carl Sandburg*.

(Note: The complete text of The Courtship of Carl Sandburg *is included in the appendix of this book.)*

12

HOBSON'S CHOICE & THE BEST OF FRIENDS

The mid '80s were, without a doubt, the most productive and successful period of Bob's career. The Courtship of Carl Sandburg *had been a great hit for Bob, he continued to be free of drugs, he was singing, playing and writing better than ever, and he was physically more fit than he had been in years. Without the aid of the drugs that kept him lean in the early days, weight had always been a problem for him, but for once he had trimmed down and looked terrific. With the play behind him, he now looked for other projects.*

Considering Bob's history in the world of folk music coffee houses, having been instrumental in their development in the Village to begin with and then his reign at the legendary Gate of Horn, it seems incredible that it took so long for him to join the ranks of club owner. Aside from a brief partnership in a club in Cleveland in the early days, this was one area he had not pursued. The time finally seemed right to him, though, and he became a partner in a place on Clark Street in Chicago that had a reputation already as a restaurant. It became Hobson's Choice.

I was trying to run a place with certain kinds of principles and goals. It was a wonderful place for people to perform with a very small intimate room and a real connection between performers and audience. Of course, I changed the nature of how they performed. Instead of doing one-nighters, I had them come in for longer periods of time, like two to four weeks.

George Matson remembers the story of how the club got its name:
Hobson was a stable keeper in Harvard or near there. The fastest horses were the ones that, of course, were in the most demand, and I think he saved those horses for certain clientele. Bob had an open mike or a feature night. The idea behind the place was to showcase new performers.

Garry Cooper wrote about Hobson's Choice in Chicago Singles *in 1984:*

BOB GIBSON: THE QUIET VOICE

We in Chicago have become used to our best performers never quite making it here in Chicago. Steve Goodman, Bonnie Koloc —

sooner or later they all come to the point in their careers where they have to leave Chicago to try to boost their national recognition. It seems as though they have to erase every trace of their Chicago roots from their public image if they are to have a chance. Bob Gibson has swum against the trend, though. Born in New York, Gibson originally came to Chicago looking for work. He likes Chicago and has made it his home. Through his long association with the Old Town School of Folk Music, Gibson has shared his singing, songwriting, guitar and banjo-playing skills with hundreds of fellow musicians and students. His latest ventures sink his Chicago roots even deeper.

As Artist-in-Residence at Hobson's Choice, 5101 N. Clark St., Gibson is in charge of booking entertainment. By booking quality entertainment rather than "big names" and by showcasing and giving opportunities to musicians who need and deserve exposure, he is rededicating himself to the cause of good music over his own career. "We want to make Hobson's Choice a place where people want to be. A place to go. A place where you don't feel you have to know who's performing on any particular night — you just know that if you go, you'll enjoy it."

Looking thinner than at any time since the '60s, healthy and younger than his 52 years, Bob Gibson is in a period of easy growth.

Writer Jeff Mintz also wrote about the club:
BOB GIBSON OPENS HIS HEART — AND HOBSON'S CHOICE

Tonight it's the second evening of activity at Hobson's Choice, a re-opened Uptown restaurant at 5101 N. Clark Street, where, as musical director, Gibson hopes to run the neighborhood bar in the tradition of the Gate of Horn, exposing new talent in an intimate setting. It's just one of several projects well-suited for one of contemporary folk music's pivotal figures.

Gibson is proud of his latest find — Anne Hills, a full-voiced songstress who has appeared with him as well as with Best of Friends, a trio project that includes Tom Paxton. Gibson produced Anne's first album last spring ('83) for Hogeye Records and is readying a new one by her for early '84 as well as his own record, his first in two and a half years. Meantime, Gibson is associated with Community Entertainment Productions, a non-profit group involved with Hobson's and one that functions to help any of the 67 community organizations in the Uptown Organization for the North East with benefits and fundraisers.

Chicago Sun-Times writer Dave Hoekstra wrote about a unique feature of Hobson's Choice on November 28, 1984:

Folk singer Bob Gibson comes at you like a bowl of his fiery chili.

Before his performance last week at Hobson's Choice, Gibson was in the kitchen hovering over kettles of Homemade Texas chili

I COME FOR TO SING - 151

and a delightful Chicago chili. The effervescent Gibson oversees the club, occasionally cooks the food and remains a legendary performer in folk circles.

And if that fails, there's always Bob Gibson's Chicago chili: ground meat, lamb, tomato sauce, assorted spices, bay leaves and Cajun pepper, covered with a few good songs.

George Matson remembers Bob's chili:
Bob also won a slot in the Terlingua Chili Contest in California. It's made with beef heart and chili powder. And he said, "not 'chili powder' but powdered chilis. It's gotta be powdered chilis." The chili was the mainstay of Hobson's Choice and then of course it had the entertainment in the evenings. It was very good chili — excellent — probably the best I've ever had.

Josh White Jr. remembers playing at Hobson's Choice and what made it stand out from other clubs:
Being solo performers, Bob and I didn't see each other too often. We had done the Soundstage show together in 1981, and then I got into colleges and didn't see him that often until we toured together in '83 or '84. Then he got Hobson's Choice and invited me to play there. Hobson's Choice was a bar that Bob took over that had a performance area and then a bar outside. It was special because it was so respectful. As I remember it, the bar was situated so that if there were people who didn't particularly want to come in or pay the cover to see the music, we were not disturbed by them. That, as I remember it, was very important. There is nothing worse than having a listening room that is not a listening room. That's the way the Gate of Horn was, too. If you were in the performance room, you did not have to deal with that noise of the bar at all. Again, it could be different when other performers were there. I know the Village Gate in New York — it was big enough that there could be a lot of noise if the performance that was being given was more jazz oriented or something where people felt compelled to talk. I remember working at the Village Gate with my old man, and whoever we were co-billing with, a lot of whom could bring in a loud, drinking crowd. The old man, if they started being noisy, would just start singing softer. It worked beautifully! Then after awhile, they're policing themselves. You don't have to do anything.

Anyway, Hobson's Choice was a family thing. Everyone knew each other. Gibson was not always there, but his presence was felt, because I'm sure he let those who were going to be there know that this was a room where professional people were going to be singing. It was not a bar where people could come in and talk and drink and not be respectful of the performer. It was a good place.

As usual, Kerrville was always a part of a musical relationship with Bob, now more than ever. Not only did Bob have the songwriting school, but he had become one of the directors of the school. Josh White Jr. remembers being recruited:

>Gibson was also the first person to introduce me to and bring me down to the Kerrville Folk Festival where he was a director during that same time when he had Hobson's Choice. One of the first things he did when he was booking that was to call me and ask me if I would like to work it. We did *Billy Come Home* and some more music together at Kerrville. For Bob to ask me to do *Billy Come Home* with him was just wonderful.

The time came to make music again. Bob had not made a record since Perfect High *in 1981, so in 1984, he went back into the studio to make the album* Uptown Saturday Night. *It came out on the Hogeye label.*

Tom Paxton was doing the *Bulletin* album which was originally on Hogeye and then was distributed by Flying Fish. I'd never been satisfied as Tom's producer with the number of records he sold compared to the number of people who showed up for his concerts. Of course, he sells some albums off the stage. He does quite well doing that. I always felt, though, that there was a bigger market for Tom than was reflected in his album sales. What happens is that the older affluent market just doesn't go to record stores and buy a lot of records regularly. A younger audience would. My thought was, maybe we should advertise Tom in some of the more avant-garde or politically conscious magazines. We went to publications like Mother Jones and Chicago Magazine and tried it. We spent a lot of money on the advertising and did not particularly gain from it. I've never known why. Maybe we did it the wrong month. We did it in the month before Christmas trying to tie in with Christmas sales. It didn't work. Tom went on to sell the same quantity of that album as he had a lot of others, but it's one of his great albums. Anyway we founded Hogeye to do that. Hogeye was set up to do Paxton albums, Gibson albums, and to begin to record and release Anne Hills' albums.

I had Anne Hills produce my album *Uptown Saturday Night*. I just turned to her and said, "You ought to produce this. It would be a good credit for you." I'd have done it, but I decided to give her a shot at producing instead. She's got good ears and she had good input.

Steve Romanoski wrote this review of the album Uptown Saturday Night:

Bob Gibson is an entertainer who has experienced artistic success, hard times and several career revivals along the road. But like most people, Gibson has mellowed with age. Thus, his latest recording, *Uptown Saturday Night,* presents Gibson as a mature performer who is content to convey expression through words rather than dynamics.

Uptown Saturday Night is a low-key collection of contemporary tunes, most of which were penned by Gibson. Gibson has a magic touch with chords and is one of the finest arrangers in contemporary folk music.

Uptown Saturday Night contains some real gems including *Let the Band Play Dixie* and *Looking For the You In Someone New.* The latter tune includes some exceptional violin work from Stuart Rosenberg blended with Gibson's smooth banjo playing.

While I can't place *Uptown Saturday Night* among the best recordings of Bob Gibson, it is light years ahead of most of the mainstream contemporary balladeers who get the glory while Bob Gibson just grows mellow like fine wine.

The song *Looking For the You in Someone New* was one of my favorite songs that I wrote. I used it as an example of my writing style and development of a song in my songwriting manual.

Also on that album was the song *Pilgrim*. I co-wrote that with Marv David, a writer in Chicago. We were commissioned to write a particular song for a medical facility, Parkside Medical Services. They had a substance abuse program and wanted a song that would be used on a film they were making. So it is a theme song really. I liked that song a lot. Marv wrote a lot of scripts for television and films. When he finished the script he said to the Parkside people, "This needs a song. I know a guy that can write it." He and I wrote the song. We brainstormed and did all the things I talk about in my songwriting classes, went through all the steps. *(This is a reference to the Songwriters School which Bob ran at Kerrville in association with Steven Fromholz and Nanci Griffith, and also to his songwriting manual written for that course which appears in the appendix section.)* We spent a lot of time manicuring the song. We wanted to make it right. Every word needed to be just right on that. It meant a lot to both of us. That was the only thing we ever wrote together.

The song, The Pilgrim, *interestingly, had made an earlier brief appearance in Bob's repertoire. In a performance at Earl of Old Town in March, 1972, Bob had sung a very different version. It, too, was called* Pilgrim. *The lyrics were not the same, the rhythm was dramatically different, but the melody and the idea behind the song were totally identifiable. Although it was a touching and beautiful song, it disappeared from his shows for twelve years until this moving, revised version appeared on* Uptown Saturday Night. *The newer version of the* song was so effective that it became the unofficial anthem of AA. The new Pilgrim lyrics appear at the end of the Demons chapter. Here are the earlier lyrics as a comparison. As Bob's daughter Meridan said, comparing the two sets of lyrics gives a textbook example of the song-writing process in which an ordinary, good song can become an anthem.

>   I'm a pilgrim of my mind
>   Spent half my life just wastin' time
>   Travelin' through that lonely void
>   Mixin' my blood with powdered joy
>   Now I'm a pilgrim — You're one too
>   You are me and I am you
>   But together we'll get through
>   What else can us pilgrims do?
>
>   I am a pilgrim of my time
>   Wasted promise, broken dreams
>   Empty future, bright foreseen
>   Empty visions, awful schemes
>   Now I'm a pilgrim — You're one too
>   You are me and I am you
>   But together we'll get through
>   What else can us pilgrims do?
>
>   I am a pilgrim of my soul
>   Spent half my lifetime to be whole
>   In so many ways I find
>   There's so much love it blows my mind
>   Now I'm a pilgrim — You're one too
>   You are me and I am you
>   But together we'll get through
>   What else can us pilgrims do?
>   What else can us pilgrims do
>   But to help each other through?
>
>   *(©Robert Josiah Music, Inc.)*

ખ ખ ખ ખ ખ

It was either on the album, *A Perfect High,* or Tom Paxton's *Up and Up* where Anne and I first worked together. Then of course came *Courtship.* She used to sing with her husband, Jan Burda. I heard them singing and always thought she was a good singer. What they did was real cute, a very traditional kind of thing. Everything they did was off records. It was a nice rendition of something you could hear somebody else do, or another duo do. She began to do back-ups, she and Cindy Mangson, on some of the Tom Paxton stuff. Those two voices with Tom's made a really nice blend, a nice effect. Then somewhere along the line, Tom's manager said, "Tom, why don't you and Bob go out as a duo?" Tom said we should do it as a trio with Anne. It seemed like a good idea. We called ourselves The Best of Friends. It was interesting music to make. We tried that for a while, but we chose not to release an album of our trio. There never was a commitment from any of us to do it sufficiently, and you've got to make a real commitment for something like that to succeed. We'd do gigs every couple of months. We'd arrive in Phoenix, Arizona, in the afternoon and start rehearsing like crazy to try to remember our parts and all. It wasn't much fun at times. If you do it in a trio and do that format regularly, you can start to have fun with the music because you know the parts.

Tom Paxton:
Bob produced ten albums of mine. He produced the two albums I did for Mountain Railroad, and he produced the album I did for the company he and Anne Hills had, Hogeye. He did a couple of the albums I did for Flying Fish and several children's things, and we worked and performed together. We had a trio with him and Anne Hills and me, so we were tight buddies.

Michael Smith looks back on the trio and the way Bob invited him to be a part in it:
When Bob started working at Hobson's Choice, he and Anne and Tom Paxton formed a trio called Best of Friends. I had vaguely known Anne because I had seen her work. From our experience doing the show *Chicago: Living Along the Banks of the Green River* in 1981, Bob called me up to work with him at Hobson's. I'm not sure how it came about that I joined the group, but I guess, I was just into playing bass — I liked to play bass, and Bob either asked me, or I asked him if I could play bass for them, because I loved his rhythm. I always loved what I had heard. I thought it was very sophisticated, and by that time I pretty much knew how his songs went, and I knew how his feeling was and I thought, "I can play bass for this — no problem!" I wasn't that facile a bass player, but I'd been attempting to play bass about 30 years, so I'd gotten sort of the feel and I started playing behind the group, and that was fun! It was really a kick to tell myself I was playing with this guy 20 years after I first heard of him on the one hand, and on the other, I was playing with him songs that I absolutely knew down to my core because I'd heard them so many times. I always thought Bob had a nice feel, and it was FUN playing bass for him. We did that for a year or so.
Then, after a while, Bob would stop in the middle of a set and he

would say, "My friend is playing bass, here. He's a very good songwriter. Can he do three songs for you?" The audience would go, "Oh, yeah." So then I'd play three songs. This was out of the blue for him. This was *his* notion. I mean I would never, EVER have said to him, "Please, let me play some songs in the middle of your set." It wouldn't EVEN cross my mind. He was the guy who turned to me and said, "I think you're very good. Let me give you a little showcase." He was so cool that way.

The trio along with Michael Smith on bass did quite a bit of touring for a couple of years, appearing at Carnegie Hall, Chautauqua Institute, Massachussetts, Minneapolis, Washington, DC and Michigan. The beginning of 1985 they toured the British Isles where they appeared on Scottish television on a show hosted by the Corries, a well known British Folk Duo. The series included appearances by Judy Collins and the Clancy Brothers, among others. The Best of Friends also appeared on Pebole Mill, a BBC television show from Birmingham, England, and also a BBC radio show called "Folk on Two" eminating from London. On their return to the States, they played in Chicago and did folk festivals. They had a wonderful blend vocally. The intention was to produce an album of the trio, either a recording of the live performance they did for WFMT, or a studio recording, but for many reasons it never happened. Of the WFMT show, Tom said:

When we listened to it, we realized that it was just too rough to release as a record.

Then problems developed that eventually ended the group before they could come up with anything else. Tom remembers:

Bob and Anne started fighting. I think there were problems stemming from Hogeye and that Carl Sandburg play. I do know that it was a constellation of circumstances that ended the group. One — we couldn't make it work financially. I couldn't stop my regular performing. I was trying to put kids through college, so I couldn't drop everything and go to square one with a trio on spec, so that made it difficult. Also we couldn't get enough jobs at reasonable pay to make it worthwhile, so it just kind of withered on the vine really.

Michael Smith adds:

What I heard about Best of Friends and why it didn't go any further, Anne said that there was an agreement as to how they were going to split the proceeds, and the agreement had to do with their relative earning power ordinarily. I don't know what the proportions were, but it was approximately, let's say, Paxton got half and Bob got 30% and Anne got 20% or something along those lines. That was appropriate since Paxton could have done those shows by himself and made the same amount because Paxton has a career that is constant in terms of work, whereas Bob, in my impression, did not have that kind of constant. For one thing, he wasn't nearly as prolific as a writer. Paxton is just always coming up with stuff. It pours out of him. Anyway there was a point at which Paxton's stance was, "I like having the other two with me from a musical point of view and a friendship point of view, but monetarily, I'm losing money from this when I could make this kind of money myself and not split it." It was a lovely sound, but Tom really had his career and couldn't afford to be paying to have the extra. In a way, I think the folks who bought Tom had been buying Tom for so long that when the trio came along, they really were buying Tom, and anything Tom wanted to do was fine with them. If it was a trio, that's fine. Gibson was certainly just a vague thought in their minds, and Anne, at that time, as now, I would say, didn't nearly have the drawing power of either of those gentlemen and understood it, but was thrilled to be a part of it. Anne realized this and once said a funny thing. She was at Carnegie Hall and working on a bill with a whole bunch of folk singers like maybe Peter, Paul & Mary, and the Kingston Trio. Anyway Anne said, "I'm the only one on this bill I've never heard of."

It is tragic that the planned record release of the trio never materialized. The harmonies produced by the three of them were some of the best ever heard, and the voices blended perfectly, with Anne's clear soprano finally completing the trio sound that Albert Grossman had looked for so many years before. That thought must have always haunted Bob, since he continually found himself in this kind of group situation. As wonderful as Bob was as a solo performer, he always hit new heights when teamed with other artists. The performances of The Best of Friends could not have been better.

Despite the fact that Hobson's Choice lasted only a year and the Best of Friends split up, Bob's incredibly productive period was nowhere near its end.

1984

L-R: Michael Smith, Josh White Jr., David Hernandez, Anne Hills (behind), Bob Gibson at Hobson's Choice, 1984

Bob at the bar at Hobson's Choice, 1984

13

UNCLE BOB

William Carlton - Fort Wayne News-Sentinel - August 4, 1988

Folk singer Bob Gibson spent 30 years trying to win over erudite grown-ups in coffeehouses. They'd give him about four songs to warm up and prove himself before asking for the check.

Today, as Uncle Bob Gibson, he's trying to wring applause from the toughest audience of all — 6-year-olds in shopping malls; they give him about one minute to make them laugh before crying for their mammas.

By 1987 my type of music was a sliver of the market it once was, but I was still getting to do what I like to do. You can't beat that if you get to make your living at what you like to do.

In October of 1985 I started directing my attention to some children's material. I put together a couple of children's concerts — family concerts at Holstein's in Chicago. I did traditional stuff from the folk music thing, and then I said, "Wait a minute! The parents love this, but the kids are real bored." I was doing traditional folk songs for kids, like *The Old Woman Who Swallowed a Fly*. The kids were bored because the songs didn't really involve them. So I started to write stuff and I got very involved and found out there really was not much good children's material. There was some, but it was classic stuff. There was too much dorky stuff. A few people were writing some wonderful things, but there was a real opening for another guy to come in and write some more songs.

Even on television there were too few good things for kids. Most of the Saturday morning kids' programming was created by toy and cereal companies. It used to be that they just advertised, but then they started getting involved in underwriting the development of the shows' characters. They were always trying to sell the kids stuff—not just Care Bears and Smurfs, but all kinds of clothes and other things. It was kind of appalling. There was enough entertainment there to keep kids hooked in, but no attempt at any real content. The idea seemed to be to just hold kids' attention until the next commercial. I set a goal of holding children's attention with stories and songs about feelings rather than odes to consumer goods.

Most of the songs I wrote were for kids from three to nine years old. I really believed that kids that age needed good positive songs.

There were three kids in my family. We all used to sing in the car, songs like *Someone's in the Kitchen with Dinah.* I still remember from my childhood, *I've Been Working on the Railroad,* and *Go to Alabama with My Banjo on My Knee.* I didn't know what the words meant then, and I don't know what they mean now, but I know the songs. Now, I thought, if I could write songs that have real positive messages and are that singable and that memorable for kids, maybe we could get them to remember all the lyrics and the music to songs and eventually they'll absorb some of these positive messages. Music is a far more effective tool with kids than people realize, because once they love a song, they'll sing it over and over and really learn it. It becomes their tune.

The first thing you need to understand in writing music for kids is that there's no such thing as a "just a children's song." Kids' music requires at least as much thought as adult lyrics. Successful grownup songs almost always deal with situations the average listener can easily identify with, while children's music should use fantasy without losing touch with reality.

Two things kids love are ghost stories that let them be scared without actually being in danger, and the chance to do something outrageous without having to worry about getting into trouble. Also kids will go along with all kinds of things if they're having fun with it because they haven't yet learned it's important to be cool, so they'll make funny sounds and faces with you. That was a really important element in what I was doing as Uncle Bob, because the songs I did for them didn't have any meaning unless the kids did their parts.

I was working with a brilliant man who was both a psychotherapist and a rabbi. I can't mention his name, because I'm not sure if he'd like me to. I'd go to him with ideas and brainstorm with him to see if I was on target. By no means were my concerts kiddie therapy groups, but there were some fundamental concepts that I wanted to get across.

I liked the three to nine-year-old range because they are the most receptive and malleable and like to identify with adults. Older kids don't want to hear from us; their peer groups are more important to them.

I appeared as Uncle Bob for the first time at Holstein's in Chicago on Sunday, February 23, 1986. We had shows for kids and their families at 3 pm on the second and fourth Sunday of each month through June. We did a show called "Uncle Bob's Clubhouse," in which the material changed from week to week.

I did about 15 shows there, honing my skills and videotaping every segment with a wide-angle lens so I could see the audience from every side. I wanted to see what they were reacting to.

In an article in the Chicago Tribune on May 14, 1986, Julie Cameron wrote about Uncle Bob:

HUSH UP, TV PITCHMEN, BOB GIBSON HAS SOMETHING TO SAY TO THE KIDS

The face is familiar: twinkling eyes, cherubic grin. The voice is familiar too. Warm, hail-fellow-well-met. Except for the red Oshkosh overalls and canary yellow T-shirt, except for the lyrics — "I've come here today to play, there's nothing else to say" — you might think the man onstage at Holstein's on Sunday afternoon is legendary folk singer Bob Gibson. If you think that, you are right.

With a banjo pressed to his girth and a Cheshire grin pressed to his face, Bob Gibson has turned his attention to small fry. Looking like nothing so much as an updated Captain Kangaroo, Gibson clearly enjoys his own act. The kids do, too — nearly as much as their parents.

A glance around the room reveals an audience full of wire-rimmed glasses, blue jeans that aren't Calvin's, beards, Indian cotton shirts and a general air of happy nostalgia.

"Yes, I'd say that a lot of the people who come, a lot of the parents, knew Bob from his days with Hamilton Camp, back when they were Gibson and Camp," says Ed Holstein, proprietor.

"I don't know. I think Bob's set would have kids who are a little older," an eavesdropping woman disagrees. "I think people just want something nice to do with their kids."

"I got into this because of my grandchildren," Gibson, himself, confirms.

"This" is a kiddy show. The set of songs — even the set itself, large, bright cutouts — were designed by Gibson to entertain. And the kids are entertained.

The whole thing blossomed into "Uncle Bob's Place", which is more of an attitude, a frame of mind, although, I eventually got a whole set and everything that I was hauling around to the malls and doing these shows. It was like a gazebo and the kids all sat on carpets in front of me. We just had a wonderful time.

Then I had a revelation. I'd look out in the audience and all the kids would be wearing these OshKosh B'Gosh bib overalls, and I decided I was going to wear a pair of those, just like them. I made a connection with OshKosh B'Gosh, Inc., and they were kind enough to say, "Listen, we love the stuff you're doing. We think there should be more positive quality for kids. Take it out!" so they started sponsoring me on tour. They sent me out to sing these songs and all, and have some fun with kids. So "Thanks to the folks from OshKosh B'Gosh," because you need some backing for stuff like this. I performed free shows in malls all over the country, and I wore bright blue or red bib overalls, just like the little kids. They were exactly the same.

One thing I wanted to get across to kids was that what they think and what they feel is OK. Feelings are wonderful to have. Everything you think is OK, but what they do sometimes may not be OK. And that's a pretty strong message for little kids. I was raised in that period where good children were seen and not heard, and today we've learned that what we can best do for our kids is just to make them feel secure, love them, hug them, make them feel wanted and loved. In my day and age, there were other things that seemed to be more important. Parents wanted kids to have the right education or the right this or the right that, and sometimes failed to make us feel as loved as we should be.

I tried to relate my songs to the child in me. All I had to do was remember that kids three to nine years old have the same concerns that you and I have got. They have the same emotions. They just have a limited vocabulary, and a limited life experience. They're not interested in abstractions at all! First of all they want to be entertained. Their first priority is they want to know, "Are we having any fun?" It's real simple! But they also are wide open to being stimulated, or educated, if you will. So fun with a message was what Uncle Bob's place was all about.

First and foremost, my goal was to get kids hooked into the music so they were enjoying it, and then if I could put a little message in there and tell them something, that would be nice, but first and foremost you've got to get to them. Once they were in a happy mood, then I could educate them by weaving healthy, wholesome values and perspectives in the song, though not in a cutesy way. I didn't use plays on words, puns, or talk at the kids and act ridiculous. I stayed focused on communication with words and music. Their feelings need to be approached in a direct manner.

I was about as excited working with kids as I was when I first started working with adults. They're very, very exciting to work with. They're real challenging, too, because the only thing you get from kids is their attention in the moment, and if you lose them, they're gone! And they're honest - TOTALLY honest! They're not the least bit moved by reviews of my last show. They just care right now! They want fun *right now!* If they liked what I was doing, they'd walk right up and stare in my face. If an adult did that, it would be bizarre. They perceive false emotions immediately, and once you lose their interest, you can never get it back. The kids will suddenly notice they are surrounded by 100 other kids and party with them.

The kids are as much co-writers as anyone. They let you know if things work or not. Of course, sometimes, I admit, I missed the mark completely with a song with concepts beyond the experience and understanding of young children. I originally set out to create a whole new body of work and that led me to write a show, a format where I could put in songs, scenes, characters, the whole thing.

The first week, I introduced this eccentric old street lady, bag lady character named Hambone, played by actress and storyteller Virginia Smith. Hambone refused to speak and only rattled her tambourine — once for yes, twice for no. I'd ask her if she was sad or lonely or what. She'd rattle 'no' to all the questions until I'd ask her if she was tired. Then she rattled, 'Yes.' I'd ask why she was tired and finally she'd speak: "I'm tired of all these questions!" That got us into a song about curiosity. It worked wonderfully.

Other approaches didn't work as well, though. We did a skit where I asked why she had all these bags full of stuff. She called them treasure, not trash, so I'd ask her what treasures were in the bag — gold? silver? She said, "Yes, an old motorcycle sprocket I can use as a trivet so the table won't burn, and a hubcap I can use to serve crackers and dip. A wooden spoon could be a backscratcher or a drumstick." The kids didn't like it. It was too adult or something. When I wrote a song about that, the adults thought it was clever and the kids thought that sprockets and hubcaps were still junk. I don't think they were interested in the ephemeral quality of what to do with old things.

I worked on one song composed of several emotions. I'd break down the sounds of laughter — "ha, ha; ho, ho; hee, hee" — and incorporate them into the chorus. But then I got to things like anger, stubbornness and rebelliousness. What is the sound of anger? There is no sound because it's not okay to express anger. Children are taught to stifle it. They aren't given indications from parents about expressing certain emotions. That's why there are more sounds for joy.

I loved to talk to kids about their feelings. I'd ask the kids, "Did you ever wake up in the morning and look out the window and you saw it was raining, and you knew that you probably wouldn't even go out if you went to school? They wouldn't even have recess 'cause it was raining, and if you got to go out, you'd probably have to wear your boots, and your raincoat and it was real frustrating." I'd ask them if they'd ever gotten real mad — you know really angry or really sad or disgusted. Did you ever get disgusted — I mean just when nothing was going right and you just felt kind of BRRAACCKK? *(This is the spelling for a Bronx cheer.)*

> Did you ever, did you ever, did you ever wanna just go
> (BRRAACCKK)
> When your shoestring broke (BRRAACCKK)
> You forgot that joke (BRRAACCKK)
> Or your bike got a flat (BRRAACCKK)

Or someone sat on your hat (BRRAACCKK)
Someone called you a name (BRRAACCKK)
Or you lost that game (BRRAACCKK)
Did you ever wanna just go (BRRAACCKK)

If someone says don't (BRRAACCKK) that way
What they really mean is don't feel that way
But what we're feeling is A-OK
So we could just go (BRRAACCKK)
'Til it goes away
Did you ever wanna just go (BRRAACCKK)

'Cause the bus was late (BRRAACCKK)
And you had to wait (BRRAACCKK)
Or your lunch got lost (BRRAACCKK)
Or you got double crossed (BRRAACCKK)
Or you were late for school (BRRAACCKK)
And you felt like a fool (BRRAACCKK)
Did you ever wanna just go (BRRAACCKK)

It's not so bad - it feels real good
To just go (BRRAACCKK) when you think you should
I love to (BRRAACCKK) when I don't feel good
Let's all go (BRRAACCKK)
There, I knew we could!
Did you ever wanna just go (BRRAACCKK)

Cause it rained all day (BRRAACCKK)
And you couldn't play (BRRAACCKK)
So you stayed indoors (BRRAACCKK)
And you got really bored (BRRAACCKK)
There was nothin' to do (BRRAACCKK)
And then the TV blew! (BRRAACCKK)
Did you ever, did you ever,
Did you ever wanna just go (BRRAACCKK)

(by Gibson — ©Robert Josiah Music, Inc.)

That song grabbed the kids right away, even those kids whose parents had just told them not to make those rude sounds. The song may be punctuated by a resounding Bronx cheer, but I wasn't trying to make rude sounds. At the end of that song, I'd tell the kids, "Now I'm not telling you that you should make that sound, because somebody may have just told you, 'Don't make rude sounds.' What I'm telling you is if you feel that way and you feel frustrated, it's OK!"

And kids would get the point that it's OK to feel that way.

Early on I'd ask the kids if they knew the story of the boy who cried wolf, and they'd all put up their hands and say, "Sure, we know it!" So I'd say, "Well let's just check out our facts and make sure we all know it the same way. A little boy was told to watch the sheep and guard against the wolves and if he saw a wolf he was to yell; "WOLF! WOLF! WOLF!" and people would come and help him drive off the wolf. Well, in the story, the little boy was out there taking care of the sheep, and there was not really a wolf, but he cried out anyway. He yelled, "WOLF! WOLF! WOLF!" And everybody dropped what they were doing and they came rushing out to where the little boy was and they saw there was no wolf and they were very upset, and they said, 'You're not supposed to yell 'WOLF!' if there's not really a wolf! So they all went back to what they were doing. Well, the little boy was out there again, all by himself, taking care of those sheep, and there was not really a wolf, but he cried out again anyway. He yelled, 'WOLF! WOLF! WOLF!' and this time half the people dropped what they were doing and they came rushing out to help the little boy drive off the wolf and when they saw that there was no wolf, they were very angry. They said, 'You're not supposed to yell 'WOLF!' if there's not really a wolf!" So they all went back to what they were doing. Well, now a little while later, what came along? And all the kids would wave their hands and they'd say 'A WOLF!' And I'd say, 'Right! The little boy saw a real wolf, so he yelled, 'WOLF! WOLF' and what happened? The kids all filled in the blank, and said 'Nobody came!' We'd go through the whole story. The kids love to illustrate that they knew the story. Then I'd say, "I always wondered, why do you suppose that little boy cried 'WOLF!' when there wasn't really a wolf? You know, that's not talked about in the story. I wonder if he was just kind of lonesome, or maybe he was bored. Maybe he was a little afraid out there all alone taking care of those sheep. Maybe he just wanted some attention, and he didn't know how to say, 'I want some attention,' and so he yelled 'WOLF'. So I was interested in him, and I wrote a song about it."

> And the boy cried, "Wolf! Wolf! Wolf!"
> He called to the people loud and clear
> He cried, "Wolf! Wolf! Wolf!"
> And the people came runnin' from far and near
> But pretty soon the folks from town
> Wouldn't stop workin', they'd only frown
> They wouldn't come runnin' from miles around
> When the boy cried, "Wolf! Wolf! Wolf!"
> He cried, "Wolf! Wolf! Wolf! Wolf!

             Wolf! Wolf! Wolf!"

        And the boy cried, "Wolf! Wolf! Wolf!"
     He didn't mean "Wolf!" He meant "Come here!"
             He cried, "Wolf! Wolf! Wolf!"
          I'm all alone and I want you near
          I want some attention of my own
       I'm just a little boy that's about half grown
        And I hate this feelin' when I'm all alone
                  So I just cry, "Wolf!"
     He didn't mean "Wolf!" He meant "Come here!"
          He felt like he wanted someone near
          And a great big hug would be OK
        And that mean old wolf would run away
        If he could just tell you what he means to say
                  And not cry, "Wolf!"
           He cried, "Wolf! Wolf! Wolf! Wolf!
                  Wolf! Wolf! Wolf!"

        Did you ever cry, "Wolf! Wolf! Wolf!"?
           Tellin' a tale that same old way
             He cried, "Wolf! Wolf! Wolf!"
       You said that you couldn't go to school today
       You told your mother that you didn't feel good
   And you couldn't go to school like you knew you should
      And it worked on your mom like you knew it would
               But you were cryin', "Wolf!"
     Ah, you didn't mean, "Wolf!" You meant, "Come here!"
          You felt like you wanted someone near
        And the very next time you feel that way
          And the feelin' just won't go away
         Why not say what you need to say
                  And not cry, "Wolf!"
              "Wolf! Wolf! Wolf! Wolf!
                  Wolf! Wolf! Wolf!"
           (by Gibson — ©Robert Josiah Music, Inc.)

   I wanted the kids to get the message that it's OK to say you want attention and deserve it, but it's not OK to yell "Fire!" or cry "Wolf!"
   Kids do seem to relate to just a troubadour, a guy or gal and a guitar. And they like it real simple. They want to get involved in the song and the idea. They want to play.
   At the shows I would give kazoos to all the kids and we'd end the show with having the kids join me in the *Rooty Tooty Kazooty*

Marching Band. I had the time of my life.

Rich Hudson, Gibson's engineer and musical collaborator, comments on the band:
> The kazoo-along had to be the last number because once they got the kazoos, the place started to sound like a hive of killer bees. It was pretty hard to get their attention back.

I wanted kids to really enjoy the songs, but I still wanted them to hear a little something too. There's a lot they ought to hear. It's terrific to use songs to open up a discussion, a song that involves the child, that the child likes and has fun singing it. But then it opens up a situation that needs to be discussed between a teacher and children or parents and children.

I eventually got to working on a bunch of songs called *Songs for Safe and Secure Kids,* that was designed to help prevent child abuse. I did this with a fellow from Chicago, Rich Hudson, who I met while teaching songwriting at Columbia College, where he taught radio and television engineering and production as well as music and writing. It was the most challenging work I'd ever done. We co-created 14 songs. These were all songs that hopefully would provide children with coping mechanisms if they were faced with an abusive situation, but they're very positive. They were not meant to scare children or make them anxious at all. It was done for a West Coast Christian outfit called "Cause Concepts and Americans for a Better Life." They were going to produce the album. I was getting a lot of help from the National Association in Chicago.

The kids on the album were all from Lake Forest, and they went to school up there. A very talented guy who I'd worked with before, Fred Cook, who was a music teacher in a grade school and had done some records of kids' stuff, knew the kids and had worked with them and brought them in. They were wonderfully talented kids. I loved to sing with the kids; with and for the kids. I really did.

Of course, when we think about child abuse, we think of the horror stories that we heard in the last 15 or so years; physical abuse, sexual abuse, but there's also another kind of abuse that we, as parents, sometimes unwittingly provide for a child. There was more stress on the emotional and psychological abuse because so many well-intentioned parents who really love their kids forget and say things they don't really mean. When the child breaks the window we say, "Why are you so clumsy? Why can't you be like other kids?" There's nothing wrong with saying, "I'm angry you broke the window," but when you say things like, "You're a klutz. You're a big bother to have around. We're sorry we had you," then you're making it the fault of the child. There's nothing wrong with being angry at stuff the kids do. But we say things that damage kids. Words can really hurt. You know, "Sticks and stones can break my bones, but words can really hurt me terribly." And we do things to the child's self-esteem that takes a lifetime to repair. Kids are so vulnerable, and they look to us for our input to tell them who they are and what they are, and when we're abusing them that way verbally, then we're making marks and permanent damage.

There was one underlying thought and message that I was trying to convey with these songs to children, and that was to tell them, "You're not wrong, you're not at fault. It is not your fault! Things can happen to you that are not so wonderful, but it's not your fault!"

My experience was that a lot of the material about abuse for children was intimidating or threatening, even to the point where one time I remember one video cassette which was telling kids, "You have to have a password so that if a policeman comes to your school and tries to take you away and says your mother and dad were hurt you'll know it's really true." Well I felt this was giving these kids a lot of responsibility and an awful lot to do. It's like, you've got to protect yourself. I really don't hold with scaring kids that much. I'm much more into, it's really okay to have the freedoms to talk to people or to run away from an icky situation, and emergency plans so you know what to do in certain kinds of situations and so forth.

There are some real tangible ways that we can teach kids to arm themselves. We can teach them that it's okay to tell someone if it doesn't feel right, if the situation feels wrong. As I say in the song, "If it's an icky situation, you tell someone." It's okay to run away if it's a bad situation. Feel free. Run away. That's a good technique to protect yourself.

One of the songs I wrote is called *Tell Someone,* and it is really just that. It's a song where the kids are talking about how they don't feel as if their parents always listen to them. It's a common complaint among children and in this song we're telling them, you know, you've really gotta go tell someone when it doesn't feel right. When it isn't right, tell someone.

> If a shooting star fell in your back yard
> You'd tell someone
> If the Northern Lights lit up the nights
> You'd tell someone
> And if your wish came true
> Wouldn't you tell someone
> Tell someone, tell someone

Tell someone what's on your mind
If they won't listen, you must find
Someone who would be so kind
To listen while you tell someone

If you got an A on your math today
You'd tell someone
You would quickly run to tell everyone
You'd tell someone
Tell mom or dad, you'd be so glad
To tell someone, to tell someone
Tell someone

Tell somebody, tell a friend
One who'll listen till the end
Tell your mom or tell your dad
If you hurt or if you're sad

And the way you deal with an icky feelin'
Is to tell someone
If someone touches you like they shouldn't do
You tell someone
If they try again, no matter when
Just tell someone
Tell someone, tell someone

Don't hold back, just let it out
Whisper it or give a shout
Your heart will tell you what is real
Tell somebody how you feel

If a shooting star fell in your back yard
You'd tell someone, you'd tell someone
You'd tell someone
(by Gibson — ©Robert Josiah Music, Inc.)

You know, the unkindest thing of all is that kids who are caught up in abusive situations and sexually abusive situations are told, "Don't tell anyone. Keep the secret." They're told to keep the secret, but if they don't keep the secret, that's when that situation can be corrected and straightened out.

You've Gotta Have Friends is the next to the last song on the album, and the whole point of that song is to say to kids that if they've tried to tell an adult about a problem, and they don't listen then they have to be able to tell their peers. You have to be able to tell other kids, and the best way to have a friend you can to talk to is to be a friend. And that's what it's all about — you've gotta be a friend.

It's not okay if somebody tickles me when I don't want to be tickled.
I wish they knew a better way of paying attention to me.
Sometimes all I need is a hug to tell me I'm okay just the way I am.

> I only wanted hugs a lot
> Hugs a lot, hugs a lot
> I only wanted hugs a lot
> Why don't you give me one.
>
> I thought I'd failed the baseball team
> I felt lower than a rat
> My eyes were full of tears of rage
> I'd struck out each time at bat
>
> Mom thought maybe I was hurt
> I was crying tears of shame
> Dad assured me he would show me
> How to win that baseball game
> *(by Gibson — ©Robert Josiah Music, Inc.)*

The message behind this one was to parents, "If your son struck out three times in a row at the Little League game and felt so bad he cried, would you (1) give him a batting lesson? (2) give him a lecture? or (3) give him a hug? Number three is, of course, the best choice. Being a good parent is easier than we think sometimes. We don't have to respond to everything with our heads. We should do a lot more with our hearts.

Kids need to be aware of what an important word "No" is. One of my songs was about how much fun it is to say "No!" I've heard that the first word kids learn is "Mamma" and the second word is "No!" It's a way of asserting self-identity. Kids have to learn to say it about drugs and alcohol, too. In Chicago, around the time I was doing the Uncle Bob shows, a 10-year-old boy drowned in a YWCA pool after he took a fatal dose of crack. I was shocked to read that, and to hear a friend's 4-year-old daughter who said, "Mom, I don't feel good. I think I should take a Tylenol." Parents shouldn't wait until their kids are 14 to teach them to say "no" to drugs and alcohol.

I was honored to sing for the National Committee to Prevent Child Abuse at their big annual year-end meeting they have at the

Ambassador West. I got to introduce these songs which, of course, all apply to just the issues that these people are dealing with day in and day out, so it was a real honor and a real pleasure to get to sing these songs for them.

One of my proudest achievements related to all this was the Uncle Bob television series we put together. The name of the show was *Flying Whales and Peacock's Tales*. It was carried in 1989 on WMAQ, the NBC affiliate in Chicago, and it was even nominated for an Emmy. I had a group of five kids join me in the studio, and we'd sing songs together, they'd draw pictures and we'd talk. It was a lot of fun. The master tapes were edited into a series of ten video cassettes that were sold to schools. The title of the show for that package was *One, Two, Buckle My Shoe*.

For several years I was totally focused on the youth market in music. During the Uncle Bob years, I produced four albums of original songs for children for Tom Paxton on Tom's label, PAX Records. Then finally in 1989, I released my own children's album on my label, BG Records. It was called *A Child's HAPPY BIRTHDAY Album,* and it contained twelve new and original songs about birthdays. Ten of the songs I co-wrote with Dave North, and two of them were done with Shel Silverstein.

I'd been in the music field for many years being a songwriter and singer, performer and producer, so I brought a lot to the table with me in that way as Uncle Bob, but I sure learned a lot about kids doing this — what their needs are and how to relate to them. I had my own background of being raised at a time when parents were told in the books of the day, "Don't dangle your children on your knee and don't kiss them good-night. Kiss them, perhaps, on the forehead goodnight, and by all means, shake hands with them the first thing every morning." This book was printed in 1928 and was sort of the Dr. Spock of the day. I was born in '31 so, right away I have to give my parents a pass and say they were still in the tail end of the Victorian era. I'm a parent, myself, of four kids who are all grown and have kids of their own now, but I can remember painful moments with them when I said the wrong thing without meaning to. I also recall, with sort of sadness, that there were times when I reasoned with my kids. When one of my daughters was ill and told me how afraid she was of how she felt, instead of telling her, "Daddy's here, everything's OK now," and just putting my arms around her and making her feel safe and loved and secure, I reasoned with her and told her why it was really foolish to feel this way and how she should feel OK about being scared.

I also have a fifth child, Sarah, who was born in March of 1989, about at the end of my Uncle Bob time. She is the light of my life. I was very excited about being a father again. When my other children were growing up, I wasn't as involved with them as I wanted to be with Sarah. I lost a lot and gave up a lot. I didn't want to do that again.

You know, I think one of the greatest frauds ever perpetrated in the world is the idea of quality time. I find more guilty parents who really try and dismiss their own self-involvement with their careers and their own lives by saying, "Well, we have quality time with our kids." Nothing will replace time and involvement with your children, and one of the first things that kids wonder is, "What's wrong with me that I don't seem to be lovable enough or fun enough or something that Mom and Dad want to be with a lot?"

I like to think that what I did as Uncle Bob was probably the most important work I ever did as a performer.

Unfortunately, the album, Songs For Safe and Secure Kids, *never made it onto music store shelves. A beautifully finished studio version was produced, but it did not satisfy the organization in California that was funding it. Unwilling to make changes that they wanted, Bob abandoned the project. The masters still exist, though, and hope remains that it may yet come out someday.*

I COME FOR TO SING - 173

14

ONE MORE TIME!
GIBSON & CAMP
AT THE GATE OF HORN

It's amazing how many people asked me, "Where can we get that album you guys made?" I'd say, "You can't, it's no longer in the catalog." So as a 25th year reunion concert, Camp and I made the album again. Billed as "The Gate of Horn Revisited," we played music for four nights, June 5, 6, 7 and 8, 1986, at Holstein's, at 2464 N. Lincoln in Chicago. We put three songs on it that weren't there originally. Other than that it is the exact same album. There's more energy to the second album.

Ed Holstein remembers the monumental occasion when the legendary album was recreated at his club, Holstein's:
Bob worked at Holstein's frequently, but when Gibson & Camp worked there, it was like four days of heaven for everybody. I mean, they were great, and the audience was great. Waitresses used to walk out of there with money falling out of their aprons. We all made a lot of money. It was like perfection or Nirvana! They'd do two shows a night and you'd sit there as people were walking out with the waitresses just in the greatest mood, and the people would say, "Thank you for bringing them!" like you did something when all you did was Bob called and said, "We want to come in," and we said, "Okay, when do you want to come in?" It was unbelievable. I never saw anything like it. We had a lot of great acts at Holstein's, but they really come to mind where people were just tripping out of their minds. These people in the audience were part of their history. The people watching them now were in their 40s and 50s and it was just unbelievable. It was like when I saw the Weavers, but with Gibson and Camp, all this stuff was coming out of two people. Then Hamid would sing and do some theatre stuff since theatre is his main thing — but you just don't see shows like that! They also had Michael Smith playing bass and then HE would do stuff, so you had this just unbelievable show!

George Matson:
I wasn't one of the 26,000 people who claim to have been at the closing night of the original Gate of Horn, but I did make it to Holstein's for the Gibson & Camp reunion in '86. I was determined I was going to make that one. I missed the first one. By God, I wasn't going to miss that one! It was just wonderful. It was almost word

for word like the first one. It was a packed house and the audience knew everything that was going on — every joke. I assume they were all like me, and they'd probably all worn out three albums. It was wonderful! Gibson & Camp were really on top of the game there and it was energetic and marvelous. Just fabulous!

Entertainment writer Howard Reich reviewed the re-creation:

'60S FOLK HEROES GIBSON AND CAMP STILL IN TUNE

Though the folk-music heyday of the '60s probably seems like ancient history to many of today's listeners, at least two survivors of that era are eloquently keeping the memory alive.

Granted, Bob Gibson and Hamilton Camp probably never will recapture the fame they enjoyed in the glory days, when they held court at Chicago's long defunct Gate of Horn folk club. But judging by their sweet and, in a way, innocent performance Tuesday night at George's, that's quite beside the point.

A great song remains a great song, they seemed to be saying, as they performed '60s chestnuts with a freshness and vigor that nearly belied the passing of the years. Camp's face may be more lined and Gibson's frame more substantial than in the early days, but their musical intensity and conviction seem undimmed.

No doubt some listeners will find the prospect of two middle-aged men railing against various social ills, accompanied only by acoustic instruments, positively anachronistic. This is the age of the heavy-metal drone, after all, and songs with genuine literary subtlety are hardly in vogue.

But listen closely to Gibson and Camp sing such tunes as *Well,* *Well, Well, I'm Gonna Tell God* and a *Vietnam War Trilogy* (a takeoff on their previous *Civil War Trilogy*), and it seems impossible to remain unmoved. The warmth of their voices and the urgency of their message transcend musical fashions.

Not all their material, however, is laden with social consciousness. There are lighter touches, too, as in their exuberant *Skillet Good and Greasy,* the folk evergreen *The Midnight Special* and several devilishly clever numbers by Shel Silverstein and Michael Smith.

Beyond the verbal dexterity, there's the simple pleasure of hearing them play their instruments, from Gibson's banjo and guitar to Camp's plaintive harmonica.

If the between-song patter lacks a high degree of polish, that's simply vintage Gibson and Camp. As always, the duo is a shade under-rehearsed, leaving to chance what others plan in great detail. For the listener, the joy is in the spontaneity of it all — Gibson and Camp simply do whatever strikes their fancy at the moment, and it's anybody's guess what they'll sing or say next. In an age of carefully calculated music videos and slick-surface performers, what could be more appealing?

Michael Smith:
   I played bass for him and Camp at Holstein's, and then we did some other gigs together. That was REALLY fun! Really I felt historical. For me it was a big deal. I remember we played a gig with Odetta up at the concert hall at Skokie. That was very interesting to see the attraction between Camp and Gibson and Odetta. Odetta struck me as being a highly sensitive, very, very delicate person at the time, and Gibson got along with her real good. Camp gets along with anybody! He's just an actor as he's always been. Playing gigs with them was really fun and a major experience for me, just to get to work with Gibson & Camp, because, again, that was a legendary situation.

Hamilton Camp:
   By the time of the *Revisited* tape, being that was what we did for the rest of our lives, we got that set down pretty good. On stage we were the best of friends. We're both older and wiser now — we were pretty hell-bent for leather back then. Now we can both really appreciate working together. It's better now than it's ever been. Sometimes it's metaphysical, it's so good. That's what he's given me: he has made this unique duo harmony a wonderful experience.

On the recording just before the last song, Gordon Lightfoot's For Lovin' Me, *Bob addressed the audience. He said, "We were wondering, if we did this again, would you be around in the year 2000?" The crowd roared its approval of the idea. The two men Albert Grossman had brought together twenty-six years before had come so far. While their differences and divergent paths in life kept them from ever really becoming friends, there remained an undeniable bond between them that was able to transcend it all — the bond of the incredible music they made together. Now twenty-five years after their groundbreaking album* Gibson & Camp at the Gate of Horn, *for one more time, they had come together in triumph to show the legend was still alive. The harmonies they produced in those four days of reunion soared. Never had they sounded better or been better received. If only there could be that reunion in 2000, but as long as this music exists to be heard, there will always be a Gibson & Camp and a Gate of Horn.*

There is one more note on Gibson & Camp. The reunion recording may have been the end of the music they made together, but it was not the end of the reunions.

Meridian Green:
   The story of Gibson & Camp is not complete without the story of the least known, but perhaps most important reunion, as the fathers of the groom, Stephen's wedding in 1988. But first, some back-

ground. My parents, Bob and Rose, married in 1952, and by 1959, Rose was the mother of three children, and Bob was the father of four. I was born in 1955, Susan in 1956, and Pati in 1958. And Stephen in 1959. Stephen was born to Jovita, who later married Bob Camp and changed her name to Rasjadah.

Stephen first learned the truth of his paternity when he was fourteen. I first got to know him a couple of years later when Bob, his girlfriend Debbie, Susan, Stephen and I lived on Wilton in Chicago. Stephen was having some adolescent upheavals in his life and came to live on the couch because he wanted out of Skymont, Virginia. When Stephen emerged from adolescence he was living in Los Angeles with the Camp family (on yet another Wilton). He fell in love with the girl next door, Seannie McRae, who was 16 and was considered by her parents to be too young for this relationship. But their love lasted and Stephen and Seannie's wedding was the truest ever Gibson & Camp reunion.

We were all there, the entire clans. Rasjadah, mother of the groom and Stephen's five siblings on the maternal side, Lewis, Ray, Henrietta, Hamilton, and Laksmi. My mother Rose, who had since become Rose Garden, with her three married daughters, me, Susan and Pati, and the first of the grandchildren, my son Terra and Pati's son Jordan. Bob's second wife Margie was showing a wee bulge that became Sarah.

It was a colorful event with quite a cast of characters assembled in the garden of the McRae's. The families of the former Skymonters, including the famous Arquettes attended. The bridesmaids were resplendent in extraordinary shades of orange and yellow. Dr. McRae, in full Scottish regalia, including kilt and bagpipe, escorted Seannie down the aisle. As gloriously beautiful as the bride was, as poignant as the love story that led to this wedding still is, for me the significance of the day was this — Gibson and Camp standing before God acknowledging that together they had fathered a son, Stephen.

It was the only time we ever all gathered together, the clans of Gibson and Camp. That's who Stephen is, the embodiment of Gibson & Camp. He looks a lot like Gibson, feels just like him to hug, sounds and smells like Gibson. But he has Camp's sense of family. Stephen is a gravitational force drawing his families together. He and Seannie live two blocks away from both the Camps and McRaes with their children Fergus and Sylvana. Stephen is a Prop Master becoming a film director, and Seannie is a midwife. They recently changed their family name to Gibson.

L-R: Camp, Gibson at Kerrville Folk Festival, 1987

Photo courtesy Rod Kennedy

L-R: Camp, Gibson at Holstein's in Chicago, 1986 recording the *Revisited* album (Background picture from the original *Gate of Horn* album, 1961)

1986 Photo by Kathryn Brown

L-R: Lenny Laks, Gibson & Camp at Napa Folk Festival, 1994

Photo by Antonia Lamb

BOB GIBSON - 178

Gibson & Camp perform at Stephen & Seannie's wedding, July 30, 1988

Stephen in center flanked by fathers, Hamilton Camp, left & Bob Gibson, right, July 30, 1988

I COME FOR TO SING - 179

15

THE WOMEN IN MY LIFE

For Immediate Release:
The Women in My Life, a musical collaboration by Bob Gibson and Michael Smith will preview at Holstein's on Wednesday, October 8th through October 11th, 1986. Gibson and Smith will premier twenty new songs created especially for The Women In My Life.

Thus was announced the production of the musical collaboration which was an autobiographical journey through the memories of Gibson and Smith about the women who had the most profound influence on their lives. Although the two had worked togther for five years, this was their first full-length collaborative effort.

Gibson and Smith accompanied themselves on 6-string and 12-string guitars with additional accompaniment by Mark Edelsten on bass and Julianne Macarus on violin and synthesizer. For the most part they took turns in the solo spotlight, occasionally dueting, as on the gospelish Glorious Love. *The Holstein's stage provided a theatrical setting and the performers sang and talked through wireless microphones around a bench.*

The songs represent a wide range of influence from Bob's How Could You Do This To Me?, *a painfully humorous look at mothers based on the event referred to earlier when he was arrested in Cleveland; to Michael's* Sister Clarissa, *a statement on Catholic education; to Michael's* Ballad of Elizabeth Dark, *a tribute to a long-lost beatnik love; to Bob's* Joanie Did It Better, *his adolescent view of sex; to Bob's mature but ironic* Loving You With Open Arms *and finally his tribute to his new wife Margie,* This Woman Is the Women In My Life.

In a review in the Chicago Tribune, Lynn Van Matre had this to say about the show:

> There are a number of good songs and plenty of gentle laughter. Time has a way of eventually turning adolescent traumas into amusing memories, and Gibson and Smith have come up with a collection of alternately funny, intensely poignant and insightful tunes that frequently jar the memory while they spur smiles of recognition.

Michael Smith:
   This whole project was Bob's idea. He called me up and said, "I want to do this show called *The Women In My Life*. I've had this idea for some time, and I think you and I could do this together." I said, "Great, great, and I've got a bunch of songs." He said, "No, I want us to write songs new songs. I don't want to have any old stuff." I thought, "Oh, God, that sounds like an awful lot of work!" But he was so enthusiastic about it, and he seemed to be very industrious and he got it together. We started rehearsing. We rehearsed for a couple of months. I'd go to his house, and we'd work very hard. We'd do three or four hours together and I'd go home. I'd come back in a couple of days and we'd do the same thing again, and we did that continually for about six weeks.
   In general, what happened for both of us was that we had to look at our lives and see in what ways women figured. What happened for me was that I found out that women were more important in my life than I was. The influence was so strong there hardly was a me I could call me that wasn't part of some woman's influence. For me, it was a real exploratory experience. I also found out there were women I couldn't reduce to the level of song.
   Everybody writes about women. That's 90 percent of what a male songwriter will do, or emotionally anyway. For me, the discipline of it was that we had a certain time to be writing songs. It wasn't like you could reach back and say, "Hey, I've got this one song." I could certainly do that. I've got songs about my daughter, my various lovers, but I never had to say, "OK, here's what I feel like right now." It was all new. I wish there were this kind of challenge all the time.

We'd brainstorm ideas and get a concept. Sometimes it was done independently and we'd bring them together. Other times we'd work ideas off each other.

Michael Smith:
   It was better for me to write this way because when I have to explain something to somebody else, immediately I'm more communicative. If I'm writing a song for being in a show with Bob Gibson, I write a song in a different way and that's real good for me. What Bob did was make me appeal to people in a way I would not by myself. I alienate people. Here I had a filter which was very wholesome. He made me focus in a simple, clear way as the audience who comes to see him.

I did have emotional blocks, though. I really wanted to write a song about daughters and fathers—I had three daughters at the time.

Daddies are special to daughters and daughters are special to daddies—but I couldn't write it. I made some attempts at it, but it was too close to the bone right then.

Given some years to contemplate what happened in doing the production together, Michael looked back in 1997 with some lingering questions:

We wrote some together. He would say, "I've got an idea," and I'd say, "Okay, I think these chords would be cool," or "Do this," or sometimes I'd say, "Here's an old Gibson riff," and I would play him something that would sound to me like Bob Gibson. We wound up maybe writing three or four songs together, and then he did about five or so, I did about five or so., and we had the opening song. Sometimes he'd write the words and I'd say, "Give me this," and I'd take it home, and I'd write a song that sounded like Bob Gibson and then I would bring it back to him and say, "Do this." He wouldn't have any problem with it because it did sound like Bob Gibson. There were at least two tunes that were like that in the final structure. There was one tune where he wrote a song and then I wrote a kind of contrapuntal thing in between. He'd written a song called *Glorious Love* and I wrote a thing that went with it. I wrote almost a separate kind of tune that was like a reflection on it. So that was the way it worked. It was pretty much, "I've got an idea. Let's see what we can do with it." I'd take it home. I'd bring it back. Or I'd say to him, "I've got an idea." He'd take it home. But usually it was the other way. He'd have the idea and he'd say, "Okay, run with it." I really did pride myself on *The Women In My Life* thing about trying to make things sound like Bob Gibson. Everything! I'd try to make my own songs sound like Bob Gibson, because I wanted to make it seem thematic.

We got the show together and it went very well. We did four days at Holstein's right in a row. It seemed to me Bob was quite happy with it. In the end I said, "Well, Bob, what are we going to do?" I really had always left everything we'd do up to him in general because he was the kind of person who would have plans. He was definitely the adult in this relationship. With me it was always like, "Whatever you want to do, Bob, I'm ready," because I was so kicked to be working with him on that plane. In general when he wanted to do something, I'd just go, "Yeah!" No matter what it was. At the time I had a straight job, and so he would say to me things like, "I'd like to go to Iowa and record. Can you get off?" I'd say, "Oh, yeah, I'll take my vacation." Then when the vacation would come, he'd say, "Well, I don't think it's gonna happen." He was definitely living in a different kind of world than I was. For me it was a big deal, and he was very casual about it, which I understand — it wasn't a problem for me.

Anyway, Bob had done *The Courtship of Carl Sandburg,* which had started at BoarsHead and went to Evanston to the North Light and then the Apollo Theatre in Chicago, so he'd had a little history of doing theatrical things. My picture was that we'd go the same route. We had a nice little review in the Tribune. So at the end of it I said, "Well, Bob, what are we going to do?" You want to try to get a theatre? What do you want?" And he said, "I don't think I want to do it anymore." And I was like, "WHAAAAT?! What, what, whoa, wait up!" He said, "Naaah, I don't think I want to do it anymore." It really floored me, because we'd done SOOO much work, and at his instigation. It was a good show, and the thoughts I had were, for whatever the reason, somehow he didn't get from it what he wanted, but I never did know.

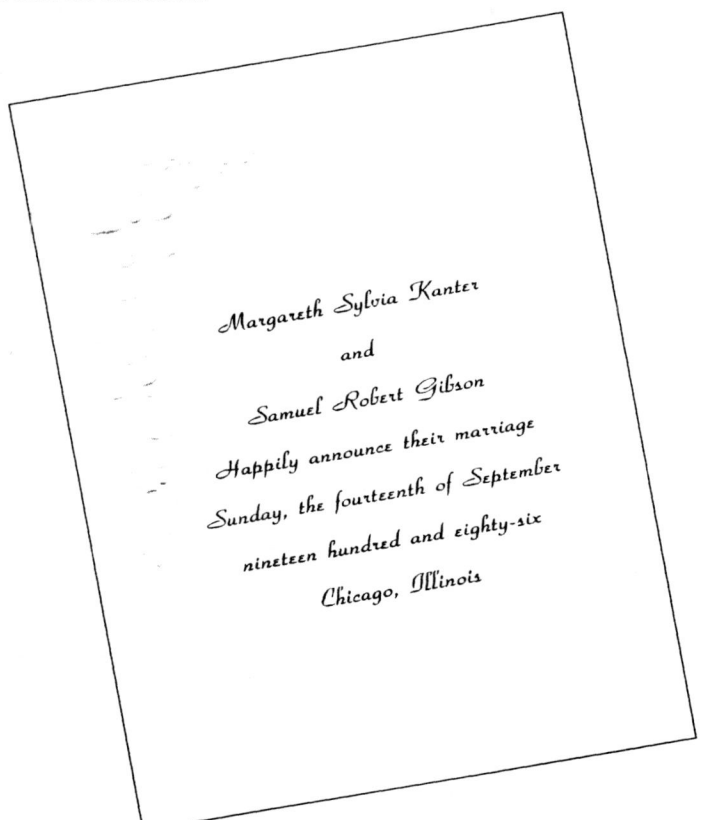

Margareth Sylvia Kanter

and

Samuel Robert Gibson

Happily announce their marriage

Sunday, the fourteenth of September

nineteen hundred and eighty-six

Chicago, Illinois

On September 14, 1986, Margie became the woman in Bob's life which led to an interest in family that he had never appreciated before.

16

AT LOOSE ENDS

The decade of the '80s was drawing to a close, and Bob could look back with great pride at his accomplishments. It had been a mere twelve years before that he had escaped the veil of drug addiction that had plagued the first twenty years of his career. In the brief time that followed, the whirlwind of activities Bob pursued was staggering. In twelve short years, he had begun his songwriting instruction career, reunited with Hamilton Camp for two albums, put out another album of his own, took part in the musical show, Chicago: Living Along the Banks of the Green River, *appeared on* Soundstage, *did his play* Courtship of Carl Sandburg, *became the owner of his own club,* Hobson's Choice, *participated in The Best of Friends, collaborated with Michael Smith on* The Women in My Life *and found a new audience in children as "Uncle Bob". In his own quiet way, he had reached the pinnacle of success in a way he never could have imagined in his earlier days. He had finally allowed himself to grasp the idea that success didn't have to mean hit records and huge audiences. Success had become the pursuit of perfection and the realization of his dreams. At no time in his life had Bob accomplished more. As the decade neared the end, though, the light dimmed for him. He quit doing Uncle Bob for reasons which are unclear and chose not to go any further with* The Women In My Life. *At the same time, he started having trouble with his marriage to Margie. Times were difficult emotionally, and work consisted of sporadic appearances at clubs, benefits and the annual Kerrville Folk Festival.*

George Matson:
> I met Bob as a friend in about 1987. I started taking private lessons from him. He was just wrapping up Uncle Bob. He was doing quite well at that time and was producing some children's recordings. But along about then was when he started having some troubles with his marriage and everything just kind of fell apart for him for awhile. He pretty much emotionally fell apart. Uncle Bob was a good gig and he was enjoying it and they seemed to like him as well. He never did tell me why he quit doing it. He explained the whole premise. It wasn't the actual show — it was the pre-show interviews and the post-show interviews, all that kind of thing that OshKosh benefited from. There were times when, because of the place where the show was, that there might only be 15-20 kids in

the audience, but it was the interviews surrounding the show that were valuable to OshKosh. From what I understand, they were real happy with him. I suspect that a lot of the reason he stopped was that things were coming apart for him.

He had been interested in doing some collaborations with an illustrator to do a children's book and so, after Uncle Bob, he was working on that. He did various gigs around.

Ian Shaw:

Bob used to have a pretty regular gig at a place called the Clearwater Saloon in the Old Town area in the late '80s. I saw the reunion show with him and Camp at the Old Town School in '89 or so. It was incredible. It was a packed house and the crowd knew every word. I remember his daughter, Sarah, walked right up on stage.

George Matson adds:

She did that quite a bit in later years. She was often on stage with dad. I think she's destined to be on stage, myself. She's learning piano, and she's really something else.

Rod Kennedy expanded his activities at the time and took Bob along:

I put Bob Gibson on the Napa Valley Folk Festival that I started in 1989 with Hamilton Camp. Hamilton and Bob played here a couple of times.

George Matson:

I think I got him involved in his last paying gig in Chicago before the effects of his illness really started to take their toll. It was a benefit for the Bluewater Boat Guild Underwater Archaeological Society, which is a restoration society for old wooden boats and stuff, and I was the emcee for the show. He asked if I'd play with him because he really couldn't play anymore so we had two 12-strings on the stage at once. He came in from California to do that show. I had to do some selling, because all of the members of that society were younger than I was. I said, "You guys, if you want to make a big splash, just get Bob in here." And it worked.

That was a magic night. He was to appear so far along in the evening that I didn't think he'd ever be able to pull that audience back. They had some very boring accounts of some various activities in the area, that kind of thing. And I thought, "Oh boy, how's he ever going to pull this audience back?" He got up there and he opened with the Great Lakes song and within three or four bars he had the audience right in the palm of his hand. It was just one of those magic nights. They just couldn't get enough of him. That was the latest I'd ever seen that place open. I was surprised they didn't get into trouble. It sounded great and it went over really well.

Then he did *The Perfect High* and he got to the last stanza and he forgot it. I was sitting there dumbstruck because I couldn't think of it either, and I know it by heart, but I just couldn't think. If I could have just called out a key word. I felt like if I'd ever let the man down, it would have to have been then. He fumbled around a little bit, but at that point it didn't really matter. The people who were there that night wouldn't have cared what he did. They were just glad to see him again. It was a very warm night.

It was a time of too few opportunities. There were no fans more loyal than those of Bob Gibson. Nevertheless, the loyalty didn't translate into enough income to help Bob through the hard times he was enduring. With his marriage over and a new life to begin, Bob was at a loss. His friend and neighbor, musician David Bragman remembers Bob's troubles then:

Bob was taking me to a meeting in his van. It was when I first moved into this apartment and I didn't have a car. He said on the way that Sarah had been sick and she needed to go to the emergency room, and it took all the money he had to take care of her. He said things were kind of slow. I said, "Have you ever thought of just getting a day job of some kind?" He looked at me and he said, "I don't know how to do anything else." That really stuck with me because here he is this legendary performer, and he's driving to a meeting telling me it took all the money he had to take care of his daughter. The song *Living Legend* comes to mind. He took it in stride. That was part of being an artist to him.

LIVING LEGEND

Ain't it great to be a living legend!
Hey, mister, can you use an old folk singer?
Would your patrons like some old time soul?
Can they dig the Foggy Mountain Breakdown?
Sorry, I don't play no rock 'n' roll.

Ah, but I can make 'em cry to Molly Darlin',
And sing along to Row Your Boat Ashore.
I'll play until the dawn, and when the crowd has gone,
Mister, I'd be glad to sweep the floor.

You shoulda been in New York in '60!
Hey, wasn't I a star there for a while?
But New York messed up my head,
And I got strung out on reds.
Bobby Dylan went and caught my style.

Ah, but I can make 'em cry to Molly Darlin',
And sing along to Row Your Boat Ashore.
The street life sure is fun when you're 21.
Mister, I ain't 21 no more.

I take the love of them that still remember.
I take the help of them that care to give.
I trade my songs for sandwiches and shelter.
Even living legends gotta live!

Ah, but I can make 'em cry to Molly Darlin',
And sing along to Row Your Boat Ashore.....

~Shel Silverstein
©Evil Eye Music

17

STOPS ALONG THE WAY

As time goes by a man begins
Looking back on where he's been,
Spending nights remembering other days.
All the old songs come to mind
Like friends and lovers left behind,
And all the stops we've made along the way.

When wine did pour and hearts did break
And chances were the thing to take,
Love was just another game to play.
When I look back I am surprised
At all the dangers I've survived,
And all the stops I've made along the way.

Along the roads that brought us here,
The footprints all are bright and clear.
Let's enjoy this moment while we may.
Let's not deny the other loves —
What we are we are because
Of all the stops we've made along the way.

Ah, the stops along the way,
Where the highway came together,
Stops along the way,
When I thought I'd live forever,
Love we thought would never end,
'Til we found out that they
Were just stops along the way.

(by Gibson/Silverstein — ©Robert Josiah Music)

    1990, the beginning of a new decade, became a time of promise and renewal for Bob — to once more emerge from the shadows and make it happen again.
    Ed Holstein remembers the beginning of it all:
        In 1990 I had a concert with Gibson and Camp at the Old Town School. It was a big deal — sold out. It was great. Just a typical

Gibson & Camp show. All the Highland Park doctors came who were Northwestern pre-med students when they were at the Gate of Horn and now 58 years old.

Allan Shaw remembers another very important event in Chicago and Bob's part in it:

In 1990, Dave Guard of the Kingston Trio was dying of cancer and requiring extensive medical treatments. He had no medical insurance. So a number of people, us included, sponsored some benefit concerts throughout the country. We were involved in two; one in St. Louis and one in Chicago. The Chicago one was held in the Old Town School of Folk Music. Bob Gibson, of course, was the logical one to ask to participate in the show for the Chicago people. Bob said, "Hey, I'd love to. I'm most happy to. Now, tell me about the show." So I said, "Well, Bob, we've got five acts," and I told him who they were; the Shaw Brothers, the Dooley Brothers and so on. He said, "And when would you like me to be on?" I said, "With your reputation, Bob, you're the best known performer who will be at this show, so I think it would be appropriate that you close it." He said, "Well, let me ask you a couple more questions. You say there are going to be five acts?" I said, "Yeah." He said, "What time are you starting?" I said, "Oh, eight o'clock." He said, "How long is each act going to go?" I said, "Oh, forty-five minutes." He said, "Allan, you know, that means that, even if you keep to the schedule, I'm not going to be until after eleven o'clock!" Then he said, "I hate to tell you this, but the people who would come to see me don't stay out that late! They're going to have gone home and gone to bed! If you want my crowd there, you better put me on no later than nine!" So I said, "Okay, thank you, Bob. We will." So he was the second act and went on about nine, and he was right! People left after he performed.

Maybe the audience did leave after the nine o'clock performance, but there can be no doubt that they would have stayed as late as was necessary to have seen Bob Gibson.

Things began to click again. Bob started putting together a show with a particular set of songs that worked well together and took it on the road performing at different venues around the Chicago area.

John Irons:

There was a big folk seminar in Bloomington, Indiana in May, 1991. It was like a gathering of all the folkies from the '60s. Lou Gottlieb, Oscar Brand, Mimi Fariña were all there. Bob and Mimi put on a show at Bear's Place in Bloomington, Indiana. The way they did it, Bob would do a song and Mimi would do a song and they'd talk a little bit about "Oh, this reminds me of this song," and just traded off for about an hour. A long time ago — many miles ago. I was his manager then. I was his manager about eight months or so.

May 16, 1991 was the date of the show Bob did with Mimi Fariña at Bear's Place. On May 20, the Indianapolis Star carried a review of the evening written by R. Joseph Gelarden:

A FOND VISIT TO WHEN WE WERE SIMPLE AND SO WAS LIFE

My neighbor, the big-time executive, and I took a road trip last week. It was a bona fide, laugh and sing, stay-out-late road trip.

Last Thursday after work, we kissed our wives and then drove to Bloomington to see a couple of folk singers. At least that was the excuse we used. In truth, the executive and I joined together for a secret journey back in time.

As the sun set, we arrived at a tiny club. We sat back in the wooden booth and a pleasant lady collected a $7 cover charge. The instant she stamped our hands, pixie dust fell from the ceiling and an unknown Hoosier spirit waved a magic wand over the room.

Suddenly it was 1963 and we were in a tiny folk music club. Only this time the crowd was balding and slightly overweight. There were more greys than blonds. Almost no one smoked.

There were no signs of the '90s. It was a simple time — before our lives were complicated by Vietnam, drugs, politics and decisions we were too scared to make, and too scared not to make.

On the tiny stage was a gray-headed fat little guy named Bob

Mimi Fariña & Bob in Bloomington, 1991

Gibson who played a banjo and a 12-string guitar. Next to him was a stunning 40ish woman named Mimi Fariña with dark hair. She accompanied herself on a fine Martin 6-string.

They sang simple songs of love, of relationships, of shipwrecks and nonsense. And we chuckled as Gibson sang of the *Mermaid from Ontario* who "loved a bass named Larry-O, who lived under the Ferry-O somewhere in Lake St. Clair-E-O."

As we sang along with them, the executive and I were no longer caught up in what he calls the real world. We didn't think of mortgages, or taxes, or the land mines that wait for our kids after they walk out the front door, or ChemLawn or Saddam Hussein and Scud missiles or the recession and layoffs.

As we sang along, the executive and I were once again 22 years old. Our eyes were clear, our heads had hair, our bellies were flat and our backs no longer hurt.

So for a couple of hours, we sipped beer, and sat stone still swaying with the music and pretending the moment wouldn't end. But after a two-hour show, we all sang an old Southern gospel hymn, filed out of the club and rejoined the '90s.

The next morning, as the sun peeked in the bedroom window and National Public Radio barked to life with tales of famine in Bangladesh and cholera in South America, I was jerked out of slumberland and kicked back to reality.

But for a moment — an evening — reality was Gibson and Fariña singing about the Mermaid from Ontario. And no one had an Excedrin headache, or reached for the Maalox or complained about anything.

And it was marvelous.

The momentum was building and just three days after this show, before the review had even appeared, on May 19, 1991, Bob was at Charlotte's Webb in Rockford, Illinois, for a show which would become, albeit on a small scale, a commercially released cassette called I Hear America Singing. *The tape consisted of sixteen songs recorded live that night. The audience was one of the most lively ones he had had and laughed and sang enthusiastically right from the start.*

Once again, Bob Gibson was back! John Irons spoke of how the emotional pieces came together:

> I've got a fairly big place, and I've got a completely finished basement. I ran cable TV downstairs; Bob had essentially his own shower and bathroom, laundry facility in another room. He had a bed and dresser and table and chairs down there, color television. We set up a sound system down there and that's where he started practicing getting *Stops Along the Way* ready.

November 16, 1991, on the occasion of Bob Gibson's 60th birthday, he invited about 80 friends to a recording session party at Bill Goldsmith's Paramount studio. John Irons made the arrangements and hosted the evening. Speakers were set up around the room directed so that the audience could hear themselves as they sang along with Bob. As Lynn Van Matre of the Chicago Tribune said, "The mood was warmly informal, with guests singing along from time to time. The songs were a mix of old and new, including traditionals such as Michael Row the Boat Ashore *and* No More Cane on the Brazos, *as well as more contemporary, socially conscious fare."*

The songs were designed to represent "stops along the way" in the career that, at that point, had lasted 38 years. Backing Bob on bass, once again was Michael Smith. He remembers:

> It was very unusual for me to say, "Bob, why don't you do this?" If I did say anything it had to do with the medlies he'd do. He had that *Play Me Some of the Old Songs* routine that used to DRIVE ME NUTS! As a musician, I don't want a minute of a song and then move to something else. I'm just starting to get the feel of the song when

it's time for him to go on to something else. I'd say, "Let's do the whole damn song all the way through and then stop and get some applause and then do the next song all the way through." In general, when I would talk to him about this, he would just ignore me in a kind of nice way, but he made it clear, you know, that "although you may have your opinions, I'm gonna do what I do." And that was fine with me, because he was a lot larger than I would ever understand or encompass.

The result of the concert was a CD called Stops Along the Way. *John Irons comments on the recording:*

In my opinion, *Stops Along the Way,* because of material, is one of Bob's best albums. It almost became *Stops Along the Road.* Bob and Shel wrote that song over the phone. Shel had been writing all these country-western songs so he was thinking more in terms of the word "road". I guess for the last 30 years I had been kind of toying with Zen, and my favorite book was *The Way of Chang Tzu.* I think in terms of the song itself, there are a lot more words that fit in with "way" than "road." That was my major contribution to *Stops Along the Way,* making it *Stops Along the Way* instead of *Stops Along the Road.* I was never too much into getting credit, though. I figured anything that I could do for Bob I would.

When we initially started talking about this, we realized if you're going to make any kind of a comeback, you have to have a CD because radio stations would not play tapes. They want CDs so they can go right to the specific cut. So once we decided to make a CD, I put together the material that I thought would make a good set and arranged it in order. Bob thought about it, and I even got a little note that said, "I'm going with John's set." The only variance made in the plan was that I wanted him to do *Easy Now.* I thought that would have been a really nice one right before "*How Could You Do This To Me?*" Bob used to deliver a rap on stage about how the song *Easy Now* was about his mother, but it was really her on *How Could You Do This To Me?* I thought that was kind of nice, but he dropped *Easy Now* because that was another song in the key of D and he didn't want too many songs in D on the record. If you listen to the whole CD, there are some comments in between the songs, and I thought that gave it a nice rounded affect. The way I set it up, the CD started off with his big hit *Michael Row the Boat Ashore* and then ended with *Living Legend* which ends with *Michael Row the Boat Ashore* and then *Stops Along the Way* which brings that kind of full circle of Zen back around again.

George Matson:

Bill Goldsmith had the place where *Stops Along the Way* was recorded. It was a corporate studio which, at the time, was really going strong doing a lot of commercial work. It was really slick and wanted for nothing in the way of recording equipment. There were about 80 people invited there that night and everybody knew the songs, so when he asked them to sing along, no one fumbled along.

To this Allan Shaw adds:
And then at the end we had birthday cake.

Following the release of the CD, Bob started making appearances to promote it and to recreate the mood of the party where it originated. He and Michael Smith kicked off this tour with a record-release party at the Clearwater Saloon in Chicago (3937 N. Lincoln Ave.) in early March, 1992. One of these promotional stops was reviewed in the April, 1992 issue of Boston Seniority *in an article by Jim Murray:*

AMERICA STILL HEARS HIM SINGING

In 1959, Club 47 in Harvard Square, Cambridge, was the center of the revival of folk music in America. It was there that a young Bob Gibson first heard an even younger Joan Baez sing and play. That same year Gibson brought Baez out onto the stage at the Newport Folk Festival, essentially launching her career.

Gibson, one of the original founders of the folk movement, yet not a commercially known recording artist, often jokes self-effacingly that his only claims to fame "are stuff like that I introduced Joan Baez — and now people are saying, 'Who's she?'"

A few weeks ago, Bob Gibson returned to the old Club 47 (named for its location — 47 Palmer Street, now known as Passim's) with a new album of songs, old and new (including his timeless *Abilene*, a commercial success for George Hamilton IV) addressing issues such as the environment, AIDS, and homeless Vietnam veterans.

On stage, Bob Gibson's crackling banjo and mastery of his trademark 12-string guitar are still awe-inspiring to folk music fans and folk musicians alike. "There's no one who can touch him," one of his contemporaries enthused recently. And just a few notes of *Daddy Roll 'Em*, a classic crystallized by Gibson's furious, yet seemingly effortless strumming and picking, is enough to convince any doubters.

Gibson's latest release, on his own label, is called *Stops Along the Way*. Recorded on his 60th birthday, last November, the album was made "live" with an "invitation only" audience of about 80 friends and family members. The material on the new release comprises the major part of his new one-man tour.

Gibson's voice remains confident and strong, unmistakenly that of the good-natured Chicagoan who burst onto the music scene while Eisenhower was still President. (For some unknown reason, folk performers of that era always "burst" onto the scene.) As the decade quickly turned to the "New Frontier" days of the Kennedy administration, folk music reflected the issues of the day with an increasing departure from traditional songs to songs of protest.

In 1964, Gibson and the late Phil Ochs co-wrote a stirring anti-war anthem entitled *Start the Parade*. The war in Vietnam was just beginning to "heat up," notes Gibson as he sang:

Cold hard stares on faces so proud,
Kisses from the girls and cheers from the crowd
While the widows from the last war are cryin' in their shrouds
Here comes the big parade, don't be afraid, the price is paid,
Start the parade.

As the packed audience applauds, Gibson speaks wistfully: "That was 28 or so years ago. We all know that 58,000 Americans were killed in Vietnam. But I recently heard that 112,000 Vietnam veterans have committed suicide."

Gibson is more than compassionate on the subject. A few years ago he played a benefit in Boston to aid homeless veterans of the Vietnam War.

"As a country, we still haven't come to any conclusion about the Vietnam War. You can have your position. You can be either for it or against it, or whatever. . . . How about all those guys who've come home? We've never recognized the contributions that they've made. So many of them are homeless now. We've never really come to grips with that. . ." He begins to strum his guitar as he launches into *Get Away*, his personal ode to homeless Vietnam vets.

Get away, get away, can't use you no more
Don't stand at my windows,
don't knock at my door.
'Cause we're tryin' to pretend there was never a war
And you're just a constant reminder.

Heavy stuff, but Gibson's deft chord changes and his soft rendition of those haunting lyrics bring home the message of pain without inflicting any.

The crowd is hushed, deeply moved, as Gibson flashes a bright smile and reminds one and all that folk music is also about "having a good time." He then barrels into a cheerful and whimsical tale of *The Mermaid of Ontario* whose boyfriend liked to sit around in his "underweario" and "read books from the fish librario." Gibson rapid-fires another little ditty about the computer age which is best left for hearing on compact disc, the lyrics being "grown-up" but riotously funny.

As our own world has changed much since those days of sit-ins and peace marches and "broadsides" at Newport, so has life changed for Bob Gibson. He has worked hard to overcome many personal challenges and strives to live a day at a time, having given up alcohol some 14 years ago.

"It wasn't that I was afraid of dying. I was afraid of living that way."

He has a three-year old daughter named Sarah for whom he sings an updated version of *Stella's Got a New Dress*, substituting, of course, "Sarah" for "Stella." "She just *loves* that," he beams, as he prepares to hit the road for yet another stop along the way.

For everyone in attendance the night the CD was recorded, it was a magical moment. So, too, it was for anyone listening to it later. For one last time, Bob was at the peak of his game. His head thrown back, singing from his soul, every movement he made at one with his guitar — and that smile! That infectious smile that won audiences everywhere he had ever performed. As he sang those familiar songs for his friends once more, did his mind return to those early days? Was he transported back to a time when the world was at his feet and the next step would have been the lasting fame that was to fall on Peter, Paul & Mary, Gordon Lightfoot, Bob Dylan and all those other legends who paid homage to him? How could he not be flashing back? Certainly the audience had to be reliving those days. Back to the time when Gibson & Camp at the Gate of Horn was the hottest album around. Back to Arthur Godfrey and Carnegie Hall. Back to the time, when for all outward appearances, Bob Gibson was reaching the peak of stardom.

Bob at Old Town School of Folk Music 1991

In 1964 Bob Gibson released what Rick Neely calls his best album, Where I'm Bound. *Judy Bell began her career at TRO Publishing Co., which then published Bob's music, and she remembers her first job there was to put together* The Bob Gibson Song Book, *which contained the music from that album. Bob knew, and those near him knew, that at that same time he had nearly self-destructed from his drug use and was soon to disappear. Ironically, in that same year the illness that was, forty years later, to be his final destruction, was first diagnosed in America and given a name. Now, nearly 30 year later, again at top form when he'd finally conquered all his demons and was embarking on one more comeback, Bob was to be hit by something over which he had no control. The symptoms began to appear around the time he did* Stops Along the Way.

John Irons:

Right around the time we made *Stops Along the Way*, we made one big tour. We went to Arkansas and Indiana and up to New York. The timing of the whole thing was just a little off, though. That was right around the time Bob was starting to show some symptoms. He was falling over a lot and he was also losing sensation in his left hand. He'd have to shake it to get the feeling back into it so he could play the guitar. His illness starting was a contributing factor to the end of his performing then. The other thing was that that was right around the time of the divorce, and Bob was getting desperate. Unfortunately there were just not a lot of venues to book to. I was making calls but it wasn't worth driving a whole bunch of miles to make $200.

If you walk away with say $200 and you're in a strange town — you've got fifty bucks for food plus whatever gas you used trying to get to the place, and then you've gotta eat while you're there, so by the time you accumulate the overhead, you've got maybe seventy-five bucks left. The other kicker is, it's not a 365 day job. It's primarily weekend work on Friday and Saturday. That makes it really rough because you have to make enough money on Friday and Saturday while you're on the road to carry you through Monday, Tuesday, Wednesday and Thursday. So that was what really doomed what Bob and I were trying to do. We could string a whole bunch of things together, but the real money that Bob made on those trips was from sales of CDs and tapes. That's really one of the reasons to go to some of these low-paying gigs if you've got product. That's where Tom Paxton and Peter, Paul and Mary are brilliant. They've got a jillion things to sell.

The falling got worse. Doctor after doctor disappointed Bob with their inability to diagnose his problem. He became difficult to be around and one by one, people dropped out of his life. His marriage to Margie had come to an end, but Bob kept pushing himself. He continued to perform as long as he could, promoting the CD. At that same time there was also a pilot for a Saturday morning TV show starring Gibson in the works, and work got more serious on the album that had been planned for so long with Shel.

He prepared himself for his annual visit to the Kerrville Folk Festival, which, for 12 years, had been the highlight of every year. This year was to be different, though, and must surely have seemed like the hardest blow of all. Rod Kennedy:

I was getting a hint that there was something wrong with him because he was not remembering faculty and students' names. I knew there was something wrong. In fact I called Tom Paxton in New York and I said, "You know, there's something wrong with Bob. He's having brain showers or little strokes or something. He's not remembering people's names, and he's just not doing what he used to do and he doesn't know it." I talked to him about it and he didn't have any answer for me, and I said, "I'm going to have to replace you in the songwriting school because the kids are not getting their money's worth out of this." After I asked him to step down I heard that his critiques had become damaging to the students.

Everything seemed to be falling apart for him. He broke up with Margie; he was nasty to Anne Hills and they split and didn't work together anymore; Tom Paxton quit producing his records — all right in that time period there. Nobody knew what was going on except they just didn't want to be around him. One of his favorite expressions was, "I'll break your knees." He got that from his drug and alcohol days, and he used that quite a bit. Then I don't know, I guess he actually quit playing the festival about a year after that. We talked on the phone but I didn't have any more contact with him. That was just toward the end though that he was like that. We had a whole bunch of great years. Bob spent a lot of happy years at Kerrville. He was an engaging performer. *Looking for the You in Someone New* — God, that was a great song!

George Matson remembers the agony he went through not knowing what was happening to him:

Bob had been with Leslie Korshak for a while. That's when his disease was really starting to take its toll. She had told me about several shows that he had done where he forgot lines and lyrics and couldn't play as well — couldn't do the things that he used to do. He was really quite ill, and nobody could figure it out. He had gone to many, many different doctors including his former brother-in-law and nobody was able to pinpoint this thing. Bob was under the care of a Russian herbalist in Milwaukee for awhile before the diagnosis had been made. He had some really potent herbal medicaments — nothing in pill form. It was all fresh. He was also a visualist who was able to visualize what was going on in your body. I didn't know how sound this whole thing was, but it seemed to lift his spirits, so I figured, "Go for it!" He told Bob that he had to sing everyday because that was what he really needed to be well.

Leslie Korshak:

I'd known Bobby since the Gate of Horn days. I met Bobby and Shel when they were 28 and I was 14. I was the one in the liner notes "who said nothing," and, oh, have I made up for it. I knew at 14 that Bobby and I were going to end up together at the end of his life, because I never met anybody who was so alone in the middle of so much. I used to tease him, "You're the most alonest critter I've ever met." With Bobby and Shel I was just a kid — like a little mascot. First of all, the care and feeding of Bob Gibson involved total concentration, but there was just such an element of totality when Bobby and I finally did get together and we did this wonderful little romance.

With things falling apart for him, Bob finally decided to pack up and move back to his beloved Mendocino, which had been a place of creative rebirth for him before.

Leslie Korshak:
Right after *Stops* we decided to leave Chicago together. We had to move my house in New Orleans and then we had to pack up and move his office. Bobby had been living at John Irons' house, and he moved out and put a mattress in his office on Hood Street, and we just stayed there while we went through sorting, saving, tossing, packing and left from the office. We rented a big Ryder truck. The tag on the side said "A Moving Experience" and in Bobby fashion, he rearranged the tape on the M so it said "A Loving Experience." We left and headed west during the blizzard in Feb of '92.

As we travelled to Mendocino he was doing a lot of house concerts which he loved because, unlike a lot of performers, he loved listening to people who were talking to him. We went across country sleeping in basements and bedrooms and I watched people turn young in front of him. I've watched as gray-haired car salesmen, bankers, doctors — you know, the middle aged groupies — so often just disappear, and you could see their young critter selves as they listened to Bobby do *Baba Fats [Perfect High]*. There were a couple of talk songs like that that were really important in those last few years because Bobby could do those and rely on his character and involve people in conversation. In fact the conversation before and after took twice as long as the concert. He did a lot of larger venue concerts, too, but the more this disease got hold of him the more comfortable he was in smaller and smaller venues. Even in Bobby's heyday, he was always an intimate performer. The Gibson magic was that he could take a big room and make it small and a small room and turn it into a concert hall. He was one of the few people in the world who could do that. Sammy Davis could do it, but very few people have that ability.

For a long time he was the only one who knew he was sick. We spent four years going across the country getting misdiagnosed. Then, of course, the medication that goes with the diagnosis that was inappropriate also got introduced. Everybody else gave up. Most doctors gave up because they didn't know what it was, and so we kind of grew more isolated.

I thought we were going to end up taking a quick exit from the left lane on a freeway and both of us were going to be smashed on one of those dividers because he had no business driving. But when the doctors are telling you it's blood pressure, or eye problems... We must have changed his eyeglasses

Bob doing *Perfect High* in a house concert

12 times in a year. It had nothing to do with his eyes! It was the muscles controlling them that weren't working. So we'd drive and he'd be changing glasses all the time. He was determined he was able to drive — he wasn't able to play the guitar, but by-God he was able to drive — and he wasn't!

We spent an awful lot of time planning, although we knew he was never going to do it, a one man show using the backdrop of the old Gate of Horn.

Bobby became heroic as he came back to Mendocino and put together his life. He did that with grace and humor. He was a man who came to terms and did it very well. In those four years as the music diminished, he became his own man. There was no more hiding behind that big 12-string.

L-R: Gene Parsons, Bob and Meridian Green - 1992

18

Makin' A Mess

Bob's problems continued to intensify after Stops Along the Way. *Living in Mendocino and then Ft. Bragg, near Mendocino, he became unable to play his instruments, and was still no closer, at that time, to knowing what was going on inside of him.*

Michael Smith recalls seeing Bob again after the Stops Along the Way *times:*

>The second to the last time I saw him was in San Francisco. He was living out there and I was working a gig and. Bless his heart, he came down to see me. It was a surprise. I didn't expect that at all. By that time we had not done much together for awhile. He was living in Mendocino then, and I guess it was a couple of years before he died. There were two other times he did something like that. After *Women In My Life* I got a gig with Steppenwolf to do *The Grapes of Wrath*. I invited Bob, and he came and was very complimentary. We went on tour with it, so after that I didn't see much of him for two or three years. Then right after that I started doing a biographical play, *Michael, Margaret, Pat & Kate,* and he came to that also. He was very nice to me about both of these things. I definitely consider him a mentor in a sense that it was real important to me that I have a good opinion from him. The situation was a little tense, though. On both these occasions, he had difficulty and was different, and this, I assume, had something to do with his illness. There was almost a shyness in his appearance — like a little kid in some way. I wasn't aware at the time of his illness yet, so it made me rnervous. He was really physically retired. I was used to this guy who didn't really care what you thought of him, and who was very direct and businesslike in the way he approached things — kind of cold and closed. He used to walk into a room, and he wasn't like "Tah-Dah!", but he was sure of himself. Now. by contrast,suddenly it was as if he was thinking, "Do you still like me?" I was confused, but he was a very close individual and you couldn't ask him flat out.

Uncertain of how he fit in anywhere anymore and whether he ever would again, plans kept being made around him. A sense of panic must have overwhelmed him as he faced life not knowing if he would ever recover or just keep deteriorating. For some time, Bob and Shel Silverstein had talked about doing an album with Bob singing Shel's songs. Bob recorded several different demo versions of a variety of

Shel's songs, but as time went by, he became uncertain that he could pull it off. Shel finally insisted it could work. He said he could get Nashville studio musicians and friends to help out on instruments and vocals. Then he got together with Kyle Lehning of Asylum Records and plans started to finally become reality.

George Matson:

At that point, Bob was in the throes of trying to discover what was wrong with him. He was very distraught and cranky and tough to deal with.

Diane DeVry, long time friend:

The Bob Gibson story has been an odyssey for me. I had known him since 1955 at the Off Beat Room. I started to lose track of Bob due to his abuse of drugs, but mostly due to my not being anywhere he was or with anyone who cared about my love of his music and what it added to my life.

I heard from him again in 1994 when he was in the middle of trying to find a diagnosis for his illness. He came to my home in Florida, played for my sixtieth birthday party, and I took him to the Mayo Clinic in Jacksonville on April 19. I gave him my bed so he'd be comfortable and then went off to a pallet. He was so sweet and always shy. I felt after all these years, I had him to myself and was, before, during, and after his stay, on an elevated plane of gratefulness for the gift he gave us.

Allan Shaw:

Glenn Yarbrough called me about six weeks after that and said, "Did you hear about Bob? He was at the Mayo and they diagnosed it as 'Progressive Supranuclear Palsy.'"

Work was nearly complete on the album when Bob received his diagnosis. On one hand, it was a weight off his shoulders to know at last what he was facing. On the other hand, the news was grim, and everyone now knew this would be Bob Gibson's last recording effort. The one song remaining to be cut was I Hear America Singing. *Shel put out the word, and in no time had assembled a magnificent tribute to Bob.*

Josh White Jr. remembers the call:

When Gibson was doing his last album down in Nashville, that's when we first heard Bob had a problem, and Shel had this one tune that he was going to ask people if they could come down to Nashville and all do a choir thing for this song. If this was what I could do for Gibson — come in and sing along with him — I'd do it. We all came together. We met at the studio and there were lots of interviews about the album. I'd not seen Spanky McFarlane in years, so we reminisced, and then we did just the one tune, *I Hear America Singing*. Just to be able to be there when someone called and said, "Can you do it" for someone you've admired and loved for so long, it was a pleasure. There's a good feeling to sing around good singers, some that you've admired, some that maybe you've not met, and those you've not seen for a long time. It was great for me to be in Ed McCurdy's presence. He's a wonderful, wonderful man!

The press package put out by Asylum Records on the release of Makin' A Mess, *described the session and its significance:*

On July 25, 1994, many of the greatest names in folk music, past and present, gathered in Nashville to record *I Hear America Singing,* the final song on *Makin' a Mess: Bob Gibson sings Shel Silverstein.* The album, released by Asylum in January, 1995, is in one sense a tribute by one of the most influential and enduring voices in folk music to one of the most unique songwriters ever to embrace the format. The climactic Nashville session, though, was a loving homage solely to Gibson, himself.

After recording the bulk of the album, Gibson was diagnosed with a form of Parkinson's Disease. Thus, the addition of *I Hear America Singing,* an inspirational anthem in its own right, took on deeper significance as a celebration of an artist who has not only touched all those who made it their duty to come to Nashville to sing along, but so many of today's top singer/songwriters, who, like Silverstein, credit Gibson as a mentor.

Indeed, the participants read like a "Who's Who" of folk and beyond. Besides Gibson and Silverstein, they include Tom Paxton, Spanky McFarlane, Ed McCurdy, Josh White Jr., Glenn Yarbrough, Oscar Brand, Dennis Locorriere, Emmylou Harris, John Brown, John Hartford and Peter Yarrow of Peter, Paul & Mary.

"There are other families in show business, but the family of folk musicians turns out for each other with such naturalness," Yarrow says. "We really do care about each other. We are here to celebrate Bob and the music and honor this connection."

"It was a celebration about him down in Nashville," says Ed McCurdy. "We all got together — almost all the singers you can think of who associated with that type of song — and we spent a couple of days loosely associating, and then we all got together and sang.

"All these people from my shady background," joked Gibson, one of the few folk singer-songwriters to come out of the '50s and still impact heavily on the '90s. "It's been wonderful to see them. I'm so moved. Some of these people haven't seen each other in 30 years."

The album was co-produced by Shel Silverstein and Kyle Lehning, who heads Asylum Records in Nashville and also owes much to the Gibson-Silverstein connection.

It is an inventive, eclectic collection, running from the sublime to the ridiculous. The album offers 13 shining examples of trademark Silverstein, as sung by his longest-lasting musical friend and collaborator.

Bob said, "It was so hard to narrow it down, because Shel had so many good songs. There's the straight-ahead, vulnerable Shel

Silverstein of *Whistlers & Jugglers,* and *Stops Along the Way,* and the funny, caustic Shel Silverstein of *Still Gonna Die, Killed By A Coconut,* and *Makin' A Mess of Commercial Success.* The thing about Shel is, he's always kept his integrity. I attribute all my success to him — as he does me."

The fruits of their relationship have never been sweeter. *Makin' A Mess* is an irreverent, poignant, worldly and passionate look at life. And on many levels it is as complex and compelling as the two men who made it possible.

A wonderful addition to the Bob Gibson collection is a radio interview that Studs Terkel did on his WFMT radio show to promote the release of the Makin' A Mess CD. *A Chicago legend, Pulitzer Prize winner and long time fan of Bob's, Studs Terkel had interviewed him many times over his nearly 40 year career and had written the liner notes for his* Yes I See *album. This particular interview went so well, not to mention the fact that it captured a moment in history in which three of the most monumentally famous Chicagoans sat down to talk, that it was released as a limited edition CD itself. Following are excerpts from this interview which aired on July 28, 1994.*

Studs Terkel: This album is, in a sense, autobiographical, a reflection of the world, funny... Put out by Asylum — What a great name for a record company!
Bob: Sanctuary! Sanctuary!
Studs: In a sense *Stops Along the Way* is Bob Gibson's saga. It's Bob's autobiography, and at the same time, it's everybody's. It's the common denominator. It's the kind of people we've met along the way. I know we all can recount it. That's one of the, what I call, poignant songs on the album. All of us are thinking about health and diet and food, but everything else is processed. So I'm thinking about this song *Nothin's Real Anymore.*
Shel: You can spend a good part of the day and never touch anything that's the way it was.
Studs: So this song captures it. I'm thinking now about you two collaborating, Bob as the performer and Shel now and then coming in in your gravely chorus — a bass baritone/tenor/alto all rolled into one.
Shel: No, Bob never allowed me to sing with him. He drew the line there. *(Actually the voice that sounds like Shel singing on this CD is that of Dennis Locorriere.)*
Studs: Then, one of the funniest songs I've heard, which Bob offers in a dry kind of humor, combined with Shel's zany kind of humor, is *Killed By A Coconut.*
Shel: It just has to do with fate coming along and dealing with you no matter what you do. I wrote it with Even Stevens in Florida.

Studs: This is the best example of fate ever put into song! But then again we have the juxtaposition of the sentimental in the best sense songs, the memory songs.

Bob: These are the ones that I love to do, the ones where Shel is very vulnerable. He's doing *Whistlers and Jugglers,* and nobody can write like he can.

Shel: This really has to do with my observation of performers. Most performers or successful show people — men — the women that they wound up with started out as fans, groupies. And the thing about a groupie is, that a groupie can also be a groupie of somebody else, too. So somebody who is attracted by performers, could be attracted by a new performer. And the men know that. Certainly the reality of the life together was not as glamorous.

Studs: At the same time, it's almost as though the world were a clown show, too. And Bob's interpretation of Shel's observation is very moving.

Shel: The gratifying thing for me, when Bob sings my songs, is that he can get the humorous stuff and he can get the dramatics. He just feels all of it.

Studs: One funny, dramatic one is very pertinent to the world we're watching today. It's called *Makin' a Mess of Commercial Success.* Now we know, day after day we are inundated with the beer commercials with those young oafs and their consorts there, and we see them again and again and the vulgarity and the commercial aspects — it's quite obvious.

Shel: Well, this one I wrote with Mickey James and it just has to do with what could be a reality in doing a beer commercial when you try to make it authentic, what could very likely happen — what I wish would happen! And, incidentally, it came very close to happening. It was based on a commercial that they were shooting in Key West while we were there, and they did indeed take the saloon and fix it up and they started bringing in people and it got a little out of hand.

Studs: So on this one, Bob Gibson is a storyteller. He narrates it and tells that story. And this has to do with the nature and the arrogance of TV.

Shel: They assume that you should be honored that they are shooting on your street and being there, blocking off traffic and not letting you park, and they couldn't get away with it for any other reason. But somehow the word "TV" is supposed to — and it DOES — people do respect it and they worship TV that much that it just becomes a holy experience.

Studs: You know, they suffer all sorts of humiliation and inconvenience just the fact that they're being celebrated. They're on TV! Not just the commercial - that, of course, just makes it even more grotesque — but features, newscasts go into homes, interviews, and you're supposed to be honored. You know, sometimes a guy who's gone crazy — he might be a returned vet or someone else — holding hostages, and you don't know what to do. He'll give himself up to the TV anchor man! So the, "Ma, I'm on TV!" Basically that's it. This has happened — I'm not kidding — this has happened very often.

Shel: It's going to be more and more so with the greater love and respect people have for TV.

Studs: That's why this song is so good. It's something you hoped would happen. We've touched on life, food, lives of jugglers and whistlers, comic songs about fate and stops and those we've met. But then there's technology, too. Nothing escapes. The song is called *The Man Who Turns the Damn Thing Off and On*. So he's a guy, he's a tender of a machine.

Shel: He's the last working man.

Studs: That's what we're seeing, isn't it, to some extent? Less and less of the human touch. This is beyond automation.

Shel: This is pretty positive, too. We're assuming that they're still gonna need one person to start the machine. They may not, though. They might be able to beat that.

Studs: In this album, there's a connection of all these songs. *Nothing's Real Anymore,* the automation song, the beer commercial, and then you have the human ones, the clowns and jugglers, and people along the way. So it leads to life, itself, doesn't it? Life and what follows. And so, we come to the song, *You're Still Gonna Die*. No matter what you do, what sort of life you live — it could be a celebrate life, it could be any kind of life, you could be following all the foods, you could be any age — now this is universal.

Bob: You aren't going to get out of this one alive!

Shel: Well, a lot of us live as if we aren't going to. They think that by taking enough good care that they're gonna. I'm very healthy in my diet. I just don't want to kid myself that it's gonna do more than I think.

The idea of the song is to have some fun in your life if it's possible, with all the information we have now. I don't know if it's possible. I think we have too much information. I mean, knowing what we know, that anything pleasurable can kill us, I don't know how much pleasure it's possible to have — how much total pleasure. When you didn't know, you could just have some fun and if you keeled over that was okay. Now we know that everything can hurt us, so I think that stops us from having total pleasure.

Bob: For over 35 years I've been leading people singing and trying to locate the anthem, and I finally found it, and I got to lead all my friends singing! It was wonderful!

Studs: This is a song that Shel wrote, of course, based on an old vision of Walt Whitman, *I Hear America Singing*. In a way, that's what Bob's life and those of the singers who preceded him were, whether it be Woody or Pete Seeger or down the line of Blues singers that all influenced you and those who followed. So Bob it's a tribute to you, and your rich and rewarding and gifted life.

While a distinct departure from the Bob Gibson folk style, this CD, recorded in the capital of country music, was well-received and generated many favorable reviews:

Jonathan Takiff - Philadelphia Daily News - March 3, 1995

The first great pop-folk singer, Bob Gibson, and a hip humor-warped folk original, Shel Silverstein, have been good buds and occasional collaborators for more than three decades. So it's no surprise that this project goes down like buttah, with lots of laughs and bittersweet insights about time's passage spread along the way.

Silverstein, known equally well for his kiddie yarns and Playboy contributions, amuses both contingents with songs like *Nothing's Real Anymore* (from fake eggs to fake breasts) and the calypso beat *Killed By a Coconut*. The latter's one of several clever songs about nature's way of catching us when we least suspect. Bemused and bitter are ditties like *The Man Who Turns the Damn Thing Off and On*, the tale of a poor sap reduced to flipping a big mama computer's power switch.

Jimmy Buffet devotees should check out this set; these are the guys who really wrote the book. (★★★ - Worthy)

Steve Matteo - New Country - April, 1995

While the urban coffeehouses of Greenwich Village and Cambridge, Massachusetts, may come to mind when one thinks of folk music's heyday, Chicago once boasted a folk hotbed, The Gate of Horn. There Bob Gibson became one of the most important folk figures of the late '50s and early '60s as both a solo artist and as half of the duo Gibson and Camp. Now 64, Gibson has made a record that picks up where his folk recordings left off, but he has injected just enough modern commentary and smooth country twang to see him reborn as a '90s artist.

Gibson is more than comfortable interpreting songs. His choosing the songs of artist/author Shel Silverstein is natural, since Silverstein has a long-standing relationship with Chicago and the two men wrote songs together during the heady days of '50s folk.

Gibson doesn't sound anything like his 64 years, and he clearly enjoys singing Silverstein's songs, which effectively poke fun at many current fads. On both *Still Gonna*

Die and the sweet, fiddle-filled *Nothin's Real Anymore,* Gibson sings about how all the diets, workouts and polyunsaturated fats still won't bring immortality. Given that Gibson has a form of Parkinson's Disease, he seems to face his own transience with every word.

The highlight is *I Hear America Singing,* something of a tribute to the true American spirit, folk music and even Gibson himself.

For anyone who thinks a 64-year-old ex-folkie can't make a record that's fun, funny and contemporary, *Makin' a Mess* is proof to the contrary.

Mordecai J. Hines II - Country Star - March, 1995

Bob Gibson's more than 45 years in show business have been spent primarily as a folk singer/songwriter/acoustic guitarist/banjo player, but he has also taught at the Chicago Conservatory of Music, Portland State University and the Kerrville Songwriters School.

Between them, Gibson and Silverstein have written some interesting and humorous country classics in the past 35 years.

Makin' a Mess: Bob Gibson Sings Shel Silverstein honors the remarkable gifts of songwriting and humor. This pure, traditional combination will make this album hard to beat at next year's Grammys.

Dan Bennet - North County Blade-Citizen, Oceanside, CA - March 3, 1995

Joining the king of American folk with one of the genre's most skilled songwriters, *Makin' a Mess* is sublime seduction for those who grew up cherishing this music.

Gibson is the undisputed master of the form. Gibson delivers Silverstein's songs with impeccable understanding and phrasing, joined in the end by some of the greatest names in folk history on *I Hear America Singing.*

Bill Jarnigan - Times Daily/Sunday - February 26, 1995 - Alabama Beat

ALBUM SURE TO TICKLE FUNNY BONE

One of the funniest, delightfully musical albums to debut lately has been a collaboration by Nashville singer/songwriter Bob Gibson as he sings tunes created by the eccentric artist Shel Silverstein.

Lisa Grider - Easy Reader, Hermosa Beach, CA - March 9, 1995

Those of us who can recall our childhood years might remember reading a story entitled *The Giving Tree,* or another called *Where the Sidewalk Ends.* For those people the name Shel Silverstein holds dear memories of fantasy and happy endings.

But you might not realize is that Silverstein is also an accomplished poet, cartoonist and songwriter as well. Silverstein's wisdom appeals to the child in everyone.

If the name Bob Gibson sounds familiar, that's because it is. You've probably been exposed to his musical talent more than you realize. He was a big part of the '50s Greenwich Village folk scene, where he met Woody Guthrie. One of the most notable songs he is responsible for is *Abilene*. Through the early 1980s, however, Gibson focused mostly on children's music.

This collaborative album is yet another spirited achievement, with songs that will make you laugh and that will make you feel good. The farcical world of Silverstein coupled with the musical talent of Gibson should appeal to nearly everyone.

George Matson:
I thought he did a nice job on some of the songs like *Never Be This Young Again,* and *Fancy Ladies* — that was one of his songs that he'd recorded many, many years earlier and had always been a one of my favorite songs of his. One of the lines in that song is, "Ghost wreckers spread dishonest lights." What they used to do is put lights out over by reefs to run ships up on the reefs, and they would pick all the flotsam that came in — called them ghost wreckers. I never caught the significance of it, but Bob did because he was really into Great Lakes history.

Leslie Korshak:
Whistlers and Jugglers wasn't even supposed to be on that album, but a last minute replacement song was needed, and while they had a couple of hundred to chose from, the time seemed right for the true love song of Bob and Shel. That's a really precious gift from both of them — not gimmicky. It was a Saturday, and there were no other musicians in the studio. Kyle Lehning and Joey Bogen worked the console. Bobby did it on the first take. Then he kind of edged onto a stool in the recording studio about three feet away from the glass that separated the studio from the control room. I sat facing him just below the work area occupied by Joey, Kyle and Shel. We were all crying, and when Joey turned the last dial, Kyle said, " If you don't like that, you don't like Christmas."

The title of that album, by the way, was supposed to be *Still gonna Die,* but when it finally became all too apparent that Bobby *was,* "Gibstein" (as I called Bobby and Shel) got their heads together and decided on *Makin' a Mess.* Nothing pretentious, no *Bob Gibson's America* — just Bobby and Shel, hanging out and makin' a mess. Not unlike *The Train that goes To Morrow,* which everyone thinks is funny, but Bobby always thought the most profound song he ever wrote. The final title of that last album is far more than a line from a song. It's who they were, how they viewed and lived life, how they each created careers and friendships.

Glenn Yarbrough's daughter Holly had known of Bob all her life, and she recalls with fondness the one time she went to see him:

The only time I remember spending time with Bob on my own was when Folk Era asked me to write something about *I Hear America Singing*. I went and met with him in his apartment in Chicago. Well, he wasn't living here, he was visiting his ex-wife and his little girl and they were going out to see the *Lion King* for the third time, and his little girl was all excited. This was shortly after he was diagnosed, and it was about probably no more than a month or so after they finished up recording in Nashville. I don't remember what I wrote quite honestly, but I remember how incredibly excited he was about the song *I Hear America Singing*. He was just like a little kid. A lot of artists are like that. They have this thing, and they just want to share it so badly, so we sat and listened to the song. I was so moved by it. It's just a wonderful song. I really got the feeling at that meeting that he felt that that song was the pinnacle of his career. He seemed really peaceful — just with his daughter and his music. It was really nice.

The group that gathered for the Bob Gibson folk reunion July 25 in Nashville: (top row) Cathryn Craig, Tom Paxton, Peter Yarrow, John Hartford, Emmylou Harris, John Brown, Kyle Lehning; *(second row)* Dennis Locorriere, Oscar Brand, Bob Gibson, Ed McCurdy, Glenn Yarbrough; *(bottom row)* Barbara Baily Hutchinson, Shel Silverstein, Spanky McFarlane, Josh White Jr.

Photo from Bob Gibson collection

Photo from Bob Gibson collection

Photo from Bob Gibson collection

19

THE ILLNESS

With great physical difficulty, his voice nearly gone by this point, Bob Gibson spoke in June, 1996, about his illness — its symptoms and its devastating progression — from his apartment in Portland, Oregon:

The symptoms of my illness started to show up about five or six years ago. I started falling a lot and I went through all these twists and turns with the doctors there. I tried all kinds of alternative therapy from diets to everything else. By 1993, when I was living in Fort Bragg, near Mendocino, I had deteriorated to the point that finally my daughter, Susan, said, "Dad, why don't you just realize that the doctors in Fort Bragg are not helping you?" That is when I made the last move of my life to Portland. Mendocino was my favorite place to live. Northwest California. It's gorgeous. I would be there yet, but there was more work being done on PSP in Portland, Oregon. That, combined with the fact that my daughter Susan lived there, prompted my move.

George Matson:
   Once the diagnosis was made, it was like a load was lifted off his shoulders, because for so long he hadn't known what was going on. After the diagnosis he was fighting the enemy he knew and not the unknown fear. He felt that "now we know what's going on, let's deal with it." That seemed to give him some focus and direction. Then he came back to Chicago for awhile and then finally went back west to live in Portland. When he would come to Chicago after that, he would stay at my house for the most part or sometimes with Margie.
   Somewhere in there also he made amends with Meridian because they were estranged for quite awhile. Then when things fell apart with Leslie out there, he went out to Fort Bragg and just put everything in storage. At that point he was needing some financial assistance. I bought his banjo from him and he was trying to put things together a little bit, but it was not working real well.

PSP — Progressive Supranuclear Palsy. Supranuclear means part of the brain stem. It doesn't do well. It's supposed to take messages from the eyes quickly — but no more. This disease has really hampered me and, one stage at a time, has taken away all my faculties. The first thing that is affected is the balance, then the eyes, and then the voice goes. Now it's the voice — the breathing control and stuff. I was very appalled by it the last couple of months when I've gotten quite a bit worse. The only pain involved is just from slamming myself around. I lose my balance and fall a lot and end up with all these bruises.

Sometimes I cough and I pass out. It feels like the days when I'd shoot a lot of cocaine and stuff. I feel so similar that I wonder if they're not related. I don't know if my drug use has caused what I have now, but I'm waiting for some reason to be this way. I don't know any. They say it's like a virus. There are only 20,000 people in the United States who have my symptoms. There aren't 500,000, like Parkinson's disease, so there's not the money to research it. They know that the MRI — magnetic response imaging — study shows the black nerve brain stem as having some white spots on it. Oh boy!

Physician John Rumler commented on the history and effects of Progressive Supranuclear Palsy:
PSP wasn't diagnosed until 1964 and is only about two percent as common as Parkinson's disease. Symptoms include a loss of balance, forgetfulness, trembling hands and blurred vision. Slurred speech and an inability to maintain eye contact often give the mistaken impression of senility.

According to Dr. Lawrence Golbe of the University of New Jersey School of Medicine, a small percentage of PSP patients suffer mental impairment which is misdiagnosed as Alzheimer's. "The symptoms of PSP are caused by a gradual deterioration of brain cells in a few tiny but important locations in the brain," he said.

Scientists are unable to determine what triggers the deterioration, and there is no known cure.

I have such a hard time. I used to be such a verbose guy and loved to tell my life story. There's so much quaking with this. I don't like it at all. It's really a drag. I'm realizing that I'm failing very quickly now. I fall down a lot, sometimes several times a day, and I'm not supposed to get out of the chair unless I'm with somebody. The eyes are blurry in terms of vertical. Side to side it's OK. The vertical takes a long time to reconcentrate. That's why if I see something low, I can manage, but that means that I've gotta get my eyes in focus when I look up. It's made it impossible to read. I can't read, and I got a computer a year ago — I gave it all up. Oh, thank God for television.

Susan Hartnett commented on the toll the illness took on her father:
With the onset of PSP about five years ago, Dad quietly slipped

from the performing stage into the shadows. It ended his career. His voice was once a very clear tenor, but it changed. His hand-eye coordination deteriorated, along with his stamina, to a point where it was impossible for him to continue.

It's very sad to me, that at this point in his life he has nothing that has any real meaning to him. He hasn't written anything and he hasn't shown any indications that he'd like to write anything. From my observation, it's just that since he can't be what he was, he doesn't want to be anything at all. Over the last three years he's gotten so he couldn't play and he couldn't sing and he couldn't write — I mean literally write as opposed to think of the music. About 18 months ago, maybe more, he was playing the banjo and he made a comment about how he couldn't stand the way he sounded or something. I said, "Oh, Dad, that sounds great!" He said, "No, it doesn't sound the way it did before!" I said, "Well, maybe it's not as good as it was before, but it's still very good music!" And he said, "Well, if it can't be what it was, I don't want it at all!" To me that was a very revealing comment of how tied he was to the perfection he once achieved. He felt that how the world thought of it was more important. It wasn't like he was performing for anyone, but that was his feeling about playing. If he couldn't play, if he couldn't be what he had been as a musician, he didn't want to play music at all. It was a drag for him that he couldn't find a way to find some enjoyment out of what he had done for so long.

George Matson:
I told Bob one time, "I can't imagine what you're going through." And Bob said, "It's nice for you to say that, because everyone always says, 'Oh, yeah, I know...', but you don't know." I said, "I can't imagine what it would be like to be on top of your game and then not be able to play anymore at all."

John Irons:
Bob had a lot of material that he wrote that he never really sang anywhere just because he thought it wasn't really that good, but he figured "Later on if I ever need it I could always go back to it" because he thought the voice and everything would always be there. I suppose we're all like that. We think that everything should be there forever. I guess the whole concept's a joke — all that stuff that doesn't kill me makes me stronger. Oh? Stronger for what? The next miserable thing that's gonna happen? None of us gets out of it alive. I'm not quite sure that was ever the goal. In a lot of ways Bob kind of followed his own drummer, and there's nothing wrong with that.

Bob had spent the early part of his life as an inovator in the music field. With music now behind him, his breakthroughs didn't stop.

Leslie Korshak:

So many of the things that Bobby pioneered in medicine he didn't know he was doing. I've spoken with doctors all over the world who said, "You know more about this than we do." PSP patients fall backwards. He used to fall in slow motion — how he never killed himself is a mystery to me. He was going to physical therapy which he was religious about and he fell leaving a bus on his way to physical therapy and so now he had the reality of the falling plus the anticipation and the fear of it. So we were talking and I said, "You need to tell the doctors that you've added this fear, because if it stops you from physical therapy you'll disappear. It has to be dealt with. You have got to keep the body working. There's a world full of medication that won't do a thing for you other than block those fears." At which point he said in true Bobby logic, "Well honey, you know I have 600 Zanax. I just can't take them. I might get addicted." And he didn't know why I was laughing for 5 minutes. That was Bobby.

Rick Neely:

There was an enormous period when I was kind of out of the scene and didn't have anything to do with Bob at all until that day that I opened up the paper and was stunned by the news. I had thought for a while something was wrong, because I always used to read the Reader and the entertainment listings to see what was going on, and there was a long time where Bob didn't play anywhere. I was concerned and though maybe I should call, but then one date showed up in '91 or so where he played the Chicago Historical or Cultural Center downtown, so I thought, "Oh, everything's okay." I didn't think anything more of it until this article came out. Like a lot of other people in the area, I didn't know what was going on with Bob until I opened up the paper and there was a big article about Bob being sick and a big benefit concert for him. I scrambled around to get a ticket. By the time that article had come out, it was already almost completely sold out. Bob was so weak, but still at that point able to navigate and was walking around under his own steam.

Leslie Korshak:

There are those who tend to back away when they know something's wrong, but they don't know what it is. There were a lot of people that stood away from him, but in that isolation and backing away, the people that didn't back away were Odetta and Peter Yarrow. Looking back, I think they are the two people who knew Bobby the best and who really understood the spirit of him. Peter listened to Bobby's fears and Peter was the only music friend that really listened. Peter's a really special man.

Peter Yarrow remembers his part in the benefit concert in Chicago for Bob:

When Bob acknowledged the fact that he was beginning to deteriorate neurologically, I was called upon to spearhead an effort to create a celebration in Chicago honoring Bob. In the past I had organized many benefits for a variety of causes. I co-organized the March on Washington in 1969, events at Shea Stadium, Madison Square Garden and other places. To put the benefit for Bob together in Chicago, I worked with Jim Hirsch, who is an exceptional organizer and the head of the Old Town School of Folk Music, an incredible institution. Bobby was one of the founders. Jim and I organized a fund raiser for Bob to to help cover some of his unforeseen medical expenses. The concert included Hamilton Camp as well as Spanky McFarlane (Spanky and Our Gang), Roger McGuinn, Josh White Jr., Peter, Paul & Mary and, of course, Bobby. Bob was in tears. He was deeply moved by it, as were we. We were able to show our admiration and our love for him at a critical time when we needed to do so, knowing that he was soon to pass away. .

Josh White Jr. looks back on the night:
It was from working on *Makin' a Mess* that I was called the next year and asked if I could come up and do that benefit for him in Chicago. It was one of those things that you said, "Sure!" I didn't know who else was going to be there and it didn't really matter. It could be everybody — it could be whomever. That was one of those things where it's a built-in audience anyway. I mean, if there was nothing wrong with Gibson, just to be doing a showcase for him for whatever reason was just — you could do no wrong. I think that was the last time that Gibson ever put a guitar on himself. It was an ensemble, so he didn't do any solo things, so he might have just strummed. I remember putting it around him, but I don't remember seeing him play a lot. It's one of those feelings of your denial, you know, that that's not really going to be, you know, you'll always see Gibson playing his instrument.

The Chicago Tribune carried an article about the benefit concert which was at 7:30 pm Tuesday, September 27, 1994, at the Vic Theatre, 3145 N. Sheffield Ave. The feature was written by Lawrence Rand:

OLD FOLKIES; A GATHERING OF THE GATE OF HORN CROWD

Bob Gibson was back in Chicago from Oregon because the Old Town School of Folk Music and WFMT radio, home of *The Midnight Special,* had organized a benefit for the 12-string guitar and banjo strummer. Half a lifetime ago, he and actor Hamilton Camp were the hippest act at the Gate of Horn, the hippest night spot in town. The lineup at the Vic was stocked with "the old Gate of Horn crowd," as they called themselves — Peter, Paul and Mary, who had worked the Gate on their quick rise to stardom; Gibson and Camp, the

Gate's crown princes; John Brown, a folkie who ran the Centaur, an early Old Town coffeehouse; Roger McGuinn, an early "graduate" of the Old Town School of Folk Music and founder of the Byrds; Elaine "Spanky" McFarlane of Spanky & Our Gang, but best known to Gate of Horn folks for her work with the New Wine Singers; and folksinger Josh White Jr., son of a blues and gospel musician who picked guitar with all five fingers of his right hand and so smoothly captivated the mostly white "cafe society" crowds, including the Gate of Horn's, that other black bluesmen angrily ostracized him. In 1962 you could easily have filled the Auditorium Theatre for this crew, and in '94 they still sold out the thousand-seat Vic at a stiff ticket price.

Nowadays they really are old, the Gate of Horn crowd, parading into the restored vaudeville house at Belmont and Sheffield in their suburban finery. Some of the balding men wear gray ponytails as well as beards to compensate — the women are much more willing to look their age. Some suited graybeards have come straight from the office. The surprise, however, is the guys in the slacks and synthetic sweater uniform of the retired. "Gibson & Camp's Retirement Village Hootenanny" is not what the old Gate crowd wants — they want the wild old nights at the Gate to return.

The Old Town School of Folk Music and 'FMT had pushed the right buttons, so the Vic was SRO. There were a few Gate ghosts flitting about, I believe — former Gate proprietor Albert Grossman drooling over the take (about $50,000 was raised to help Gibson, according to Jim Hirsch, who runs the Old Town School); the incomparable Lord Richard Buckley, who jazzlated literature into hipster, whether it be Willie the Shake or the New Testament "Naz"; Lenny Bruce, who embodies the Gate of Horn ethos in many ways and whose arrest closed the place; and maybe singer-songwriter Phil Ochs, whose self-destruction overshadowed an important body of work. A notable corporeal no-show was songwriter, cartoonist, and playwright Shel Silverstein, Gibson's longtime friend and sometime collaborator (he worked on the new CD) who doesn't like crowds and is shy about performing.

Josh Jr. led off starting with "Loving You," a lilting Gibson/Tom Paxton composition. He got the audience clapping on the Bill Withers tune, "Lean on Me," half choosing the black backbeat and half the white downbeat, the latter carrying the day toward song's end.

By the time Spanky was into her classic blues tunes, other performers were sneaking out front to size the house. Peter, Paul and Mary are amusing because their offstage personalities seem opposed to their characters onstage. Offstage Mary is chatty, huggy and maternal — during PP&M's glory years she had been silent and sexy. Peter, so warm and emotional onstage, seems intense, reserved and cynical off. Paul, real name Noel, the rubbery comedian onstage, is shy, stone-faced and aloof backstage.

Camp seemed smaller than ever. He was no less intense, however, a winged Mercury scurrying back and forth across the standing room in the rear reconnoitering the audience, a winning soul.

As Camp and Mary flitted around out front, Josh Jr. updated me on his life. "I'm still in Detroit," he told me. "I have ten grandchildren there now, so I can't imagine moving anywhere else." He has gravitated to doing more children's shows, and of all the performers seemed the least timeworn — bald and bearded, as he has been for the 30 years we've been acquainted, fit and slim — a dark, handsome man resembling his dad and his son, who was with him.

While male ponytails abounded in the crowd, Roger McGuinn's was gone. Of all the musicians on the bill he was the youngest and most instrumentally talented, and his skills have not eroded with time. The Byrds tunes worked extremely well as solo acoustic material, which didn't surprise me — I can remember him doing an acoustic guest set at It's Here coffeehouse about 30 years ago and getting lectured that he "shouldn't Elvis up perfectly good Bob Dylan songs." Lucky for him, he didn't listen. His acoustic version of "Eight Miles High," a highlight of the evening, revealed how cleverly he had absorbed Gibson's 12-string style, just as PP&M's second tune, "Sinner Man," bordered on harmonic thievery from Gibson & Camp. It was a revelation PP&M seemed to set before the crowd purposefully.

Peter, Paul and Mary have retained a strong desire for social justice, their musical technique continues unabated and audiences love them.

Before them was Camp, who I can count on for brevity almost always. Then came Himself. Bob Gibson looks heavier than when I last saw him, and is balding in front — a plump old rogue of an Irishman as he bows stiffly to the standing ovation. Life in the fast lane started catching up with him physically some years ago; or as Edgar says in *King Lear,* "The gods are just, and of our pleasant vices make instruments to plague us."

It is a terribly ironic moment, Gibson's entrance, this outpouring of emotion for a rascal who scandalized staid folk circles with his womanizing, drugging, flip attitude, and "commercialization" of folk music, which meant something a lot heavier than just making it marketable — it implied a lack of political correctness. The Errol Flynn of folk music was receiving kudos for chutzpah — or were we all just smiling at surviving?

"Does anybody play music anymore?" the Quiet Knight's Richard Harding had bitched earlier. He caught himself and added, "Ah, I'm just sayin' that because I'm an old fart."

McGuinn is riveted to a plastic mike box now that Gibson & Camp are singing, and the gals in the wings, including Mary, Spanky and Rasjadah (Camp's wife of many years), are misty. Gibson & Camp sing *I'm Gonna Tell God How You Treat Me,* and Gibson, who's sitting and singing but not picking, knocks off a Silverstein ditty called *Nothin's Real Anymore.*

Then they do *Well, Well, Well,* a harmonizing gem that a young Simon & Garfunkel (calling themselves Tom & Jerry) tried to cover on their first album, and they nail it terrifically right up to the last note, which they blow but the crowd doesn't care. Gibson & Camp shoot each other a glance as the audience explodes, Camp's mug breaking into a swift smile, jolly Gibson beaming, and that's the moment some folks shelled out $125 for; the flash of magic between two men who have made music together for 35 years and done horrendous things to one another and overcome everything — a look of reassurance, respect, trust, and love, a two-second glimmer right out of Shakespeare's *King Lear;* "We two along will sing like birds i' the cage; / When though dost ask me blessing, I'll kneel down / And ask of thee forgiveness; so we'll live, / And pray, and sing, and tell old tales, and laugh / At gilded butterflies, and hear poor rogues / Talk of court news; and we'll talk with them too — / Who loses and who wins; who's in, who's out — / And take upon's the mystery of things / As if we were God's spies."

Another article appeared about the concert, also in the Tribune, on September 29, 1994. It was written by Dan Kening:

FRIENDS STAR AT BENEFIT TO AID BOB GIBSON

The FOBs (Friends of Bob) were in abundance Tuesday at the Vic Theatre, both on stage and in the audience. The Bob in question was seminal folk musician Bob Gibson, and the occasion was a sold-out benefit to help pay the medical expenses of the musician who was recently diagnosed with a neurological disorder similar to Parkinson's disease.

A standing room only crowd paid $25 to $125 a ticket to hear such luminaries as Peter, Paul and Mary, Roger McGuinn, Hamilton Camp, Josh White Jr., and Spanky McFarlane pay tribute to a man who was a huge influence on a number of folk and rock musicians.

Gibson, who spent much of his career in Chicago, is credited with popularizing both traditional folk songs and the 12-string guitar. That latter credit was underscored Tuesday by White and McGuinn, who both said they picked up the 12-string because of him.

McGuinn reminisced about being a Latin School student and hearing Gibson play at a concert there. "When I saw Bob that day, it changed my life," he said. McGuinn then sang his touching "The Gate of Horn," about the famous Chicago folk club where Gibson regularly appeared, while playing arpeggios inspired by Gibson on his 12-string guitar. McGuinn later founded the Byrds, whose direct influence today on artists like Tom Petty and R.E.M. means that a little bit of Gibson is in their music as well.

Although the headliners were Peter, Paul and Mary — whose Peter Yarrow, together with emcee John Brown and the staff of the Old Town School of Folk Music, organized the event — the reunion of Gibson and old partner Camp was the night's highlight.

While his condition makes

playing the guitar impossible, Gibson's voice is still robust, and he and Camp harmonized as if time had stood still on *Well, Well, Well,* and *Abilene.* Gibson also sang the whimsical *Nothin's Real Anymore* from his upcoming album, as Camp backed him on harmonica.

Following Peter, Paul and Mary's harmonious segment, it was Gibson who fittingly stole the show in the all-star finale. Strapping on a guitar that he played with some difficulty, he sang a rousing *I Hear America Singing,* which underscored that this folk legend isn't giving up without a fight.

David Bragman hadn't seen Bob since he left Chicago a few years earlier. He recalls the shock:

When he came into town a couple for the fund raising show at the Vic Theatre, some friends of mine had a catering company, and I volunteered to help with the catering for that just to get a chance to be there. I remember seeing Bob being assisted onto the stage. It shook me up.

George Matson:

That was really quite a magical evening. It was so cute. Bob came on stage probably about midway through to say a few words and brought his daughter with him. She was kind of shy, kind of hanging on his leg and kept tugging at his coat. It was real cute and very moving. Most of that show, Bob was in a wheelchair. He was able to get up and move around, but not for great distances or for a long time. He was able to sing and he did play the guitar a little bit, but it wasn't "Bob Gibson" playing the guitar. It was just chords, kind of strumming. It wasn't that rolling thunder. He used to have a kind of contrapuntal where he used his fingers and his thumb. I don't think he could feel his fingers at that point.

The benefit was a really emotional performance for Roger McGuinn, and it was quite a performance.

The benefit in Chicago was not the only one. Kerrville Folk Festival director Rod Kennedy remembers Bob's last visit to the event he'd loved so much:

Bob's last date here was at the 1995 Folk Festival. Actually, he came to the '95 festival so we could do a big benefit/tribute to him with Peter Yarrow, Tom Paxton, Josh White Jr., Allen Damron, Anne Hills and Michael Smith. It was at our Threadgill Theatre, and we were trying to raise enough money to get him an electric wheelchair — $2,500. One of the American Indian craftspeople heard that we were going to have this benefit, and she was concerned that we wouldn't raise the money, so she went around to all the craftspeople exhibiting at the festival and got something from every one of them. There were about 60 of them. Then she printed raffle tickets and personally went out and sold about $1,700 worth. Unfortunately, we only made about $700 or $800 at the concert. The problem was the concert was already a part of the festival, and if you bought your ticket to the festival, you were in. So there was a problem of how to raise money, and we decided that we maybe ought to just do it as a tribute. Then she walked up and gave me a check for $1,700 or $1,800, so we just wrote the check for the whole amount and he got his wheelchair. That was a pretty touching gesture. Her name was Nantiki Rose. She became a dear friend of mine, but she just disappeared. I don't know where people go.

The excitement of the concerts over, Bob quietly returned to Portland, passing his days in introspection. Rick Neely:

After the benefit concert, I had told Bob that episode in 1977 was so hurtful to me because I had managed to stay so far away from drugs, and that was his indirect doing. I think in some ways that pleased him, and we kind of parted that way. Ever since the benefit I had been talking to him on the phone pretty regularly. We talked about a lot of things, and after the party, I said, "If you can still sing and you are asked to go somewhere to perform and you think you can do it, I'll be happy to come and play." I said, "I can play whatever it is that you want to play, I can play and we'll go and we'll do it." My thinking was that this is a person that needs to somehow keep going so I made that offer. There was some talk of doing another benefit concert deal either in New York or something else with Camp in Chicago or Los Angeles or somewhere which never panned out. After that concert he got so much sicker so fast that it was unbelievable.

Bob was living in Portland in a retirement kind of home, and I was kidding him, and I asked him if he was terrorizing little old blue-haired ladies, and he said, "Yeah, fat chance!" Then I asked him what kind of place this was, and he said, "It's a place for fucked up old people!" That was a real uncharacteristic kind of response for someone who always, in the face of all kind of adversity had been pretty up in his public persona, and he didn't reveal stuff like that very often. Shortly thereafter he moved into a different apartment, which was much better.

At that point I realized you learn things as you go through life, and one of the things you learn is that it's important to tell the people you love, that you love them while they're there, because when they get away from you, it's permanent. So I had kind of on the one hand vowed to make peace, and on the other hand I vowed to get back into music for myself because it was always something that I wanted to do and somehow never got around to. It hadn't had much of a priority, but then when Bob got sick it got obvious to me that you lose things real fast. Also I had gotten sick with a circulatory disease, and I had an operation in '94 where I had a grafted artery and a pulmonary embolism. Then a lot of things happened to me after the surgery that drove it home that your life is only a temporary passage through here, and so there are some things that you need to pay more attention to. The most important thing in life is to tell people that you love them when you do while they're there. So I started playing music again.

Allan Shaw remembers Bob's participation in the Folk Alliance Conference in 1995:

The 1995 Folk Alliance Conference was held in Portland, Oregon. Knowing that Bob was living in Portland then, I invited him to participate, and he agreed to attend the conference. Dick Weisman, who was with the Journeymen back in the '60s, was one the artists who was going to be there. We also had Erik Darling of the Tarriers, Weavers and Rooftop Singers there, and although it wasn't pre-planned, Alex Hassilev of the Limeliters was there. So I had gone to the Folk Alliance program committee and said, "Hey, you know we've got some real legends of the folk era coming here, why don't we have a panel discussion?" That's what we did, and it was very exciting. Bob said almost nothing because he was feeling the effects of the disease. It was hard for him to talk. He talked some but not as much as I would have liked or he would have liked. He had expressed a willingness to do a couple of songs in our showcase and just felt he couldn't, so he had Meridian fill in and do them for him.

Pete Seeger and Bob at '95 Folk Alliance

'95 Folk Alliance panel in Portland, OR.
L-R: Dick Weissberg, Bob, Erik Darling, Alex Hassilev and Allan Shaw

L-R: Bob's daughter Susan, Bob, Erik Darling, Bob's daughter Meridian

I COME FOR TO SING - 221

As it turns out, this was to be Bob's last professional appearance. He lived a quiet, simple life two blocks away from his daughter Susan. The electric scooter he got with the funds raised at the Kerrville benefit gave him the freedom to venture out into the world. He frequently went to movies, and daily went to the coffee shop at the hospital across the street for latté. The walls of his apartment carried few reminders of the celebrity life he had once lived. On the wall over his bed, there were three pictures. One was of him from The Courtship of Carl Sandburg, another was of him with his dear friend Shel Silverstein, and the last was the group picture of those participating on the song I Hear America Singing *on his* Makin' A Mess *album. Where he spent the lion's share of every day was in the living room watching television. On the wall behind his chair were two posters — one of canoeing in the boundary waters of Quetico and one from the Kerrville Folk Festival. The only picture he had from his performance days in the living room was directly in front of him over the television. It was one of him on stage with Michael Smith at Hobson's Choice. His banjo stood sadly neglected in the corner of the room.*

He commented about his life in Portland:

Some people come from some distance to visit, but for all intents and purposes, Portland is unaffected by my stay.

Bob with his youngest daughter Sarah at the Nutcracker Ballet in Portland, OR, December, 1995

20

BOB GIBSON — THE MAN

The gift of Bob Gibson was that of musical genius — his natural, almost effortless ability to touch, excite and inspire his audience and his fellow performers. Without any plan or perhaps even any awareness of what he was doing, he introduced a generation to a style of music that has had an impact on everything that followed it. Who knows where this kind of talent comes from? As his daughter Susan said:

> I asked Dad what inspired him to get into Calypso music, and he said, "Oh, the beach and the warm sun." It was like he wasn't really musically motivated. I think between the drug use and what I describe as the hole . . . . I don't think he ever really understood what was going on. I think his fame and his music and the attention that that brought him was at a real basic level for him — was trying to fill that hole that his mom didn't fill for him.

Nevertheless, there was something within Bob Gibson that was able to identify music that had significance, and there is no disputing the fact that he had a true genius where songwriting and performing were concerned.

The sad part of all of this was that between a childhood filled with emotional abuse and twenty years of an adulthood numbed by self-inflicted drug abuse, Bob found it difficult to master the interpersonal skills required to maintain relationships. Up on a stage no one was better with an audience, but one on one was a different story. He turned his back on two marriages, lost his chance at being a father to four of his children, and went through scores of friends. Tragically, the illness that ended his career and life kept him from enjoying the second chance at being a successful father that he had hoped for in his last daughter Sarah.

Meridian Green:

> I think one of the hardest things for him in the five or six years before he died was that I think he absolutely got, in the process of bringing up Sarah, what he had missed with his first kids and just how precious that was and what a trip it is to hang out with your kids and have a relationship with them and then to realize that he wasn't actually going to get to see Sarah grow up. He got in on one end with her and he had started to work out relations with his adult

children, but he wasn't going to be able to stick around long enough to have a relationship Sarah as an adult.

Had he been able to apply his stage charisma to all aspects of his life, there is no telling how far he might have gone. Family harmony was something that eluded him most of his life, though.

Meridian Green:
One of the things about my dad that was always really odd was that he had two different personas. One was the family persona and the other was the unbelievable charismatic and engaging fellow that went out into the world. At home he didn't bother to turn any of that on, and he was the ultimate couch potato.

Bob as a father was different at different times. It was interrupted enough that there was a discontinuity there. I found it very frustrating and difficult to deal with somebody who was really never clear with just how grown up I was. Probably some of that was that he was always kind of relating to the kid he saw a few months ago when I was little because I didn't live with him with any consistency between two and seven, so by the time I was seven years old, we were already having major difficulties when he came around. Part of it was that when he came he usurped my position because I was the eldest child, and when he came around he was the eldest child. It was really a problem. I was very much used to being in charge. It's funny. My mom is quiet. There's a self-effacingness that my mom has that kind of makes it really possible for whoever's around to end up being rather dominating because she doesn't dominate back. So as a child I probably expanded on that a lot. Everytime my dad would show up it would really rock my boat. He also didn't bring any great parenting skills to the party. I remember a couple of bonding experiences that I had with him that were very cool. When I was a kid I had a lot of tonsillitis and I had very high fevers. I remember one night he was sitting up with me keeping me company while I had a raging fever and helping me get my fever down. We watched old movies in the wee hours of the morning — just hanging out and having a nice time. I guess he was just happy to have somebody to hang out with because the house was usually quiet that time of night. I remember the first time he took me out for a lobster dinner when I was eight years old. That was a pretty nice little treat.

I always had a longing just to have my dad be really excited and pleased to see me, and I didn't get that when I was little. Those people who light up when they see their kids and are pleased to see them give their kids something really important in this world which is a sense of being treasured and a sense of joy that I didn't get from him. I don't think it was personal, but it was really hard when I was little not to have it feel personal.

I'm somebody whose emotions are so close to the surface that I have a tendency to think that people whose emotions are very low key or not obvious, simply aren't having them. By the time I was heading into adolescence, I think that I caused my dad an enormous amount of pain because I was trying so hard to get a response and he didn't respond. Somewhere along the line, I actually got that the things that I said that were hurtful, did indeed hurt him, and that was a shocking revelation. I would have stopped if he'd said, "Ouch!", just once. I just kept trying to figure out how he could be so impervious, and it turns out he wasn't. It was an optical illusion.

Leslie Korshak:
Bobby was always a little rebel and loner and he was always looking for the simple — not the easy, but the simple. Bobby was of his time when he was a child and of his parents where everything was complex. That was the intellectual approach, and the women were put away with, "There, there, dear, don't worry your pretty head about it." Bobby was thought to be incorrigible and it was written on his report card. He was sent to Catholic school and was abused and the priest still sent notes home saying he was incorrigible. Bobby never fit even within folk music. He was a very difficult person to pigeonhole because Bobby hated labels or anything organized. Organized religion made him crazy and so much of it came from the rage at such a young age of being called incorrigible. What happened with Bobby from the beginning to the end was that he finally figured out that he was his own thing — he wasn't supposed to fit in. It was part of the baggage of being the troubadour — the pioneer. He really became heroic.

That rage in a 14 year old, no church, no parents, no family — he had no family skills. Of course he abandoned his first family and they have terrific issues to this day with that. He didn't know — he was abandoned as a child by everything. He had no idea how to be a family man, because he never had those skills. He knew how to be an adolescent and that's where it stopped and that adolescent kept getting physically older but the adolescent behaviors stayed.

Rick Neely:
When Bob's oldest daughter Meridian was a teenager, she was real upset with Bob one time about something and she went fleeing from Chicago. She went out to live in Connecticut with a guitar player and his wife for a while. I remember I wrote her a letter, and in it I said, "We're not related, but I feel like your big brother, and I'm going to say things that probably are off base. I think your father really loves you, and I just don't think that, in some ways, he always had the ability to show it in the right ways."

But I think that he loved her tremendously, and I don't think it was until the end of his life that she finally realized it or came to terms with it.

Susan, in many ways, is the oldest of Bob's daughters, even though she is the second, and Pati is probably the most responsible of all, but they all had their problems with Bob as a father.

As for his second marriage, there are two sides to every coin, but I think Margie genuinely loved Bob a great deal. Why they came to a point in their life where they could no longer be together I don't know. Only the two people that are involved can really tell you that, and sometimes, while deep in your heart of hearts you know the reason, you can't get it out. You can't tell anybody else, but you know. I think that the little voice inside you always tells the truth.

Bob and Sarah 1993

I've spent a lot of time with Margie and Sarah, especially Sarah, and I've told Margie that as long as Sarah is a young adult and if she needs help in anything, I would be willing to help her, because I feel that for all of the years that I took from Bob and his music, there needs to be some kind of humble repayment in some way. All his other girls are grown now, but to be available for Sarah is the smallest thing that I can do. The irony of the whole thing is that she was the one chance he had to do it right, because I think the other girls really got short shrift because they had to share him with the drugs, and they all have their story to tell.

Gibson clan gathering 1995 - *L-R back:* Rose Garden, Bob, Susan
Middle: Pati, Meridian, Pati's son Jordan, Stephen's wife Seannie holding their son Fergus, Stephen; *Front:* Pati's daughter Mackenzie and Sarah.

I imagine that sometimes Bob felt trapped within himself, unable to understand why success came to him with such ease in the beginning. Perhaps he didn't feel he deserved the recognition he received. He certainly didn't know how to handle it. Despite these problems, he continued to be a quiet force in the world of folk music.

Leslie Korshak:
People often talk about Bobby's self-depricating nature, and it was true. It all came so easy to him that he'd sometimes get very upset and think he was a fraud.

Even though he did have problems in communication and relationships, he also was able to reach people on a personal level that made many of them forgive the cruel mistakes a friend of Bob Gibson would many times have to endure. Nevertheless, people who knew Bob Gibson feel a depth of love for him that few people have ever commanded. To dwell on Bob's personal shortcomings would be pointless, but to ignore them totally would not give a complete picture. To look at Bob Gibson the man helps to understand why he made many of the choices he did in his career, and, perhaps, why the world doesn't know him the way it should.

Dave Samuelson:
I think Bob is a significant figure, but his story is very complicated. He's a man who should have been on top but he blew it in many ways and it's sort of ironic that his last album should be called *Making a Mess of Success*. That's the way it is. The main thing is he's a man everybody loved and he hurt a lot of the people who he loved, but the man was just incredibly charismatic and his music generated such power it was overwhelming and inspirational.

Bob, God love him — everybody loved him but he was not really always that nice a man, and basically I attribute that to the kind of old time low level philosophy of "do what you could just to survive." To explain Bob to people who don't know him, you have to understand the culture that Bob operated in. It's radically different from Pete Seeger's and Eric Darling's or, for that matter, Dave Van Ronk's. Bob was never part of that whole intellectual scene like the Van Ronks and some of the New York people were. That was the whole coffee house thing. Bob's was pretty much the underbelly of small time show business. He was basically a vaudeville type performer, and as a consequence he did a lot of things that nobody could be proud of, but that's just the way it was. That's why a lot of boarding houses would not rent to vaudevillians because they'd take the towels and anything else. I've hired a few old vaudevillians and they'd do things like run up a huge room service tab and then stick you with it when they'd leave town and the whole shebang. That's just the code of old vaudevillians, I guess, and that was carried on with the small time nightclubs. I know there are a lot of people that were hired to work as side men for Bob and they were never paid. He'd just grab the check and split, and the side men, who usually played bass, were left holding the bag. That's the way Bob did things. Bob didn't talk about that. I got that from other people. This was just par for the course that "if you work with Bob and backed Bob, don't expect anything from Bob." People learned the first time. They'd get burned once, and if they opted to do it again, they recognized that they weren't going to see any financial reward.

Also a lot of things that he said were basically not true. I don't think he really lied about things. I think that by a certain point he was becoming befuddled because of all the chemicals or whatever the case might be, and started thinking a lot of things were true that really weren't. I don't think it was malicious on his part by any means. I don't think he was a malicious man. I just think that he tried to scramble and survive. I'm a big fan and always will be, but I also realize the man's faults. That's part of the whole picture, though. This was a man scrambling to survive and do whatever he could to survive. He never had a whole lot of money.

He had so many wonderful things fall his way and he'd screw them up. That's the way his luck tended to be. It's a very curious story how things were offered to him and fate would just play a hand. A lot of it was his own doing. Bob was never one to be part of a partnership with anybody.

Writing about Bob is a complicated situation. It's almost like a guy like Godfrey who was pleasant to some people and sort of nasty to others. I don't think Bob was ever nasty to anybody, but he hurt a lot of people, and that's part of who he was and how he survived.

Rick Neely:

There were two different people in Bob Gibson. There was a public guy who was always Mr. Up and the center of the social activities wherever he was, and there was a very private insecure other person who was very shy and kind of awkward in some social circumstances, and so he adopted this kind of thing where sometimes he just didn't talk. He'd just be this kind of ambience that was there with his hands kind of stuffed in his pockets looking around at the world and everybody thought that this was a very benign little person, but I think that was his shyness coming through. Bob was very shy around tiny little groups and he had real good command of bigger where the shyness didn't come through at all. The confidence, the savoir faire really came flying through.

I was trying to think of specific things that we talked about, and it's been so long that I don't remember anymore specifically. But I remember talking to Bob's son Stephen the afternoon after the memorial service, and I said, "When did you first have contact with Bob and know that he was your father?" He said he'd just kind of found out he was his father and was going through all these resentful things when Bob took him on an engagement trip where they went to Cleveland and stayed in somebody's cabin somewhere out in the semi-wilderness. They spent the weekend together there. I said, "Well, what did you talk about?" He said, "You know, I really can't remember. We didn't talk about much, but you kind of just absorbed this aura that emanated."

Michael Smith said that they also didn't talk much, and then he he pointed out that as Bob got sick, he got hard to talk to because it was physically difficult and enormously frustrating for him to try to carry on a conversation.

Of course the years on drugs affected his personality and his ability to communicate and deal with people, and this is why you hear people say things like, "That son of a bitch! He screwed me out of . . ." You know, you gotta realize THAT'S NOT THE GUY! That's the addict, that's the drugs doing their thing because the drugs are so powerful that you do whatever you have to do.

I think that in my life I knew the real guy. You know how sometimes you meet somebody and right away you feel connected and you have no idea why you're connected? One thing I learned from Margie that just blew me away, was the story about Bob being incorrigible as a small child and his mother putting him on a leash. My mother did that to me, too. This was something that never came up in any conversation while he was alive, but wouldn't his mouth have dropped open?! Wouldn't he have just freaked out to find out somebody else wore those same shoes? Why is that? What in the cosmos does that? So he's either my father or my brother or something in the universe somehow. We were kindred spirits in many ways, our childhoods, our shyness in small group situations. I just miss him enormously.

Ed Holstein remembers the Bob Gibson that he knew:
My relationship with Bob was like so many musical relationships. There are different friendships based on when you're gonna get together and play together on the same bill or you run into each other. That's how my friendship with Bob was — we'd just bump into each other every once in awhile and we'd talk. I don't think — and this is coming from a guy who's been behind a bar a lot — I've met a more interesting person to talk to than him. He was just the greatest story teller. A lot of times people have a lot of information and can just be simply boring. They know a lot of stuff but it just doesn't translate. There are two people that come to mind that can tell stories based on not only what they know personally or maybe what they read. They are Dave Van Ronk and Bob Gibson. There are only a few people that come to mind who really capture you, because

you've heard it all, especially as a bartender. But Gibson — when you think of him — he really is part of a whole — I don't want to use the term counterculture or alternative culture — but another option in show business. It was him and Second City and Elaine May and Mike Nichols and just all kinds of different options in show business that he represented. So my relationship with him was limited, but everytime I was with him I just wished I had a tape recorder. I never met anybody who was that charming as a storyteller who would talk about stuff that would normally bore me, but he was able to interest me in whatever he talked about. He was so intimate with his audience, too.

Ramblin' Jack Elliot told me a story about Bob. Bob was such a gentle guy. It was in the Village, and Bob was living there at the time. Jack's wife had left him or something like that, and he went and knocked on Bob Gibson's door and stayed with Bob for the night. They talked all night. Gibson was a real friend.

His mind was always so active that he just couldn't stop thinking of things to do and I think he had trouble focusing on stuff. He was gonna publish, he was gonna manage, he was gonna run clubs, he was gonna do this, he was gonna do that. He reminded me of a story. I came to him with *City of New Orleans* because he had published *Jazzman* and that was a big deal because everyone thought Bob would get to all these artists and stuff. So Steve Goodman asked me if I would talk to Bob about *City of New Orleans* and he turned it down! It's been recorded in 100 different languages, you know!

Josh White Jr.:
There was a time when he had drug problems, and I know I knew him when he had all this, but I never saw it. I kind of respect the fact that, whomever else he might have known about or done any stuff with, I never experienced him doing anything. I think I might have seen him nod out a couple of times at a party or something after, but it was a different thing. I really respect the fact that he just didn't flaunt this to anyone. That was very respectful.

He also did something that was very kind that I didn't ask him to. I did a play of my father — the play was written about my dad. I did it in '83 in Lansing, Michigan for five weeks. Bob and Sam Freifeld, a lawyer who did work at the Gate of Horn, went to see it. They drove to Lansing from Chicago to see it. I did not even know they were there until, I think at the end I looked up. We used to have talk-backs there. When you finished the play you talked to the audience and explained things and there he was - they both were. That was just a nice thing to support me in that respect that I didn't even have any idea he was coming. I thought it would come to Chicago one day and he'd see it, but I didn't know he'd make a special trip — he and Sam. So he holds a very special place. I thank him.

George Matson fondly remembers what Bob was like:
He also took youth groups on canoe trips up to the Quetico boundary waters up in our area. He was an accomplished canoist. As a scout as a youngster he had done that. I don't know much about it other than he got a big thrill out of it. He told me about some of the kids he had worked with. He thought it was really a marvelous way for them to connect with something outside of where they were.

One thing many of Bob's friends share is a treasured memory of the humor.
Leslie Korshak:
His humor! So much of Bobby's legacy and spirit is his humor. We had a rule, if we could get to the punch line we were okay. So many people find songs to write about depression and he would step back and find the humor. He used to say, "People think *To Morrow* is a funny song. They don't know that it's probably the most important song I ever wrote because you can't get anywhere." The thing about Bobby's humor was that it wasn't so much the funny anecdotal Shel story as it was if he let you in his life you were on some kind of the same radar and it was just take a look. It was the absence of all the verbiage, it was getting the joke, it was just a look in the middle of an otherwise serious situation and you knew what he had pulled out of the ether that was funny and you were so focused on it that the enormity of the big thing became much more palatable to take. It was the spirit of humor.

I would come home from the grocery store and he would be playing and I would have 10 bags and with that big grin and that big guitar he would open the door and serenade me as I lugged the groceries. Very early on I realized I could put the groceries down and say "For heaven's sake, put the guitar down and help me or I could realize there was great beauty and humor to the fact that number one, I was being serenaded, and that number two, it never entered his mind.

To the day I die I will be grateful. Anybody could have picked up a grocery bag but only Bobby could have serenaded me. It was that kind of not knowing he was funny funny.

We went out one time and there was some specific dried mushroom that was like $80 a lb. We had to drive someplace in Wisconsin to find it, and I don't know if that place had even been discovered yet — it was still fur trappers. We went into a little general store and Bobby was loading up bags and bags of those $80 a lb. mushrooms because, after all, we were going on the road and don't you always make soup when you're travelling? It was just the nuttiness of it, but then what he did was pure Bob. I said, "Look, they've got fresh thyme." It was just a little tied bunch of it and it was 79¢. I put it on the counter by the bags of mushrooms, and he looked at me and he said, "Do you really need that?" He just had no idea. It was an innocence.

The humor pervades everything. Those big old blue eyes set the tone. When he was comfortable with the other person in the room, it was no holds barred. That's how we got through those years. He kept his grace and humor. There was a joy about him even in the darkest days when he was so attacked by his own symptoms. We had a lot of fun. We kept the laughter.

John Irons:
There's probably not a day that goes by that I don't think about Bob. He was a very important person in my life. He was such a card. He made me laugh. He'd punch all my funny bones, and he was somebody that I could talk to and I knew that he wouldn't say anything, and he could talk to me and I wouldn't say anything. That's true even to this day.

He worked for Earl Pionke at his club and he'd make a grand there on a weekend. He went to Earl to get paid one time and Earl was standing there flipping this silver dollar. He said "You want to go double or nothing?" Bob said, "Sure." So Earl flipped the coin and Bob lost.

Bob could gamble, though. He was living in Chicago on Wilton in the 3600 block around Addison right in back of the ballpark. He was living there with one of his daughters — either Susan or Barbara. He got a job playing in or around Las Vegas so he went up there and something happened to his guitar. The airline dropped it or something. He had to send it back to Chicago which was where his guitar maker Bozo was living to have repair done to it. So he sent the guitar to his daughter. He figured she'd panic because she knew he'd gone to Vegas and would figure he'd lost everything gambling and sent the guitar back before he lost that too.

He owned some beautiful land between Aspen and Denver and he managed to hang onto it long enough to sell it just before everything skyrocketed. He always said the reason musicians are so bad at money deals is because they can only count to four.

George Matson:
Bob told the story of a fellow at the Mustard Seed named Indian Joe. Early in his sobriety he was having trouble stringing any dry time together, and on one of his many relapses, he had been out for about 30 days and he was laying half in and half out of a doorway on Canal Street and lying in a pool of his own discharge in clothes that he hadn't changed in 30 days. The commuters were stepping over his outstretched sprawled out legs and he remembered looking up at them going to meet their trains and thinking, "I wonder if these people realize that I'm a perfectionist?" Perfectionism is a common thread running through alcoholics. They all like to do it right or not at all.

The Perfect High was an anthem that he did at AA meetings in

Chicago. He was pretty active and he died sober as far as I know. I've got his last coin. I used to make wooden watch fobs for him out of exotic wood. I made one out of amaranth which is heart wood and that's what he kept his last coin in.

There were the difficulties in relating to Bob Gibson, too. Poor communication skills, shyness, awkwardness about closeness. Michael Smith remembers what Bob was like to be around:

He was a very private man. Certainly to me he was. I was definitely the bass player, and as much I would like to have thought otherwise, in truth his peers or his contemporaries were Paxton and Odetta and Joan Baez, and I was his bass player. It was a different, hierarchical relationship, and it was as if he was saying, "You're not in this crowd." He would do things like, he'd say, "Joanie's coming to visit me next week." And then I wouldn't hear from him. It was like, don't say to him you'd like to meet Joanie. No way! It wasn't going to happen. He definitely kept his levels separate. It wasn't like he was going to tell me anything personal, and yet, now and again he would really open up to me in extraordinary things he would say to me about his views or about situations he had been involved in. He would be extremely personal. It was sort of a shock to me because he would just suddenly stop being distant and just confess stuff, but then it would go back to the other way.

Sometimes it was like trying to move a turtle working with Bob. I went into our relationship thinking, "I'm going to play bass with this guy, and he's going to be happening all over again, because we're going to make some groovy tunes. We're gonna spice up his arrangements, and we're gonna . . ." I had this picture which you get when you're a young person, and you think you're really going to change this person and you're going to be the one who's going to make this person kick-ass once again. And in truth, people are the way they are. You're not about to change the way they are, especially if they've been that way for 50 years.

Now, I see, it was just cool to play bass with him. And the fact that he NEVER let me say a word about how the arrangements were going to go, as far as his tunes were concerned, it was pretty much, you do what he does and you cope. And it was fine, because he played great. It always sounded like Bob Gibson. I'd think, "Hey, this sounds just like this record I heard, and it'd be the way I would swing with it. Whereas I might say to someone who played that way now, "You know, hey! Let's do something a little different now." But at the time, you know, this was Gibson, and I'm gonna go with this so it was really fun. It was fun to work with him and Camp.

I always felt like I was on the outside, but it was appropriate that I was. There was a big difference between us, and that was, he had established his niche in the folk music world and nobody was going to take that from him, and nobody was going to get in there and mess with it. I don't know that that was necessarily his conscious attitude, but that's what happened. It came down to, "Shut up, you're the bass player." And that was fine with me. It really was fine. The only time it bothered me was *The Women In My Life* because it was so much work.

David Bragman remembers Bob in almost reverential terms:
It wasn't until the late '80s that I got to know Bob personally. One of the contexts under which I got to know him was recovery from addictions. He and I shared a lot of stuff and started talking about, particularly at that time, compulsive eating. He was dealing with it a lot so we used to talk about the way we felt and things that were troubling us. By that time he had been clean for several years from other stuff. I was, too, and so we had a lot in common. He became a real good friend. We shared the same kind of problems and we used to talk very specifically about those. Right around the corner from where Bob lived, there's a White Hen Pantry which is open 24 hours and full of junk food. We used to talk about how when we were feeling good, we'd never go in there, but when we were really struggling that was the place to go.

In the winter of 1991, I went into a 6-week eating disorder treatment program. When I came out from it I needed to have a sponsor in Overeaters Anonymous, so I asked Bob, and he agreed, and took me to OA meetings. Actually I ended up meeting a woman at the first OA meeting that I ended up dating for a couple of years. Again, as an aside, she and I had been dating a few months and I told her, "Hey, Bob Gibson's gonna be playing at Clearwater on Friday night and I don't have a gig. How'd you like to go up and see him?" And she said, "I've always liked his music." So I said, "Let's go," and she agreed and said, "I've always wanted to meet him." And I said, "What do you mean?" And she said again, "Well, I've just always wanted to meet him." I said, "You've been sitting across the table from him at meetings for months!" And she said, "That's Bob Gibson?" She had no idea what he looked like or anything and she said, "I always thought he was a plumber or something." So we went to the show that night and before Bob went on that night, we told him about that and he just busted up. He thought it was funny as hell.

He used to perform at the Unity Church, and the minister there was a kind of a crazy guy. At the age of about 55 decided he wanted to be a minister after holding 86 different jobs, none of them having to do with anything. Bob fit right in at this church. He used to sing there once in awhile, and I can remember him singing *How Could You Do This To Me* and *Still Gonna Die*. So Bob became a personal friend, a confidant, where I could talk about, you know if I was having a bad day just dealing with things. I could call him up and just bitch about everything and he could do the same with me and did.

I've heard a lot of stories about how in the past Bob had pissed a lot of people off in dealings with them. I got to know him when he was in a different place, and I always felt real fortunate about that. I always have wonderful, wonderful memories as well as an acceptance because we were dealing with a lot of similar struggles.

I realize that there's a connection between all of the artists throughout history who struggle to do their art and provide for themselves and their families, and somebody as notable as Bob had to deal with the same shit. There's something in me that says it shouldn't have to be that way. He shouldn't have to go through that. All that he did, all that he gave, he shouldn't have had to deal with things like that, but he did, and he accepted it. He always had something going on.

It was seeing people like him that helped me put together my career. I'm just so grateful. He was a sweet man.

I remember, also, the delight he had with Sarah as a little girl. I mean, he was an old fart at the time and he had this two-year-old and playing with her and talking about her, he became so animated.

There has also been much made of Bob Gibson's reputation as a "womanizer."
Leslie Korshak:
Bobby was not a womanizer. His view of women ended as did his upbringing at the age of 14. This was ignorance. He didn't know. He didn't learn how. He didn't abuse or womanize intentionally. There was never anything malicious in Bobby's nature. Instead he gave. He just didn't waste time with that malicious stuff. It wasn't in him. It was so foreign that he couldn't do it. When people responded to him in a negative way because of something he may or may not have done or that they interpreted the wrong way, it was just this total innocence.

BOB GIBSON'S PHILOSOPHY OF LIFE:
You can be happy or you can be right,
But you can't be both!

Leslie Korshak:
It was a philosophy that angered a whole lot of people, but it was his way of coping.

I'm only expert at one thing. That is the inner me. If I'm sitting in the middle of a pile of shit with nothing to my name—but I'm happy—how can anyone tell me that I'm not in the right place. Who says I should be somewhere else? No one can make me do anything different.

When I learned that, rather than trying to cope with something I didn't want to deal with, I could escape through sex or drugs or a geographical change. If I have a tendency toward low self-esteem, why do we need to know why? Living our lives is the most important thing we undertake. We have just enough time for it; it begins and it ends at just the right time.

At one time in my life, if I would be unsuccessful at something, one of the possibilities was that I had taken on something that I couldn't be successful at in the first place. That was terrible before. Somehow I had to succeed. If I had set the goal and couldn't succeed, first, I couldn't do it and, second, I was stupid to set the wrong goal. It became a lot easier not to set up any projects to do, because that way I couldn't fail. You don't take the test, you don't fail. You know that you are going to be wonderful at something—a one-man show, a new career, a hit record, a lot of acclaim. You're not really working on anything, but you know the next thing you do will be a success. It will be as successful as you choose to perceive it.

That became my thought process when I was using chemicals. The reason I don't have to use drugs is that I made a whole lot of mental health moves in my life. I was in emotional pain all the time—resentments, jealousies, anger, depression, self-pity. It used to be I would have a few good moments in my life, but mostly bad times. Now I have a few bad moments, but they're all good days.

I believe that as we grow, we change. There are only a couple of things that are inevitable, birth and death. There are two things that are optional, growth and change. Our sense of our self, the sense of how we perceive ourself in relation to the world, whether we're comfortable or not, that is subject to a lot of growth and a lot of change. I ceased doing that. I ceased to confront and cope with life. I ceased to develop as a person.

My only agents of change were drugs and alcohol. It affected my banjo licks, guitar licks, my writing, my performing. It was not a comfortable place to live in.

I used to list the frustration, things that were denied me by fate, the bad breaks, things that I worked for that didn't come out right. The list became overwhelming. There was no point in trying anymore. But when I started to make a positive list, it became a long one. Now when something doesn't come my way, even if I do all the work and do it right, it's okay. As Lincoln said, 'We're about as happy as we make up our minds to be." For years I didn't want to hear that sort of thing. It wasn't as simple as that. I felt life was very complicated.

I've gone a lot of places and been with a lot of people and done a lot of different things. I rest pretty easy, no matter where I am now. I'm grateful that I have done so much and my life has been such an adventure. The lows have been as low as they can get and the highs have been as high as they can get. There were times when I perceived life as absolute hell and times I perceived it as heaven.

It's been glorious. It's been intense. I've never been much for 'sipping' life. I take gulps. For that reason I've liked it even when I didn't like it. There were some gulps of some stuff I didn't care for, but they really weren't handed me by fate. I have dealt with incredible obstacles, all of which were self-inflicted. They might have been awful, but they weren't hopeless and they weren't unchangeable.

There is something working on me now called peace of mind. At one time I thought that concept was as square as it could be.

Meridian Green:

For many years of my life, I was angry with my father for not considering anybody else's concerns as if it was a choice he made. But now I think that human beings come into the world with variable levels of ability in certain arenas of perception. Just as vision varies from eagle-eyed to nearsighted to blind, other senses of perception also vary greatly. Bob was very nearly blind to other people's wants and needs, although at some point he noticed that he was blind and began to try and perceive this part of the world. The particular arena of perception that Bob was myopic in had to do with people in the singular, one on one, family and friends, the little dance of give and take.

Bear in mind that who and how I am surely colors my perception of my father. I came into the world with an acute sense of fairness. How I am is predisposed to weigh and measure and tally to see if things are fair. My father always seemed surprised, not only that people could keep track of picayune details like who owes what to whom, but that they would, seemed utterly foreign to him. In order to disregard an obligation or a debt most people need a justification. Bob didn't. His sense of entitlement made him innocent and childlike in his quest for immediate gratification.

Maybe it was the same quirky brain wiring that made him such a master of pleasure in the present. He had an amazing capacity to connect crowds of people with their own joy. Bob Gibson could turn a group of people into a celebration, an extraordinary event, a party where everyone is witty and beautiful, all the jokes are funny and the songs are all well-sung. There was a surge of electricity, a shot of adrenaline, a charged atmosphere; whatever that thing was that he brought to performances that made the very air sparkle, it was unique. I love my father's music. He made great music, and I'm grateful for all the recordings. But what I miss most is the rush of being in the room with him when he'd turn the magic on.

21

FAREWELL PARTY

Want no tears shed for me when I'm gone.
Don't want to hear you sing those melancholy songs.
Don't let your parting words become my eulogy.
Have a ragtime band play to say good-bye to me.

I want no organ music bringin' people down.
I want no long faced mourners always hangin' 'round.
Don't want your candles — ah, but let the flowers stay.
The girls can wear them in their hair when they see me
on my way.

Roll the carpet back now boys and let the dancin' start.
Sing the good old songs — don't forget my part.
Invite all the girls I've known — make sure they have fun.
Hug and kiss them all, you know, the way I might have done.

Keep that whiskey flowin' boys
and raise your glasses high.
Pleased to see you're here to say "farewell"
and not "good-bye".
Keep that whiskey flowin' boys
and raise your glasses high.
Damn the man that dares to let
my farewell party die.

Bob Gibson (©Robert Josiah Music, Inc.)

Bob's friend Shel Silverstein, in the liner notes of the Gibson & Camp at the Gate of Horn *album, referred to Bob and Camp as the "social directors" of the Gate of Horn. It was time for Bob to throw one last party. He envisioned a good old-fashioned Irish wake with his song* Farewell Party, *which he had recorded on* Funky in the Country, *as the theme.*

From the Computer of... Bob Gibson

August 15, 1996

Dear Friends,

As my health has declined, I have found that I may miss music more than anything else. I miss making music, listening to music and being around others who have music in their blood. So, I'm going to have a party and invite everyone to bring their voices, instruments and songs!

Please join me, just north of Chicago, at the Sheraton North Shore on Friday, September 20, 1996 to visit and jam! I've arranged for a small sound system, a no host bar, light refreshments, and a view of the Chicago skyline. I would really like to see you, hear you and just say hello.

This may be the last chance I have to see many of you. I am finding it increasingly difficult to do the simplest things and traveling is really a challenge. I won't be able to play and sing with you, but I'm really looking forward to being an audience of one!

I hope I see you all there.

Bob

Rick Neely remembers how the party came together:

Bob called me saying he was having a party, and I asked him if there was anything I could do. He said Bill Goldsmith was handling all the arrangements, so I called him and said, "I'm local and I'm available and what would you like me to do?" He had given me a list of jobs and when I had gotten those kind of in hand, I called Bob's daughter Susan, and I said, "What do you want me to do?" She said, "We're trying to find a list of people." I said, "I can be a detective." So I called a lot of people.

Bob's daughter Meridian and I set up the room for the party and found we both had the same vision of what this party should be like — that it should be a kind of cabaret setting with flowers on the table and very hip. Once that vision was agreed upon then we could put the party together really easily. It's hard to do something for somebody when they have an idea and you're not sure, but the concept was absolutely correct.

Then my little job was to coordinate the entertainment which really amounted to me showing up at the door with a clipboard, and anybody who wanted to play could. It was fortunate that enough interesting people showed up. I thought it was, the topic not withstanding, a pretty exciting evening and very interesting to people who were there in that time period. It was pretty off the cuff and a lot of fun. John Brown being there was pretty interesting, because I had made the statement at the party that if I was the last Bob Gibson clone, John Brown was the first. They say back in those days Bob and John started to look alike after awhile. They'd hang around and you couldn't tell one from the other because everybody was looking the same, dressing the same, had the same moves and all that stuff. Camp was like that, too. You look at pictures in the early days and if you look real quick you don't know who's who.

Because of the short notice and conflicting fall performance schedules of the kind of people involved, many of Bob's old friends were unable to attend, but they all contacted Bob. Tom Paxton wrote him a letter. Josh White Jr. had talked to him before the party and tried to call during it. Bryan Bowers also called Bob. Rick Neely, who acted as emcee for the evening, read a letter that was sent by Bob's friend Marty Peifer, who is listed in the credits on Bob's album Uptown Saturday Night *as the "snaps":*

Rick Neely

I remember the time I sat up in Al Day's parents' house and listened to you and Hamilton Camp wailing out *Daddy Roll 'Em*. I knew you were one of the true folk heroes. Probably many articles about you have listed you as a great influence in the folk music scene of the times. That is certainly true, but I think of you as one of the inspirations of my own career. Everytime you walked on the stage you filled the room with confidence of someone who really knew what you were singing about. You always made everyone feel that they were a part of each song, and you made me feel excited about the music. I wanted to get up there and let the late night bunch drunks at the Earl's have it with both barrels. I watched you and I learned how to do it.

A few days before I heard about this gathering on the North Shore, I was driving home across the mountains of north central New Mexico feeling nostalgic for old times. I was listening to Tom Paxton, Anne Hills and you singing together. It put a smile on my face. I just wanted to send you this short note to let you know that you are remembered with great respect and admiration, not only for the power of your music, but for the many smiles it has put on my face over the years. I know that times are tough for you these days, and I hope that you will have the strength to hang in there, just as you have shared the strength of who you are with all of us through all these years.

Thanks for being one of my heroes. God bless.
Very sincerely,
Marty Peifer

Fred Holstein performed that evening and paid this tribute to Bob:
I think the first LP I ever owned was *Offbeat Folksongs.* He and Pete Seeger are the reason I play music. He influenced a lot of people — two generations of them. He helped change the face of American music. No question about it. Even the Beatles said that Gibson and Camp helped influence them when they were kids. Look at his chord progressions. He was a god.

Fred sang a song of Bob's and then a song of his own which included the chorus:
> This is a song for all the good people
> All the good people who touched up my life
> This is a song for all the good people
> People I'm thanking my stars for tonight

Studs Terkel went to the stage and delivered the toast for the event:
I was thinking this moment listening to Bob's grandson Jordan playing piano that this is known as continuity. Bob, your legacy is forever! It's very moving of course - and kind of exhilarating, too. There's an old English music hall song called *Your Old Brigade.* And the Old Brigade is gathered, heads bloody but unbowed, all here, and the magnet of course is Bob Gibson.

So naturally a memory comes to me at once. People say memories deceive — memories don't! Memories italicize — are indelible. And to me the memory is 1956, 40 years ago. Al Grossman opened the Gate of Horn in the basement of the Rice Hotel, across the street from the YMCA. And so Al Grossman, the impresario, the first two weeks — it didn't work those first two weeks. Two good artists were there but it didn't work. In the third week appears a young guy with crew cut blond hair, an infectious grin, a banjo on his chest, and he sings *Abilene* among others. Suddenly the place is electricity. From that moment on the electricity of Bob Gibson caught on, and Gate of Horn was established as a citadel of folk music in the country, and Bob's role as many of you said was that of a troubadour of ancient days, but of now.

And in hearing Bob, I think of that young guy then and then of now, because what you'll memorize, what you'll remember of not only then, but it's now, and it comes alive at this moment here. And there's Bob then with Bobby Camp, Hamilton Camp, doing *Daddy Roll 'Em* and there's nothing as exciting as that and then at Newport Folk Festival, just a kid from Boston — Joan Baez, and they sing *Virgin Mary Had a Baby* and all of a sudden that song explodes. And then there's Bob of course and Shel Silverstein, genius in his own right, very special right, and their songs. So there's a continuity here. And all that comes into play in hearing Jordan play tonight.

All rolled into one.

Holly Yarbrough filled in for her dad, Glenn Yarbrough, that night:

> I'm real sorry my dad couldn't be here tonight. He's on tour in North Carolina, but I'll tell you, he'd much rather be here than singing in Annie Get Your Gun which is what he's doing these days. But he did ask me to send you his love, and I'd like to sing a song for you, and since he's not here to do it, it's with love from him and from me. I also wanted you to know that I grew up singing your songs. Instead of your typical nursery rhymes, I'd sing Bob Gibson songs, and from a five-year-old, some of them could sound pretty funny. Your music has enriched my life and my dad's life, and I'm happy I could share this day with you.

Following this, Holly sang a beautiful a capella version of Amazing Grace.

Michael Smith came briefly but did not perform that night. He had very mixed emotions about the party:

> He was very encouraging to me when he was healthy and that's what I'll cherish. At the time of the party, I hadn't seen him in a long time, and I'd finally gotten the word about his illness. It was a shock to see his condition. It was a really tough night for me. That was partly me being the way I am at parties with just a whole bunch of people I don't know. I felt real sad that night, too, seeing the show where the people played all his songs to him. That was a very powerful, emotional experience and one that I couldn't sustain for a long time. I got out of it as soon as I could. There were a couple of things that struck me. One was when John Brown did his tune Sweet Bobby from Chi. That was a lovely, wonderful song, and it made me cry. I did not know John Brown well, but I didn't expect that of him. I thought that was really beautiful.
>
> Another thing that I saw at the party was the tremendous impact Bob had on people. Look at this world of people that loved and that were affected by him, worked with him, did songs with him, based their whole musical careers on his style.

It was an evening, not just of friends and fellow performers paying tribute to Bob, it was also a time of reunion and reconciliation of a family that had been too long apart. Bob's brother Jim came from Doha-Qatar for the evening, and his sister Anne Colahan came from New York. All of his children came, Meridian (who had changed her name from Barbara), Susan, Pati, Stephen and Sarah, and four of five of his grandchildren were there, too. Meridian took the stage and prepared to sing. First she spoke to the audience:

> This whole thing started when my dad said he wanted to have a party, and it's unfolded here in spades. It's just a pleasure to see you

all here. I've got relatives here I haven't seen in 32 years. We recognized each other right away. Last night we were sitting in the lobby and schmoozing, and I discovered the roots of the word familiar. I don't know why, I used to think we were a family that was distant. We're not. We're just very casual about keeping in touch. But I think I might actually get very serious about staying more in touch. Thank you for putting us all together for this event.

Those of you who I don't necessarily know but who've just been heroic figures on the horizon of my whole life, thank you so much for coming and honoring my dad. He's always been one of the heroic figures on my horizon, too.

She sang her song and left the stage. As she made her way through the crowd, Bob's seven-year-old daughter Sarah rushed up to her and whispered something. Reluctantly, Meridian once again took the stage and said:

I was kind of hoping I could get out of this. I wrote this song as a wish. When I first found out I was going to become a sister again seven years ago, I had mixed feelings about it. So I want you to know that I wrote this song as a wish, and everything I asked for has come true, more than I ever could have asked for. Thank you, Sarah. You opened up something very extraordinary.

Sarah Lou
(by Meridian Green/Gene Parsons — © StringBender Music, Inc.)

*Sarah Lou, what can I do
I hope the world makes you welcome
And your daddy learns how to love you
Sarah Louise maybe you hold the keys
When your daddy learns to love you
    Maybe he'll love me too*

*Chorus: There is another little girl
      and she cries
I want to light up my daddy's eyes*

*Sarah you've got what I always dreamed of
A daddy to hold you and tell you
    You are loved
Let him bring you up and
    never let you down
Take him by the heart girl
    Bring your daddy around*

*Sarah, my sister, it's a scary old world
I hope that your daddy loves
    His little girl*

That he protects you, loves and respects you
And when you need him
Your daddy will always be there
Chorus

Sarah Lou, what can I do
I hope the world makes you welcome
And your daddy learns how to love you
Sarah Louise maybe you hold the keys
When your daddy learns to love you
Maybe he'll love me too

At the end of the song, with everyone in the audience in tears, Meridian spoke again:

Sometimes, there's stuff that you just don't get, you know, because the fact of the matter is, my dad's always loved me. I just didn't get it for a long time.

One of the greatest thrills of the party was the arrival of Shel Silverstein, Bob's best friend and favorite collaborator. Known for his shyness, he declined to attend the benefit concert, but he would not miss this opportunity to be at Bob's last party. A wave of gasps rippled through the crowd as Shel walked to the front of the room where Bob sat right in front of the stage. Later Shel took the stage to sing one of his songs, Cuddlefish, *and to pay tribute to his friend:*

OK, I'll tell you how Bob got me started. Bob had a song — well it was about half finished — three-fourths finished. He'd heard that I'd written something, so he tossed me this and said, "You can try this." I was able to finish it — a Bob Gibson song, and another Bob Gibson song, and then we wrote some songs together, and then I was able to write some songs alone. And what I owe him, I will tell you, for all of us I think — for me, I shouldn't say all of us — what he did for us was he set the time for us and I know that at the time of the Earl and the Gate, John Brown's club — to be there was to be the best place in the world. To be where we were at that time — I've never had anything better —

I've never known anything better. I think it's important, you know, for us to know that — that we were at the best place at the best time.

So what more do I say about Bob? I had a band once that had a clarinet player — his name was Joe Moriani. Later on when Louis Armstrong passed away, they interviewed Joe on TV, among a lot of other people, and they said that we know how much you loved Louis Armstrong. Joe Moriani said, "No, I don't love Louis Armstrong." He said, "I am Louis Armstrong!" And this is true. This is true. I don't just love Bob Gibson. I am Bob Gibson. Because what he was comes into me and it comes out in the other stuff that I do, and maybe what I am goes out to some other people, not just to affect them or to entertain them — but that's enough if it was that — but we do become them and pass them on. So I thank you for coming into me and letting me pass that on.

Not having the stamina that he would like to have had, Bob tired early and went to the microphone to say good night. Seated in his scooter, he struggled to rise as much as he could in response to the tumultuous standing ovation he received. He said simply:

If you have to get a disease, don't get this one.

The party continued into the small hours of the morning. No one ever wanted it to end. George Matson summed up his feelings after the party was over:

I woke up the morning after that party Sept. 20 feeling totally alone, totally frustrated. My wife was sleeping, the kids knew Bob by name, but there was nobody that I could get hold of who understood. It was kind of like the letdown after a big class reunion. You're immersed in all those feelings and all these memories and then the next morning, everybody's on the plane and going and it's all gone. It just vanishes, and that's just the way it was with that party. It brought back so many wonderful memories of times we had on Rush Street and in Old Town. It was my whole social life. I just loved it there.

Also in attendance at the party was Roger Ebert who had been a fan of Bob's for some time. He wrote about the party in the Chicago Sun Times:

One week before he died, Bob Gibson hosted his last hootenanny. He flew in from Portland, Oregon, with his wheelchair and his fulltime caregiver, and attended his own wake.

It was exactly the feeling Bob had set out to achieve.

There is one more comment to make about the party to close this chapter — singer and former club owner John E. Brown (and as Rick Neely said, the first Gibson clone), got up to perform:

Elaine "Spanky" McFarlane and I started writing this song to the tune of *Sweet Betsy From Pike* in a hotel room one day. We got about three verses done. We were anticipating the benefit that was two years ago this month, but we never got it together. Well she called me about three weeks ago, and she dictated what we had on paper and I wrote three more verses. Then I had to learn to play it because I never played it back in the '60s. But the lyrics are just a little sort of historical account of Bob at the Gate of Horn about 1959. There he was singing *This Little Light of Mine*, and I said "I want to do that!" Three months later I had a job in a coffee house, and I just followed in his footsteps.

The lyrics to the first five verses are included in the Gate of Horn chapter. Here is the last verse of the song:

Oh, don't you remember sweet Bobby, my friend?
We'll be playing his music from now 'til the end.
Now, here's to you, Bobby, a toast from the heart,
May you play for St. Peter on your
12-string guitar!

(CENTER PICTURE FROM BOB GIBSON COLLECTION)

BOB GIBSON - 246

Sarah & Bob

L-R: Bob, Seannie, Fergus & Stephen

Stephen, Sarah & Bob

Bob's daughter Sarah & grandson Jordan

Sarah & Bob

Meridian & Bob

I Come For To Sing - 247

PHOTO BY CAROLE BENDER

L-R: Bob's daughter Sarah, Pati's children Jordan & Mackenzie & Stephen's son Fergus

Antonia Lamb & Meridian Green

PHOTO COURTESY ANTONIA LAMB

Carole Bender & Shel Silverstein
(Yes, that's Studs Terkel & Roger Ebert in the background!)

PHOTO BY JACK BENDER

Left — L-R: Jack & Carole Bender, Bob & Sarah Gibson

PHOTO TAKEN BY MARGIE GIBSON

The Gibson clan gathering in Chicago on Sept. 21, 1996.
Back L-R: Jim Gibson (Bob's brother) & his son Sam, Margie Gibson, Alexandra Colahan (Anne's daughter). Susan Hartnett, Anne Colahan (Bob's sister);
Center L-R: Pati, her daughter Mackenzie, Meridian, Bob, Sarah, Pati's son Jordan;
Front L-R: Stephen & his son Fergus and wife Seannie.

PHOTO BY ANTONIA LAMB

BOB GIBSON - 248

22

FAREWELL TO BOB

Full of the excitement of the party Bob returned to Portland, totally satisfied with what he had accomplished. He had lived a life full of passion, exploration, peaks and valleys — a life he could look back on alternately with amazement and pride, but never with a regret. In the quiet of the night on September 28, 1996, one short week following his farewell party, Bob Gibson succumbed to the ravages of PSP.

Josh White Jr. :
    I really didn't expect him to go as fast as he did. It was sort of like my old man. You'd just kind of take him for granted and just expect them to be around, but it was a privilege to be able to know him as a person and call him a friend and be one of the many that he touched and he brought up on stage to share the spotlight with.

Rick Neely looks back on the day of the Memorial Service on Saturday, October 5, 1996:
    The memorial service was a hard day. There was conflicting stuff that came out in the media. One said there will be no memorial service, and then another said there would be but that it would be private and another said there would be a public service. It was announced over the radio that it would be open to the public and actually it was supposed to be in one chapel at Rosehill and somehow that had gotten goofed up and it had gotten moved into a smaller chapel and there were people inside all the way out to the street. Studs Terkel spoke. A number of Bob's friends out of the entertainment circle from different recovery programs came and spoke. Tom Amandes came and spoke and there were some people that I had no idea who they were had talked about vignettes of their life where Bob was connected to it, and I sang. I sang the *Pilgrim* song and then Holly Yarbrough and I sang the *Wayfaring Stranger* together and then I played *Joy, Joy, Joy* on the banjo. It was so hard to come up with that kind of energy and do that and not look at the girls because they were losing it. It was a very strange, difficult day.
    I took the whole family out to dinner after the memorial service. We went down to Greek Islands and got a big table and they were all there — Sarah, Stephen, Meridian, Susan and her husband, Jeff, and Pati. We went for a long walk along the lake front, went down to Montrose Harbor and walked and walked and talked about different things — what everything meant, the party, the devastation of the

whole chain of events and how ironic the whole thing was.

What can you say when a legend passes? My mind is frozen right now, lost somewhere reaching for ways to express the feelings I have when my musical idol, my friend has died. I had not known Bob Gibson long, but his words, his music, his talent spoke to me in such deep ways, that I instantly felt I had been connected with him forever musically. When I was fortunate enough to meet him, despite the fact that he was suffering greatly from his illness, he made me feel with his warm smile and sparkling eyes that I was welcome and as much a friend as anyone else. I could see right away why everyone loved him.

I think perhaps sometimes an artist has a difficult time dealing with the everyday details of life as a human being. Once in a great while, a person comes along with such a rare gift of talent, that he seems to be on a different plane than the rest of us. Genius, perhaps, can be a burden. The talent, creativity and drive that make up such a person exact such a toll that sometimes there seems nothing left inside to give to personal relationships.

Maybe that's not it. Maybe being a common person with such gifts makes one sometimes feel uncomfortable. Learning about Bob, it seems almost as if he felt he didn't deserve the success that his talent seemed to be demanding he would have at the start. Could that be what led to self-destructive turns with drug use that interrupted both his career and his personal relationships with his family and partners? Was he maybe afraid to succeed? After all, if you get to the top, there's only one way left to go.

Whatever went through his mind through the ups and downs of his life, there is one thing that is never in question. Bob Gibson was a man of immeasurable genius, and the world of music owes him a tremendous debt. Whether we are aware of it or not, most of what we know as popular music today, would not exist if it had not been for his influence. Those he touched directly went on to influence others down the line in a chain that leads directly to today's music.

Certainly Bob Gibson had some personal demons at work on him throughout his life that provided many obstacles, some of which were almost insurmountable. He made choices of his own that drove wedges between himself and his family, and other choices that continually put his career in jeopardy.

Perhaps in the end, though, a man's character should be judged not by the mistakes he made in his life, nor his wealth by the amount of money he made, but by those who are left willing to rally enthusiastically in support at a moment's notice after the spotlight is turned off. In that case, Bob Gibson was indeed a man of the highest character and rich beyond measure.

The world is definitely a richer place having had the honor of Bob Gibson passing through. His music will live forever.

So if you want to write a song,
It shouldn't take you very long,
Though it's primitive and innocent
And wobbly at the start.
It's not a case of right or wrong,
'Cause the gift is in the song.
It's from your heart, oh yes,
It's from your heart, oh yes,
It's from your heart, oh yes,
It's from your heart!

Bob Gibson
Chicago - Living Along the Banks of the Green River
1981 ©Robert Josiah Music, Inc.

23

THE CONTRIBUTION OF BOB GIBSON

I think my greatest contribution to folk music is the relative minor chord - going from a C to an A minor or some such to an E minor. I used it a lot and I don't know that I would say that upon reconsideration, but it'll do. My main thing was the relative minor chord.

I don't think I'm that important in the folk revival. I don't think of myself that way. People were generous with me. There was a period when I started playing when I started hanging out in Washington Square which was an outdoor park in New York City. There were a lot of pickers and singers there — a lot of old time music. I'd see people like Woody Guthrie hanging out there. I'd stop someone who was playing and say, "How do you do that?" and they'd show you. It was great. There was a lot of transferring of information. People were always very generous with me. I just passed it along.

Bob's influence on folk music, and indeed popular music as a whole, is undeniable and profound. Despite Bob's modesty about his importance, it is a fact that whether people realize it or not, almost all of the popular music they listen to today has been touched by Bob's influence. This impact could be from something as direct as songs Bob wrote or co-wrote, artists he introduced, records he produced or from artists who say they owe their original inspiration musically to Bob's work. He was an artist who did it all: sang beautifully, played both the banjo and 12-string guitar with virtuoso skill and wrote wonderful music about topics of universal appeal, like falling in love and coping with life's struggles. And yet with all his personal talents, perhaps his greatest contribution was his willingness and eagerness to spend time teaching what he knew about writing, performing and playing.

John Irons:
Bob would regularly go to inner city Chicago schools to introduce the kids there to songwriting. It was a way he would try to teach them an appreciation for language skills.

Ed Kislaitis:
Once a year he'd take a group of inner-city kids canoeing and camping up North for a few weeks (thanks to his own efforts and his knack for getting

people like Gordon Lightfoot to do benefits).

His generosity is also legendary because of his love of introducing and creatively nourishing exciting new performers. Instead of looking at them as competition, from the beginning of his career, he took the greatest of delight in being able to introduce, manage, produce or co-write with new talented people.

Shel Silverstein:
I think what it was with Bob was he was so confident in his own output, in his own presence that there was enough left over for others. It's the frightened people, the insecure ones who wouldn't dare to give anyone else any credit because it may take away from them. For Bobby it was just like a very rich man giving away a dollar. He always appreciated talent. He's a great teacher for me.

If it were left to Bob's own assessment of his place in folk music history, the world would be painfully unaware of just how important he was. To truly understand his contributions, his influence, his greatness, one must listen, instead, to what his friends have to say about him:

Pete Seeger:
He was one of the people way back when folk music was just known to a small circle of friends and he helped spread it across the country. Keep in mind that what we call folk music is a branch of pop music whereas the scholars look upon it — they don't call this folk music because we're city people. The old definition of folk music is "music of the peasant class, ancient and anonymous." And the word, the phrase, was expanded by people like John Lomax who collected cowboy songs and lumberjack songs. And along came Woody Guthrie and a whole string of people following him like me and Bob and others who were all called folk singers. However, we were professional singers whereas most of the old people simply sang for their own amazement. You can recognize different definitions. I explain this way: You put a glass of Guinness Stout in front of an American and he'll spit it out and say, "Give me some beer!" If you put a glass of Budweiser in front of an Irishman, he'll spit it out and say, "Give me some beer!" They both have a word they call beer, but it's two quite different things.

Joan Baez:
I first met Bob Gibson when I sang at the Gate of Horn nightclub in Chicago. He invited me to sing with him at the first Newport Folk Festival in 1959. I was petrified. There were more people there than I had ever seen in one place. I sang two songs with Bob and it turned out to be a big thing.

Naturally I reveled in it. It was like a dream to me.

He was marvelously sarcastic and funny, drank too much, sang both serious and silly songs, and cracked jokes in between them; he actually 'entertained' people. When he brought me up to share the stage with him, he was giving me a bright and cheery smile, and his cocky look which meant that life was only one big joke anyway, so not to worry.

In August of 1963, I went out on tour and invited Bobby (Dylan) to sing in my concerts, following the example set for me by Bob Gibson four years before. I was getting audiences of up to 10,000 at that time and dragging my little vagabond out onto the stage was an experiment and a gamble. *(From Joan Baez's autobiography,* And A Voice To Sing With, A Memoir, *©1987, Summit Books, used with permission)*

Gordon Lightfoot:

I could certainly confirm that Bob influenced me. As a matter of fact, the album of *Gibson and Camp at the Gate of Horn* was what got me interested in folk music.

Back around about 1962 there was a real folk scene in the San Francisco, Chicago, New York — and Toronto was the Canadian center, and we had a couple of real great clubs here. One of them was the Purple Onion, which was really not named after the one in Los Angeles, and the other one was a place called the Fifth Peg, which was a very good one. Those were the two top clubs in town, and Bob came up from New York and played both of them at one time or another. Since I was just a fledgling artist at the time, I would go and watch his shows. I saw several of Bob's shows during that very formative time in my life in those two clubs in Toronto. During the next three ensuing years from the first time I saw Bob, I was recording for United Artists and gaining a bit of a reputation as a songwriter and one of the times when he came back, I went and met him and we got to know each other. He came to visit me, my wife and my family over at the house a couple of times. I knew him quite well. He was a great person to hang out with in terms of his knowledgeability. He was also a great teacher which he proved exceedingly well in the ensuing years at the Old Town School of Folk Music in Chicago.

Bob was a major figure in the folk revival and yet somehow, even though he had all the tools at his command, he was never able to break beyond the bonds of the folk during that five years just before the Beatles came in. Bob maintained a steady course after that. He did lots of shows, but nobody really heard about it. He was a true underground type of artist.

He was a standout performer in the *Hootenanny* series. Some performers shied away from that show, but Bob did it a number of times, and everytime he was on it, he was a standout. He was the king of stage presence among the folk singers, and he was a very fine musician too.

We always got along. We would meet from time to time through the years. One night in the late '70s, he and Steve Goodman and I did a set at the Earl of Old Town in Chicago. That was great.

There's no point of going into a great eulogy because Bob wouldn't like that anyway probably, but he took his friends seriously, and he had lots of them, and he was a great teacher. That's what I've got to say about Bob Gibson. His greatest contribution to folk music was instructor and teacher. He was always a friend, even when he wasn't feeling so good, and that could be from time to time too. Always a friend, always a smile.

Just a truly amazing person. You know, when I think back, it's him and it's Dylan — and that's about as far as it goes.

Tom Paxton:

My first contact with Bob came in the summer of 1959. I'd just graduated from the University of Oklahoma, and, together with some friends, I went up to Cripple Creek, Colorado, to try out for the melodrama. We got in the melodrama, and I spent the summer in Cripple Creek. We had one kind of sparsely furnished house for the actors and one for the actresses. My pal, John A. Horton (not the singer), had a reel-to-reel tape recorder. One night somebody came through and flopped at our house which happened pretty often, and he had a couple of seven-inch reels of tape and he played them. They were Bob playing at the Limelite in Aspen. This was the first we'd ever heard of Bob, and we were blown out of the water by his recordings. It was the first time we'd heard a lot of the songs that he sang, like — I remember *Virgin Mary* because it had such a gorgeous progression of chords. He sang it so beautifully. He was doing kooky stuff like *The Foolish Frog*. He had a whole lot of stuff, banjo and 12-string and we just thought this guy was great! Then I met him the following summer. I guess it was 1960. I was in the Army stationed outside New York, coming in on weekends working wherever I could. One night I came in a place called *The Commons* and there were two people on the stage. One of them I knew and that was Bobby Camp, who later changed his name to Hamilton Camp, but I didn't know the other guy, and they were just cookin'! I turned to Hugh Romney who later became Wavey Gravey and was my roommate, and I said, "Who's that?" He said, "Hey, man, that's Bob Gibson!" They were singing some of Bob's new stuff, *Well, Well, Well; You Can Tell the World;* and it was phenomenal. The thing that we all loved about it was that it had a driving rhythm, it had a kind of a gospel exultation, and it was right smack dab in the tradition. It was fresh. And they were on their way up to Newport. The previous year he had introduced Joan Baez and now he was going to introduce Bobby Camp. After Newport they went back to Chicago and kind of residenced at the Gate of Horn and did that amazing album. So I met Bob that night and wound up hanging out with him very late into the night and swapping songs.

First of all, Bob has been (wrongfully) criticized because a lot of young singers imitated certain elements of his style. Many coffeehouse folksingers, primarily in the midwest, misread what he was doing. They took the fact that he was a super-confident, sophisticated, urban performer, and latched onto all those things without bothering to understand that the guy really had his roots, really knew his instrument, really knew folk music, and really knew how to perform.

The things they didn't learn about were, in fact, his greatest strength. His sense of time is the best - it's absolutely flawless. His sense of the beginning, middle, and end of a song — the need to finish everything that is begun — is the kind of thing you rarely see in a tremendously casual, basically amateur form of music like folk music, which has so much of a living room quality to it. Bob can sing beautifully in a living room; he can also get up and quite unashamedly play the music for a living and knock the socks off people. It's that quality that all the young guys were trying to copy, but they couldn't copy the dramatic chord changes and one of the best right hands I've ever heard play the guitar.

His real influence, I think, is a lot harder to put your finger on. It has more to do with the personality of the guy, which was indomitable. He went though a lot of changes — he went though a lot, period — but he was still there doing shows as good as any I'd ever seen him do. He carried on.

He very successfully conveyed on stage the impression — which also happened to be true — that he'd rather be there, singing those songs, right then and there, than be doing anything else in the whole world.

I would say Bob's great contribution is his professionalism, that's what I would think. His professional approach to music and performing. He was really a model for me in stage craft — how to construct a performance, how to get the timing that goes into a performance I learned from watching him. Bob was a consummate professional in a musical field that often glorifies amateurism and a studied incompetence. I always appreciated his standards — he had professional standards that I admired — still do. He's a pro! Nothing wrong with that. And one of the best guys to hang out with too — funny guy. I loved spending time with Bob, laughing with him — quite a guy.

Glenn Yarbrough:

I loved his work, and I loved to work with him. He was a wonderful guy to work with.

Bob changed a lot in his old age. He's a lot like Lou Gottlieb, who was not a very nice person to be a partner with in the beginning of our arrangement, but he changed his whole life and so did Bob. He really did a wonderful thing in beating drugs. How he was able to do it I don't know, but it took a lot of guts for him to get out of that. There were a lot of times I helped him out when he'd get in trouble over drugs, but I could have put $100,000 into Bob Gibson and I'd still be ahead because he provided me with songs that were loving, beautiful songs that I sang and, you know, nothing's better than that. He and Shel and just he himself wrote some wonderful, wonderful things and I sang them for years and years and years, and all he really got out of it was the recording residuals, the mechanicals and stuff. The funny thing about it was that the exterior that he sometimes showed people was so ugly, but his soul was so pure and beautiful.

I don't know how that works, but it really was true. But everybody loves him. I don't care what he did. His music makes people love him so much.

Shel Silverstein:

Bob has been as strong an influence on me as anyone; he was one of the people who got me to start writing songs. I didn't know anything about songwriting, but Bob helped me. I got my publisher through him, and I learned the fun of songwriting from him. I've collaborated with him over the years many times.

His spirit was an important influence as well. He had a sense of joy about him. He approached his music in a very good way. He approached it with love, the same way he approached life. I learned a lot about music just by being around him.

He was always very encouraging and very pleased about what I did, which made me get better. It gave me confidence.

He's also always been a real gentleman — that's a funny word, but it's true. He had class then and he had it to the end. He had a strong sense of social and human responsibility, with sensitivity toward other people — other musicians, his audiences, people he's been personally involved with. He never played "star" or "freak." It was never "fuck you — I'm a musician." Not with Bob.

Roger McGuinn:

The first time I saw Bob I was going to the Latin school in Chicago. My music teacher was part of the Chicago folk scene. She played a little guitar and knew some of the people around, and she invited Bob to play for us in our school. It was, I believe, about 1957. He came over and did about an hour show. It was right around his *I Come For To Sing* album. He was doing those songs from *I Come For To Sing* on the banjo. He just had a banjo with him that day and I thought he was really cool. I was into Elvis and rockabilly and the rock & roll scene at that point, and when I saw that that banjo come through the door, I thought with a stringed instrument, maybe he'd do something like Elvis and that would be cool. He was wearing a brown shirt with a black tie. He looked really cool, and he played the banjo and he just knocked me out. I couldn't believe how great it was. After the concert I asked my music teacher, "What was that?" She said, "That's folk music." She said, "There's a school that just opened up called the Old Town School of Folk Music. Why don't you go over and check it out?" So I went over there and it changed my life — I totally converted to folk music at that point, and it's all because of Bob. I would say he's the major influence in my life. I was already playing guitar at that point. I taught myself a few chords and how to play some lead lines, but I didn't know how to play very well. When I went to the Old Town School of Folk Music I learned the five-string banjo, the 12-string guitar and obviously all kinds of folk songs and the folklore behind it, and I just fell in love with folk music. Bob wasn't teaching there then. My teacher was Frank Hamilton, who was later in the Weavers. He played on a couple of albums with Pete Seeger. In fact, I was walking in Greenwich Village with Pete Seeger one day talking about Frank, and Pete said "You know, Frank was the person who came up with the arrangement for *We Shall Overcome*." He just hadn't gotten credit for it, but it was Frank's arrangement that we all know.

I met Bob finally about a year later when I got good enough to start playing at the hootenannies at the Gate of Horn, and I would go down there at nighttime. I got a little job working at a coffee house, and I'd go down after my coffee house gig to the Gate of Horn. Bob was playing there. I met him at that point, really just as a fan. He didn't really know me, but I was hanging around enough to go into the back dressing room and talk to him. I remember one time I picked up his Vega 12-string guitar and took the capo off of it and played it a little bit and put the capo back on. Well when you take the capo off a guitar and put it back on it knocks it out of tune. He'd been out somewhere between sets and he came back and grabbed his guitar and went onstage, and it was totally out of tune. He came back offstage and he said "Who's been playing with my guitar?!" I didn't confess, but I think I told him later.

I got to really know him when he was living in Greenwich Village back in 1962. He was working sort of a long running engagement at the Bitter End. In fact I married his secretary, Susan. It was a very short marriage, but I knew him pretty well at that point.

Bob's greatest contribution? I think it was imparting the excitement and the enthusiasm for it to other people on stage. He was able to generate that better than any other performer I thought, maybe except for Pete Seeger, who was his major influence. And he took a lot of what Pete did but he kind of polished it a little bit more. Some people thought he was too slick for it but I really liked what he was coming up with. He had a very professional, polished approach. I always loved his sense of melody. Bob had the greatest sense of melody. He'd pick traditional songs with wonderful melody. It's hard to put it in a nutshell. He was really an extraordinary performer, and his greatest contribution was the ability to get people interested in folk music or whatever music he was doing.

I really got to like him in his latter years. He was like an uncle or something to me. He was a family member.

Hamilton Camp:

Bob Gibson introduced folk music commercially to America. I know that's been said before. But he is also the best entertainer I ever saw. I think it's his sense of conviction about what he's doing. He has a very big inner self, and he has the ability to let it come through. Sometimes, early in his and my careers, he would have shot his voice, and it would be good for only one or two notes — half a scale maybe — and he would keep an audience spellbound for an hour and a half. I would watch him every night, and I never got tired of seeing him.

He gave me the ability to let myself go on stage; there were very few restrictions I ever felt working with him. Over the years, we became like one musical organism. When we got together in 1970, ten years after we'd last sung together, we shook hands, went over four numbers once, and went out and did the show like we'd never stopped doing it!

What's amazing is the staying power of someone who stays and just keeps contributing. He'd teach and share. He worked with young people so much. I think, really, that his most important contribution was that he was never been too busy to talk songwriting with a young writer, to sit down with a kid and help him. He was the most sharing man I've ever known.

Lou Gottlieb - Limeliters:

Bob Gibson is really a great natural resource in this area. I had heard some of his albums, and I was working in a little club in San Francisco called the Purple Onion. I was doing comedy at the time. I saw him come in the club and he sat in about the third row. I was doing my "A" material, and about 15 minutes into the act, he got up very obviously and walked out. That cut me to the quick. So when we got together at the Limelite, Bob was working at the Hotel Jerome in Aspen, and I thought, "I'm gonna go over there, sit in the front row and walk out on him, and that'll be it, Olly!" So I sat down and he came out and the first thing he played was *Pastures of Plenty*. You know, music is really a great goose bump hunt, and I got a terrific attack of goose bumps! I stayed the whole show and it was marvelous, and he continued to be so!

Studs Terkel:

From the young have come excellent professionals. Among the best of these is Bob Gibson. Aside from his clear, strong tenor voice and his deftness with guitar or banjo, it is his impact upon the young that is so salutary. Probably the key to Bob's big score is involvement. As a result, his listeners become engaged. Certainly Bob is one of the major influences in this direction. Kids, who might otherwise have been restricted to the music of Irving Berlin and company, have now had new avenues opened for them. Gibson's value then is twofold: as performer and as ground-breaker. There was always an ebullience to Bob's way with a song. It makes you feel exhilarated. I guess you'd call it a life force that Bob has. When I think of Bob, I think of a time of hope and delight. Even for old gaffers like me. It is that contageous.

Judy Collins:

Bob Gibson was one of the most important influences in my early career. He's a marvelous singer who has led us to extraordinary songs and continues to be one of the most important influences in the resurgence of folk music.

Ed McCurdy:
   Bob was a very good natural singer. I mean he just showed up there and sang. I performed with him once or twice over the years. He had a very natural talent for song and he had good taste. He also did some writing and he was a very good banjo player. I felt a certain kinship with him because he was an alcoholic and also on drugs at one time. It wouldn't be a full story of him if you didn't mention that. I never got terribly intimate with him except in the beginning. I don't know what else I could say other than he was a good singer and a friend of mine. I'd say Bob's greatest contribution to folk music was singing. I don't know that I can say any more. I speak from the mind of a singer. I haven't been singing for years, but I still have the mind of a singer, and that's all a singer can say. He sang. He had a good song. Most of the people that got close to Bob and liked Bob were also performers. Most of us sang because we couldn't help it. We sang because we were singers.

Gamble Rogers:
   Bob Gibson exerted a huge influence on folk music in the 1960s, and for that matter, on American music in general, as folk music was a strong force in the music marketplace at that time. During those years, there was scarcely a record released by a new or established folk music group that wasn't inflected with Bob's style, particularly in the matter of musical arranging.
   His sense of arranging derived, I think, from the use of "power chords," that is, chord progressions far more complex and interesting in their structure than the three-chord simplistics common at the time. There were echoes here of white gospel, swing, and Dixieland, fused with an unerring gift for orchestration, particularly as regards variegated rhythmic texture. Bob's sense of rhythm, his instinct for dealing with the "hinge points" of rhythm, is what invests his musical arrangements with their peculiarly satisfying elements of power. The fact that this forthrightness of attack was accomplished on the 12-string — itself a difficult instrument — is most impressive.

Bryan Bowers:
   Gibber — bless his heart, man — he was just a bright, positive spirit. When I started getting a lot of press, Gibber didn't get weird. As a matter of fact, Gibber was very kind. He told me, "Look out, man, there's a lot of press coming your way. You've got to keep your head on straight. Don't start believing your press. That's the easiest thing in the world to do, and then you turn into an asshole. Just take it easy. You're good, but don't get the idea that you're the only thing that ever came down the pike." He was like a father figure to me. I had some musical chops at that point, but I didn't have any savvy about how to deal with the world and the music business and stuff. He was very kind to me at a vulnerable stage in my life. When that Chicago scene started for me, after I'd played a couple of weeks at the Earl then nothing happened, nobody came. Then Mike Seeger got me on at the Chicago Folk Festival, and in two days I got three major reviews in three major papers in Chicago, and I was made! Gibson took me under his wing and said, "You're

never going to be as good as they say you are, and you're never going to be as bad as they'll say later on that you are. Just keep your shit together, keep playing your music, try to be even-handed and be fair to everybody." He was just very good to me. There was a period of almost a year that was uncomfortable. I'd walk into Chicago and people would whisper, "There's Bryan Bowers!" It was unreal, and I often thought of Gibber's advice to me.

The funny thing to me was that by the time I met Bob, all the glory days of the Gate of Horn and all that were over. You know, it was just stories to me. When I met Gibber he was just kind of a frumpy old guy with a great sense of humor who could still play and sing great. I loved his music, but you know what I loved about Gibson the most? His laugh! When he'd get amused, he'd have this laugh that was just great. Gibber and I delighted in telling all of the jokes that you can't tell in public. We used to sit down and drink and tell these really bad jokes and stories and laugh. He was fun to hang out with. We drove from Chicago to Cleveland one time, and we talked the whole way. I couldn't tell you what we talked about, but we had the greatest time — talked and talked and talked.

I loved watching him and Hamilton Camp sit around a work up stuff. They were always chasing after the glory days that had already gone by, but, man, they could still play and they could still sing. It was just great! I remember him talking about going to see Richie Havens. Richie had invited him to come play and open some shows for him. Bob hadn't practiced in a long time, and all of a sudden he was playing and playing, and I said, "What are you doing?" He said, "Richie Havens invited me to open some shows for him, and if he thinks I'm gonna get up there and just do a pork pie, he's wrong!" So he was busy getting his act together, and I went, "Get it, Gibber!"

Michael Smith:
Bob was a cool guy, and the contradiction, I think, is somebody who is a very bright man and also a very adventurous man, certainly when he was younger. I think what I encountered was that enigma that makes somebody unforgettable on some plane and at the same time makes him very difficult. My whole relationship with him was waiting for him to do something and then try to help him. That was my relationship.

But he was very good to me, and the ways in which we conflicted disappear when I think about the ways in which he helped me. He really did put me forward when I would not have been out there myself. He didn't have to say, "Do some songs." And it was his notion to do that. I would never have suggested that. I mean, I'm aggressive at times, but I just couldn't have said, "Bob can I do something in your set?" After all, he was the big name. But with all his talent and his conflicts and his separate life, he did afford the time to be encouraging to me and gave me a showcase at a very important time when he didn't have to, and that's how I'll remember him.

Josh White Jr.:

The first time I ever saw Bob was, I think, in 1956. My old man was going to be working at the old Gate of Horn in Chicago. My very first impression of Bob was not a very nice one because I saw at the other end of the bar that my old man was having a heated argument with a short white guy, and I didn't care who it was. I didn't like him because he was having an argument with my old man.

Then several years later, I saw him and Camp at the Gate, which was truly memorable. At least for me, he was the reason why I started playing a 12-string guitar. I'd heard the 12-string guitar before. I'd heard Pete Seeger and Leadbelly and others play it, but it was Gibson's way of playing, his approach to the instrument that really got me. So I went out and I actually converted a six string guitar into a 12-string guitar — removed the bridge and saddle and had them replace it with a 12-string bridge and saddle. That was influence enough for me that I started playing 12-string.

I loved the way he would arrange traditional stuff that was so non-traditional. As for myself, I've never been a traditional folk singer at all, and it appealed. Both Gibson and Camp had great timing in their singing and playing and scatting back and forth. It was just innovative. I'd not heard folk music done before the way they worked together, learning later on that they never really rehearsed a lot. That even adds to the beauty of it. Their instincts were just tremendous. I know that there's a freedom that you have when you're just singing and you don't play. Sometimes there can be a little restriction because you are not only playing the instrument, but you are scatting or going back and forth with the other singer, but Gibson was able to do that so extremely well. He changed the way we look at folk music.

In 1965 I went on tour with Bob Gibson. It was my first big-time tour, and we went from San Francisco ending up in Detroit where I now live. On our tour, Gibson, being the gregarious person he always was in music, asked me to do a duet with him. I'm sure we did some Gibson & Camp tunes. At this point I don't remember which ones we did, but I was thrilled — one because the only other person I'd primarily sung with was my old man. For over 17 years when I'd started at age four, he was the one that I sang with on stage. I didn't really do a lot of stuff with other people and then to have Bob Gibson ask me to get up and sing with him was just a thrill. I was prepared to be just one of the performers on this tour, but it was Gibson who said, "Come up and do something with me." If it was left up to me, I never would have thought of it. But he did and it was wonderful, and I thank him everyday because he helped me, again, still maintain my own self in my presentation of music.

It was fun to work with someone where you kind of get a look and you know where you're going, where they're going, or you think you know where they're going. There is fun not always knowing exactly where you're going with the next person and see how you're going to work with it.

On stage I used to say, Gibson is the reason I'm playing a 12-string guitar and if I ever see Gibson again. . . . ." because I had to tune so damn much — so we decided to use that funny thing about him a lot. He was the one! He was the man! He made an indelible touch on a lot of us. I admire him. In fact, since he died, and I'm sure I'm not the only one, I'm getting some of the old Gibson songs out. It even made me get out my old 12-string— because I'd stopped playing it — to do *Fog Horn* and some of his other stuff from the album. It's just so choice! Because one of the best ways to keep him living for me is to do something of his on stage for those, like my dad, who might not have heard him, but this is something that he did, and if you want to know more, go get some.

Bob was a person who made it a point of letting you know, if it was not a song of his, who wrote it. A lot of people don't always do that, but he always gave credit to people.

People say, "Who are your influences?" I started so early — before a lot of my age contemporaries. I'd already been singing by the time the — '60s came along, but it was only two years into my solo performances which started in '61 that I had my 12-string because of Bob Gibson. I thank him, I thank him.

It is a source of great pleasure to sit at home watching the first annual folk music awards knowing the first three inductees are Pete Seeger, Woody Guthrie and Bob Gibson, for having the most impact on generations of performers and their contribution to humanity.

Odetta:

I was called to Chicago's Gate of Horn to sing on the bill with Paul Clayton, the most recorded folksinger, and Bob Gibson, the most energetic, joyous and charismatic performer I had ever witnessed. Gibson was open, generous and welcoming to me. I'm eternally grateful because I was one scared puppy in those days. The celebration coming to us as Bob performs is something that cannot be taught or learned. This gift is his very own, and while there are hundreds of thousands of us, too few of us have partaken of it.

George Carlin:

I only saw Gibson and Camp once. I think they did a sort of a special appearance or something that I saw 'cause people had always talked about them, and it was the folkie era and everything, so I was curious. Like a lot of people, I just thought they were wonderfully entertaining, good singers, good musicians, and I enjoyed 'em. *(Note: Carlin also hosted the WTTW Gate of Horn reunion broadcast in 1972 which included Gibson & Camp.)*

Bonnie Koloc:

I really didn't know Bob that well, but I knew him because we played at the same clubs. I'll tell you the one thing that struck me — I hadn't seen Bob in a while and I went out to California in the late '70s, and I heard him play in a little club. He was just so professional and so wonderful that it just knocked me out. I'd seen him periodically in Chicago, but for some reason I hadn't seen him for a long time and that night he was just so wonderful and so real. I sure admired him. I really believe that Bob is the one that brought folk music more to the attention of people like college people, and he really helped get the commercial ball rolling. Of course he was a really wonderful writer, too. I thought his performances were very authentic and really wonderful — just great. You know, you get used to people and you see them play, but he just knocked me out. His show was totally fresh, totally entertaining. I don't know, when you see people a lot and you see them again and they continually continue to blow you away . . . It was real honest and a real delight.

Rick Neely:
Bob and I had a strange relationship. There are fans and there are fanatics, and I'm somewhere, strangely, probably towards the fanatic end. I think, now, as an adult, I think what Bob did through his music was he replaced my father at that particular time, I always had that real connected feeling to him.

I was going to say a thing at Bob's farewell party — without Bob Gibson, folk music would not have E minor. I think Bob probably enriched the musical language of folk music because he was so far ahead of his time. Whatever anyone else was doing at that time, he just stretched the limits. He was more jazz oriented, chord formations were different and everybody was playing simple one-, two-, three-chord songs and that was it, and here comes Gibson with his handful of harmonic ideas and just changed everybody's outlook. That would be the one important contribution of his more than anything else. Great, indomitable, showmanship-like spirit.

Bob and I sang together one time at the Earl of Old Town. I was awful. I was so nervous and we did *Skillet Good and Greasy* and it was probably right on the edge of being awful, and when we came off stage, I said, "Oh, that was so much fun! Let's do this again sometime!" He didn't say a thing. He didn't say a word. He just looked at me and shook his head, and that was it. We never approached the subject again. I just went my own way and I got better and better. I got more confident. It'd be like you all of a sudden had an opportunity to say prayers with God! It was that nervewracking.

Now I'm the keeper of the strum. I try to sound just like him. For a long time I tried to deny it, but I've been trying to play this stuff since I was 16 years old and I'm almost 50! So you've either got to do it exactly correct or don't do it.

Fred Holstein:
In Chicago, at least, Bob Gibson **WAS** the folk revival. He turned so many people in the midwest on to the music. I just loved his banjo work. He influenced me to start playing that instrument. Back then he was playing Pete Seeger-type stuff. One of the first albums I ever owned was his *Off-Beat Folk Songs*. I had never heard those songs in my life, and they were fantastic the way he did them. For the rest of his career he'd still gets requests for songs from that album which was made in 1956!

I don't think anyone played the banjo like Bob. He had so many great ideas on it — and the banjo is a hard instrument, because of its limitations, to develop new ideas for.

He's a classic performer. Just watching him perform is a pleasure. He has a warmth, and real charisma. He knows what to do; he knows how to please the audience. That's what a performer is supposed to do. When I watch him play, he looks like he's having fun up there, like he's having a good time. I can always learn something by watching him perform - just the way he moves! He's an original. Anybody who really wants to learn how to perform should watch Bob Gibson.

Did he influence me? I wanted to grow up to **BE** him at one time; I really did. I had all his moves down, and I started smiling like him . . . I was just one of a string of many other musicians who wanted to be Bob Gibson. I still love to sit and watch him perform. He's so great at it.

It's so interesting what he did for folk music. He was one of the first people to put the music into saloons, he and people like Josh White. He showed that you could have fun with it without its being totally academic. That's very important to me, because to me the essence of it is having fun with the music. That was a contribution of immense magnitude. Over the years he's brought a lot of pleasure to a lot of people, not only through being a musician, but through being a teacher. He's always been a warm and charming performer, and a warm and charming person. He makes you want to say, "Yeah, Bob; I want to go where you're going."

Ed Holstein:

I graduated from high school in '65. Mainly people older than me were into folk — people who were Northwestern students in the '50s. I was aware of it though because I started buying records like Rosemary Clooney at a very early age — about 7. Then in '57 Fred brought home the *Offbeat Folksongs* album because of the calypso thing basically. I was 10 and I had teachers who were 21 or 22 who talked about the Gate of Horn who were amazed that I knew who Bob Gibson was. I started listening to the Midnight Special so I knew a lot about the Gate of Horn in my mind.

At first when Freddie brought home the record I couldn't figure it out because I'd been listening to Little Richard and Fats Domino, so at first it was a little bit odd for me. Then I started to listen to *Lula Gal,* soft, mellow not modal like I really liked and that was the start of my involvement. He made folk music accessible as he progressed on and took songs and did arrangements. If you listen to *Gibson & Camp at the Gate of Horn,* you'll hear a guitar arrangement on songs like *Skillet Good and Greasy* are C, Em, Am - boom ba-ba boom ba boom and that *Civil War Trilogy* and I think at one time that John Lennon mentioned that he had listened to that. Everybody had listened to that record. I remember I was in Carly Simon's apartment one time and the record was there. It was really sophisticated stuff. Of course the purists were going crazy, because Gibson & Camp were accessible and urbanized.

I think Bob's biggest contribution was making the music accessible, music that people might not have been interested in that a lot of people aren't interested in, but the idea that he was such a good storyteller and he could take a subject that would ordinarily bore you - he did that with music. He'd take these folksongs of the Civil War because he was a Civil War fanatic and he made them accessible with those chord changes. They were incredible. That's why if you listen to John Lennon and Paul McCartney, I think they must have heard him because those chord changes were there — C, Am, F. Before it was C to F to G, but he threw the minor chords in there. So taking something that would be otherwise dry and maybe not interesting and making it very interesting to people. The minor chords were striking. He did a version of Sweet Betsy from Pike that you can hear in a Rolling Stones song, where he went from D to C to G — very dramatic. Heck, the Beatles used his riff in *You've Got to Hide Your Love Away*. Very close to that sound — D to C to G.

Dave Samuelson:
Bob was just incredibly charismatic and his music generated such power it was overwhelming and inspirational. People have different takes on Gibson. So many people think that the Riverside era was the peak. Some think the early Elektras were. It was almost like he kept reinventing himself in many ways maturing as a performer. He came back with the *Funky in the Country* album and his powers were back. The Capitol album is superb, as are many of his others. He was a genius and everybody loved him. His impact on American music was enormous. Look at a copy of the second Buffalo Springfield album — probably the most important seminal LA country rock band with Neil Young and Stephen Stills and all these powerful people. They thank a lot of people who influenced their music. Most of them are in tiny little letters and with Bob Gibson they put it in great big letters on the back of that album. These are heavyweights in modern American music who single out Bob Gibson as being probably one of the most important of 50 or so people they thank on the back of that album. It'll just jump out at you. His impact has been enormous and the secret of his music was in his power and later years he lost some of that power and it sort of baffled people because that was what was so intriguing and every so often he could summon all that power like he did on the *Revisited* album.

Mick Scott:
I first heard Bob on WFMT's Midnight Special radio show — tapes of him and Camp from the Gate of Horn, and then the album *Gibson & Camp Live at the Gate of Horn*. That record very strongly influenced me; its energy blew my mind. What really struck me was the urbanization of the folk music, how he was able to carry that off without being crass. There were a lot of songwriters who would revamp *Wildwood Flower,* and it would come out sounding like disco. He did it tastefully. He cross-fertilized urban influence with traditional music, and created those very sophisticated settings for his songs. Whenever I find myself getting too slick, heading too much toward a rock-like sound, I'll listen to that album and remind myself to come back to earth.

His use of chords — of clean major and minor chords — contains such simplicity! He constantly changes chords, basing it all on simple triads; that's what makes his style unique. He also plays up the neck more than most 12-

string players; more, in fact, than most six-string players! He uses a banjo frailing method of playing the 12-string but is still very melodic without being erratic.

He's very easy on stage. Working with him I always felt very comfortable. He has a very quiet but loud-speaking joy. He always encouraged me to have a good time onstage. Something else I also noticed a lot about the Gibson & Camp album, basically Herb Brown was back there just pecking away and that was a part of it and obviously Bob must have really enjoyed that, too. That's the way I felt when I was playing with him.

Emmylou Harris:
I'm primarily known as a country singer, but really, I got into it through folk music. Bob Gibson was there at the forefront of the folk movement and he was, and is a modern day troubadour.

Richie Havens:
When I first came to the Village, Bob Gibson was the first inspiration for me to pick up a guitar and it was his song that did it for me.

Jo Mapes:
There is a magic that happens when this man starts to sing.

Ian Tyson:
Bob Gibson is my hero. I bought all his records in the '50s. He's one of the reasons I got into folk music.

Noel Paul Stookey:
I was late coming to the folk "scene", but both Peter and Mary knew Bob Gibson and his music well. My first glimpse of the Gibson magic was the night that the three of us arrived in Chicago for our first gig at the Gate of Horn folkclub in Chicago. Our week was about to start; his week was just ending.

That first time and subsequently whenever I saw Gibson on stage, he always seemed to have this sparkle — a twinkle if you will — as if he knew a secret about life that caused him to bubble from the inside...it was so easy to be drawn to his music and manner.

But you know how sometimes you look back at your life and realize just how much impact someone had on it even though you didn't know it at the time? Well, Gibson was like that for me. I mean, when my solo album was released in the early '70s, and the *Wedding Song (There is Love)* became a top 30 hit, some folks thought that I was the first to be presenting a contemporary gospel message in a folk style, but they forget that Bob was writing and performing folk/gospel originals like *Well, Well, Well* and *You Can Tell the World* in the sixties!

It seems so little to be able to contribute to such a great influence.

George Matson:
I was a camp counselor one summer and had just been getting into folk

music and Peter, Paul & Mary. My co-counselor pulled up in his truck and started to unload stuff and I saw this *Gibson & Camp at the Gate of Horn* album on top of his things, and I asked him what it was because I'd never heard of them. The guy said, "You've never heard of them? Listen to this!" He played it and it knocked me out. It's a magic piece of showmanship. It transends time and generations because it's so genuine and such pure entertainment.

There are lots and lots of technicians who could dazzle you, but nobody could make a guitar thunder like he could. I don't know, it was him and the guitar together — there was a melding that came out. You know, technically, he wasn't brilliant, but he just had a feel for that instrument.

David Bragman:

I first heard *Gibson & Camp at the Gate of Horn* when I was a junior in high school on the phonograph at my high school library, and I thought, "WOW, this is incredible!" Musically, he became one of my big mentors. I had started playing guitar by that time and learned most of the songs on that record. I wanted to get a 12-string guitar and not too long after that did. I grew up listening to folk music on the Midnight Special and so Bob Gibson was one of the names I always knew. I remember being a kid at summer camp, the first sleepaway summer camp I ever went to and one of the counselors played guitar and banjo, and I remember hearing *Abilene*. I was about seven or eight at the time. I was thinking how much Bob has done for folk music, and it's very humbling to me that I've been able to get to know him personally and to be able to tell him that was a very significant moment to me. There are two musicians who really indirectly influenced my becoming a professional musician. They are Bob Gibson and Art Thieme. And I'm very proud that both of them have become very good friends to me. I only performed with him once at the Clearwater with Bob and Josh White Jr. I got a chance to play banjo for Bob and that was such a thrill. I remember at the Philadelphia Folk Festival, one of the songs that I came away with was his version of *Sweet Betsy From Pike* where he played it in the key of D and he dropped the low E down to D and I still play that.

I try not to be too ego-bound with all this crap, but it makes me so proud that Bob and Margie and Sarah know my name. There's something there that's really incredible.

People are going to keep singing his songs. In the musical scheme of things, most people don't know who Bob Gibson is, but people who do, know how important he is.

Christine Lavin:

He's encouraged a couple of generations' worth of songwriters through his involvement in the Kerrville Folk Festival's songwriting school. His influence as a songwriter will be held for generations to come, with all the new writers that he's personally encouraged.

Don McLeese:

If the genial Bob Gibson can't be considered the patriarch of contemporary folk (we'll leave that to Pete Seeger), he's at least everyone's favorite uncle.

Allan Shaw:

Gibson & Camp at the Gate of Horn, released December, 1961, became a benchmark by which other folk records of the era were measured. It was everything one could hope for. Critics rate it with *The Weavers at Carnegie Hall* and it is included on almost every discography of folk music. Whether as a source for songs, for style, or for arrangements, there is probably not a popular folksinger or group of the folk era that doesn't owe something to Gibson.

Art Thieme:

Bob influenced me primarily by setting a grand example. When I first saw him in the late 1950s, he was doing almost all traditional songs - mostly with banjo. I think he was only doing one song with the 12-string guitar — *Matty Groves*. His show was very traditional, yet extremely entertaining. He combined a fresh, hip showmanship with these old songs in a way that made unlikely audiences much more receptive than they would have been otherwise.

Later, Bob changed his style radically. He moved away from the traditional songs I loved so much, but I still love to watch him. He's still GIBSON, and the charm is still there. He represents my adolescent youth, and I bring all of that with me to a Bob Gibson concert.

Most of all, Bob Gibson showed me how much fun it could be singing the great old story songs, the folk songs. Bob went on to other things, but somewhere back in 1958 he planted a seed that started me on the folklore road. My God, he was a fine folksinger. You know something? He still is!

John Irons:

In some respects, Bob Gibson was the Segovia of the folk scene. He was the right guy in the right place with all of the right talents, a great set of vocal chords, great lungs, great musical interpretation and technical skills on the instruments. Bob came on the scene and things changed, and he wasn't a one man crusade, but he was definitely one of the leading generals. The other important part of the story was when it changed again. Look at some of the Beatles' early material. They were a bridge between folk songs and soft folk rock. Take away the drum track and you've got folk songs. It wasn't until the bubble moved even further that folk dropped off and the population moved into the more heavy metal sound. The effect on that was that whenever it changes, usually the people at that point in time are left out in the cold. Where Bob missed the boat was he didn't realize how far ahead of the scene he was. Instead of Simon & Garfunkel, it could have been Gibson & Camp. Look at their harmonies!

Lenny Laks:

Bob was important because he was one of the bridges. He was like a link from folk music to rock & roll. Because he was like the Kingston Trio and Josh

White — there was folk music and folk music was square. Bob was not square. When Bob played that music it was alive and it was bluesier — and I don't mean Black bluesier — I mean it had a feeling that was very easy to get next to. It wasn't intellectual. Most folk music is intellectual, or it's people copying folk music, and they're intellectuals so that's what the music sounded like. When Bobby did it it wasn't intellectual. Plus he's the kind of guy who could write folk music. I mean, how can you write folk music? But he could write a song and you'd swear that that song was public domain. Who could write *Abilene?* Give me a break! You know that that's a campfire song that comes from some guy in Kansas City in 1885, and it's not! That's his biggest contribution — he could write folk music. He wrote music that sounded like no one wrote it. But he really was the link. He took that music up tempo and made it rock! All by his lonesome.

Steve Clayberg:
I went to Kendall Elementary, the oldest elementary school in Tulsa, near Tulsa University. The year was probably 1956, and I was in the fifth grade. We didn't have a music class per sé. We had what we called a speech class, but Thursday was music day and the teacher, Miss Rubenstein, loved music. Music day was a big day for her because that was her favorite subject, so we had all kinds of choirs and stuff like that. One time I specifically remember that she was all excited because there was a person who was going to come and entertain our class on music day. We knew about it two weeks ahead of time, and the parents were invited to stay if they wanted to. That particular day. The person that was coming was a folk singer. At that time I didn't know what folk singing, or really any kind of singing was. Mr. Gibson showed up. He came early and he left late. He had two or three instruments. He had a ukelele and he had a banjo. I can tell you he LOVED what he was doing, and from the first I literally loved it so much that I asked about a hundred thousand questions, and, actually, I stayed for the second group, too, and he took me aside and taught me a Russian folk song called *Ivan Skovintsky Skovar.* You could tell that this was his life and that he enjoyed every single aspect. Anyway it piqued my interest in songs in general and finally songs that had a reason to be sung. Even at that age I could certainly see what he was talking about. He took extra time with me, and I was so moved I'd have probably been a folk singer after that if I'd ever taken the time to learn. I was much better than average in sports at that time, and that sort of consumed my life, so I didn't go into music, but what he DID do was legitimize people who did things other than become engineers. I remembered him forever.

He was an inspiration in my life, because I saw him as someone who loved doing something artistic. It literally opened up another side of my brain, and I always appreciated that. I thought about it back in college. I could tell this guy really believed in what he was doing and that it was the only thing he wanted to do. That's exactly what came across. When you see someone who's in love with their job, it's so infectious. It makes you enjoy it. He affected at least one person in his life. He affected me.

24

THE ASPECTS OF GENIUS

What was it that made Bob Gibson so special? What about him made everyone come forward to say what an influence he was? His gift was multi-faceted and can basically be broken into three categories.

BOB GIBSON — THE SONGWRITER

My earliest work was for the Ohio Folklore Society, singing mostly to college professors. In the process, I decided that a lot of traditional songs needed some reworking, some rewriting. And pretty soon I was writing songs.

There was no real decision to do it. There was no moment when I realized that this would be quite different from adapting and arranging traditional music or writing new words or new verses for them. There was no point at which I thought, "I'm going to break away." It was just that I was working with Camp and the possibilities were greater, and I responded to the possibilities. My first was, *Who Shall Serve Me?* Then Camp got together with Shel Silverstein, who was coming in a lot. They wrote *The First Battalion.* Then Shel and I started writing together. Then Camp and I were writing together, and then I wrote with everyone, but Shel was the first. I always think of him as my mentor, but he says I'm his mentor. He says I taught him everything he knows about songwriting. I don't know about that. I think he taught me everything I know about songwriting.

I got very turned around by Shel. I hung around with him awhile and did a bunch of writing with him, and I said, "Wait a minute. This guy is still writing the greatest songs in the world, and he **may** know four chords, and if he does, he doesn't push it. Less is more. His music is not unsophisticated. It has gone beyond that to the point where the purity shows. I really think less is more. I think that the simple thing can make it sustain the facts and fullness. There's a certain rightness of absolute predictability when the the melody goes in, when the chords move in, when the words move in, the idea moves in. Even though it's a surprise. Even though you say, "WOW!", you say "Yes! Of course!"

Shel Silverstein:

It isn't true that I started Bob songwriting. I didn't start singing or writing songs until after I'd heard him. It's just a fact. If he wants to give me credit for helping his writing - sure! That's the idea. You get better when you collaborate. You start learning how they think. That's when you grow. And so pretty soon I'd start learning a little bit how Bob would make a change here, or do some musical movement. I can do a little of that. I can't do enough. I can't do what he does. But you become better because you absorb from him.

When I met Bob he was working at the Gate of Horn and I was hanging out. Everybody was hanging out. You know, at that time, you knew that when he would get on stage, something totally exciting was happening - something really dynamic. And then when he and Camp were singing together, there was nothing like that and it was that level of excitement. But it was also a social life around Gibson, and all the girls just swarmed him. I mean, you know, that was just like some kind of super stardom and it wasn't so much that you wanted to play like him - you wanted his life! You wanted girls to come around you. At that time not many girls came around when you were sitting alone in a room drawing pictures of naked women.

So that was all an inspiration and then Bobby Camp (Hamilton Camp) and I wrote our first song. He was just learning to play the guitar. He'd been singing with Bob Gibson. He was starting to play the guitar and sing a little bit alone, and he and I wrote a song. And then Gibson heard that and liked it. One day he said, "Well, you know, you write pretty good. I've got this half finished song, and he gave it to me. I guess *Frankie & Johnny* or *Tellin' Those Lies About Me*. I can't remember. I think it was *Frankie & Johnny*. But he let me finish it. I was thrilled to get a chance to work on a Bob Gibson song. And then we did more stuff, and then we started writing a lot of stuff together.

Later when Bobby was not writing that much, he started singing my songs. Always in collaborating, certain attitudes are necessary, certain personalities. There are certain people that I admire greatly, but I could never collaborate with them because of the attitude. For collaboration you cannot be too worried about whether the song expresses all your feelings. You've gotta just say, "It wouldn't have been finished without this other person. It wouldn't exist." And you have to just let it go. If it turns out to be a great song, you take full credit. If it turns out to be a flop, you say, 'Well, it's 'cause he wrote half of it." Not really! And you can't pick at it. And Bobby was the best at that. He just gave me what he did. I didn't mess with it. I gave him what I did. He didn't fuck with it. It was JUST fun! And it wasn't hard work. And it wasn't agony. I know it couldn't have been, because I know he sure wasn't gonna put up with any problems and I sure wasn't gonna do anything that was painful. The whole idea for all of us was avoiding pain at every turn of the way. So I don't take our collaborative artistic things - and with a lot of people that's what you get. I don't say it don't work. But it don't work for certain personalities. And that's what made that fun.

I would say most of the songs generally Bobby started and then I'd come and do my stuff. And then some of them I started. He did primarily music. But he did a lot of words. And the few musical ideas I had, he welcomed. But I would say that he did primarily music and he did words, and I only did words. And I did concepts sometimes.

He also taught me how to divide a song. A lot of people — a lot of my friends over the years — have had a lot of trouble when two people collaborate. The question often comes up, "Who did what?" So "How much of the song belongs to you?" Did you write three lines, did you write the chorus? And that causes a lot of pain, a lot of stopping of collaboration. I remember with our first song, Bob came to me with a contract with his publisher who is my publisher today. I'd never seen a contract. He said, "Well you gotta sign this contract." I said, "OK, I'll sign it." I looked at the contract and it said "50% Bob Gibson, 50% Shel Silverstein". And I said, "Wait a minute. I didn't really contribute 50% of the song, and I can't take 50% of the proceeds. Little did I know there would be no proceeds, you know. But I said, "I can't take 50%." He said, "Well, what percentage can you take?" I said, "I don't know," and he said, "That's the point. That's why you gotta take 50%. You can't start to figure who did what. If you contribute to the song, you're a co-writer — an equal co-writer." It's something I always quoted to all my friends in Nashville. Do not get into picking apart percentages of who did what. If they added anything to it, they're a co-writer, because the song would not exist without them. Would not exist. So it's just easier that way.

When writing with someone I think it's collaborating even if it turns out that the other person doesn't even write a verse or a word. You wrote it because they were there. Shel's my favorite songwriting partner - bar none. He's been working with me over the years.

During the period 1970-74, there weren't many jobs for me other than in clubs in the Old Town of Chicago. I was just hanging in there. I had been doing the same set of songs for several years. And I wasn't writing, I wasn't learning.

Shel Silverstein was very helpful in jarring me out of this. I just ran into him and he said, "You want to write some songs?" I said, sure, let's write a song. He said, "We're not writing one song — we're writing two of them." Shel is a very wise man. You can write just one song, but it may not be very good.

To show how he works, one time he was having something to eat in a coffeehouse in Nashville and Mac Davis came up to him, saying, "Hi, Shel, I've always hoped that someday we could get together and write a song." Shel said, "Let's do it right now." When Davis balked, Shel insisted. And they wrote two songs right then. One of them, *Pour Me Another Tequila, Sheila,* became a big hit. Shel's a very creative guy, an inspiration to be around. One of his best known songs is *A Boy Named Sue,* that was Johnny Cash's big hit.

We wrote *Stops Along the Way* for the album. That song is sort of autobiographical. Shel wrote *Living Legend.* About me? I don't know. But I know when I first heard it, I said, "I can't sing that. It's too open! It reveals too much." It was just too close to my life. He insisted. "Go on, sing it," he said. I had a tape of it and listened to it a few times. I tried it once and that was it. It felt good.

Writing a song, the first inspiration comes from God. Then you just work on that, but there were a lot of ways I would check it out. I had a list of about 17 things to do on a song, and I'd check through the song to make sure I got them all accomplished. Reversals were very important. Often you wrote the punch line first and then tried to top it. If you couldn't, the best you could do would be set it up and let it pay off. Therefore it was essential to go to work and see if your reversals pay off and so forth. There wasn't a set way I wrote. Sometimes it would be music to words and then I wrote words first. Sometimes I would have a song that just came out the way it was.

Easy Now and *Looking for the You in Someone New*— those are my two favorites of the songs I wrote. *Abilene* of course was my biggest commercial hit. *Abilene* has also probably been recorded by the most people, although *Frankie and Johnny,* which was written by Shel and me, amazingly enough has about 36 licenses on it. It's incredible. I'm still making money from *Abilene.* I get royalties about twice a year. Maybe thousands total at best. I'm not a wealthy man. Another song I wrote with Camp, *You Can Tell the World,* which Simon and Garfunkel recorded on their *Wednesday Morning 3 A.M.* album, still makes me money to this day. Oh boy, am I glad they recorded that. Camp and I recorded that on the *Gibson & Camp Live at the Gate of Horn* album.

> *You can tell the world about this,*
> *You can tell the nations about that,*
> *Tell them that the master has come,*
> *Tell them that the gospel has won,*
> *He brought joy, joy, joy into my heart.*

By 1974 or so, I was starting to get involved in teaching songwriting. I love it. I'm good at it. The difference between the pros and an amateur is in the rewrite. To face a blank page of paper, you have to be free, almost innocent, and let it flow. Then you go back and get critical. The urge to write is the most important thing. If you enjoy the experience, then you can get better. I've had a lot of fun trying to help people get better.

For many years, my course was offered for credit through DePaul University in Chicago and Portland State. I was at Portland State in the summer program teaching songwriting on the beach for two years, which was nice. It was called the Haystack Series and consisted of two-week seminars with graduate credit. It was also possible to take the course indirectly through a network of local colleges, but the course was taught either in Chicago or Oregon.

> **American Conservatory of Music**
> presents
> **Successful Songwriting**
> with
> # Bob Gibson
> A Songwriters Workshop
>
> Saturday & Sunday
> November 12 & 13
> 9am-6pm
>
> Registration Fee: $95
> American Conservatory of Music
> 116 S. Michigan Ave., Chicago
> (312) 263-4161
>
> This workshop is designed to provide a stimulating learning environment in which to learn the craft of songwriting.
> • How to release the 'creative flow'! • Form, structure, editing! • Making a demo! • Getting a song published! • Getting performers to sing your songs! • Critique, performance, review of student works!
>
> Bob Gibson, who has spent several years developing this workshop, has more than 150 published songs. He has influenced the careers of performers such as Simon and Garfunkel, Bob Dylan, Gordon Lightfoot, and others.
>
> **Bob Gibson will bring the craft of songwriting to life!**

Meridian Green:

Bob taught a song-writing workshop and a performance workshop as part of an arts program sponsored by the University of Oregon, in Cannon Beach in the summer of 1980. Bob and Margie came out from Chicago, Susan and Jeff came from Portland, and I drove up from Mendocino with my son Terra who was three years old. We all spent a week together in a house on the beach. It was the first time I'd seen Bob since he'd started A.A. and he was very different. He was attending meetings everyday. He was very real, very humble, and very brave to have asked me come. I found myself cautiously intrigued by the possibility that Bob was really clean and intending to stay that way.

He invited me to attend the performance workshop and arranged for Terra to attend the program's daycare. It was an extraordinary opportunity to spend some time with my Dad in the serene and focused space that he created in the workshop. He shared his insights into stagecraft, how to engage an audience, how to develop patter, how to pace a show and most important, his philosophy regarding performing as a service to the audience. I'm so grateful to have been there. The finale of the workshop was an evening performance at a local pub where my classmates and I each performed a tune or two with our brand new breakthroughs in stagecraft. It was transcendent experience for me, especially when my Dad gave me an appraising look followed by a joyful grin and said, "You really are a chip off the old block."

Around 1981 I did a one-day seminar at the Iowa Writers

Workshop in Stone City, about an hour away from Cedar Rapids. It's a beautiful section of Iowa, real rolling, real hilly with rivers and stuff and some limestone quarries some Irish brothers had. They gave it up around 1920 and Grant Wood, famous for his painting "American Gothic," took it over and opened it as an artists retreat. In addition to teaching, I performed in an old limestone building that once was the general store but by then was a small club and restaurant. It was pretty exciting stuff. They're nice folks.

The songwriting classes really took off and were really rewarding for me. Of course, I always took the greatest pride in the songwriting school I started and ran for twelve years at the Kerrville Folk Festival in Texas which I mentioned earlier, but I did seminars all over. In addition to those I already talked about, I did songwriting workshops, seminars or courses at the Old Town School of Folk Music, Governors State University and American Conservatory of Music in Chicago, Minneapolis Songwriters Association, Washington, DC Songwriters Guild, William Rainey Harper College in Palatine, Illinois, The Fret Place Folklore Center in California, Golden West College, Huntington Beach, CA, University of California at San Luis Obispo, and the National Education Conference in San Luis Obispo.

Bob Gibson was not a prime mover in the protest era. Much of the time he was off fighting his personal battles with drug addiction. But he did write significantly with Phil Ochs during that period.

A lot of good songs were being written in the early '60s. They were anti-war songs. The Vietnam War was just beginning to warm up then, in 1964. You can say what you want about the administrations that we've elected to office, but they sure did keep those anti-war songs alive.

Somewhat tongue in cheek in a live performance Bob said:

It seemed then that if you wrote a good enough song, the powers that be would see the errors of their ways and say, "Oh, I see now!" And they'd put down their weapons and countries wouldn't fight anymore. And if they didn't respond to your song, then obviously the song wasn't good enough and you'd have to go back and write another one. So it also kept the flow of songs coming.

As he was to so many young creative talents throughout his entire career, Gibson was especially influential on Ochs. As Steve Aldrich writes in The All-Music Guide *(2nd edition, 1994):*

> Depending on your point of view, You might find Phil Ochs to be an idealistic American hero or the ultimate '60s casualty. Relocating to New York City from Ohio with a college journalism background and

already well-versed in the emerging political left, Ochs found his niche as a topical singer-songwriter and quickly became a favorite in the Village's blossoming folk scene of the early '60s. When Bob Dylan eventually moved into the rock arena, Ochs became the folk protest movement's defacto king.
Ochs died in 1976 at the age of 35.

I was a real mentor to Phil Ochs, musically. His very first gigs as a performer were in Cleveland. I was the headliner and he was the opening act. I heard some of his stuff like *The Battle of Billy Sol Estes* and it was nice stuff. We began to talk and got to know each other.

Michael Smith had this to say about the relationship between Ochs and Gibson:
One of the things I became more aware of as time went by was how everything Phil Ochs did sounded like Gibson. That was the first thing I noticed — like in the sense of the openings of songs. You'd hear it over and over again — the same chords. Even the later Phil Ochs, like *Pleasures in the Harbor* or *Crucifixion* there were still elements for me of Gibson and the elements were hard to pick out. Certainly when you heard certain opening chords sequences, you'd say, "Oh yeah, that's something that I never heard before in a folk music context until I heard Gibson do it." There were elements like the E minor.

A year later, I had a piece of music and I said, "Hey, I got this thing here, you got any ideas?" He just hammered a lyric. We wrote *Killing Martyrs,* which became a big song. Then we wrote *That's the Way It's Gonna Be.* I recorded that, as did Glenn Yarbrough and John Denver. A couple of others were *Can't Stay Around Here Anymore* and *Start the Parade. (By Gibson/Ochs, ©Robert Josiah Music, Inc.)*

Hup, two, three, four
Marching down the street,
to the rolling of the drums,
and the tramping of the feet.
Well, the general salutes
while the widows wave and weep.
Here comes the big parade!
Don't be afraid, the price is paid.
So start the parade.

Cold, hard stares
on faces so proud.
Kisses from the girls
and cheers from the crowd.
While the widows from the last war

> are crying in their shrouds.
> Here comes the big parade!
> Don't be afraid, the price is paid
> Start the parade!
>
> So young, so strong,
> so ready for the war.
> So willing to go and die
> upon a foreign shore.
> All march together, everybody looks the same.
> So there is no one you can blame.
> Don't be ashamed, go on and light the flame.
> Don't be afraid, the price is paid.
> So start the parade!

Phil Ochs was a musician, a song writer, intense — but seduced.

It was real easy to get caught up with that liberal bunch who just love your songs of protest for political statements. I've never understood what "liberal" really meant. Unfortunately, they really want a cheerleader. Ochs wrote *Changes* and *A Small Circle of Friends,* wonderful songs, and yet he was known as a protest singer.

He was one of those who was idolized by the left wing and, unfortunately, his ability to really communicate eventually never needed to be tested. All that was needed were a few "buzz words" and a bad tune and they would all stamp their feet.

It seems kind of sad. I saw a very, very sick man there at the end, and if a lot of people were uncomfortable because they didn't try to reach out to help him, it's their problem. A lot of things might have triggered his suicide.

Those were hot times for protest. There was vindication on a lot of things, like Vietnam, and Nixon turning out to be a "crook" and everything. A lot of the paranoia of the late '60s turned out to be based on fact. People were bugged and watched and photographed at rallies.

But the point is that, through it all, I don't think Phil ever had any recognition as a helluva song writer and musician. That always was peripheral. He was a great protest singer, his lyrics and music are real good, but his politics were often very naive. When you get into complexities, it's very hard to break down into good guys and bad guys.

That's what happened to Josh White. Josh was seduced by a lot of left wing organizations and causes. If there was anybody who was politically naive and really didn't care about causes, it was Josh White. The man didn't care about race relations. There were no civil rights, but he often would mouth those sentiments and sing songs that were great pieces of entertainment or were well received by the audience. He was not singing them for their information, he was singing them because they moved the people. He would mouth the proper sentiments and all. During the '30s and '40s, he sang for all kinds of organizations.

When the House UnAmerican Activities Committee called him up, he told them everything he knew, which was nothing. They were looking for an international conspiracy and who'd they get? A guy who would sing songs.

Who doesn't? I know. I've done much of the same. You write a song out of a moment of passion, but it relates to some kind of political position you want to take. It's the buzz words that make them work. Cheap shots. They work. But it's a hollow victory.

There was a period around 1970 when everyone just wanted to hear depressing songs. You just got up on stage and sang these long sets of depressing songs. You'd have a whole audience sitting there, getting depressed with you. When you were finished, they'd all just walk away, saying, "Wasn't that just wonderful!"

Gibson cared more than some of those words might indicate, however. Sprinkled throughout his performances were songs relating to the Civil War, many of which were original Gibson songs or re-writes and re-arrangements, and which, of course were analogies to any war (the Vietnam War, in particular) and its aftermath. Gibson's Let the Band Play Dixie *was one of the highlights of Gibson's musical play,* The Courtship of Carl Sandburg.

During a performance in 1991, from which the recording Stops Along the Way, *was made, Gibson remarked to his audience:*

It's been almost 30 years since we wrote that song (referring to *Start the Parade,* which he co-wrote with Ochs), and as a country we still haven't come to any kind of conclusion about the Vietnam War.

You can be either for or against it, or whatever. But that was years ago that the thing was over. How about all the guys that have come home? We have never recognized the contributions that they made. So many of them are homeless now. We've never come to grips with that. So LET'S!

Constant Reminder
(by Gibson - ©Robert Josiah Music, Inc.)

When Johnny comes marching home again, haroo, haroo!
We give him a hearty welcome then, haroo, haroo!
Ah! The boys will sing and the girls will shout,

and the ladies they will all turn out...

Get away, get away, can't use you no more,
Don't stand at my windows, don't knock at my door,
'cause we're trying to pretend there was never a war
and you're just a constant reminder.

When you called us, we answered.
Where you sent us, we went.
What you asked us, we did.
Now that's not what you meant.
We believed when you told us
'bout the right and the wrong.
But now we're back home
where we thought we belonged.
This is our welcome home song:

Get away, get away! Can't use you no more.
Don't stand at my windows; don't knock at my door.
For we're trying to pretend there was never a war,
and you're just a constant reminder.

You pass us each day
on the streets where we lay.
You throw us a quarter, then you hurry away,
leaving us bleeding right here where we fall.
You leave us the shame and the blame for it all.
Without even our names on a wall.

Get away, get away! Can't use you no more.
Don't stand at my windows; don't knock at my door.
For we're trying to pretend there was never a war,
and you're just a constant reminder.

If there's ever a war, why we'll call you for sure,
But now you're just a constant reminder!

So often I got involved in political issues that had to do with eternal verities. We really felt like we could get the war to end if we wrote the right song, and had a pure enough heart. Maybe it's youth that tells us a good song can change the hearts of man. If that song didn't work, maybe the next one will. But we never realized that there are a lot of complicated motives going on. People are doing things in the world for a lot of reasons.

BOB GIBSON - 280

I wrote a few songs with Phil Ochs. Some were protest songs, songs of youth; preachy songs telling people where it's at. Now, I like the songs by Tom Paxton that just try to tell a story and let the idea form in the ear of the listener.

I remember the rage of 1973 and appearing at the Ann Arbor peace rally after Nixon had mined the harbor at Hai Phong. The peace rallies had dwindled from thousands to just a few hundred. It was awful because we felt powerless. And the powers-that-be were out of control toward the end. No wonder there was outrage and acts of violence.

I've never thought of myself as a topical songwriter — I've never chosen to write topical songs. Really when something's come up that's moved that part of me, whatever part that is writes a song. To me I consider songs a bit of mini theatre. They're what a musical is supposed to do. There is a beginning and an end and something going on in between.

I rather enjoy polarizing people. It's really fun to entertain people but one begins to feel like a whore after awhile and if you're good at it, it becomes easier and easier to manipulate people. But sometimes it's really neat to kind of shake them up. I'm not there to make them think or change their minds or anything like that. I gave that up years ago. Music will not change a damn thing. It will not affect anyone's thinking about anything. I'm sorry. I wish it did. Phil Ochs and I used to write songs together and think that, "Wow, this will change everybody's mind!" The only people who want to hear that kind of stuff are those of that attitude or persuasion. But they're good for that reason, that kind of reinforcement of the group ideas.

I don't know that you have to agree with everything people are singing. I sing songs that aren't necessarily my real commitment, my philosophy. You're looking to pull people's strings, you know. You're trying to move them. I'd much rather move them than awe them. I think it has to do with the fact that I'm a person of great emotion myself. I really like to be moved by things.

One of Bob's favorite writing collaborators was Tom Paxton. He had this to say about Tom's importance to him:

He's incredibly articulate. I gave him a typed draft of my lyrics for a new song. He went through and fixed it, writing notes by hand over my typing. Then I sat down with a banjo and made the grammar a little more colloquial. His doctoring was just perfect.

I'm a great starter of songs. My threshold is that I always question whether or not it's good. That's why I like to collaborate with Shel Silverstein. That's why I collaborate with Tom. Most of my songs are written with other people because I'm most comfortable with that feedback.

Tom had this to say about his writing affiliation with Bob:
    Bob and I started writing together in 1978 after he had finally quit drugs. We wrote songs together, sometimes in the same room, sometimes by mail or phone. Bob and I had no formula that I can think of — just the pleasure of bouncing ideas off each other — a "how 'bout this?" exchange that sooner or later produced something we both liked. Our collaboration on the song *And Loving You*, on the other hand, it was fairly separate. I heard Bob noodling the melody in the dressing room at Navy Pier in Chicago before he, Anne Hills and I were about to perform at Chicagofest (I don't remember the year). I liked it and asked him what it was. "Something he'd just come up with," he said. I said, "Put it on a tape and send it to me." He did, and I wrote the words over a couple of days and phoned them to him. ***Bob adds,*** "Tom called and said, "I've cracked the code!" That version is the one he recorded. I subsequently added the verse that begins, "We heard John Lennon play," and recorded the song that way.
    Somewhere in Bob's papers is the manuscript for *A Box of Candy And A Piece of Fruit*. I frequently mention it to my students as an example of how much re-writing is sometimes required of us. Bob very often did his first drafts in a deliberately undisciplined style — which I also urge my students to try. In this case he handed me four or five typed pages of lyrics about his incarceration in Toronto on a drug charge. No verse was like another verse, some had no real rhyme scheme, the scansion (metrical pattern) was haphazard...it didn't matter, because the story was a funny one. Bob handed it to me as I was leaving on a trip to Ireland, saying, "See what you can do with this one."
    I kept it with me on the tour and took it out often to chip away at it and by the time I saw Bob again in Los Angeles (this would be late September, 1980) I'd put everything in a kind of unity of rhyme schemes and scansion. We took it with us up the coast to Berkeley where we were playing the Bread and Roses Festival. The following day we sat down in my hotel room in San Francisco and started tearing it to shreds, our method being to sing it through and stop at every false note and replace or rewrite. Before long the pages were absolutely covered with new lyrics, crossed out passages, entire verses written in spaces the size of a large stamp. When we finished, we had a song, but we were the only two humans who could have pulled the finished song out of that mess.
    We wrote *Another 'I Love Texas' Song* in Chicago, I think, at Bob's place. It was the kind of song we loved to do — just letting the wild ideas flow and then shaping them back and forth. Like every good collaboration I've ever seen, the egos were checked at the door and the only thing that mattered was not who came up with the line, but that the line worked for the song. It's never clear after the dust settles who

wrote which line, anyway. We sang the song together at Kerrville and they put it in the Kerrville songbook.

Writing is my life. This is where my soul is. I'm thinking about it all the time. It doesn't take a special effort. From the time I discovered I could do this, it has been the most important thing to me. It has never let me down.

I try to write every day. I've got boxes and boxes of notebooks. If you're going to be a writer, you have to write every day. If you don't get into a writer's habit, are you really a writer? If you're not writing, it's like actors in New York driving cabs or waiting tables. Are they actors or are they cab drivers and waitresses? All I can tell you is that it works; it works for me.

It sure was fun to write songs with Bob. I've never done too much collaborating over the years. Most of what I've written, I've written myself. I did some pop song collaborating in England, none of which satisfied me. But the three or four things that I've written with Bob have been unalloyed pleasure. He brings out the best in me as a songwriter and editor and critic and we've written a couple of things that we've just torn to shreds and reassembled quite a few times. It's so much fun, that it's almost indecently terrific to come out with a good song in the end of it.

Rick Neely:

There were old traditional songs that Bob used to sing in the early years, and then it would come around again and become something else. Bob used to write things by formula. He'd fall into something and then he'd write a bunch of things that were all kind of the same. Then he'd have enough good sense to know that he could only go so far, and then he'd think up something else. Then he'd get hot on something and he'd do a bunch of songs all the same.

We did a songwriting workshop at the Old Town School where we talked about songwriting. There were a bunch of people on the panel, and I was one of them. We'd talk about songs that we'd written and then sing a song and talk about where it came from and how it was put together — that kind of stuff. It was at that point I was working on an old guitar thing that I'd just started playing. I had one line of a song. The next time I saw him he had a sheet, which I still have, of line after line after line after line after line of stuff that would fit the song. So I edited part of it and kind of put it together as a song. I tried to play it some, but it just never seemed to quite come together. It's the damndest thing. When you learn something of somebody else's you almost never forget it, but when you perform things that are your own, sometimes your brain — you've gone through such a process of getting from the beginning to the end that sometimes things get mish-mashed, and I could never perform it well so I dropped it after awhile. I finally just recorded it in 1997 on an album with a group of people so there's actually a finished, carved in stone rendition. That's the sum and total of our collaborative effort. Anyway, I don't think he ever heard it in the finished form, because he was off to California or off somewhere and we didn't see each other for a long time. It's my tune, my first line, but the rest is Bob. The song is *A Day is a Circle of Time*.

John Irons:
   A long time ago, I was at Bob's house and Shel was in town and came over and dropped a bunch of songs off. He said, "Bob, I wrote these songs. Play them and make them pretty for me. So Shel understood, "Yeah, Bob could make it pretty." And that's probably one of the reasons there were so many collaborations there, because Bob could deliver Shel's ideas better than anybody. I have a personal theory about why more of Bob's songs weren't recorded by other people. Who else could do them better? A lot of the material Bob did, nobody could do it as well as he could, and once he recorded it, it was the definitive version. Now someone like Bob Dylan has the right words that anybody else could deliver, because Dylan's voice isn't good enough to do a definitive version.
   In terms of songwriting, Bob taught it at Columbia here in Chicago for awhile. Then he was also teaching songwriting in the public school system, not as a full time thing, but as kind of a special treat to kids, going into the inner city schools and having them write a song. This was for primary grades. He had quite a bit of success with that, I thought, because he was really giving those inner city kids an appreciation of the language and how you could use it.

Josh White Jr.:
   I remember there was a club here in Detroit, the Raven Gallery, that ran from '63 to '80 and Gibson worked it a couple of times. We happened to be in town at the same time, and he invited me by his room to write a song. I felt so incompetent because I did not write songs. It was just too much and I somehow begged off and didn't do it because I didn't think I had anything to offer or to contribute. I've learned that not to be the truth at this point in time, but back then when I was in my early twenties . . . I was so thrilled that he asked me but I was so afraid of not being able to contribute anything that I just bugged out. But again, there he was offering again, willing to work together. And I'm sure we would have gotten something good, eventually we would have, but anyway... I did my first album in 1964 and I wrote my very first song there and then all I did was put new words to an old blues, but I didn't even intend to write. It was just in the early '70s that it started coming out of me, and before that I just couldn't see being able to contribute anything. So that's another Gibson thing that he did.

Josh White Jr. recalls Bob's natural brilliance as a songwriter:
   In 1981 Bob, Tom Paxton, Odetta and I performed on an episode

of Soundstage. During the show, Bob and Tom performed *Here Comes Another I Love Texas Song,* one of the songs they wrote together. Bob Gibson and Steve Goodman are the persons who come to mind first when I think of someone who could put out words off the cuff. You see people lose words, and I'm certainly one of them, and my mind, not being a prolific writer, does not run fast enough to put in words that'll fit. But on that song, it showed that Gibson lost a verse, and you would never have known it until the end when he was telling you as he was singing, not missing a stroke, that he screwed up. The audience didn't know. Only Paxton knew, because I didn't know the song that well, and he didn't miss a stroke and the people went wild. That is a testimony to his skill with words. Everyone cannot do that. You have a lot of good writers out there who can do some stuff, but get them to forget a lyric . . . We'll vamp while we think of it or I don't know what extremes people will go to. I know with me one time I just jumped right into another song that was in the same key and laughed, and after it was all over, I just said, "You just experienced the occupational hazard." But again, with Gibson and with Stevie Goodman they had that ability to put it together so fast and so well. Gibson not only kept the beat, he kept the rhyme too.

The actual lyrics to the verse in question are:
>Texas has its twisters
>Texas has its drought
>But when hard times come to Texas
>There's folks'll help you out
>Seldom is heard a discouraging word
>From a true-born Texan's mouth
>And everyone who's a loyal son
>Lift up your head and shout

Then it goes into the chorus of:
>Here comes another "I love Texas song."

With the first line out of Bob's mouth, he knew he'd blown it completely, because he changed the order of the elements involved requiring him to have a different rhyme scheme. What he sang was:
>Texas has its droughts
>And Texas has its twisters
>I blew that line quickly
>I should have written about my sister
>We could start this tape all over again
>But we're almost through with the verse
>Anyway I might make another mistake
>And it could be much worse
>Here comes another "I love Texas song."

The audience erupted!

Yes, it's fun to be a songwriter! That's what it's all about. You write a lot of bad ones to get off one that you like. One thing I tried to impress at my songwriting workshops was that if you want to write some good songs, you have to also write some bad ones. Unfortunately, no one's been able to figure out a way around that equation.

BOB GIBSON THE MUSICIAN

My voice is not that good an instrument. I have pitch problems. As a matter of fact since I stopped singing the songs that I first started being interested in, which were much more pitch relevant, I got more into anecdotal, story songs, which come from a different kind of place. They're much less pitch relevant. In other words, if I don't quite hit it, it's okay.

I think when I started to write, the way I wrote was kind of backwards. I would find chord progressions — lush progressions, one chord to the other, they would roll, there was a great logical feel to it, a great rightness about it. And you can almost hang any one of several tunes to it. You put a tune to it, but it's kind of arbitrary. You put another tune to it — take a harmony line and call it a tune — that would be okay too. They weren't tuneful tunes or walk-away-whistling-singing kind of tunes. It was more like they were hung like decorations on a Christmas tree onto that chord progression. So the 12-string guitar was almost an inevitable choice for me eventually. The 12-string is kind of sophisticated, as opposed to the 6-string guitar. Your highest tone is in the middle of your chord because you're G-high, so that it isn't just multiples of strings that do it. It's the fact that the highest tone is well within the middle of the instrument. It's a much more fascinating inversion. It lends itself, too, to stuff that I like to do with relative minors. The 12-string really gives you a chord. You don't have any 6 tones. You've got 12 fat ones and you've got a great range of sound there, so that you can play a lot more sophisticated chords and exotic intervals and still maintain your basic triads so you know it's C or C9. On the banjo you've got to imply. It could be C9 or it could be a couple of things. So for that reason the banjo kind of plateaued out for me. It was really hard for me to find what I was looking for on it.

I didn't play the banjo for a long time, but then I went back to it. It's a great instrument. It's one of the only indigenous American instruments. Many people don't realize that. There are only two indigenous American instruments. One is the 5-string banjo, probably constructed first in 1847 by Joel Walker Sweeney, and of course, the synthesizer is the other.

The style I developed wasn't conscious. It just happened. It was very exciting at first for me because there was a world of music out there and there was a place that was half way between traditional licks and the showman. The traditional way is you pick up a few tunes in a very untutored way, and you play them all your life, and you play those few tunes better than anyone else in the world. The other end is Eddie Peabody or the performing musician. You pick up a whole bunch of razzle dazzle and use constantly dazzling footwork, borrowing the best of what a whole lot of people have put together. You borrow a lick here and a lick there and you become the most proficient athletic exhibition of how fast you move your fingers and hands. But in between there, in between doing those two directions, there was a place to kind of stretch the folk music thing a little further and reach out a little more. Of course I came at a time when there were all these influences. There was the Bahamian, the Sea Island music, chain gang music, which lined out pretty damn well, and gospel music. All this stuff was coming together like crazy. Then on the other end, not that far removed, was Ray Charles. So it was not an uncomfortable bridge — it was not a big long reach to be in that place in between those things. It was comfortable. As a matter of fact, it was too big a jump maybe to go from chain gang music to Ray Charles, but if you went through us folk singers, it was logical. We were a nice stepping stone. I don't think Ray Charles came out of us or anything. It was just a comfortable place to be in musically. We had input coming in and yet we had somebody out front saying, "Hey, take a look at this." You know, you had Ray Charles saying, "Strings can be gorgeous," in *The Genius of Ray Charles,* an album that changed my life. Like Tom Lehrer says, "Life's like a sewer. What goes out of it depends entirely upon what you put into it."

John Irons:

The voice was always there. He didn't have to practice a lot. He could learn a song in a couple of days and bring it up to a performance level. He got a lot of mileage out of his chords. Very smooth on the guitar. One of the big things he really did was he tuned his instrument. A lot of them didn't in those early days. Nothing sounds worse than a 12-string out of tune. It's almost better hearing a couple of cars collide, but he could keep it in tune, and he sang on pitch. All of those things were contributory, and I guess from a musical standpoint, one of the big contributions was he'd take the folk songs with 300 verses and he'd pull out the four that meant something and he'd make it a single song that really got the whole message of the other 98 verses across.

Rick Neely:
You have to remember, when Bob started out there were no quaint little folk clubs or coffeehouses. He was playing saloons and places where they had no idea what to expect, and here comes this rosey-faced crew cut kid singing these lolly-tu-dum songs. I'm sure his row to hoe was very difficult in the early years. He used to play a banjo instrumental piece, *Andalusean Dance.* I was working on that and I asked, "Did you write that piece?" He said, "Yep, yep, I wrote that piece," and then he kind of laughed and said that he wrote it because in the early days, the banjo people would ask for songs that were made popular by Eddie Peabody, a plectrum banjo player. One of his big hits was *Lady of Spain, I Adore You.* Bob said he wrote this piece because he didn't want anybody to think that any old "Eddie Playbody could pea better" than he could!

In the early days he used to play a few tunes with a 6-string guitar. Art Thieme said he saw him in the '50s and he played almost exclusively banjo, just one or two songs on the 6-string guitar and that's all. I'm not sure exactly when the 12-string came in, but if you consider that his professional career began in '53 and he became pretty well-known in Chicago in '54 or '55 and the Riverside recordings started coming out in the the late '50s window, the 12-string guitar is not that common. He plays a couple of tunes on it — *Jordan River,* the duet with Joan Baez at Newport and *The Virgin Mary Had One Son,* also a duet with her, and it was released as a single too. That was the only time early that he used the 12-string and it was very elementary, just real simple strumming, nothing fancy, no stylistic developments — a lot of interesting chords but nothing terribly exotic really until the *Where I'm Bound* album which really defines his mature guitar-playing style. Then, when you get to the '70s, he's pretty much abandoned that thumb pick strummy kind of thing and has gone to just using a flat pick and once again a real basic strum. He used these really big, heavy triangular picks but the style was just simple strumming.

There are different ways that he played. One kind of strum evolved from banjo playing. It has a thumb pick, one on the middle finger that's flattened out upside down or backwards and then there's a third one which is plastic or tortoise shell that goes upside down on the ring finger of the right hand and that just drags along. I suspect that in the early days he probably didn't go through all the trouble of changing all the picks on all the fingers all the time because the Vega 12-string that he played was real cranky, real hard to keep in tune. Bob played a number of different banjo styles. He played a Pete Seeger banjo style mostly. You pluck up on a melody string and you brush down across the rest and then you play the thumb note. It's what's called bum-diddee-bum-diddee-bum. That's a real simple form, and he used the picks because I think in the early days most of the times you'll notice from photographs, there was only one microphone.

It took a number of years before sound amplification got sophisticated enough that they had multiple inputs. So they had one microphone to the amplifier and it was a kind of a broad ranging thing that they put kind of half way between your mouth and your instrument and a lot of times in those days people wore their instruments higher on their physical person in order to take advantage of being heard. Bob also used the picks a lot because it's more piercing, it's more cutting.

Bob was hard on guitars, and went through a lot of them. He used medium gauge d'Angelico strings. I think that that heavy a string contributed to the short life of his instruments, but it also contributed to the great power that he got out of them. Bob's hands were big, very big — huge —and they were very strong. They looked like my hands with gloves on. He didn't do a lot of fancy single string work. All his stuff was based on chords and strange harmonies within chords. The one guitar style he did with the thumb pick and the single finger pick, a kind of brushing thing, evolved out of the banjo. I am convinced that that's where it came from. You can hear the origins of this banjo strum on *Wayfaring Stranger* where instead of the thumb being the leader, it was the finger. Other than that, it was very simple and strange harmonies.

The arrangement for *Sweet Betsy from Pike* was very revolutionary for its time because it used all these strange moving chords that were brand new. Nobody did those! It's a derivative of a Gm chord. It makes very good sense musically, but nobody did it in a bass run in those days. Everybody said, "WHAT IS HE DOING?!" His mature arranging playing style had finally come out at that point, and then later, unfortunately, he abandoned it. My favorite song of his is *Cindy Dreams of California,* because musically it's so interesting, but it's based on the same exact principle, a moving bass part.

He used weird chords. He'd kind of invent chords nobody used as in *Fog Horn,* but they're harmonically all very correct if you analyze them from an intellectual approach. Bob used chord substitutions and the classical rule of chord substitutions is anytime you have a chord that shares two notes with another chord, they can be substituted for each other. Bob used to bend the rule and say, "Well, if they've got one note in common, let's try it." And that's how he'd come up with exhilarating chords like on *Just a Thing I Do.* That chord does not necessarily belong in this key but it fits. Or another great one is the *Town Crier* song. All those chords relate to each other phrase by phrase but not necessarily in the context of a key. A lot of it is modal and that also carries over from the banjo.

I read in an interview one time that there used to be a great banjo player named Fleming Brown who used to teach at the Old Town School. He said Bob Gibson made a career out of G to F or its relations. For example: The G, F, G relationship is a whole step which does not normally occur in a major scale. In a major scale you have C, D, E, F, G, A, B (the 7th tone is a leading tone and it drives itself up to the top) C again. In modal music or in some minor form, the relationship is a minor third, a whole step from G down to F as in *Super Skier* and *Whoa Back Buck*. All it is is G to F. He worked these things and he made a career out of it.

One of the things that Bob used to do was repeat chords in different registers as in *Kathy O'Grady*. It sounds interesting, but it's just the same chord in three different places. That's a thing that's a carryover from the banjo too, because he used to play lots of things where the range would go up and down the neck, but it's all the same chord. It looks really flashy, but there's really nothing going on other than the same chord changing register. Most people playing the 12-string didn't venture that high up the neck because most of the instruments were so bad that you couldn't. You could barely play. You could barely squeeze the strings down in first position let alone mash them up on the twelfth fret.

To this day, I think Bob has proliferated 12-string guitars more than anyone else at least in the midwest. Go to any kind of folk venue that has an open stage, and I'll bet you that better than one third get up with some kind of 12-string. They might not even know why, but maybe their dad played and was a fan and had one around the house so this is what they're used to hearing. Bob had a Martin 12-string that I'm sure was a conversion, because Martin in 1960 did not build a 12-string. I have seen a photograph of him playing a Martin guitar that you can tell was converted because it had too many tuners and went through the Martin decal on the guitar — stuff that the factory would have never gotten away with. I think he got into trouble because he had a contract at the time with Vega. He got promotional consideration that said, "Bob Gibson plays Vega banjos exclusively," but Vega didn't build guitars in that time period. The Vega 12-string guitar that you see on the cover of the *Gate of Horn* album and the *Where I'm Bound* that you can identify because it says Vega on it, had to have been made up by someone. I don't know the story, but I'll bet you Bob was involved in producing this instrument, because the neck was built by Vega. The body was from a Harmony Sovereign which was a cheap bottom layer guitar built in Chicago at that time period. I'll bet you anything that in his travels he had acquired a Harmony Sovereign guitar and said, "This probably would make a pretty good 12-string and had the Vega people make a neck for it and probably change the bridge and the bracing inside. But that's what that guitar was, with an old-style Gibson pick guard that was put on in that funny shape. That's what he played until the late '60s when he met Bozo *(the Yugoslavian guitar maker)* and started off on that relationship and he played only Bozos after that.

As for his banjos, Bob always played long neck Vega banjos in the early years. At the end of his life he was playing a Deering Black Diamond banjo.

I sat with him one time on a really hot Sunday afternoon in his apartment on Wilton by Wrigley Field. I was hanging around playing his guitar. Bob was sitting in a reclining chair in his bathrobe reading a paper, and I said, "What is the secret to your great guitar playing?" It was a half tongue-in-cheek question. He kind of folded the corner of the paper down and said, "Boom chucka," and just went back to his reading. And I said, "Boom chucka?" He said, "But you've gotta go real fast." And if you slow it down to boom chucka, that is exactly what it is — it is no more, it is no less.

I knew Bob's oldest daughter Meridian (Barbara, at that time) when she was a teenager. She was aspiring to be a songwriter. She came to stay with Bob, and came over to my apartment because we were going to write some song. She put out her ideas and I would arrange them, and right away she got real mad at me and said I "Gibsonized" everything, because I do. I choose chords that are his because that's what I know, and even to this day, if I pick something up, suddenly it gets twisted around to where it comes out sounding something like that, no matter what I do. When you've done that and it's perfected, it's pretty hard to deny it and I don't see any reason to. I give credit where credit's due. I'm not stealing anything. In fact, at this point, I consider that I'm preserving something, because I think that I do it exactly. There are other people that do it kinda, but I think I do it exactly, for what it's worth.

Michael Smith:

When I hear Rick Neely, I think, "Jesus Christ, that right hand — that's Bob Gibson! My God, he's got it down." I don't know what it was, kind of hesitant or kind of a dry quality to the rhythm. I don't know what you'd call it. And it may have been simple, but the thing is that nobody was doing it. At the time it was THE big deal to hear that Gibson guitar and to hear the elan with which he did it. Most young people when they play are very nervous and very sincere. Then when you hear somebody with a kind of, you know, "I don't give a damn" attitude and they're still rhythmic, and they're still swinging, then there's something about it — that's what makes people say jazz. It sounds like an old guy in that willingness to kind of be groovey. A lot of people, like young people, don't want to be groovey. They want to be exciting, but "exciting" a lot of times keeps you from being groovey. Bob was willing to be groovey right from the start in a world where people all thought they should be like Pete Seeger and the Weavers in this frenetic style. It was either frenetic or very simple. With Bob all of a sudden there was this cool guy. At this point we were all in denim, and we'd been talkin' like Pete Seeger or we'd been all frenetic like the Kingston Trio or the Limeliters. Here came Bob in the middle, kind of shufflin' along like Dean Martin! It was like in pop music where there were the rock & rollers and the guys that were very straight, and here was Dean kinda doin' that thing. It was very down the middle and he got big hits. Long after Tony Bennett and those guys were down, you know, there was Dean still having those kind of easy swingin' kind of hits. It was a quality Bob had and continued to have past all the Beatles and the Kingston Trio and the Rolling Stones and Peter, Paul & Mary, and still there was Bob going boom-chicka-boom. There was something specific to his rhythm that lasted through the years that I could still recognize after 20 years.

There's a whole section of kinds of songs that have a certain feel to them that were Gibson ragtimish. I read an interesting thing recently in a book, where the author talked about who he thought was going to make it in the new folk rock world. They talked about Dylan and how he made that transition very easily; how Phil Ochs and Ian & Sylvia attempted to; how Peter, Paul & Mary attempted to on occasion, but that Dylan did the best at that. But this person said Gibson had a problem because his music was so ragtime related. It's a lot of ragtime influence with a little jazz — a more swinging feel to it.

Ed Holstein:
He really was kind of a jazzy guy with his chord changes. There are some jazz chords in there if you listen to some of his tunes, they were heavily influenced by Dixieland/Ragtime music. He played the Blue Angel in New York and the Village Vanguard, and he was going into the jazz thing.

Josh White Jr.:
I'm always curious as to why with Gibson he always used a thumb pick and three finger picks. I had not seen him for years before he got sick, but he'd gone to using a flat pick. It was so odd to see him using a flat pick. I always wondered why he switched. A lot of his fast guitar style wasn't there anymore. Things were a little slower.

(Actually the reason for switch in picks was largely related to physical needs. Bob started having the effects of carpal tunnel syndrome in the '70s and he said, simply, that it became easier for him to control the flat pick.)

Gordon Lightfoot:
In the 12-string department, he taught me some of the rudiments of capoing the 12-string which is an art unto itself. He used to like to tune his guitar down a whole step and then put the capo on and bring it up into concert. I misread that and I started to capo on the second position so that got me up a tone and that stayed with me for the rest of my career. The reason for that really was in concert to make the strings a little softer. He explained that to me when I saw him last which was a couple of years ago and while he was playing for me backstage in Chicago at the big amphitheatre. We had a little get-together there. He sang *Let the Band Play Dixie*. He sat there and played it, and I was amazed as always because I there's one thing that I really always thought. I know the song *Living Legend* says that Bob

Dylan copped his style, but I don't know if that's true. I think that I copped his style more than Bob Dylan did.

BOB GIBSON — THE ENTERTAINER

BEIN' ON THE ROAD
(by Gibson — ©Robert Josiah Music, Inc.)

Won't you sing me some new song
That I ain't heard before?
Your "poor boy on the road" songs
Are such a bloody bore.
If it's so lonely at the top,
What you up there for?
Won't you sing me some new song
That I ain't heard before?

Ah, you say you came through rain and snow
And never ever missed a show.
Tell me 'bout the rigors
And the mortise on the road.
Ah, but don't complain to some poor lame
Who's stuck in Terre Haute.
He'll get feisty if he's got
No other place to go.
And if the weight's too great to carry,
Please put down the load.
Quit your belly achin'
'Bout your bein' on the road!

You come in on your own Leer jet
To a waiting limousine,
Your liveried chauffeur holds the door
Like you're some king or queen,
And then he whisks you down the boulevard
To the best hotel in town,
Where 14 pre-pubescent groupies
Wait to show you around,
You have an interview with "Rolling Stone" -
You got some heavy stuff to say -
Then everyone adjourns to dinner
At the famous *Chez Gourmet*,
Where the manager picks up the check,
Then it's time for you to go and play

> Some music for a couple of hours
> For ten thousand bucks a day!
> With ladies for your pleasure
> And cocaine for your nose,
> It's hard to be a music man,
> It's hell out on the road!
>
> Hey, won't you quit your bitchin'
> 'Bout your bein' on the road.
> Go, tell it to the Eskimos,
> 'Cause they love to be snowed.
> But I ain't really goin' for
> Your terrible tale of woe.
> I've traveled on that highway
> Just a few miles of my own.
> And if the weight's too great to carry,
> Please put down the load.
> Quit your belly achin'
> 'Bout your bein' on the road!

What Bob did, perhaps, better than anything else was relate to his audience. He had priceless words of advice for entertainers on how he approached that relationship to make it work so well.

Some performers arrive in a limo. There are literally spotlights on them. They're given microphones so that their every whisper is amplified. Everything they do is larger than life and made important. They get the idea that they're the center of attention. To the guy that just paid five bucks to sit there, they are not. He is. And they forget that.

For me it works to remember that that guy paid five bucks to be the center of attention. And my job is to make him be somewhere else for awhile, take him on a trip. He can either sit and look at me and view me as an oddity in a zoo, or he can get caught up in my trip. I'd love to move him. I'd like my work to be so serious that I move them. But if they just watch me do my dance and are fascinated, that's okay, too. Either level is okay as long as it works. It's okay as long as I like it to work.

The Summer 1986 edition of <u>Transformation,</u> wrote about Bob's uniqueness on the stage:

> Besides, Bob's fearless innovations, the other element that made Bob such a special joy was his boundless delight in music and his feelings about the responsibility of the performer to "provide a service."

There is something else he was always credited with, and that's his stage presence—the enthusiasm, the joy and the energy—his way of seducing an audience Is that something like that learned or does it come naturally?

It's a gift. I'm very grateful for it, but it's a gift. I can give all kind of hindsight and maybe why, but I really don't know. It's also a great mystery to me and it's fascinating that some nights when I've really worked my hardest and done my damnedest, it isn't spectacular, and another night when I didn't exactly phone the show in, but something broke my concentration or for whatever reason I'm not able to concentrate, I'm just not on, then I get great feedback that it was one of the greatest shows I ever did. It's a mystery. I don't understand it. It isn't always that way. There are nights when I just feel great and I get great feelings coming back, but there are mystery nights where I go, "Gee that was wonderful!" And everybody goes, "Yeah, that was a pretty good show." And there are other nights I just groaned and said, "I wish I'd done that better," and everybody'd say, "That's the best I ever heard you!" And I'm talking about people who were qualified because they'd heard me a lot. I can't understand it. It probably has something to do with where they're at, too.

I don't know how you'd learn something like that. I think you do it over a long period of time. You get different feedback that's all non-verbal, and if you've got some smarts and you're concentrating on some less than conscious level, you respond, and you register that when you're in that place and you're head's in that place, you get a better response from the audience. So if it's that way, what device can you use to get yourself there? Devices are very important. I have a lot of them. For example, one Labor Day, I spent three of the loveliest days of my life at the Bread & Roses Festival — I mean three days of ecstasy! It was wonderful. The music was wonderful. My face hurt from smiling. That's how it was. So when I got to Dayton, Ohio, and only 16 people were there, all I had to do was tune in on what I got from Bread & Roses, and that would sustain me. There's a whole lot to draw on, and it really makes a hell of a difference.

Another thing is that sometimes something will be a little aggravating. A guy will be mixing grasshoppers in the mixer in the middle of a soft song, or maybe there's a loud table — something's wrong. And then I've got to remember that, although the spotlight's on me, I've got the microphone, my name is written in letters two feet high, my picture is in the paper, and I'm getting grossly overpaid to do what I do, I am still not the center of attention. The guy who pays five bucks to sit out there thinks that HE should be the the center of attention to me. He's come to me for a service. I'm in the service business, and if I can remember that and get humble enough to say, "Wait a minute, what is the relationship between me and that guy," that's what it's all about.

It is not art. I would like to have art overtones, and I would love it if people would sit around and discuss old Gibson's art. That'd be fun. But, you know, I'm a saloon singer, basically. I wouldn't mind singing in bigger halls and doing all that, but I'm there to relate to the audience in that environment. It's good for me to continually remember or be reminded what the relationship's really about and that although I'm in a really nice line of work, I am not the center of attention. I know that to be true, because I'm a hell of an audience when I go out. I don't like to go too much to hang out. I go to hear, and I want the guy to give that service to me. I'm there for a reason, and that reason is I want to be entertained.

I was getting nutted out in the '60s. I did what a lot of performers do — I was looking for approval. You want to feel good about yourself and you want a couple of people to approve of you. If you get a couple, you want more. Then you want hundreds, thousands, always seeking to feel OK about yourself.

It never really works. While you're looking for approval from all these people, you're isolating. I was more and more isolated up in front of people and also unable to deal with people on a one-to-one basis. It was a long, long time before I was able to come to terms with that. Now it's so easy. I'm just in a service business. I have the pleasure of making music, which is a nice thing to do. It's no big deal. It's not the big deal I once thought it was.

Around the early '70s a lot of us were into angst, self-examining our songs, and the pain. God, there was something noble about sharing the pain with the audience. A lot of people came out and I don't know what they were looking for because I only had misery to share. I got back to a more well-balanced point of view with a little irony in it.

There have been changes in the audiences over the years since I started. I know I don't have the energy anymore that I did have. I think that has something to do with it. I think it's partly youth, but I think that there was a willingness of people to go out and do stuff that there isn't now. I don't know what that's about, but they would take on their nemesis whatever it was.

I've seen some incredible changes in folk music, too. The number one thing is I think the audience has changed. I think that we were looking for the roots of our country — where we were coming from — our soul — in the late '50s, early '60s. We were going back to folk music. There were two Republican administrations and it was a recession and the changing technology, very similar to today. But they were looking for the spiritual quality in songs.

Today I find young people going to more rap concerts and so forth and so on — rock & roll concerts. They want a more visceral experience and technology.

Studs Terkel commented on these changes and the performance quality of Bob Gibson in a radio interview in 1994:

Young Bob Gibson. I say young Bob Gibson, because in 1956 was when he really opened Gate of Horn, the first of folk palaces, you might say, in the country in the old Rice Hotel. The Bob Gibson I remember was a crew cut blond kid, so I still refer to him as "young Bob Gibson". And I'm thinking of his life, the changes he's seen in that world we call folk music.

There were certain movements, too, at the time of the popularity of folk music. There was the civil rights movement, there was the anti-Vietnam war movement, big ones, but Bob used the word energy. That may be the key — the energy of Bobby Camp — more than just physical energy. There was a vitality, and that aspect, one way or another, has worn thin.

That question of "Whither the young?" in the music we hear and technology; volume of sound as well. We talked about dizziness among people, our rock contemporaries; I think that deafness may be the ailment next forthcoming.

Roger McGuinn:

As a performer, he was very disciplined. He had a lot of energy. His intonation was really perfect vocally, and he had a good sense of dynamics. When he'd start a song, he'd always build it up like a fireworks display with a big, big thing at the end on every song and then that would carry over to the whole show too. He did a lot of interesting synthesis things with music where he would combine different forms of music like ragtime and jazz and blues and traditional Appalachian sounds and bring them together into one thing that was unique to him at that time. I guess a lot of people copied it because the Kingston Trio and the Limeliters, the Chad Mitchell Trio and others would be doing his material. He was extremely dynamic. He was very entertaining to watch — he looked great and sounded great.

Michael Smith:

One thing that struck me was I had bought this picture of him for years of being the kind of person who was disdainful of his audience, and would go on stage and didn't care. When I finally experienced him onstage it was totally different. It was like a lesson in how to relate to the audience. He was so NICE to the people who came to see him. He was much nicer to the people who came to see him on the stage than he was to anybody personally. He got very polite and charming onstage. It showed me, "Boy, you can get along with your audience, and you don't have to be a bad guy, and they'll still like you.

George Matson:
He had the best cranial cavities of anybody I ever knew. And that impish grin. God, he loved doing that! He was a small room player — he played best there. He liked the intimacy of that, because he was very soft-spoken. He was a very charming entertainer.

Josh White Jr.:
I've always considered Bob greatly influential in supporting that which my dad taught me many years ago. There are two things you have to do if you're going to be a performer — make sure you believe what you sing, because if you don't believe it, other people are not going to believe it either; and make sure they can understand what you sing.

My old man never restricted me, and then Gibson, with his ecclecticness, reinforced mine. Just to hear Bob and work with him occasionally, reinforced that idea that you do it your way. You hear it, you interpret it, and you also learn that everyone may not like how you interpret, but you still have to interpret the way you feel it. You can't wait and get approval for something that comes from you. You throw it out, and if someone is not crazy about it, that's what makes a horse race. You just keep on going, but you allow your intuitive senses to flow and come forth with whatever you feel you want to interpret.

Bob discussed his life philosophies which kept him focused on his performance attitudes:
I go through life on the grazing principle. So many of us get locked in a vice because we've determined what the nature of our life is gonna be, what we're gonna do and how we're gonna do it and what we're gonna get for doing it. It's so rigid and prescribed. Often, we have these things right in front of us that are so simple and easy to do. If you do one of those things, pretty soon you get another one and then another. And soon, you've experienced all these wonderful things without having to be so uptight.

It amazes me all the people who always talk about their financial responsibilities, and the need to have a certain kind of job, so they can have possessions, and maintain the life-style they want. I believe it's very important to do what you *want* to do, regardless of the money.

It's hard for a lot of people to say, "It's okay for me to do something I enjoy." They grow up with that idea of "I've got to do some kind of odious 9 to 5 job, and in return, I get a house in the 'burbs, two and a half kids, and a nice sportscar.

But when you do something you totally enjoy, a lot of that stuff becomes very extraneous. It's quite secondary whether you have it now. If you do, it's a blessing that you're really grateful for. If you don't, it's fine because you are very rewarded and fulfilled in your life.

When you're working in something you really don't like to do, you better have all the accouterments of the good life, because you don't have much else. In other words, if you love your work, you can get in an old car and drive to work and it's okay. If you hate your work, you better have a damn good car. If there's very little pleasure once you get there, you better enjoy the ride.

It's important to remember that young performers always have it rough at first. Money is usually scarce until you have made a name. The economics of being a musician are hard unless you have big records and can draw big numbers. A lot of folkies aspire to poverty level. I mean, by the time you get done travelling around the country in your car doing $100-a-night jobs—you don't do one every night—you might have to drive to Omaha to get another one. You add it all up and then deduct your gas money and hotels, and - uh oh! - you're way under $8,000 a year. It's okay because the rewards are in doing it. But it's hard for very talented, deserving people to break in.

There have been times for me in my career that with the exception of one or two gigs, I didn't have a gig scheduled for the rest of my life. That's the nature of my business. I may never get another idea. I may never get another booking. When one idea is built to completion, a song, a show, whatever, I feel very spent. I feel very empty. The fear that I will never have another idea, it's devastating.

I think the most important thing a young performer has to do is learn his craft, what I call "woodshedding." Any money you make in the beginning should be viewed as getting paid to learn. You should keep your day job while you learn your performing craft. That's the number one priority. Then if you can get the right kind of place and audience on a regular basis, if you like doing it, and then do it with a kind of openness, responsiveness to the people you are there to serve, you will get very good. You'll get good at delivering an experience. Doesn't matter if you're making them laugh or making them cry, piquing their curiosity or lecturing—you just have to do it well.

I think a lot of us folk singers have been hiding out behind our music for a long time, refusing to really do the job. People who come to hear a singer want to be amused, they want to be moved, they want to be enlightened, they want to be something . . . . They may not be choosy what, but more often than not, they come for a service. Performers can lose sight of this.

We're really cheerleaders. We're there to convene with a group who feel the same way, and we all sing and see that we're not alone, though sometimes out there it feels like our voices are lonely. We come together for the songs, and we cheer the singer and ourselves, and we say, "This is the right way to think." Then we don't feel so alone.

In 1986 I was observing in groups like the Muskrats, The Washington Squares and Suzanne Vega that their roots were in punk rock and rock 'n' roll, but they were doing some of the old songs in a new way. The Muskrats did an old folk song I wrote with Ochs called *That's the Way It's Gonna Be*. Listening to songs of outrage by punk groups scares grownups out of their skin, but, it was the same kind of unsettling thing when I was young. Instead of wearing jeans and long hair, now they have green spiked hair, but the whole idea of being outraged and questioning is a good thing. While we still can ask, 'why?', I don't grieve for the future of America.

As far as political activism goes, I'm into effectiveness. You can march all you want, and say nuclear power is wrong and dangerous, but it was when we took a more reasoned attitude and said, "We'll accept nuclear power plants as soon as they are absolutely safe, and we'll continue to go to court and demand satisfaction," that things happened. If they try to make them safe, they're too expensive. So you ended up in the wonderful position of having gotten it done. The position of rightness alone isn't really too helpful. It's not just a question of having the attitude and the position — which is just so much noise happening in the wilderness; you have to know who to talk to, what meeting to show up at, and when to stand up and speak. It doesn't hurt to write a letter to Mother Jones, but it helps more if you know the kind of letter political people respond to.

The environment is where the jobs are going to be. Cleaning it up must become our first national priority. This is where we all live and this national apathy will soon be exchanged for a new era of caring and commitment. We've got to look at what we can give of ourselves. It's terribly important. We've gotten away from that spirit that once was America. It will be a new way of life. But we must realize as a people, that it's not what you have, it's what you contribute.

I cringe every time someone in Washington says the economy is improving, because that's when I know more folks will be losing their jobs. It's a very confusing time for people because their lives are being changed very quickly by forces that are beyond their control. I'm finding a great parallel to the technological changes in the 1950s. People are having a hard time keeping up. I'm finding that many of the values of the '50s and '60s are more relevant than ever today. The biggest change in the '90s has been in the American corporation. The big word now is "downsizing." What the hell is downsizing? I'll tell you. Downsizing is technobabble for putting people out of work, taking away their homes and in some cases putting them out on the streets. It's taking money out of the pockets of the workers and putting it in the pockets of a few. When some company president says he's laid off a couple thousand people to protect the interests of the stockholders, he may damn well have served their interests and his own million-dollar salary, but does not serve the interests of America!

In principle, at least, American business at one time existed to create jobs and put people to work. But now? Well, the ultimate corporation of the 1990s will be the one that hires nobody, makes nothing but turns a profit.

I think there are going to be some real tough times ahead. I feel that when people get confused and the economy goes to hell, we return to our roots. We want to know who we are, as an American people. I find it a spiritual quest.

I think folk music has a more universal appeal and can have a greater effect on people than other styles, such as rock. You have more slack with folk and country music. Any song that has an attitude, a point of view, anecdotal kind of story, can get to people who might never have been exposed to that before. If what you're singing is of interest to them, you got them. Even if it's in a form that they don't understand, the content will get them. That's not true of rock & roll, which is a far more visceral experience. You have to get up to at least 80 decibels just to have your bone marrow jiggle in time with the bass.

I used to be passionate. Now I'm effective. I used to think I could do something about starving people in Biafra. I can't do anything about that. You're hungry, you need a few dollars, here, take it, that's what I can do. It took me a long time to learn this. Now I specialize in small things. I've learned to have a small effect.

Writer Garry Cooper commented on Bob's philosophy in his Chicago Singles *article* The Quiet Voice:

Small effects. Like seeds. Bob Gibson's small effects will survive long after the man, among his friends, audiences and musicians.

Sometimes there is a wide gap between a performer's public and private personalities. Bing Crosby comes immediately to mind. And who has any idea what Mick Jagger is really like? But with Bob Gibson, you have the impression that he is what you see. His business card says, simply "Bob Gibson," with his address and phone. No guitars, musical notes or fancy letters.

Photo by Paul Natkin

Photo courtesy Allan Shaw

Photo courtesy Leslie Korshak

Bob Gibson

EPILOGUE
by Peter Yarrow

I think that Albert Grossman had enormous respect for Bob Gibson, not just as a performer, but as a musical groundbreaker. I often told Bobby that the way in which he used voices, particularly with Joan Baez when he did a duet with her, and with Hamilton Camp (who was Bobby Camp, originally), was really thrilling — and very important to Peter, Paul and Mary. His arrangements were unusual in that he didn't use parallel harmonies in a conventional kind of way. It was as if there were two melodic lines being sung. An example of that was *The Virgin Mary,* which he sang with Joan Baez at the Newport Festival in 1959. And then, of course, he and Bobby Camp sang *You Can Tell the World* and *Well, Well, Well,* which Peter, Paul & Mary later recorded using the same harmony concepts. It was definitely a great gift that he gave us — to go far beyond traditional folk harmony structure. The intervals were chosen to accentuate the emotional place that you were reaching for in the song. It was all very intuitive. Much as I loved and admired the close harmony of traditional folk groups (and even the Everly Brothers), this was a step beyond. It was less linear, freer and more abstract.

Bobby also absolutely had the gift of knowing how to get an audience singing in the sense that few performers can. The united sound of an audience actually becomes almost another single voice — another artist. Singing with an audience hinges on one's ability to listen to their sound and blend with it, finding the vocal quality that shares a resonance; an acoustic resonance, but also a heart resonance. Of course, Bobby had all those capacities in great abundance.

He was also a folklorist. He was knowledgeable about songs, and he had extraordinary taste.

More than anybody, Bobby brought the 12-string guitar into broader acceptance in the '60s. He didn't play it the way Huddie Ledbetter played it or even the way Pete Seeger played it. His unique style was sort of a cross between a rhythm guitar, a harp and a hammer dulcimer. His playing felt rich and symphonic.

On the other hand, Bobby was very derivative of Pete in his banjo playing — no question about it. But everybody was derivative. I owe so much of my musical vocabulary to Josh White, Pete Seeger, Bob Gibson of course, and Woody Guthrie. They all gave me something valuable. The beginning of creativity is imitation. Being derivative is not a bad word in folk music. The folk process not only allows it, but invites us to take that music, give it our own imprimatur, and board the train of the great, great ride to wherever folk music is going. We add what we add. We take what we take. We enrich ourselves and hopefully those people with whom we're sharing the ride — and then we get off the train. But the train moves on with our music joining that of others who wrote it long before us.

And that is basically what Bobby has done for us. He's taken that ride. He's left a legacy that inspires us, that enriches us, that informs us. We embrace him, we love him in his beauty, in his pain, in his gifts, both aesthetic and personal, and we incorporate his work and his inspiration into the music that we make.

February, 1999

APPENDICES

Appendix

Notes from Pete Seeger's Manual
How to Play the 5-String Banjo

With Pete Seeger's permission, following are some excerpts from his manual "How to Play the 5-String Banjo" that Bob used to learn the banjo and, in its third edition from 1961, is still available today:

From the Preface to second edition, 1954:

"This is the second edition of this manual. It has been added to and revised slightly, and thereby, it is hoped, improved. The first edition was mimeographed, its stencils having been typed in a variety of hotel rooms while the author was accompanying Henry Wallace in the presidential campaign of 1948. The first printing of 100 copies sold out in three years. The second printing, also mimeographed, sold its 500 copies in another three years. A casual statistician might thus deduce (assuming the same rate of increase continues) that 390,000 copies will be sold within the next twelve years. As G.B. Shaw said, however, 'there are lies, damned lies, and statistics'. The author prudently limits this printing to 3,000."

From his note dated March, 1996, added to the book for the most recent printing:

Dear friends -

For 25 years I've tried to find time to really revise this banjo manual. No luck. Perhaps others will. . . .

If I did revise this book I'd start with the G tuning, not the C tuning, and start with single string playing, not chords. What I call here "a basic strum", I'd call "a simple strum" and teach it not at the beginning, but later on. For the first chapters I think I'd show the pattern I learned from Bascom Lunsford.

I'd print more complete songs. I never realized how frustrating it must be to start learning a piece, and then be told "finish it yourself."

I'm sorry I've not had time to revise this book since 1962. But its basic ideas I'll still stand by:

- Have fun.
- Learn by participating with a wide range of folks.
- Keep your banjo hanging handy so you can pick it any old time you want to.
- Stick with one thing till you learn it well - in your fingers, which will remember things your brain forgets.
- Take it easy but take it, and don't let your studies interfere with your education.

Pete Seeger
March, 1996

I Come For To Sing - 307

APPENDIX
THE PEEKSKILL RIOTS
SEPTEMBER 4, 1949

The Peekskill Riots in 1949 were symbolic of the tumultuous climate developing when Bob emerged on the scene. They embodied all of the fears that gripped Americans at that time — the Communist witchhunts, the racial unrest and the economic fear of organized labor. From a biography of Paul Robeson on the Folk Era web site:

Paul Robeson used his deep baritone voice to promote Black spirituals, share other cultures and to benefit the labor and social movements of his time. In 1933, Robeson donated the proceeds of *All God's Chillun* to Jewish refugees fleeing Hitler's Germany. At a 1934 rally for the anti-fascist forces in the Spanish Civil War, he declared, "The artist must elect to fight for Freedom or for Slavery. I have made my choice. I had no alternative." In New York in 1939, he premiered in Earl Robinson's *Ballad for Americans*, a cantata celebrating the multi-ethnic, multi-racial face of America.

During the 1940s, Robeson continued to perform and to speak out against racism and for peace. In 1945 he headed an organization that challenged President Truman to support an anti-lynching law. As a passionate believer in international cooperation, Robeson protested the growing Cold War and worked tirelessly for friendship and respect between the U.S. and the USSR. In the late 1940s, when dissent was scarcely tolerated in the U.S., Robeson openly questioned why African Americans should fight in the army of a government that tolerated racism. Because of his outspokenness, he was accused by the House Un-American Activities Committee (HUAC) of being a Communist. Robeson saw this as an attack on the democratic rights of everyone who worked for international friendship and for equality. The accusation nearly ended his career. Eighty of his concerts were canceled, and in 1949, two interracial outdoor concerts in Peekskill, NY were attacked by white mobs while state police stood by.

From the web site for Orb Total Media, http://www.highlands.com/robeson/second.html, which has a Voices of History Video Project *dealing with the Peekskill concerts. Information is ©1998 Marilyn Elie:*

What was happening in Peekskill reflected what was going on all over the country. Defense Secretary Louis Johnson visited Peekskill and spoke to the American Legion about the dangers of the Russian enemy. He complimented them on being "awake" to the dangers posed by the Soviet Union.

Many young veterans and union members felt moved to come and protect what they had gone to war for — democracy. Plans were made for two thousand men, many of them wearing uniforms or union hats, to create a living wall around the concert area. They left the city in buses and arrived at the concert grounds early on the morning of Sept. 4, well before the police. Many carried baseball bats.

Of course it wasn't all emotion and principal. Economics played a role in what was unfolding as well. Peekskill was a company town and that company was Standard Brand, the largest yeast factory in the country during the war. The two men who ran the company had hired up to 1,200 in the factory during the war. Now employment was down to 770. Union activity and anyone who supported it was not welcome in Peekskill from their point of view. They were also major advertisers in the Peekskill Evening Star and friends of the editor.

The battle lines were drawn. The day before the concert, the Peekskill Evening Star ran one last editorial entitled *Wake Up America,* a slogan that was later publicized around the world.

Excerpted from a letter dated September 8, 1949, from the Office of the Sheriff, County of Westchester, White Planes, NY to the Honorable Thomas E. Dewey provided by the Field Library in Peekskill, NY:

On the morning of September 2nd, 1949, I was apprised that Mr. Paul Robeson had announced that a concert was to be held in Peekskill on Sunday, September 4th, 1949 at 2 pm. This was publicized in New York City as a concert for the benefit of the Harlem Chapter of the Civil Rights Congress.

On this same morning a meeting was held in the office of the District Attorney with various officers of the organized veterans' groups in the Peekskill area who had already announced their intentions to hold a parade and demonstration on the highways bordering the concert area. It was suggested to the veterans' groups that the parade be held within the City of Peekskill, which is approximately four miles from the concert area. The answer to our request was that their membership had by resolution agreed to hold their parade in the area on the highways near the concert area.

At a meeting on Saturday evening at Troop K Headquarters, a plan was formulated, posts were designated and police personnel assigned to all points considered vital. "No Parking" areas were designated. Walkie-talkie and loudspeakers were allocated. Radio cars were assigned. The total police force on duty in the area numbered 904. This was the largest concentration of police officers ever brought together in one area in Westchester County to handle problems arising out of a single incident.

The property of the former Hollowbrook Country Club at Van Cortlandtville which is in the unincorporated area of the Town of Cortlandt was used for the concert. This property is an abandoned golf course located approximately two miles north of the City line of Peekskill and approximately one mile south of the Putnam County line and faces on the northerly side of Oregon Road. The concert area is approximately a quarter of a mile in length along Oregon Road and the stage of the concert area was located approximately twelve hundred feet from Oregon Road in a hollow not visible from the road. The concert area was rough and uneven and partly surrounded by trees. There is one entrance to this area which is a dirt road leading off on Oregon Road in a northerly direction and cars approaching the concert area would have to come east or west along Oregon Road or approach via Red Mill Road which enters Oregon Road at the entrance to the concert area. Both are narrow two lane roads approximately twenty feet in width.

Upon my arrival at the scene, I observed between two thousand and twenty-five hundred persons apparently Robeson guards, who were stationed in what appeared to be a circle of defense standing very close together covering almost the entire area. A large number had already arrived and were down in the hollow in the vicinity of the concert stage. People started to gather along Red Mill Road and Oregon Road who appeared to be onlookers. These onlookers began to increase along these roads and in the fields beyond the road until it was estimated that they numbered approximately five thousand.

At approximately 1:30pm the veterans' demonstration parade started. It proceeded along Oregon Road from Oregon Corners on the Putnam County line. There was an estimated 2,500 persons and they paraded directly past the entrance to the concert area to Locust Avenue where the parade reversed itself and marched back again in front of the concert area. The parade continued until 2:50 pm when orders were given by the Chairman of the Parade Committee to disband and leave the area. Cheering, cat-calls, backfiring of exhausts made a din of noise, but up to this time, no disorder took place. All seeking to gain entrance to the concert area proceeded without hazard, and no disorder was observed during the concert.

At approximately 4 pm some cars began to leave the area. Veterans had left the scene by then, but spectators who had lined Oregon and Red Mill Roads for about one-half mile converged at the intersection, completely blocking it and making it impossible for cars in the concert area to exit. Cars which had left the concert area were stoned by persons in the fields on a bank along Red Mill Road. A large group would rush from one position to another and precipitate the stoning. They had to be removed from trees and billboards from which positions they could readily cause damage and injury by throwing rocks into the cars that were leaving. Incidents of stoning of cars occurred in a ten mile radius far removed from the policed area.

The entire concert area was cleared by 10:30 pm. Three automobiles were overturned. Seventy people received minor injuries. Serious injuries reported to us were a fractured skull, a broken arm, a broken jaw and an eye injury.

Marilyn Elie:
Most accounts concur that there was no physical violence during the concert. It was when the concert was over that violence erupted. Eyewitnesses say that as the concert goers left the grounds they were all directed, by State Police, the same way down Oregon Road. There were people along the road waiting with piles of rocks. Pete Seeger spoke of a young man who stood by the roadside next to a large pile of rocks which he hurled at the windshield of each passing car. Pete's windshield was smashed as his wife and children ducked to the floor. He stopped to ask an officer to stop the assault and was told to move along, much to the relief of the driver in the car behind him who was being pummeled.

What happened in Peekskill and the surrounding area made headlines around the world. Reports were prepared and hearings were held to determine the official version of what happened on September 4th. The official report exonerated the police. The American Civil Liberties report which was issued about the same time came to very different conclusions. Some who had been assaulted attempted to pursue a class action suit with a young lawyer recently out of law school named Bella Abzug. Her advice was that, while the evidence was there, the chances of winning a suit in the current political climate was practically non-existent.

Pete Seeger
Bob Gibson knew that I had sung in Peekskill in September, 1949. I don't think he was even a teenager yet. Maybe he was — might have been 13 at the time. *(Bob was actually almost 18.)* And he said, "Oh, I know all about that concert. It was the Ku Klux Klan that organized it."

I said, "Well, tell me, how did they organize?"

He said, "Well the Klan had members in the police force in Peekskill and Westchester and they organized it like a battlefield. They had walkie-talkies all around the concert area." And Bob said, "You guys didn't have a chance."

You probably know that about 10,000 people had stones thrown at them and it was a frightening thing. I was trying to build a house, and people said, "Pete, don't you realize that in a year somebody like Sen. McCarthy's going to be the dictator of America?" And people on the left as well as the right found that this was only going to be the first of many such things happening.

But I don't know — I'm a long-time student of American history and I felt the average American wouldn't put up with that kind of violence — throwing stones at women and children, and I was right.

There were signs in all the stores, on bumpers and in houses all through Peekskill. They were like bumper stickers about six inches high and about 20 inches wide and they said, "WAKE UP AMERICA" and then underneath it in smaller letters "Peekskill did".

Now somebody pointed out that this was exactly the sign that they had after Kristalnacht in Germany. "WAKE UP GERMANY - Munich did" And it caused a great stir in Europe. "What's going on in America? Is America going Fascist?"

Within about four or five weeks all those signs disappeared, and I was proven right. The average American didn't go along with that kind of stuff. You might not have liked communism, but still you didn't throw stones at women and children.

But it was Bob who told me that it was the Ku Klux Klan that had members in the police department and they organized the whole thing.

Paul Robeson commented at the time:
I'm going to sing wherever the people want me to sing...and I won't be frightened by crosses burning in Peekskill or anywhere else.

Marilyn Elie:
Years later Pete Seeger found that he was denied permission to perform in a New York school because he had filed a law suite against the state of New York. He used the rocks which had been thrown through the windshield of his car in the construction of the chimney which warmed the log cabin he was building in Beacon, New York — *that same chimney that Bob Gibson had been "Tom Sawyered" into helping him build in 1953!*

Appendix

Bob Gibson Discography

This discography comes from Bob Gibson, himself, who graciously opened his archives, and my own collection, supplemented by information provided by Michael Dresser and Ben Cohen, who have a web site devoted to a Bob Gibson discography that can be found on Roger McGuinn's "Folk Den" page; Bob Allen, who took the Gate of Horn pictures; Allan Shaw of Folk Era Productions; and Ron Pratt's tireless internet search on my behalf.

I. Bob Gibson Albums

Following are the known Bob Gibson albums. Most were released on 12-inch LPs, at least one on reel to reel, and a few on cassette and CD. A few of them are very obscure, local releases available basically only at performances. All are Gibson alone, except for those marked with * which are with Bob (Hamilton) Camp or † which is with Tom Amandes and Anne Hills. Most are no longer available, only showing up in used record stores, but there is interest in re-releasing his music, so there is no telling how many of them might become available again. Folk Era Productions in Naperville, IL is the best source for finding out the availability of his music.

LP = long play 33 1/3 record   CS = cassette   VHS = video tape
RR = reel-to-reel   CD = compact disc

1   **Offbeat Folksongs** *(LP) Riverside Records RLP 12-802 - (1956)*
2   **I Come for to Sing** *(LP) Riverside Records RLP 12-806 (1957)*
3   **Carnegie Concert** *(LP) Riverside Records RLP 12-816 (1957)*
4   **Folksongs of Ohio** *(red vinyl 10" LP) Stinson Records SLP-76 (recorded 1955 - released 1957)*
5   **There's A Meetin' Here Tonight** *(LP) Riverside Records RLP 12-830 / 1111 (1958)*
6   **Ski Songs** *(LP) Elektra EKL-177 / EKS-7177 (1959)* *(RR) Elektra EKX 7177 (1959)*
7   **Yes, I See** *(LP) Elektra EKL-197 / EKS-7197 (1961)*
8*   **Bob Gibson and Bob Camp at the Gate of Horn** *(LP) Elektra EKL-207 / EKS-7207 (1961)*
9   **Folksongs of Ohio** *(red vinyl 12" LP - reissue of above 10" LP) Stinson Records SLP 76 (1963)*

10   **Hootenanny at Carnegie** *(LP - reissue of Carnegie Concert with alternate jacket graphics and song order) Riverside Records RLP542/RS-9542 (1963)*
11   **Where I'm Bound** *(LP) Elektra EKL-239/EKS-7239 (1964)*
12   **Bob Gibson** *(LP) Capitol Records ST-742 (1970)*
13   **Funky in the Country** *(LP) Legend Enterprises (Mountain Railroad Records, Inc.) / Universal Audio Corp. UAS 895-64384 (1974)*
14* **Gibson & Camp, Homemade Music** *(LP) Mountain Railroad Records, Inc. MR-52781 (1978)*
15   **The Perfect High** *(LP) Mountain Railroad Records, Inc. MR-52794 (1980)*
16† **Courtship of Carl Sandburg** *(CS) (1984)*
17   **Uptown Saturday Night** *(LP) Hogeye Records HOG005 (1984)*
18* **Gibson & Camp, The Gate of Horn — Revisited!!!** *(CS) B★G Records DM-87023 (1986)*
     (CD version of above CS) Folk Era Productions - FE1413CD (1994)
19   **A Child's Happy Birthday Album** *(CS) B★G Records 001 (1989)*
20   **Bob Gibson 5/91 - I Hear America Singing** *(CS) Live Music Is More Real / Snapshot Music (1991)*
21   **Stops Along the Way** *(CS) B★G Records CM4210 (1991)*
     (CD) B★G Records 1004 (1991)
22   **Bootleg Bob Gibson/Bob Gibson in Chicago 1965-1972** *(CS) J&G Reel to Real (1994)*
23   **Makin' a Mess, Bob Gibson sings Shel Silverstein** *(CD) Asylum Records 61697-2 (1995)*
24   **Bob Gibson Interview Disc/Makin' A Mess: Bob Gibson Sings Shel Silverstein/Radio Interview With Studs Terkel** *(CD) Asylum Records apcd-0021 (1994)*
25   **Joy, Joy! The Young and Wonderful Bob Gibson** *(CD) Riverside Records / The Riverside Folklore Series Volume One RVCD 9909-2 (1996, '57-58)*
26   **Perfect High** *(CD) re-release of the earlier album (1998)*

Following are the songs included on these albums. Where known, the writers of the songs are noted. In many instances, especially on the early recordings, Bob Gibson is listed as the writer because of his arrangement of the song.

Offbeat Folksongs - 1956 - Riverside

The album is an excellent collection of humor, Calypso, ballads and virtuoso banjo playing.

1A Mighty Day *(Bob Gibson)*
2A The Pig and the Inebriate
3A Andalucian Dance *(Bob Gibson)*
4A Greenwood Side
5A Delia
6A The Abdication
7A Rejected Lover
8A The Horse Named Bill
9A Snake Cure

1B Lula Gal
2B Bahamian Lullabye
3B Pretty Boy
4B Block Island Reel *(Bob Gibson)*
5B What Are Folks Made Of
    (Bob Gibson)
6B Noah *(Bob Gibson)*
7B Linstead Market
8B A Maid Went to Dublin
    (Bob Gibson)
9B The Next Market Day
10B Chickens *(Bob Gibson)*

I Come for to Sing - 1957 - Riverside

Recorded on January 24 & 25, 1957, this classic album includes the first recording of his signature song *Abilene,* and his song *To Morrow,* which the Kingston Trio recorded on their seventh album. Strangely, *I Come For To Sing* is listed on the album's liner notes as being written by Chick Young of Ann Arbor, Michigan, but TRO, Bob's publishing company from the early years, lists it as a Bob Gibson song. Most other songs are traditional, but the evidence of his re-writing, condensing and arranging are becoming more evident, most notably in *John Henry.* Assisting musicians were Dick Rosmini on guitar, Trigger Alpert on bass and Pete Berry on conga drum.

1A John Henry *(Bob Gibson)*
2A Dance, Boatman, Dance
3A Abilene *(Bob Gibson)*
4A Katie Morey
5A Lost Jimmie Whelan
6A Ol' Bill
7A To Morrow *(Bob Gibson)*
8A Take This Hammer

1B Money Is King
2B Drill, Ye Tarriers
3B I'm Going to Leave Old Texas
4B Mattie Groves
5B The Squirrel
6B I Come for to Sing *(Bob Gibson)*
7B The Lily of the West *(Bob Gibson)*
8B Springfield Mountain *(Gibson)*

Carnegie Concert - 1957 - Riverside
Hootenanny at Carnegie - 1963 - Riverside

The *Carnegie Concert* has a photo of Gibson on the cover; the *Hootenanny* edition has a drawing by Ken Deardoff. Both albums have notes on the songs by Kenneth Goldstein and a commentary by Orrin Keepnews. Both are condensed on the *Hootenanny* edition. The sequence of songs differs:

Carnegie Concert
1A Sail Away, Lady
2A Alberta *(Bob Gibson)*
3A The Erie Canal
4A Pushboat *(Bob Gibson)*
5A John Riley
6A There Once Was a Poor Young Man
7A *Some Fragments of Marital Advice:*
  Hard is the Fortune
  Marry a Texas Girl
  When I was Single
8A Mighty Day *(Bob Gibson)*

1B Day-O
2B Go Down to Bimini *(Gibson)*
3B Wheel-a Matilda *(Gibson)*
4B You Must Come in at the Door
5B Good News
6B Michael, Row the Boat Ashore

Hootenanny
1A Some Introductory Remarks
2A Michael, Row the Boat Ashore
3A Day-O
4A Go Down to Bimini *(Gibson)*
5A Wheel-a-Matilda *(Gibson)*
6A You Must Come In At the Door
7A Good News

1B Sail Away, Lady
2B Alberta *(Bob Gibson)*
3B The Erie Canal
4B Pushboat *(Bob Gibson)*
5B There Once Was A Young Man
6B *Some Fragments of Marital Advice:*
  Hard is the Fortune
  Marry a Texas Girl
  When I Was Single
7B Mighty Day *(Bob Gibson)*
8B John Riley

Folksongs of Ohio - Stinson

Recorded in 1955 as an audition tape, released by Stinson on 10" LP in 1957, and re-released on 12" LP in 1963. Most of the songs are traditional.

1A Katey Morey
2A Down in Sky Town
3A Father Grumble
4A Working on a Push Boat
5A I'm a Methodist Till I Die
6A There Was an Old Woman

1B Lily of the West *(Gibson)*
2B Over in the Meadow
3B Ninety Nine and Ninety
4B Father Grumble
5B Ohio River
6B Ninety Nine and Ninety

There's A Meetin' Here Tonight - 1958 - Riverside

For the first time Bob features the 12-string guitar on this album on *Jordan River, The Virgin Mary Had One Son* and *This Train*. He is backed on the album by Earl Backus on guitar and tambourine and John Frigo on bass.

1A Joy, Joy
2A There's a Meetin' Here Tonight *(Bob Gibson)*
3A Jordan River
4A Brandy
5A There's A Hole In The Bucket
6A Easy Rider *(Bob Gibson)*
7A Red Iron Ore
8A The Virgin Mary Had One Son

1B This Train *(Bob Gibson)*
2B Whoa, Buck
3B Pastures of Plenty
4B Titanic
5B This Little Light
6B East Virginia
7B When I First Came To This Land
8B A Wayfaring Stranger *(Gibson)*

Ski Songs - 1960 - Elektra

Planned as a ski play written with writers from the Denver Post, this album is all that was ever produced from the effort. Assisting musicians are Joe Puma, electric guitar, Russell Savakus, bass, and Eric Weissberg, banjo, bass and guitar.

1A Celebrated Skier *(Gibson)*
2A In This White World *(Sealy / Pitts / Nardin / Gibson)*
3A Super Skier *(Gibson / Rieser)*

1B Ski Patrol *(Gibson / Wurman / Fuerst)*
2B Skiin' in the Morning *(Gibson)*
3B Super Skier's Last Race *(Gibson / Abramson / Holtsman)*

4A Highland Lassie *(Gibson)*
5A Bend in His Knees *(Gibson)*
6A Talking Skier *(Gibson/Rieser)*

4B What'll We Do
    (Gibson/Pitts/Sealy/Nardin)
5B Skol to the Skier *(Gibson)*

Yes, I See - 1961 - Elektra

This was a departure in style for Bob, and he started doing things on this that no other artist did until ten years later. He was backed on some songs by the black female group, The Gospel Pearls. Assisting musicians were Joseph Robert Gibbons, Herbert O. Brown, Thomas J. Tedesco, Eddie Lee Kendrix, Joe L. Clayton, Nick Bonney and James E. Bond, Jr.

1A Yes I See *(Bob Gibson)*
2A Springhill Mine Disaster
    (Peggy Seeger/Ewan MacColl)
3A Well, Well, Well *(Gibson/Camp)*
4A You Can Tell the World
    (Gibson/Camp)
5A Copper Kettle *(Frank Beddo)*
6A John Henry *(Bob Gibson)*

1B Gilgarry Mountain (Darlin'
    Sporting Jenny) *(Gibson)*
2B Motherless Child *(Gibson)*
3B Daddy Roll 'Em *(Gibson)*
4B Trouble in Mind
5B By and By *(Gibson/Camp)*
6B Blues Around My Head (When
    the Sun Comes Up in the Morning)
    (Gibson/Camp)

Bob Gibson & Bob Camp at the Gate of Horn - 1961 -Elektra

Recorded at the Gate of Horn in April, 1961, this is one of the greatest albums in the history of folk music. There are two versions of this album. The first has the song *Butternut Hill*. The album was then reissued without Butternut Hill. That is the only difference. Gibson and Camp are backed by Herb Brown on bass.

1A Skillet Good and Greasy
2A Old Blue *(B. Goode & B. Kuhl)*
3A St. Claire's Defeat *(Bob Gibson)*
3A St. Claire's Defeat *(Bob Gibson)*
4A I'm Gonna Tell God *(Gibson)*
5A Two in the Middle *(Gibson)*
6A *Civil War Trilogy*
   First Battalion *(Silverstein/Camp)*
   Yes I See *(Bob Gibson)*
   Two Brothers *(Irving Gordon)*

1B Daddy Roll 'Em *(Bob Gibson)*
2B The Thinking Man
    (Gibson/Camp (new words))
3B Butternut Hill *(Gibson/Camp
    (new words))*
4B Wayfaring Stranger *(Gibson)*
5B Chicago Cops *(Frank
    Hamilton/Gibson)*
6B Betty & Dupree *(Gibson/Camp
    (new words & music))*

Where I'm Bound: Bob Gibson and his 12-String Guitar - 1964 - Elektra

This is Bob's last album before he dropped out of the business for three years to try to clean up. As Rick Neely said, it was the best example of Gibson's 12-string guitar work at its peak. The album is significant also because of the presence for the first time of Gibson and Silverstein collaborations. Released at the same time was the *Bob Gibson Song Book* with music and tablature for the songs on this album.

1A Where I'm Bound
   (Gibson / Thompson)
2A The Waves Roll Out
   (Gibson / Silverstein)
3A 12-String Guitar rag *(Gibson)*
4A Wastin' Your Time
   (Gibson / Silverstein)
5A The New Frankie & Johnny Song
   (Gibson / Silverstein)
6A Fog Horn *(Silverstein)*
7A Baby I'm Gone Again
   (Gibson / Silverstein)

1B Farewell My Honey Cindy Jane *(Gibson)*
2B Some Old Woman
   (Gibson / Silverstein)
3B Stella's Got a New Dress
   (Gibson / Camp)
4B The Town Crier's Song
   (Gibson / Camp)
5B What You Gonna Do?
   (Gibson / Silverstein)
6B Betsy from Pike *(Bob Gibson)*
7B Fare Thee Well (Dink's Song)
   (Bob Gibson)

Bob Gibson - 1970 - Capitol

Bob's comeback album after his self-imposed exile, he enlisted help from a power-house lineup of friends to help him sing on John Prine's *Sam Stone*. Unfortunately the inclusion of this song got the album enjoined in court which slowed the momentum of sales. Joining in the recording were Bob's friends, Roger McGuinn, Chris Hillman, Ann Goodman, Dick Rosmini, Sneeky Pete, The Cosmo Alley Choir, Severen Darden, Denny Doherty, Cyrus Faryar, Eddie Fischer, daughter Susan Gibson, Cynthia Goyette, Mark Hammerman, Bernie Leadon, Spanky McFarland, Nigil Pickering, Kay Reynolds, Rick Roberts, Linda Woodward, Mike Deasy, Earl Ball, Mike Bohs, Steve LA Fruer, Hamid Hamilton Camp, David Crosby, Emil Richards & Bud Shank. Also included on this album is *Easy Now,* which Bob said was one of his two favorite songs that he wrote.

1A Fog Horn *(Silverstein)*
2A Sam Stone *(John Prine)*
3A Leavin' for the Last Time
    (Jo Mapes/Gibson)
4A For Lovin' Me
    (Gordon Lightfoot)
5A A Hard Rain's A Gonna Fall
    (Bob Dylan)

1B About Time *(Camp)*
2B Just Like a Woman *(Bob Dylan)*
3B The Ballad of Fred and Mark
    (Marion Fischer/Gibson)
4B Easy Now *(Gibson)*
5B If I'm There *(Silverstein/Gibson)*

Funky in the Country - 1974- Mountain Railroad
This album, considered by many to be Bob's best, was recorded live at Amazingrace in Evanston, Illinois.

1A Cindy Dreams (of California)
    (Silverstein/Gibson)
2A I Never Got to Know Her
    Very Well *(Silverstein)*
3A Come on Back Baby (Lovesick
    Blues) *(Silverstein/Gibson)*
4A Funky in the Country *(Talbot)*
5A Dime a Dozen Times *(Afterman)*
6A Living Legend *(Silverstein)*

1B Abilene
    (Acuff/Loudermilk/Brown/Gibson)
1B Blues *(Gibson)*
2B I Can't Hide the Way
    (Gilbert/Gibson)
3B Farewell Party *(Connelly/Gibson)*
4B One and Only *(Gibson)*
5B Brownsville *(Gibson (new words))*
6B The Tarot and The Banjo
    (Hott/Gibson)
7B That's the Way It's Gonna Be
    (Ochs/Gibson)

Gibson & Camp, Homemade Music - 1978 - Mountain Railroad
   This is the first album of Bob's clean rebirth, his first reunion recording with Hamilton Camp, and it was literally homemade in Dick Rosmini's house.

1A Jimmie Rodgers *(Silverstein)*
2A Lookin for Trouble *(Goodman)*
3A Self-Satisfaction
   (Monty Dunn/Karen Cruse)
4A Dogies *(Gibson)*
5A Dead on the Run
   (Silverstein/Gibson)
6A Billy Come Home *(Gibson)*

1B Sing for the Song
   (Silverstein)
2B Spoon River
   (Michael Smith)
3B Fancy Ladies *(Silverstein/Gibson)*
4B Light Up My Lady
   (Douglas Steiger)
5B Homemade Music *(Gibson)*

I COME FOR TO SING - 319

The Perfect High - 1980 -
Mountain Railroad

Very important record released after Bob's creative rebirth in Mendocino. He also makes some very powerful statements about drugs on this album.

1A Just A Thing I Do
    (Kathy O'Grady's Song)
    (Silverstein / Gibson)
2A Yes Mr. Rogers
    (Silverstein / Fred Koller)
3A Leaving for the Last Time
    (Gibson / Jo Mapes)
4A Army of Children
    (Gibson / Irma Brown)
5A Rock Me Sweet Jesus
    (Silverstein / Gibson)
6A Heavenly Choir
    (Silverstein / Gibson)

1B Mendocino Desperados
    (Silverstein / Gibson)
2B Cuckoo Again *(Silverstein)*
3B Middle Aged Groupies
    (Silverstein)
4B Box of Candy (and a Piece
    of Fruit) *(Gibson / Paxton)*
5B Baba Fats (The Perfect High)
    (Silverstein)

Courtship of Carl Sandburg - 1984 -
Courtship Prod. Inc.

This was a cassette of the Chicago production of the play with Tom Amandes in the role of Carl Sandburg, with Bob Gibson and Anne Hills as the "Greek chorus." Chicago lawyer Ben Cohen was privileged to see the show and bought the cassette at the performance.

Songs in the play are a combination of songs collected by Carl Sandburg and originals for the play written by Bob Gibson. Songs include:

Horse Named Bill
Wizard Oil
Hallelujah, I'm a Bum
I Went Up in a Balloon So High

He Really Said A Lot To Her
Let the Band Play Dixie *(Gibson / North)*
Down In the Valley

Uptown Saturday Night - 1984 - Hogeye

This album is especially significant because it includes Bob's song *Pilgrim*, which became an unofficial anthem for AA, and it also has the second of Bob's two favorite songs that he wrote, *Lookin' for the You In Someone New.*

1A Let the Band Play Dixie
    (Gibson / Dave North)
2A Rest of the Night *(Gibson)*
3A Tequila Sheila
    (Silverstein / Davis)
4A And Lovin' You
    (Gibson / Paxton)
5A Pilgrim *(Gibson / Marv David)*

1B Uptown Saturday Night
    (Gibson)
2B Baby, If You Don't Know
    Now *(Gibson / Silverstein)*
3B Lookin' for the You *(Gibson)*
4B Tom Cattin' Time *(Gibson)*
5B Bein' on the Road *(Gibson)*

Gibson & Camp, The Gate of Horn — Revisited! - 1986 -
B★G Enterprises, Inc.

25th anniversary reunion of the benchmark album re-created and recorded at Holstein's in Chicago in June, 1986. It is nearly identical to the first album with the exception of three songs that were not included the first time around. These are *You Can Tell the World, Well, Well, Well* and *For Loving Me.*

1A You Can Tell the World
   (Gibson / Camp)
2A Well, Well, Well *(Gibson)*
3A Skillet Good and Greasy
4A Old Blue
   (B. Goode / B. Kuhl)
5A St. Claire's Defeat *(Gibson)*
6A I'm Gonna Tell God *(Gibson)*
7A Two in the Middle
   (Gibson / Camp)
8A *Civil War Trilogy*
   First Battalion *(Camp / Silverstein)*
   Two Brothers *(Irving Gordon)*
   Yes I See *(Gibson)*

1B Daddy Roll 'Em *(Gibson)*
2B Chicago Cops *(Gibson / Frank Hamilton)*
3B The Thinking Man
    (Gibson / Camp)
4B Wayfaring Stranger *(Gibson)*
5B Betty and Dupree
    (Gibson / Camp)
6B That's What You Get for
    Loving Me *(Gordon Lightfoot)*

A Child's Happy Birthday Album - 1988 -
B★G Records

This is the only officially released "Uncle Bob" recording — as yet!

1A We're Gonna Have a Birthday
    (Gibson / David North)
2A I Wonder What's Inside the Box
    (Gibson / David North)

1B Here's to the People
    (Whose Birthday it Isn't)
    (Gibson / David North)
2B There Must Have Been a

3A The Wrapping Song
     (Gibson/David North)
4A Seymour The (Birthday) Skunk
     (Gibson/David North)
5A The Old Man's Birthday
     (Gibson/David North)
6A A Whole Year Older
     (Gibson/David North)
(Gibson/David North)

Party Here *(Gibson/North)*
3B If Nobody Comes to My
     Party *(Silverstein)*
4B Inniuk the Eskimo *(Silverstein)*
5B The Birthday Card Song
     (Gibson/David North)
6B A Happy Birthday Wish For
     You

Bob Gibson 5/91 - 1991 - Snapshot Music

Recorded at a live performance at Charlotte's Webb in Rockford, Illinois, May 19, 1991. He does his new version of *Stella's Got a New Dress,* changing it to *Sarah's Got a New Dress* in honor of his daughter who was born in 1988.

1A Cindy Dreams (of California) *(Silverstein/Gibson)*
2A How Could You Do This To Me? *(Bob Gibson)*
3A Just a Thing I Do (Kathy O'Grady's Song)
     (Silverstein/Gibson)
4A Dyin' for Love
5A And Lovin' You *(Gibson/Paxton)*
6A "Sarah's" Got a New Dress *(Gibson/Camp)*
7A Lookin' for the You in Someone New *(Bob Gibson)*
8A Living Legend *(Silverstein)*

1B Abilene *(Acuff/Loudermilk/Brown/Gibson)*
     Blues *(Gibson)*
2B Pilgrim *(Gibson/Marv David)*
3B I Hear America Singing *(Silverstein)*
4B *Civil War Trilogy*
     First Battalion *(Camp/Silverstein)*
     Two Brothers *(Irving Gordon)*
     Yes I See *(Gibson)*
5B Get Away
6B Let the Band Play Dixie *(Gibson/Dave North)*

Stops Along the Way - 1991 - B★G Enterprises, Inc.

A live recording, this was a by-invitation-only birthday party concert for Bob's 60th birthday. It is especially important as it is Bob's last folk release.

1A Michael Row the Boat Ashore
2A To Morrow *(Gibson)*
3A Abilene
    (Gibson / Brown / Loudermilk)
4A I Can't Hide the Way
    (Gilbert / Gibson)
5A How Could You Do This to Me
    (Gibson)
6A Sing Us Some of the Old Songs
    (Gibson)
7A Great Lakes Song *(Gibson)*
8A The Mermaid of Ontario
9A Row, Row, Row

1B No More Cane on the Brazos
2B Start the Parade *(Gibson / Ochs)*
3B Get Away
4B Let the Band Play Dixie
    (Gibson / Dave North)
5B Dyin' for Love
6B I Hear America Singing
    (Silverstein)
7B Living Legend *(Silverstein)*
8B Stops Along the Way
    (Silverstein / Gibson)

Bootleg Gibson - 1994 (release date)

This is an "official" (more-or-less) Bootleg Gibson album that was sold (in an unknown but not very large quantity) at the Gibson benefit concert held in Chicago on September 27, 1994. It is a compilation of Gibson performances dated from 1965 to 1972. Ben Cohen bought a copy on the way in. At the end of the concert they were all gone. Bob's daughter, Meridian Green, has the original DAT tape of this, so there's a possibility that it may become available commercially.

Rick Neely said this about the tape:

Jeff Chounard worked the sound board at Mother Blues and the Quiet Knight and recorded a lot of stuff. He came out with the *Bootleg* recording. Some of it's pretty doggone good, and some of it's pieces that have never been recorded anywhere else, and some of it's pretty bad. He does a duet with Paul Butterfield who's also an incredible musician with his blues harmonica. They do a duet where they do *Goin' Down to Brownsville,* and musically instrumentally it's together, but vocally, it steps over the edge a little bit. The improvisation got a little bit too wild, and the intonation got a little off. The crowd must have been right with them, though, because the response is great, but the tape doesn't lie. I asked Bob, "Were these recordings made unbeknownst to you?", because I wouldn't have imagined that he would let somebody record some of that stuff. I think musically, Bob was confident enough that it didn't matter. It was wild, it was free-spirited, it was the spur of the moment, and he probably understood that it would never be released commercially. Some of it's pretty good, some of it's pretty wild, but it's the essence of what a Gibson club date must have been like in that time. Guy Guilbert played bass on some of the cuts. Another guy named Bob Matthews played bass on some of the other cuts. He must have been a working bass player around town at that time period because he was on other recordings and stuff as a bass player. Guy Guilbert played bass for Bob a lot. There's another guy who played bass for Bob who I think is out in California — Wally Pillach. He was a young black guy who was more rock and jazz oriented and played very well with Bob because Bob liked that kind of stuff. His playing was the kind of rhythmic groundwork that everything else could expand around, and the more interesting you could make it, the better it was as far as Bob was concerned, vocally as well as instrumentally.

1A Frankie and Johnny
    (Gibson / Silverstein)
2A Come On Back, Baby
    (Gibson / Silverstein)
3A You'll Never Know
    (Gibson / Silverstein)
4A Can't Wait Around Here Anymore
5A For Lovin' Me
    (Gordon Lightfoot)
6A Tryin' to Make Me Settle Down
    (Gibson / Silverstein)
7A Sweet Betsy From Pike
    (Gibson)
8A Ain't No More Cane on the Brazos
    (Traditional)
9A Goin' Down to Brownsville
    (Gibson-new words)
    One and Only *(Gibson)*

1B Where I'm Bound
    (Gibson / Thompson)
2B Fog Horn
    (Silverstein)
3B Abilene
    (Gibson / Brown / Loudermilk)
4B I Like Your Song
5B Ol' Blue
6B Dolphins in the Sea
    (Fred Neill)
7B Two in the Middle
    (Gibson)
8B Well, Well, Well
    (Gibson)
9B Skillet Good and Greasy

Makin' a Mess, Bob Gibson sings Shel Silverstein - 1995 - Asylum Records

This was Gibson's last release. The backup choir that came in to help Bob on *I Hear America Singing* includes Peter Yarrow, Elaine MacFarlane, Josh White Jr., Ed McCurdy, John Brown, Tom Paxton, Oscar Brand, John Hartford, Emmylou Harris, Glenn Yarborough, Cathryn Craig, Dennis Locorriere and Barbara Bailey Hutchinson.

1   Stops Along the Way *(Silverstein & Gibson)*
2   I Hear America Singing *(Silverstein)*
3   Whistlers & Jugglers *(Silverstein)*
4   Nothin's Real Anymore *(Silverstein)*
5   Killed By a Coconut *(Silverstein, Stevens, Kanter)*

6 The Man Who Turns the Damn Thing Off and On *(Silverstein)*
7 Take Me *(Silverstein, James, Spivey)*
8 Still Gonna Die *(Silverstein)*
9 Fancy Ladies *(Silverstein & Gibson)*
10 Never Be This Young Again *(Silverstein)*
11 The Golden Kiss *(Silverstein)*
12 The Leavin' Came Hard *(Silverstein)*
13 Makin' a Mess of Commercial Success *(Silverstein, James, Spivey)*

Makin' a Mess Promo - 1995 - Asylum Records, APCD-21

At the time *Makin' a Mess* was produced, Bob and Shel Silverstein were interviewed by Studs Terkel on July 28, 1994, on Terkel's show on Chicago's WFMT. A CD was released of this interview to help promote the *Makin' A Mess* CD.

1 Stops Along The Way
2 Nothing's Real Anymore
3 Killed By A Coconut
4 Whistlers & Jugglers
5 Makin' a Mess of Commercial Success
6 The Man Who Turns the Damn Thing Off and On
7 Still Gonna Die
8 I Hear America Singing

Joy, Joy! The Young and Wonderful Bob Gibson - 1996 - Riverside, CD

This is a compilation of highlights of Bob's early Riverside albums.

1 Joy, Joy
2 Whoa, Buck
3 This Train
4 Abilene
5 John Henry
6 Pastures of Plenty
7 Easy Rider
8 Money is King
9 Ol' Bill
10 Titanic
11 Virgin Mary Had One Son
12 Wayfaring Stranger
13 Take This Hammer
14 Red Iron Ore
15 Brandy
16 Lula Gal
17 Rejected Lover
18 Block Island Reel
19 Jimmy Whalen
20 Drill Ye Tarriers
21 I Come For to Sing
22 Meetin' Here Tonight
23 Alberta
24 Erie Canal
25 John Riley
26 Mighty Day

The Perfect High - 1998 - Drive Archive, DE2-41794

This is a CD re-release of Bob's 1980 album available through Folk Era Productions in Naperville, IL.

1. Just A Thing I Do (Kathy O'Grady's Song) *(Silverstein/Gibson)*
2. Yes Mr. Rogers *(Silverstein/Fred Koller)*
3. Leaving for the Last Time *(Gibson/Jo Mapes)*
4. Army of Children *(Gibson/Irma Brown)*
5. Rock Me Sweet Jesus *(Silverstein/Gibson)*
6. Heavenly Choir *(Silverstein/Gibson)*
7. Mendocino Desperados *(Silverstein/Gibson)*
8. Cuckoo Again *(Silverstein)*
9. Middle Aged Groupies *(Silverstein)*
10. Box of Candy (and a Piece of Fruit) *(Gibson/Paxton)*
11. Baba Fats (The Perfect High) *(Silverstein)*

II 45 RPM Singles

Marching to Pretoria / I'm Never to Marry - 1956
   Decca 9-30528
Blues Around My Head / Gilgarry Mountain - 1961 -
   Elektra 12001
Sam Stone / About Time - 1970 - Capitol P-3134

III Gibson Cuts on Other Artists' Albums

Up & Up - 1979 - Tom Paxton LP - Mountain Railroad
   Bob Gibson plays 12-string and does vocal on the song **"Outlaw"**

The Paxton Report - 1980 -Tom Paxton LP - Mountain Railroad
   Bob Gibson plays 12-string and does background vocals

And Loving You - 1986 - Tom Paxton LP/CD - Flying Fish
   Bob Gibson and Hamilton Camp do background vocals

IV Gibson Cuts on Compilations

Chicago Mob Scene: A Folk Song Jam Session - 1957 - Riverside RLP 12-641
(Note: The label on the center of the record gives the title as Chicago Mob Scene: Folk Songs from the Windy City.)

A collection of Chicago folksingers including these artists: Larry Ehrlich, Pete Stein, "Samuel Hall", Pete Stone, Moe Hirsh, Blind Bill Todd, Bob March. The liner notes say this about 'Samuel Hall': '...is the pseudonym chosen to mask this pre-professional (though certainly not unworthy) effort by a young folksinger and banjoist who, shortly after this session, turned entirely to folkmusic performance as a career. Some listeners may easily recognize this fast-rising young star; others can be content to enjoy him.' "Samuel Hall" is credited on these tracks:

Mama Don't Allow - *Pete Stein and Hirsh, Guitars; Bob March and Samuel Hall, banjos; Blind Bill Todd, bass; vocals by all*

The Old Woman Who Loved a Swine - Hall, vocal and banjo.

Day-O - Hall, vocal and banjo; Stein and Hirsch, guitars; March, banjo; Todd, bass.

Life is a Trial - Hall, vocal and banjo.

Mob Blues - Stein and Hirsch, guitars; Hall and March, banjos; Todd, bass; vocals by all and Dean Gitter (producer of the LP).

All-Star Hootenanny - 1957 - Riverside, RS 7539 (stereo) and RM 7539 (mono) - 12" LP
One Gibson cut:
Whoa Buck

All-Star Hootenanny Volume Two - 1958 - Riverside, RM 7543 - 12" LP
One Gibson cut:
Titanic

Everybody Sing Volume 1 - Songs for Cubs - 1958 - Riverside, RLP1418 - 12" LP
Four Gibson cuts:
Noah
There's a Hole in the Bucket
Day-O
There's a Meetin' Here Tonight

Everybody Sing Volume 2 - Songs for Juniors - 1958 - Riverside, RLP 1419 - 12" LP
Four Gibson cuts:
When I First Came to This Land
Dance, Boatmen, Dance
This Train
You Must Come in at the Door

Everybody Sing Volume 3 - Songs for Seniors - 1958 - Riverside,

RLP1420 - 12" LP
Two Gibson cuts:
Michael, Row the Boat Ashore
Ol' Bill

Everybody Sing Volume 4 - International Songs - 1958 - Riverside, RLP1421 - 12" LP
Two Gibson cuts:
Wheel-a Matilda
Linstead Market

All-Star Hootenanny Folk Favorites - 1959 - Decca, DL 74469 - 12" LP
One Gibson cut:
Marching to Pretoria

All Time Hootenanny Folk Favorites Volume 2 - 1959 - Decca, DL74485 - 12" LP
One Gibson cut:
I'm Never to Marry

Folk Festival at Newport, Vol. 2 - 1959 - Vanguard VRS-9063 and VSD-2054.
  This is the Newport concert where Bob introduced Joan Baez.
Two Gibson cuts:
Virgin Mary Had One Son (with Joan Baez)
We Are Crossing the Jordan River (with Joan Baez)

The Newport Folk Festival Vol. 2 - Recorded on Location June 24-26, 1960 - Vanguard VRS-9084 - LP
Gibson was accompanied by Dick Rosmini on guitar and Herb Brown on bass. The jacket notes were written by Stacy Williams:
"To start the disc is a bright, hard-driving trio; Bob Gibson, with Dick Rosmini, guitarist, and Herb Brown on bass. Gibson had endeared himself to the Newport audience at the 1959 festival not only with his own performing, but by introducing the amazing talent of Joan Baez. Gibson had another surprise in store, this time, by introducing the young singer, Bob Camp. Here is popularized folk music with a city sophistication and an urban polish to it."
Four cuts on side one:
This Little Light of Mine
Wayfaring Stranger
You Can Tell the World (with Bob Camp)
Well, Well, Well (with Bob Camp)

Hootenanny - 1961 - Crestview Records, CRS-7806 - LP
One Gibson cut:
You Can Tell the World

The Original Hootenanny - 1961 - Elektra/Crest, CRV-806 - 12" LP
One Gibson cut:
You Can Tell the World

The Original Hootenanny, Volume 2 - 1961 - Elektra/Crest, CRV-807, 7807 (stereo) - 12" LP
One Gibson cut (with Bob Camp):
Skillet Good & Greasy (with Bob Camp)

Folk Box No. 2 - 1962 - Yorkshire, 27005 - 12" LP
One Gibson cut:
12-String Guitar Rag *(from his album* Yes I See*)*

The Folk Scene - 1962 - Elektra, SMP-6 - 12" LP
One Gibson cut:
Gilgarry Mountain *(from his album* Yes I See*)*

Folk Song and Minstrelsy - 1962 - Vanguard, SRL-7624 - 4 LP box set
(Classics Library Division of Book-of-the-Month Club, Inc.)
Two Gibson cuts:
Virgin Mary Had One Son (with Joan Baez)
Wayfaring Stranger

Folk Box - 1964 - Elektra, EKL-BOX - 4 LP box set
One Gibson cut:
You Can Tell the World

An Introduction to Folk Music and Folklore - 1960s - Golden GW-223
This is a children's record in the "Golden" series, narrated by Ed McCurdy, and featuring Oscar Brand, Jean Ritchie, and Bob Gibson. According to the labels, here's Gibson's contribution to the album:
Dance, Boatman, Dance
The Squirrel
I'm Gonna Leave Old Texas

A Child's Introduction to Folk Music - 1960s - Judson 3436
This appears to be the same album as Golden GW-223, also nar-

rated by Ed McCurdy. Judson appears to have been yet another label in the Riverside/Bill Grauer stable, specializing in records for children. Most of the songs appear to have been taken from various Riverside LPs. Bob Gibson shows up on these tracks :
Dance, Boatman, Dance
The Squirrel
I'm Gonna Leave Old Texas

Anthology of the Twelve String Guitar - 1968 - Everest/Tradition, 2071 - 12" LP
Album features Glen Campbell, Mason Williams, Joe Maphis, Howard Roberts, Billy Strange, James McGuinn and Bob Gibson.
One Gibson cut:
12 String Guitar Rag

Something to Sing About - produced by Milton Okun (probably in conjunction with his book of the same name which was published in 1968) - 3 LP box set
One Gibson cut:
Virgin Mary Had One Son (with Joan Baez from Newport Folk Festival 1959)

40 Great Folk Songs - 1974 - Vanguard for Radio Shack, 50-2031 - 4 LP box set
One Gibson cut:
This Little Light of Mine

Riverside Folksong Sampler - Year unknown - Riverside, RKP 12-802 - LP
One Gibson cut:
Chickens (from *Offbeat Folksongs*)

A Golden Treasury of Legendary Folk Songs - Year unknown - Longines Symphonette Recording
  Society, LWS 176-180 - 5 LP box set
Two Gibson cuts:
Lily of the West
There Was an Old Woman

Greatest Folksingers of the 'Sixties -1982 -Vanguard VSD 17/18, VCD17/18 - 2 LPs in gatefold jacket
Two Gibson cuts:
Well, Well, Well (with Hamilton Camp)
Virgin Mary Had One Son (with Joan Baez)

Greatest Folksingers of the 'Sixties -1987-Vanguard, VCD-17/18 - CD
  One Gibson cut:
  Well, Well, Well (with Hamilton Camp)

Folked Again - The Best of Mountain Railroad Volume One - 1987 - Mountain Railroad,
  MR-52781 - LP - MD-52671 - CD
  Two Gibson cuts:
  Box of Candy and a Piece of Fruit
  Jimmie Rogers (with Hamid Hamilton Camp)

A Folksinger's Christmas -1995 - Vanguard, 73132-2 - CD
  One Gibson cut with Joan Baez:
  Virgin Mary Had One Son (from 1959 Newport Folk Festival)

Joan Baez Rare, Live & Classic - 1996 - Vanguard, VD1026 - 3 CD box set
  One Gibson / Baez cut:
  We Are Crossing Jordan River (from 1959 Newport Folk Festival)

Troubadours of the Folk Era - Current - Rhino CD 8122-70262-2 - CD
  One Gibson cut:
  Well, Well, Well (with Camp)

V GIBSON ON VIDEO

Bob Gibson In Concert - 1980 - Shanachie Ramblin' 819 -
  60 minute VHS
Concert for public television, Athens, Ohio, this video is still available from Stefan Grossman's Guitar Workshop, P.O. Box 802, Sparta, NJ 07871.

One, Two Buckle My Shoe - 1988 - C.T.I. Glad Productions - VHS
  Assorted episodes of the Uncle Bob television series *Flying Whales and Peacock Tales* were made available to schools on video.

VI BOB GIBSON SONGS RECORDED BY OTHER ARTISTS

The Kingston Trio,
  Album - *String Along* - Capitol T1407
    I COME FOR TO SING - 331

To Morrow

The Chad Mitchell Trio
    Album - *At the Bitter End* - Kapp KL 1281
    Blues Around My Head
    You Can Tell the World
    Album - *Mighty Day on Campus* - Kapp KL-1262
    Super Skier
    Album - *Best of Chad Mitchell Trio* - Kapp KL1334
    Super Skier
    You Can Tell the World

The Mitchell Trio
    Album - *That's the Way It's Gonna Be* - Mercury SR-61049 (1965)
        Reissued as *The Mitchell Trio, Violets of Dawn* - Mercury SR-61067 (1965).
    That's the Way It's Gonna Be
    Album - *John Denver with the Mitchell Trio, Beginnings* - Mercury SRM1-704
    That's the Way It's Gonna Be

Simon & Garfunkel
    Album - *Wednesday Morning, 3AM* - Columbia CS 9049
    You Can Tell the World

The Limeliters
    Album - *Sing Out!* - RCA Victor LSP2445 RE
    Gilgarry Mountain (Darlin Sportin' Jenny)
    A Wafaring Stranger
    Album - *Our Men in San Francisco* - RCA Victor LPM 2609
    Yes I See
    Album - *Tonight: In Person* - RCA Victor LPM 2272
    Molly Malone
    There's A Meetin' Here Tonight
    Album - *Fourteen 14K Songs* - RCA Victor LPM/LSP-2671
    Sweet Betsy From Pike
    Faretheewell (Dink's Song)
    John Riley
    Album - *Best Of* - RCA Victor LPM/LSP-2889
    There's A Meetin' Here Tonight
    Wayfaring Stranger
    Album - *Reunion / Glenn Yarbrough & The Limeliters* - Satx Records STS-5513
    That's the Way It's Gonna Be

Easy Now
Album - *Alive! In Concert* Vol. I - GNP Crescendo Records GNPS-2188
John Henry
Album - *Alive! In Concert* Vol. II - GNP Crescendo Records GNPS-2190
Wayfarin' Stranger

Glenn Yarbrough
　Album - *Yarbrough Country* - Warner Bros.-Seven Artd Records - WS 1917
Abilene
Album - *One More Round* - RCA Victor LSP 2905
Baby, I'm Gone Again
Ten O'Clock, All Is Well (The Town Crier's Song)
The New "Frankie & Johnnie" Song
Album - *Come Share My Life* - RCA Victor LSP-3301
That's the Way It's Gonna Be
Album - *Time To Move On* - RCA Victor LPM/LSP-2836
In This Wide World
Album - *Live At the Hungry i* - RCA Victor LPM/LSP-3361
What You Gonna Do?
Album - *The Best Of* - RCA Victor LPM/LSP-4349
The New "Frankie & Johnnie" Song
Album - *And the Havenstock River Band* - Impress Records IMPS-1612
Easy Now
Funky In The Country
Album - *Easy Now* - Brass Dolphin Records BDR 2203
Easy Now
Funky In The Country
Album - *Live at Lou Weston's Troubador* - Brass Dolphin Records BDR 2204
　Reissue - *Live at the Troubador* - Folk Era Records FE 1704 CD
That's the Way It's Gonna Be
Sing Us Some of the Old Songs
Just A Thing I Do
Don't Let It Rain On Me

The Brothers Four
　Album - *Sing of Our Times* - Columbia CL2128
Daddy Roll 'Em

Peter, Paul and Mary
>Album - *Album* - Warner Bros. WS1648
>**Well, Well, Well**

The Serendipity Singers
>Album - *Take Your Shoes Off* - Philips PHM200-151
>**Foghorn**
>Album - *The Many Sides of the Serendipity Singers* - Philips, PHM200-134
>**The New Frankie and Johnny Song**

The Seekers
>Album - *Georgy Girl* - Capitol T 2431
>**Well, Well, Well**
>Album - *The New Seekers* - Capitol (S)T 2319
>**Well, Well, Well**
>Album - *A World Of Our Own* - Capitol (D)T 2369
>**You Can Tell the World**

The New Christy Minstrels
>Album - *Sing and Play Cowboys and Indians* - Columbia CL 2303/CS 9103
>**Betsy From Pike**

Tom Paxton
>Album - *And Loving You* - Flying Fish Records FF414
>**And Lovin' You**

The Tarriers
>Album - *Tell the World About This* - Atlantic SD-8042
>**Jordan's River**

The Byrds
>Album - *Fifth Dimension* - Columbia CL 2549
>**John Riley**

Roger McGuinn
>Album - *Live From Mars* - Hollywood Records HR-62086-2
>**Daddy Roll 'Em**

Phil Ochs
>Album - *There But For Fortune* - Elektra 960832-2
>**Power and Glory** (written by Gibson/Ochs)
>Album - *The War Is Over* - A&M Records CD 5215 - DX 003704

I Ain't Marchin' Anymore (written by Gibson/Ochs)
Album - *Live At Newport* - Vanguard 77017-4
Ballad of Medger Evers (written by Gibson/Ochs)
Power and Glory (written by Gibson/Ochs)
I Ain't Marchin' Anymore (written by Gibson/Ochs)

Odetta
    Album - *Odetta Sings Folk Songs* - RCA Victor LPM 2643
    Yes I See

Judy Collins
    Album - *#3* - Elektra EKL-243/EKS-7243
    Ten O'Clock All Is Well

George Hamilton IV
    Album - *The Best Of* - RCA Victor LSP-4265
    Abilene

The Highwaymen
    Album - *The Spirit & The Flesh* - United Artists UAS6397
    Well, Well, Well

Joe & Eddie
    Album - *There's A Meetin' Here Tonight* - GNP Crescendo
      ST 90034
    There's A Meetin' Here Tonight
    Album - *Live In Hollywood* - GNP Crescendo GNP 2007
    That's The Way It's Gonna Be
    Skillet Good & Greasy
    You Can Tell the World
    2:19 Blues
    There's A Meetin' Here Tonight

The Just IV
    Album - *The First Twelve Sides* - Liberty LRP-3340/LST-7340
    Gonna Be Singin' In That Land
    Midnight Special (Gibson adaptation)
    You Go Thisaway (new words/music by Gibson & Silverstein)
    Doggies (Gibson adaptation)
    Stella's Got A New Dress
    Foghorn
    Ten O'Clock, All Is Well

The Brothers Four
    Album - *B.M.O.C.* - Columbia CL 1578/CS 8378
        I COME FOR TO SING - 335

Well, Well, Well
Album - *Roamin'* - Columbia CL 1625/CS 8425
Abilene
Betty and Dupree
Album - *In Person* - Columbia CL 1828/CS 8628
Darlin' Sportin' Jenny
The Thinking Man, John Henry
Album - *Cross Country Concert* - Columbia CL 1946/CS 8746
The New "Frankie and Johnnie" Song
Album - *Sing Of Our Times* - Columbia CS 8928
Daddy Roll 'Em
Album - *The Honey Wind Blows* - Columbia CL 2305/CS 9105
Nancy O
The Waves Roll Out

Sally Rogers
Album - *Closing the Distance* - Flying Fish FF425
Quetico

Steve Addis-Bill Crofut
Album - *Such Interesting People* - Verve V/V6-8519
Mighty Day

The Travellers 3
Album - *The Travellers 3* - Elektra EKS-7216
Well, Well, Well

The Four Preps
Album - *Songs For A Campus Party* - Capitol ST1976
Abilene

The Modern Folk Quartet
Album - *The Modern Folk Quartet* - Warner Bros. W(S)-1511
Yes I See
Album - *Changes* - Warner Bros. W(S)-1546
St. Claire's Defeat

Johnny Mann Singers
Album - *Golden Folk Song Hits Volume Three* - Liberty Records LST-7355
There's A Meetin' Here Tonight

The Kinsfolk
Album - *Up on the Mountain* - RCA - Camden Stereo CAS-2365
You Can Tell the World

The Womenfolk
   Album - *Never Underestimate the Power of the Womenfolk* - RCA Victor LSP-2919
   Ten O'Clock, All Is Well (The Town Crier's Song)

Meridian Green
   Album - *in the heart of this town* - 1998 - StringBender Records
   Abilene

VII   GIBSON AS PRODUCER

Bob Gibson
   Funky In The Country - 1974 - Legend Enterprises - Universal Audio Corp. UAS 895-64384
   Gibson & Camp — The Gate of Horn Revisited!!! - 1986 - CS - B★G Records DM-87023
   CD - Folk Era FE1413CD (1994)
   A Child's Happy Birthday Album - 1989 -
   CS -B★G Records 001
   Stops Along The Way - 1991 - CS - B★G Records CM4210 - CD B★G Records 1004

Tom Paxton
   Up & Up - 1979 - Mountain Railroad MR52792
   The Paxton Report - 1980 - Mountain Railroad MR-52796
   Even on a Gray Day - 1983 - Flying Fish, FF280
   Bulletin - 1983 - Hogeye, HOG004
   One Million Lawyers ...and other disasters - 1985 - Flying Fish, FF356
   And Loving You - 1986 - Flying Fish, FF414
   Politics LIVE - 1988 - Flying Fish, FF486

Anne and Jan Hills-Burda
   The Panic is On - 1982 - Hogeye HOG 001

Just IV
   The First Twelve Sides - 1964 - Liberty LRP-3340/LST-7340

Curiosity note: There is an album called **The Great Gerry Mulligan** on Crown, CST, 363 (year unknown) There are no liner notes. The only information about the contents is the cover it says "With Bill Robinson, Dick Hurwitz, Bob Gibson and Mel Pollan." It is all instrumental. Nothing on the record sounds like Bob's banjo or 12-string, so I am inclined to think it is someone else, but I haven't heard of another musician named Bob Gibson....

APPENDIX
SONGWRITING MANUAL
An Introduction
By Bob Gibson
(prepared for Kerrville Songwriting School 1978)

There is a need for a book about the writing, rewriting and editing techniques that I teach in my workshops. This book will help you learn and review the material covered in this class.

This book should become your permanent record of what is taught in this class. It is a catalogue of skills and ideas you will find helpful when writing.

There are many useful ideas covered in this book. You will understand some of the tricks and shortcuts of songwriting more fully when you have finished this class.

I hope the techniques suggested in this book are as helpful for you as they have been for me. I hope they are as useful for you as they have been for the many songwriters who contributed to this book.

I hope that your songwriting will benefit greatly.

THE ORIGINS OF THIS BOOK

I am a songwriter with thirty-five years of experience in the music business. With more than thirty years as a published songwriter, I have several hundred titles in my catalogue. My songs have been recorded by many different recording artists. I have recorded sixteen albums as a singer/songwriter. These albums have consisted of my own songs or collaborations with other writers.

My royalty checks have been a welcome portion of my income. I have had a lot of fun and made some money, too. That's what I think it's all about. Having fun and making money.

Those are my qualifications as a songwriter. They are neither my qualifications nor my reasons for writing this book. This book has grown out of my teaching experience.

I found that there are more SIMILARITIES between beginning and experienced songwriters than DIFFERENCES.

It is apparent that there are repetitions and patterns to the problems facing inexperienced writers. These problems are exactly the same as those confronting experienced songwriters.

This holds true for beginning songwriters I have taught. Perhaps it holds true for you, too.

When I saw that inexperienced songwriters face the same problems as experienced songwriters, I sought solutions from songwriters

I knew. Many of them were able to articulate their experiences. Some analyzed their own writing and had helpful suggestions to make. Their insights make up this book.

That is the source for this book. The techniques come from experienced, professional songwriters who deal with the same problems in their writing as do beginning writers.

These techniques were suggested to me and I pass them along to you. I hope they will assist you in better, easier and more profitable songwriting.

I am indebted to Shel Silverstein and Tom Paxton for teaching me that if I want to be a writer, I must write. The quality of their songs and the quantity of their output has always been awesome.

I want to thank Hamilton Camp who showed me how much meaning could be contained in the lyric of a song. I am grateful to Peter Yarrow who showed me the ways he uses to break out of the confines of "folk song" writing. And thanks to Phil Ochs, who cared, perhaps too much.

There are many others who have contributed to this book, knowingly or otherwise: Fred Koller, Paul Simon, Fred Neil, Bob Dylan, Roger McGuinn, Les Brown, Jerry Jeff Walker, Al Brachman, Al Grossman, Ricky Neff, Ray Tate, Gary P. Nunn, John Ims, and, of course, Rod Kennedy of Kerrville, Texas, who values songwriters so much.

I am grateful to each of you.

THE WORKBOOK AS A PROCESS

This book contains a PROCESS of editing and rewriting songs. The process is a series of steps that you must experience to realize their benefits. Abandon skepticism and try each exercise in this book.

You will find many ideas that will be profitable to include in your own system of writing songs.

I repeat! This book is a PROCESS. It is a step-by-step path through the maze of songwriting. You will find your way through the maze as you read this workbook.

DO YOU HAVE "IT"?

I am approached by beginning songwriters who are not interested in learning about the craft of songwriting.

They have written something that sounds like a song, in the form of a song.

They want me (or the class) to pass judgement on their songwriting. I am not a music critic. I am a songwriter, so I don't wish to do this.

What they really want to know is, do they have "IT". They want to know if they are ordained to be songwriters because they possess some unique talent.

I don't know what to tell them. I know I don't have "IT". My friends don't have "IT". You probably don't have "IT".

This book is about things you can learn that will make your songwriting better. It is about dedicating yourself to this art form until you have mastered it.

Learning the skills and techniques of successful songwriting requires commitment. It is not a question whether you have a special gift that determines whether you should become a songwriter. The question is, are you willing to practice the craft until you can write successful songs?

THE DIFFERENCE BETWEEN AMATEURS AND PROFESSIONALS

The greatest difference between the amateur songwriter and the professional songwriter is the professional's acceptance of REWRITING AND EDITING.

You may consider that the first draft of your song is the completed song. The experienced songwriter knows that when the first draft is finished, the real work just begins.

When your first draft is written, it is time to refine, define and focus your song. You will learn how in this book.

YOUR FIRST DRAFT IS NOT A FINISHED SONG

What the amateur has completed, and considers a finished song, a professional considers a first draft.

That is the difference that this book will teach you about.

Inexperienced songwriters always try to write the best songs they can but they lack either the years of experience necessary or the counsel of other writers to achieve their goals.

Their songwriting may be charming, moving and quite "near the mark", but it is not what a publisher, record producer or recording artist would consider a successful song.

I repeat. Usually, what the amateur has completed, and considers a finished song, a professional would consider a first draft.

The elements of songwriting which this book will concentrate on are the techniques of REWRITING AND EDITING.

You will also learn how to analyze your songs and judge them for content, development and completeness.

You will learn how to fix the flaws and fill out the thin spots.

You will learn the skills that separate the amateurs from the professionals.

ANYBODY CAN WRITE A SONG

Anybody can write a song. At least anybody with a little creativity and imagination can write something that seems like a song.

You can identify it as a song written by a beginner. You hear they have not learned how to make their songs memorable.

Their songs may contain good ideas, fine melodies or poetic phrases, but in the end, they are not memorable.

Songs must contain all the elements of a good song and the elements must work together to make the song memorable. It is frustrating to hear a song with the individual components necessary to be successful but that doesn't seem to work.

And if a song is not memorable, it does not work!

SEPARATING THE WRITING FUNCTIONS

Beginners try to do two things at the same time. They try to create the first draft of their song and at the same time to rewrite it.

It's a little bit like a man who is trying to stand up and sit down at the same time. It can't be done.

You can do one or the other but you can't do both things at once.

This is true of songwriting.

You are not free to create your song while you are simultaneously trying to rewrite it. These are separate functions. Let us examine them separately.

RELEASING YOUR CREATIVITY

Beginners place limits on their creativity. Limits such as, "Is my idea 'cool' or 'hip'? Will my idea seem funny to some people? Is my idea sophisticated? Does it make me look good?"

Do you ask yourself, "Does this sound like a good (appropriate) idea for a song?"

Do you throw out ideas you write because they are so "different"?

Are you willing to chance your idea being considered "strange"?

These are EDITING AND REWRITING questions. They have no place in the creative phase of your songwriting.

These questions are limitations on your imagination. They pose obstacles to your creativity.

In the early phase of writing, remain free to write anything that you think about. This is not time for self-criticism.

BE AS FREE AS A CHILD

You have seen the unselfconscious ease with which a young child can create a poem, a song or a story. Children are completely uninhibited by the same considerations that limit adults.

The first draft of your song should be written the way a child writes, without judgement and criticism. You must cultivate the innocence of a child.

Learn to achieve child-like freedom when you are using your imagination.

Remember how easy it was to "Make up things" as a child? When a child composes a song or story they have no hesitation. They just do it.

The first draft of your song needs to be non-judgmental, too.

Soon you will don your other hat, as it were. This book will teach you to develop the attitudes of a critical song publisher. You will learn to become a beady-eyed skeptic that will judge, analyze and edit the weaknesses in your song.

Then you will then have TWO people on your songwriting team. You will have both the unencumbered innocent who creates lots of ideas, and the merciless editor, that will look at every line in your song to see how it can be improved and made better.

There are two distinct parts to your songwriting. Consider them separately.

There is the initial phase of writing that is non-judgmental and as free as a child. There is also the Rewriting and Editing phase which is different and places different demands upon you as a writer.

When this book has become second nature, you may be able to combine the different functions; first draft writing and rewriting. It will be easier for you to consider these as entirely separate functions.

You will be able to see if you are trying to do two different things at the same time.

WHERE IDEAS ORIGINATE

Writing creates a vacuum and new ideas will replace the ones you write down on paper. Get your ideas on paper.

Don't fix your song before you finish writing it. Reserve these rewriting skills for the appropriate time; after your imagination has had freedom to play, create and write.

I began to appreciate the importance of a good idea when I was talking to a writer friend of mine recently. I asked if he'd written any songs lately. I was curious because he's currently involved in writing screen plays and stage plays, having been successful with everything he has created, from hit records on the country charts to the largest selling children's book ever published.

He said, 'No', that he hadn't written many songs lately. He said (with more than a little wistfulness), "Writing a song has become so easy for me".

And then he added this observation that told me much about the way he viewed songwriting. "It's so hard to think of things to write 'em about".

This is a dilemma that you face all the time. "What shall I write about? Where will the ideas come from for new songs?"

I suggest this possibility. The reason there are so many songs published in Nashville these days with as many as three and four names on them is that some of the older, more experienced songwriters have chosen to collaborate with newer writers. The professionals need the new ideas and directions which are provided by new writers. The experienced writers provide the craft and the skills of songwriting while the inexperienced writers provide the IDEAS.

Those collaborations have produced some very successful results.

I am a firm advocate of collaboration. I collaborate on many of the songs that I write. I like the structure that collaboration provides.

I find it is much easier to make a date to write with someone at two P.M. tomorrow afternoon than it is for me to sit down and write, by myself, at two P.M. tomorrow. I am able to find something that will keep me from writing. I will discuss the drawbacks and the advantages of collaboration in another section of this book.

The anecdote I mentioned and the possibility I submitted to you a couple of paragraphs ago both make the same point; that a song will be good if it is based on a good idea.

IDEA SOURCES

One obvious source for a song idea is your life experience.

A situation that you experienced (or watched someone else experience) provides you with information about the feelings, facts and characters for your song.

Another good source for song ideas is OTHER SONGS. I am NOT suggesting plagiarism. I am suggesting the ideas behind the song will sometimes provide a direction for your writing. If you feel that a song contains a great idea, but that the writer hasn't expressed it well, you might have found the inspiration for a wonderful song.

Use no WORDS or NOTES of music written by another writer. Do not use another person's work and call it your own. If the lyrics of the song didn't work for the other writer, why do you think that you can make it work?

What I am suggesting is that if you are moved or inspired by the ideas expressed in a song, the ideas and concepts that are the basis for that song can inspire your own work.

Other sources for you to consider for song ideas are short stories, poems, TV shows, movies and the overheard conversations of other people. I cannot stress the latter too much.

Other people's stories, concerns, peccadilloes, anecdotes, and the ways that they phrase their ideas are excellent sources of ideas for songs.

Be a good listener. Listen when folks tell you what happened to them. When they are telling you something you are identifying with, and telling in a spellbinding fashion, you are listening to a song that needs to be written.

Listen to yourself, too.

If you find yourself repeating the same story again and again, it means that the story has great meaning to you. You either have a lot of feeling about the incident or perhaps it still poses an unanswered question to you. Either way, it is a story that means a great deal to you and you have all the elements of a great song right at your fingertips.

At this stage of your writing, it is the ideas that are of primary importance. It is not the time to worry about the completed, graceful or poetic nature of your work. This is the part of songwriting where you identify what you are trying to say in your song. This is the stage in your writing for you to find out how you feel, what you know and what is most interesting to you about your idea for a song.

OUTLINING THE INFORMATION

When I am "brainstorming" for ideas, and when I am developing ideas, I use a journalistic technique called "OUTLINING". I was taught in school, when writing an essay, story or letter, it is a great help to first outline the points to be covered.

This is the 'WHO, WHAT, WHEN, WHERE, WHY AND HOW" of newspaper writing. It is a listing of the basic information for your story. It provides you with a check-list of the facts you need to write your story.

This is a helpful technique when used by a creative writer who wants to explore his understanding of the information needed to write a song. The storyline, the characters and the situations in a song are important. You need to know them to be able to write well.

When you are stuck with questions of what to write about, perhaps you haven't explored your own imagination enough to know what it is you want to write about.

Have you really identified WHO is the teller of the story? Do you know who your characters are so that you will have them say and do things that are consistent with their personality and background?

Do you know WHAT happened? Remember, it's never the breakup of the romance that's the song. It's the bittersweet sadness of the breakup that really tells the story.

Have you identified the WHEN of your song? The sound of a door slamming after midnight tells a lot different tale than the sound of a door slamming at noon. If the WHEN is important to your story it will help you to identify it clearly.

Is the WHERE an important part of your story? To use the analogy from the previous paragraph, isn't a breakup different when the person walks out of your house than it is when they get out of your car in front of their house?

Actors sometimes use the theatrical device of creating a WHOLE PERSON for the character that they are called upon to portray. They create an entire background of information for themselves about the role they are playing so that everything that the character says and does is consistent with WHO the character is supposed to be.

They can tell you much information about their role that does not appear in the script or the lines that they read. They can probably tell you what the character likes to eat, where the character went to school, what the character's childhood was like, and various other information that helps them to better get INTO CHARACTER.

Please refer to the section of this workbook containing the ten tips for rewriting and editing your songs for more about OUTLINING.

OVER WRITING

Often beginning writers stop writing just when the going is good. They stop writing when the lines seem to be about as long as a song ought to be. They are afraid their song will become too long. So they stop writing.

They stop writing before they have exhausted their ideas on the subject.

Write down your ideas and thoughts, putting down all the lines that come to you, all the feelings and all the images; perhaps writing far more and far longer than a song needs to be.

But you should not stop writing your ideas until you have wrung the subject dry.

This part of the process is called OVERWRITING. You should continue OVERWRITING until your thoughts and ideas become redundant.

That is the signal that you have written everything that you have to say about your idea. It means that the first part of your creative process is completed.

It is time for you to switch hats. It's time for the beady-eyed editor and song critic to go to work on your material, improving and rewriting it into a complete and wonderful song.

The feeling that you have wrung out a sponge as completely as possible, right down to the last drops of water that you can squeeze out of it is the signal that you are done with your initial draft.

It is a good feeling having completely explored your song idea or concept. You will have lots of raw material with which to work, perhaps even MORE good ideas than you can use in just one song, certainly enough material to begin the fashioning of your song.

Remember: Don't judge. Don't edit and rewrite as you go along! Wait until it is time to employ these skills. Some of your lines or ideas may seem awful. That's okay. Some of them are bound to be terrible.

You are writing quickly and in a non-judgmental fashion. Everything that comes to mind will not be wonderful.

Right now, your assignment is to CREATE.

At this stage of your writing, don't be a critic and don't be a judge. You will get to that soon enough. Remember, critics and judges don't create. They only criticize and judge the work of creative people.

Remember, some of your first draft writing may be awful. It must be that way. You are trying to write freely, unencumbered by how the finished product will sound.

The inescapable truth is: NO SONGWRITER EVER WROTE GOOD SONGS WITHOUT WRITING A LOT OF BAD SONGS.

That's basic truth. Everything you write will not be wonderful. Some ideas and lines will be embarrassing to read to ourselves.

The only way for you to find out everything you have to say about a subject, though, is to write down all the ideas that occur to you. You can't wait to write only good songs or you may write NO SONGS AT ALL.

You have to try. You have to dare. You must allow yourselves the freedom to create thoughts and ideas that are less than wonderful. You must have courage to be creative.

USING A TIMER

I have discussed using a common kitchen (or photography) timer in my writing. It helps me. It provides me with some limits to the quality I try to achieve.

By this, I mean, without the timer I feel that I must write a wonderful song. I don't know how long wonderful takes. No matter how long I work on a song, I feel that if I had a little more time I could make it better.

The use of the timer relieves me of this problem. The timer becomes the arbiter of how long I shall write. I will stop when the timer rings.

I find that my best ideas are pretty accessible and easy to write. More time does not produce more quality. This is not to say that I don't return to the piece of material upon which I am working. I do, but only when I am ready with more ideas to write.

FREE WRITING EXERCISE

Try writing for ten minutes. Without any terms or conditions, just put down your ideas as they come to you.

What you write may (or may not) be in the form of lyrics or it may be in a prose style of writing. Do not be limited by considerations of rhyme or meter. The lines or ideas can come out in any form and in every form. The main thing is to get your ideas down on paper. What are you feeling to write about?

The only rule is: DON'T LET YOUR PENCIL STOP WRITING.

Write down everything you think, the good ideas and the not so good ideas. Don't chew on your eraser and search for BETTER ideas than you are having. Just write them all down. Make no judgments or editing decisions. Just write.

Let's discuss what has taken place here. What did you experience? What did you find out? Were you surprised to find out how much you had to write about when you had no direction in mind when you began?

MORE FREE WRITING

Write for another timed ten minute period. This time, pick a direction or an idea that you would like to write about. Use this "brainstorming" to find out what you think and feel about a particular idea for a song. This is a self-discovery time.

What you are writing is a "rough draft" or a "brainstorming" outline of ideas. As you have discovered, you do not need inspiration to write a song. You need commitment. An inspired idea will help, sometimes even make writing easy, but as you have learned in the above exercise, it is not essential.

SEPARATING THE WHEAT FROM THE CHAFF

Years ago, harvesting wheat was done by hand. It was done this way long before the huge combines that we use today were employed.

The process of separating the wheat kernels from the straw "chaff" was called "winnowing". The wheat was placed in a large, slightly flat, tightly-woven basket and tossed gently into the air. The breeze carried away the wheat chaff (bits of straw and stems) as it was lighter than the wheat. The kernels of wheat were left behind in the basket.

The process of looking at your "rough draft" or "brainstorming" outline should be similar to "winnowing". You should read over your lines and ideas lightly, without trying to justify or defend any of them.

Let the ideas and thoughts that have more substance "stand out" in your mind. Let the rambling ideas and thoughts with less substance simply blow away in the breeze. You should save only those lines that you cannot bring yourselves to discard. Don't worry about whether they "work" with each other. Only consider whether they say something that you feel belongs in your song.

Then you will be able to enlarge, rewrite, rhyme and reorganize your ideas so that they take on the shape of a song. Expressing ideas and feelings are what make it YOUR SONG.

You have experienced that as you kept your pen moving, the ideas just keep flowing, not always great ideas, but ideas nevertheless.

Your mind is fertile and active and only needs to be "let loose" to find thoughts, inspirations and ideas that flow quickly and freely.

The same thing is true when you begin to write your lines for a song.

If you are unhampered by considerations of rhyme scheme, meter, structure and whether the line is "cool" or sophisticated enough, your ideas and lines for your songs will flow with incredible ease.

At this point, and not until this point, you shall begin to rewrite and edit your material. You have created and assembled your ideas and will now find that the rewriting and editing part of the songwriting process is in the appropriate place.

UPON FINISHING FRAGMENTS

Do not enter the conflict I pointed out to you earlier in this workbook. Don't try to be creative and judgmental at the same time. It isn't possible to do two things at the same time. One thing will cancel out the other.

This is how you end up with lots of songs that you have begun and very few that you have finished. The FRAGMENT SYNDROME I call it.

If you have a notebook full of songs that you have begun and never finished, then you have "THE FRAGMENT SYNDROME". If you begin work on a song, and then, because it isn't as good as you expected it to be, you drop it, then read this carefully.

Lots of writers end up with notebooks full of songs that are begun and not finished. They become burdened with notebooks full of one or two verses to their songs, most of the material only pieces and fragments and all of it incomplete.

Too many unfinished songs can be a millstone around the neck of a songwriter. Song fragments hang like dead weight around writers' necks keeping them from moving forward.

When you have a body of incomplete material, it can stop you from writing anything else. You have so many "defeats" behind you, why try again? Each unfinished song is a small "defeat" to your creative selves. You feel, "Why start another song, I have so many to finish as it is." You put away your pen, discouraged.

FINISH ALL YOUR SONGS

Finish the song that you are working on. Even if you know that it is not turning out to be a "keeper", finish working on it. You may create good ideas and lines that you can scavenge from this song and include in other songs. However, you will not be creating more fragments of incomplete songs.

When I advise you against being a critic or a judge, I mean that you shouldn't stifle the creative person within you. At this point in your songwriting process you should be giving yourselves lots of room. Take joy in the good ideas and ignore the less than wonderful ideas. Don't criticize the writer for writing them.

Be kind and supportive to your creative self.

REWRITING TECHNIQUES

Now that you have a "rough draft" of your song, it is time to take a look at some other techniques that will help you to further perfect it.

RHYME SCHEMES

Many songwriters make the mistake of placing too much importance on the rhyme scheme of a song. They mistakenly put the RHYME scheme before the idea of their lyric.

The result is one you can see frequently in songwriting workshops; a song which has been written around a rhyme scheme.

The writer has placed primary emphasis on rhyming the words so that the rhyme scheme ends up writing the song. The writer creates a line that says what he means to say, and them searches for a rhyming word that "works" with the rhyming word that "works" with the rhyming word of the line he wrote.

At this point the writer has to figure out what he can say that will accommodate the rhyme he has chosen to use. THE RHYME SCHEME IS WRITING THE SONG.

If you have ever worked with a rhyming dictionary, you will know what I mean. With a rhyming dictionary, you can discover some wonderfully clever rhymes. With these rhymes in mind, as an afterthought, you then try to figure out what you can say that will use this particular series of rhyming words.

MAKING A RHYME SCHEME WORK FOR US

Look at how your rhyme scheme can control or determine the direction of your song, IF YOU LET IT. Haven't you all had the experience of "writing to the rhyme"? Did you ever think of a line you like, one that represents a good development of your song idea, then think of WHAT RHYMES WITH THE LAST WORD OF THAT LINE?

If you first come up with the rhyme, then try to imagine what you can say to end with that rhyming word, you are abandoning the creation of your song to the mechanics of the rhyme.

Do you see how you are letting the rhyme write the song when you do that?

Instead you should be writing lines that say what you want to say in your song, and then making them rhyme with each other.

CHANGE THE RHYME WORD TO FIT THE SONG - DON'T CHANGE THE MEANING OF THE SONG TO ACCOMMODATE THE RHYMING WORDS.

Sometimes you will need to change the RHYME WORD of a line that you wrote for a song. The rhyme scheme is not working with the ideas that you have had.

If the line you are trying to rhyme is so constructed that it is a play on words, or a pun, you may be sacrificing the entire song to try to accommodate a structure that is difficult to work with in the first place. Word play is fine for Cole Porter, but it's not a very effective way for a beginning writer to create a song.

Some "hook" lines are wonderful by themselves, but it's nearly impossible to write a song around some of them.

For instance, suppose I wrote this "hook" line: THE TIME BETWEEN THE LEAVING AND THE LOVING.

I intend to write about relationships, past or present. Easy? Yes, it's a standard kind of song idea? But where do I go from there?

Let's look at this rhyme scheme. LOVING is the key rhyming word in line, so I will have set up idea lines that end in words that rhyme with LOVING.

From "Woods' Unabridged Rhyming Dictionary" I find:
Above
Dove
Glove

Shove
Of
Be love...

This is not much to work with, if I stay with direct rhymes. Can you add any I might have missed? Perhaps I must turn to ASSONANCE or "near rhymes", sometimes called "vowel rhymes."

Some "assonances" (near rhymes) would be:
Loving
Stuffing
Subbing
Supping

Are there other assonant words that could be used in my problem line?

If you don't question the effectiveness of the rhyme scheme you have decided to use, you may end up with a rhyming sequence that's very difficult to sustain in subsequent lines.

The answer is to change your rhyme scheme. You don't need to think of another idea with a different rhyme scheme . . . rather REWORK THE IDEA YOU HAVE ALREADY WRITTEN.

For example:
THE TIME BETWEEN THE LEAVING AND THE LOVING can become:
THE LOVING AND THE LEAVING AND THE TIME THAT'S IN BETWEEN.
Or perhaps:
THE TIME BETWEEN THE LOVING AND THE LEAVING
Or even:
THE LOVING AND THE LEAVING AND, IN BETWEEN, THE TIME.

Are there other ways to rearrange this line?

Try changing the words to accommodate a different rhyme scheme?

Maybe you can rewrite the line to set up an entirely different rhyme scheme.

Explore some possibilities of changed rhyme schemes that will make the above exercise easier to write.

HEADLINING

An important technique we can use to help us identify whether we have completely understood and filled out our song idea is a tool borrowed from the Newspaper business.

Every newspaper story is introduced by a HEADLINE. This Headline is a brief statement of what the following story is about. It is the means by which the reader can decide (or be made interested) whether a story has relevance and interest. The person who creates headlines must be able to reduce the entire story into an abstract or a cogent, shortened and very succinct few words that state to the reader the general direction and contents of the story that follows. The reason that this HEADLINING technique can be helpful to songwriters is that we can better understand what it is we are trying to cover in our song if we can state the theme and content of the song in just a few, cogent words. If we can't state the meaning and direction of our song in these very few Headline words, we may not be fully aware of what it is we are trying to write about. Conversely, if we can state our song theme in a Headline, it can often help us to ADD new material to our song that makes it more complete, descriptive or satisfying to the listener.

HEADLINING EXERCISE

Try to identify the central theme and idea of a few songs and invent the appropriate Headline for them as if they were newspaper stories. The Headline we create should be just a very few words that tell us very briefly what the song that follows is about.

CHANGING THE TENSE OF THE LYRIC

Another possible change that may yield a dramatic difference in your song lyric is to change THE TENSE of the song. If you have written your lyric (or story, or poem) in the PAST TENSE it is a good idea to see if a CHANGE OF TENSE will improve your song.

It is sometimes a very powerful tool of lyric rewrite!

If the song or story line is written in the PAST TENSE, i.e. from the perspective that everything has happened already, you might see if changing the "TENSE PERSPECTIVE" will improve your lyric.

You would rewrite the lyric, changing the "TENSE PERSPECTIVE" to the present or future tense.

Sometimes a lyric will be cast in the "TENSE PERSPECTIVE" in which it is the simplest for us to create a story line. But upon examination you may discover that by altering whether "IT HAPPENED - IT IS HAPPENING - IT WILL HAPPEN" you can strengthen your lyric substantially.

INSERT SOME "TENSE CHANGE" EXAMPLES. SAMPLE SOME LYRICS OF WELL KNOWN SONGS CAST IN ANOTHER PERSPECTIVE THAN THAT IN WHICH THEY WERE WRITTEN.

CHANGING THE "PERSON" OF A SONG

Another improvement is to change the personal pronoun you are using. For example if your song is written from the "I" point of view, it might be improved to change it to a second person or third person song, i.e. changing the "I" point of view to "he" or "she" or even to a "they" perspective.

You may write a tale of someone else's situations that can be made more powerful in its impact by changing it to a first person "I" song.

Conversely, the song you write from your own point of view may be made to have greater impact if it is rephrased so that it is told from the "he", "she" or "they" perspective.

PROJECTIONS

If you find your song doesn't "GO ANYWHERE", here is a tool to help you with this problem.

Look at the characters or the situation of your song from the point of view of the future or the past. What will this story develop into if you project ahead many years or went back into the past to compare those times with the "NOW" of your song.

If your song is about a hope or wish for the future, you can look at what it would be like if IT HAPPENS OR COMES TRUE. You can imagine what it would be like IF IT DOESN'T HAPPEN OR COME TRUE. Perhaps you should include a 'THEREFORE" in your song.

After you have established your theme there might be a conclusion or "therefore" reference. This might even be a statement of the "moral" to the tale. The "don't let this happen to you" or the "if you let this happen here's what will come to pass" ideas may help you with your song.

Put your unfinished song to these tests to see if there is more information you should add to your song. Information that can help you produce a more complete or artful piece of material.

ADDING COLORS

Television journalism uses "color commentary", i.e., a news broadcaster or sports announcer provides commentary about the "colorful" aspects of the event. This can be asides that don't affect the basic story, but help listeners become more involved. Helping listeners to know some of the information that makes the event more interesting.

By adding "color" to your lines and ideas, you make the song easier to understand and, more important, more interesting for the listener.

The "color" is the flavor of a song. You wouldn't want to eat food without any seasoning at all. You want your songs to have flavor, too.

"Color" is: What did it feel like? Was it rough or smooth? Wet or dry? Warm or Cold? Hard or soft? Did taste bitter or sweet? Was it slow and languishing or quick and abrupt? Was it red or blue or striped?

Was it black as a tunnel or fuzzy and grey as fog? Was it loud or soft? Shrill or LIFTING? Was it night or day? What was the light like? Bright or dim? What was the weather like?

Was it like anything you ever knew before? Was it different from what you imagined it would be? How did you imagine it would be? What do you think it will become? Tomorrow? Next week? Years from now?

These are the elements that will "fill out" your song and make it complete. Your vision, your description, is what is endlessly interesting to other people. When you identify with an artist's song, you feel it is your story, your song, your life they are talking about.

FROM SPECIFIC TO GENERAL - FROM GENERAL TO SPECIFIC

It often happens in the third verse of a song, you're stuck with endlessly repeating the same idea that you stated so eloquently in your first two verses. To restate it again would be boring.

Your theme is begun with a strong first verse, "I love you so much". And in the second verse you amplify or enlarge upon the idea that "I love you so much".

You know that if you state the idea again, "I STILL love you so much", than it will be counter-productive. So you need to find a slightly different, slightly skewed direction for your next verse.

Check to see if going from a "specific" verse to a "general" verse, or from "general verses to "specific" verses will help your problem. This means if you have written a verse or two that is talking about loving a PARTICULAR person, how the loving of that person is SPECIFIC ("her eyes, her hair, her savoir-fair") and about things that are specific to loving THAT PARTICULAR PERSON, then you add variety by writing a verse that is GENERAL, i.e. about "love" IN GENERAL or about "women" IN GENERAL.

If your verses have been GENERAL in nature, about "love" or "women" or any other GENERAL approach to the subject, you can write a verse that is SPECIFIC to what you are trying to express, SPECIFIC to one particular person or "love of your life".

"LOOKING FOR THE YOU IN SOMEONE NEW"

This is the time to look at a ROUGH MANUSCRIPT of a song I wrote called "LOOKING FOR THE YOU IN SOMEONE NEW". It has elements of the last three writing skills we have been discussing: OVERWRITING • REWRITING • RHYME SCHEME • REVERSALS.

Candlelight and caviar
Watching for a shooting star
Dancing cheek to cheek, two by two
And all the time I just compare
Their savoir faire, their eyes and hair
I'm Looking for the You in Someone New.

   some new
Starting with the old promise
Ending with a good night kiss
It's all I seem to know to do
   I might
Seeing if I could replace
   easy laugh
Your look your walk your funny face
Just looking for the you in someone new
   * * *
Maybe someday I'll discover
Another
The person who's the perfect lover
Then I can close the books on me and you
Concentrate on my new friend
And never have to go again
Looking for the You in Someone New.
   * * *
So I flirt and carry on
A not so satisfied Don Juan
Sorry I
I guess I just don't know what else to do
   seem
To some it must look pretty sad
   To miss what I already had
To search so hard for what I had
Looking for the You in Someone New
   * * *
I'm blind to what's in front of me
It could be Miss Wonderful

   * * *

I invent new fantasies
Of brand new thrills I think I need
And then I see them out; but when I'm through
It hurts me to realize
It's just a futile exercise
Of Looking for the You in Someone New
   * * *

I just need a substitute
It's just a matter of a substitute
   I need that
So don't you flatter yourself you're the one I need
   that you're so cute
   * * *

Sometimes there's a sweeter curve
A different way to touch the nerve
Exciting just it's strange and new
But the novelty wears thin
I have to face the fact again
I discover someone else but it's not you
I've found another one that isn't you

A SUMMARY OF SOME WRITING AND REWRITING TECHNIQUES

1. OUTLINING - Follow a journalism outline for story writing, using the WHO, WHAT, WHEN, WHERE, WHY and HOW checklist to see if you have omitted information that could add facts and/or color to your song.

2. USING A TIMER - The timer provides you with a structure for your writing. Without it, you might feel that you've got to sit with a pad, chewing your eraser, until you come up with some "good" ideas. Using the timer, write whatever comes to you inside of ten minutes. Then you can stop and review what you have written to see which ideas you want to explore further.

3. OVERWRITING - Write down all your ideas and thoughts, put down all the lines, all the feelings and all the images; writing far more and far longer than a song needs to be. This will provide you with more options and directions for your song.

4. HEADLINING - Outline briefly in three to five words the essence of the story you are telling in your song. The HEADLINE gives you a new perspective regarding the song you are writing. It may suggest areas of information that are not covered that would be important additions to your lyric.

5. PROJECTIONS - PAST OR FUTURE - Change your lyric direction or content so that it looks ahead in time, into the future, or back in time, into the past. See if projections into the past or the future help you to find additional ways to deal with your story line. This will also suggest verses in the nature of, "If it happens", "If it doesn't", "Therefore", "The moral to the story is" and "The conclusion is".

6. CHANGING TENSES - Check your lyric to see if it can be improved by putting it in a DIFFERENT TENSE; Future, past or present. Also check that you have been consistent with the tense in which you have written your lyric and that any changes in tense are accounted for within that lyric.

7. CHANGING THE PERSON (PRONOUN) - Check your lyric to see if it can be improved by putting it in a different person, i.e. ME or I to THEY or THEM, or even HE or SHE to ME or I. When this technique is applicable it usually changes the lyric dramatically for the better.

8. COLOR COMMENTARY - Check your song to see that you have used all the "sense-memory" specifies that make your lyric powerful. Have you left out descriptions that would help with the setting or texture of your song, i.e. "where, what time, the light, the smells, the sounds, what was worn, or what was done."

9. REVERSALS - Check if your lyric is in the BEST order for the ideas to flow. You often make your best statement of an idea prior to the one that you put at the end. It is like telling the punchline of a joke before revealing the story. Very often the second line should be 'REVERSED" and put in the number one position. This puts your good ideas and statements where they belong, at the end.

10. RHYME SCHEME CHANGES - Keep the good ideas, change the rhymes that don't work. Don't let the rhyme scheme write your song. Your ideas are more important than the rhymes (though they are an important part of the craft) and rhymes are easier to find than good ideas.

11. FROM SPECIFIC TO GENERAL - FROM GENERAL TO SPECIFIC - If your verses have been GENERAL in nature, about "love" or "women" or any other GENERAL approach to the subject, write a verse that is SPECIFIC to what you are trying to express, SPECIFIC to one particular person or "love of your life". Check to see if going from a "specific" verse to a "general" verse, or from "general" verses to "specific" verses will help.

All material ©Bob Gibson Trust

The completed version of the lyrics of
LOOKING FOR THE YOU IN SOMEONE NEW

Sometimes there's a sweeter curve,
A different way to touch the nerve,
Exciting just because it's strange and new.
But then the novelty wears thin,
I have to face the fact again
I'm looking for the you in someone new.

So I invent new fantasies
Of brand new thrills I think I need.
Then I seek them out but when I'm through,
It hurts me then to realize
It's just a futile exercise.
I'm looking for the you in someone new.

Chorus: And all the time I look for you,
I'm blind to everything I see.
I could miss Miss Wonderful
If she were standing right in front of me.

So I flirt and carry on,
A not so satisfied Don Juan.
I'm sorry I don't know what else to do.
To some it must look pretty sad
To search so hard for what I had,
Looking for the you in someone new.

Chorus

Maybe someday I'll discover
The one who is the perfect lover.
Then I can close the books on me and you,
And concentrate on my new friend,
And never have to go again
Looking for the you in someone new.

~ *Bob Gibson ©Robert Josiah Music, Inc.*

APPENDIX
THE COURTSHIP OF CARL SANDBURG

ACT I

A banjo quietly starts to play the theme song of the play.
Bob Gibson and Anne Hills, a sort of Greek Chorus, begin to sing:
He told us of the things he'd seen
Across his native land
He spoke of the injustices
He couldn't understand
He wrote of fields and factories
And he knew the pride of man
And he told a lot of people how things were
He told us how they oughta be
With promises and poetry
But he really must have said a lot to her
Lovely Lillian
He really must have said a lot to her

Sandburg (singing - accompanied by a banjo):
Oh I had a horse and his name was Bill
And when he ran he couldn't stand still
He ran away
One day
And also I ran with him
He ran so fast that he could not stop
He ran into a barber shop
And fell exhaustionized
With his eye teeth
In the barber's left shoulder

Chorus (both Bob & Anne):
They talk about his poetry
Talk about his books
I think you'll find a hero
If you care to take a look
This prairie boy from Illinois
With a sense of great adventure

Did it all
He did it all
Carl Sandburg came from Illinois
Raised in Galesburg as a boy
And as he dreamed his poet's dreams
He tried a million jobs it seems.

Sandburg (speaking - reciting his sales pitch):
"Stereographs, as seen through a good glass, are the best possible substitute for travel. They bring a scene before the eyes with startling reality and impart much of the same inspiration that the original scene would. These, when studied in the same spirit of investigation and love of beauty that one should have in the study of art, history, geography, books of travel, are of inestimable value. To neglect them is to forego a genuine pleasure and a real addition to your stock of knowledge. They are the connecting link between illustration and reality."
(Now speaking as himself)
I have been selling stereographs off and on since I was a boy in Galesburg, and in this manner I have supported my various activities; wandering socialist, itinerate poet, vagabond songster on the highways and byways of life. But after all is said and done, I'm a pretty good part time stereograph salesman.

Chorus (both):
On the sixth of January in 1878
He made his first appearance
On that auspicious date.
A poet and a writer and a dreamer on run
A prairie son
A prairie son

Raised in Galesburg as a boy
In the prairie state of Illinois
Grew up under prairie skies
Saw the world through a poet's eyes

Sandburg:
When I was a lad, one night at home I heard that the opera house was burning, and I ran down to the corner of Main and Prairie to watch it. I stood across the street until midnight. Saw the second story go; heard the roof crash. Saw the fireman try to keep the fire from spreading. I didn't like to see the place go. I could remember so much about it.

On that stage I had seen the Kickapoo Indians. They stayed for six weeks. I went there at least once or twice a week; saw them in buckskins and feather headdresses. *(An Indian drumbeat plays in the background)* They danced and stomped, howling their war songs. Then the white man that they worked for would put on his schpeel. He claimed if you had rheumatism or aches in your muscles or bones, you eased it away with "Kickapoo Indian Snake Oil"! If you had trouble with your stomach or your liver, you took a few spoons of Kickapoo Indian Sag - why your insides felt better and a bottle or two cured you! He was a slicker!

Chorus (both):
I'll take another bottle of wizard oil
I'll take another bottle or two
I'll take another bottle of wizard oil
I'll take another bottle or two

(Bob)
I love to travel far and wide
Throughout my native land
I love to sell as I go along
(Anne)
And take the cash in hand

(Both) I
love to cure all in distress
That happen in my way
And you better believe I feel quite fine
When the folks rush up and say

Sandburg (Speaking as Snake Oil Salesman):
I'll take another bottle of wizard oil!
That's so wherever, ladies and gentlemen, the wizard oil is used. The people all are thriving. And whenever I get up to sell the second time in a town, I'm interrupted by the sweet silvery voice of a young lady or the sonorous tones of a gentleman. They rush up to me with a dollar in their hand and soon I hear their sweet exclamations, which sound very much like . . .

Chorus (Both):
I'll take another bottle of wizard oil
I'll take another bottle or two
I'll take another bottle of wizard oil
I'll take another bottle or two

Sandburg (as Snake Oil Salesman):
Music to my ears, and let me tell you this much, folks. Your requests for wizard oil shall not be denied! Remember the good lord helps those that help themselves so help yourself to a bottle of Kickapoo Indian Snake Oil. A buck a bottle. Get . . .
Well my goodness, ma'am! It's good to see you again! As a thank you for coming back again this year, take this bottle of wizard oil absolutely free of charge. If you could have seen this woman just one year ago today, the sorry, sorry, condition I found her in, you'd swear that five dollars, heck twenty dollars was not too much to ask. But a dollar a bottle!

Now there is a gentleman that looks like he needs help. A gentleman whose get up and go looks like it got up and went. A gentleman whose crushed spirit is crying out for rejuvenation. Sir, tell me, how much would you spend to put the lilt back in your voice, the twinkle in your eye, the spring . . . don't tell me. Because I'll tell you what I'm going to do. Absolutely free of charge, take this bottle of wizard oil, if you will. Now stand up, by God, stand up if you can. Hold it high over your head. Now you tell me - doesn't he look better already?! *(Cheers from the chorus)*

I could go on and on, ladies and gentlemen. But now, here to tell the tale of two testimonials of tribute to that treasured tincture that is Kickapoo Indian Snake Oil, direct your attention once again to my two musical counterparts.

Chorus (Both):
I'll take another bottle of wizard oil
I'll take another bottle or two
I'll take another bottle of wizard oil
I'll take another bottle or two

Bob:
Now once while traveling way out west
In the state of Illinois
The people all came running up
To see what made the noise.

Anne:
The merchants from the counting rooms,
Farmers from their hoeing
Both:

Among the rest a Dutchman came
A-puffing and a-blowing . . .

Sandburg (as Dutchman):
Mine Got in Himmel, vat a country und vat a peoples. Shtab me in ther back mit a double barrelled buchek. He's ther same man I saw in Chicago last week. I buys one bottle of oil from him. I takes it home, und my darling, that's good shtuff!
So. . .

Chorus (Both):
I'll take another bottle of wizard oil
I'll take another bottle or two
I'll take another bottle of wizard oil
I'll take another bottle or two

Bob:
Soon after this a lady spoke
Fresh from the Emerald Isle
She said, "Mister, if ya will,
I'll speak with ya awhile."

Both:
Why certainly, madam, speak right up
What's the matter, anyway?
Are you sick or lame or blind?
Or what have you to say?

Sandburg (as Irish woman):
No, no, no. It's me husband! Bad luck to the lazy divil! Divil a bit a work has he done for the past six months! He lies about till ten in the mornin'! And I'll take your oil of profitable quality to pull the lazy divil outa bed! So . . .

Chorus & Sandburg:
I'll take another bottle of wizard oil
I'll take another bottle or two
I'll take another bottle of wizard oil
I'll take another bottle or two

I'll take another bottle of wizard oil
I'll take another bottle or two
I'll take another bottle of wizard oil
I'll take another bottle or two

After a slight pause, the Chorus returns to the original theme:
Anne:
Agitator, socialist,
With a poet's pen in hand
He ventured forth to ramble
And to see his native land
Both:
Bought himself a ticket
On the Chessie boxcar line
Doin' fine
Doin' fine

Well he rode the rods
And he hit the roads
From the windy city of Chicago
The hobo poet with a cause
Went to see . . . America . . . !

Sandburg (speaking as himself):
You know, I hoboed some. Out to Kansas. Out to the wheat field harvest. I rode the rods. What a great adventure that was! Picked up some of the color of it - picked up the flavor of hoboing!
(Banjo starts to play the tune of "Hallelujah, I'm a Bum!")
I listened to the language of America! *(Laughing)* Picked up some other things, too, riding the rails. The dirt and the grime and the cinders in my eyes. But mostly, I picked up the feeling of what it's like to hear myself referred to as a bum!

Chorus (Both):
Hallelujah, I'm a bum
Hallelujah, bum again
Hallelujah, give us a handout
To revive us again

Well, I like to work
Like the other men do
How the hell can I work
When there's no work to do?

Hallelujah, I'm a bum
Hallelujah, bum again
Hallelujah, give us a handout

Sandburg:
I was once called a bum by my own people! Swedes - how about that? I was really a hobo! I kept moving around, but I was ready to work. A tramp won't work.

Chorus (Both):
(Chanting)
Tramp, tramp, keep on trampin'
Nothin' here for you!
Keep on trampin'
Keep on trampin'
It's the best thing you can do.

Sandburg joins in (still chanting):
CS: He walked up and down the street
Anne: Uh Huh!
CS: Till the shoes fell off his feet.
He spied a lady cookin' stew
Told that lady "How'dy do!
Can I chop some wood for you?"
What she told him made him blue

Chorus (Both):
Tramp, tramp, keep on trampin'
Nothin' here for you!
Keep on trampin'
Keep on trampin'
It's the best thing you can do.

Carl Sandburg: Tramps can't even think about workin'!
Chorus (chanting): Tramp, tramp, keep on trampin'
CS: Gives a tramp a pain in the ass to think about work.
Ch (chanting): Keep on trampin'.
CS: And a bum won't do anything at all.
Ch (chanting): Tramp, tramp
CS: He won't move and he won't work! Ahhhh ... but a hobo ...
Ch: **Tramp!**
CS: Prince of the Road!
Chorus (Both - singing):
I went to a house
I asked for some bread
The lady come out
Says the baker is dead

Hallelujah, I'm a bum
Hallelujah, bum again
Hallelujah, give us a handout

Sandburg:
Once there was a hobo at the back door of a house, hungry for two days. He asked a hatchet-faced woman for a bite to eat. She said she'd get him something. He waited. Eventually the door opened again. She stuck out her skinny hand - offered him a single dry crust of bread. She said, "I give this to you, not for your sake, or for my sake, but for Christ's sake." He looked at the bread, said, "Listen, lady, not for your sake or for my sake, but for Christ's sake, put some butter on it!"

Chorus (Both - singing):
I went to a house
I knocked on the door
The lady said, "Scram, bum,
You been here before!"

Chorus & Sandburg together:
Hallelujah, I'm a bum
Hallelujah, bum again
Hallelujah, give us a handout
To revive us again.

Sandburg alone:
Hallelujah, I'm a bum
Hallelujah, bum again
Hallelujah, give us a handout
To revive us again.

Chorus (Both - singing):
My daddy is an engineer
My brother drives a hack
My sister takes in washin'
And the baby balls the jack
And it looks like
I'm never gonna cease
My wanderin'

Sandburg:
One time, unshakeling myself from all of the conventions and the

elegances, swinging clean to the extreme of Bohemianism, I wandered across Pennsylvania, along the beautiful Susquehanna River, past the coal mines, along the mountain sides where I could look down on smelters and lurid lights much like the pits of hell - at least according to orthodox descriptions. In Pittsburgh, I was captured by the railroad police and sent to the Allegheny county jail where I put in ten days. Now, the warden, he got 50¢ a day for each prisoner he was supposed to be feeding. And as said feeding does not entail the expense of a nickel a day, well, he can shake the plum tree and fill his own pockets. The charge against me was riding a freight train without a ticket. I was thrown in a cell along with a young Czech who didn't know 40 words of English and a gray haired Civil War veteran. Though it was a lark on the whole, I think it gave me a new light on the evolution of the system, as it works in this country.

Chorus (Both):
Oh, I went up in a balloon so big
The people on the earth
They looked like a pig
Like mice
Like katydids
Like flieses
And like fleases
The balloon turned up with its bottom side higher
Than on the wife of a country squire
She made a noise
Like a hound dog
Like a steam whistle
And also like dynamite

Sandburg:
Seems to me there are going to be some great times on the political firing line in this country. There is some splendid blood in the socialist party and such reckless zealots. I feel that whether I ever get a dim glimpse of a cooperative commonwealth, I'll certainly witness some grand assaults on capitalism and you know as sure as your blood is red, there will be a recession of some sort from the present arrogance. I cannot stomach the bland easy assumptions of the powers that be.

Chorus (Both):
Oh what do you do in a case like that
What do you do but jump on your hat
Or your toothbrush

Or your grandmother
Or anything that's helpless

Chorus (Both - returning to the main theme):
A poet agitator and a hobo socialist
Even sold some stereopticons a little bit
Anne:
Then he was a travelin' man
And a lecturer, you know
Both:
On the go
On the go

So this boy from Galesburg town
Followed his star where it was bound
So many things he tried to do
He even tried the lecture circuit, too . . .

Sandburg:
They are sort of crazy here about the lecture on Whitman I gave yesterday. You know, I have dreamed and welded and laughed and prayed with it. For me and for the audience, it was an occasion. They drew out of me my best. Mr. and Mrs. Hubbard say I have a "world beater!" Well, the crowd caught things right on the wing, all the way through, and when I was done, had seated myself, was talking nothing with somebody, Hubbard grabs me by the arm and pulls me to the front again. They were clapping, yelling for an encore. For the tribute I don't care any particular damn, but I am now sure that I have trained my powers so that they can be of service to me. This presentation will get me a number of engagements next winter. I have changed it from a strong literary lecture into an **ORATION**, and I now know that I have a winner!

(sings) I'm goin' out in the woods next year
To shoot for beer - Not for deer
I am
I ain't
I'll be a great sharp shootress.

Chorus (Both):
At shootin' birds I am a beaut
There is no bird I cannot shoot
In the eyes
Or in the ears

Or in the teeth
Or in the fingers

Anne (Reciting):
To Ruben W. Burrow:

Sandburg (Writing a letter):
Dear Ruben,
    Glad to hear the buggy sales are coming along well. Is it now Burrow & Sons Buggy Sales or have you not made that much of a commitment yet to the family firm? I hope you still dream of a literary career. I think you have great promise, good friend. It would be a loss to the world of letters if you remain forever in the buggy business.
    You mention the probability of you living on the farm. Ruben, I envy you. It is the right place for a man to be. On the land a man is safe and comes nearer to being one soul and one body than anywhere else under present conditions. I hope she won't mind the liberties I've taken with your name in my new circular. It contains flattering comments attributed to one Ruben W. Burrow or the Marshall, Michigan News. I quote, "It says that Sandburg was tall, lean, proud, strange. Epithet denunciation and eulogy leap and pour from him. There are times when Sandburg means what he says absolutely."
    It is a high ambition to want to be an orator - to move people with my words. High ambition, I think, because sometimes I feel myself standing in the shadow of another son of the prairie state, Abraham Lincoln.
(In the background, the melody line of Dixie begins, played on a 12-string guitar)
Sandburg:
On the final day of the War Between the States, the rumor swept Washington that it was over.
Bob sings:
The news was run from Richmond
In that fading April sun
That Lee had handed Grant his sword,
The war was finally won.
Into the streets the people spilled,
Feeling the excitement build,
And the crowd around the White House milled,
Asking, "Is it true - it's finally done?"

Inside the White House
Lincoln heard them calling out his name.
He sat there wondering what to say
To ease their years of pain.
Someone yelled, "Come out the door,
And tell us what you've got in store
For the rebels who have lost the war,"
So out upon the porch Abe Lincoln came.

He said, *(Anne joins in harmony)* "We are gathered not in anger,
But in celebration.
Let's be grateful we are once again
A single nation.
Let's stand together reassured,
Now that peace has been secured.
Our nation's illness can be cured,
And I suggest the overture for this occasion.

He said, "Let the band play *Dixie,*
Play that tune that holds its head up
High and proud,
And let our nation once divided,
Bloody but unbowed,
Take the swords of war and beat them
Back into a plow."
On the day that Lee surrendered
Mr. Lincoln told the crowd,
"Let the band play *Dixie.*"

A tired Union soldier hobbled
On his only limb
Filled with bitter memories
The war had left with him
He dragged his wooden leg and cane
His face was set and creased with pain
He stumbled, fell and rose again,
And he wondered what the future held for him.

He spied a black child kneeling there
In humble gratitude
He knelt down right beside her
To share her thankful mood
Grateful words were raised in prayer
"God, in your sweet, loving care,

Our broken lives now please repair,
And let our wounded nation be renewed."

And let the band play *Dixie,*
Play that tune that holds its head up
High and proud,
And let our nation once divided,
Bloody but unbowed,
Take the swords of war and beat them
Back into a plow.
On the day that Lee surrendered
Mr. Lincoln told the crowd,
"Let the band play *Dixie.*"

Sandburg:
Now there was an orator! *(The guitar once again plays the melody line of "Dixie")*
I don't know if I'll be an orator or a poet, maybe a socialist politician, maybe a writer. For now I'm a pilgrim. I don't know the tasks the gods would have me perform, but I hope I'm granted the boon of being effective.

Chorus (Both):
I've been a-wanderin'
Early and late
From New York City
To the Golden Gate,
And it looks like
I'm never gonna cease
My wanderin'.

Been workin' in the army
Been workin' on a farm
All I got to show for it's
The muscle in my arm
And it looks like
I'm never gonna cease
My wanderin'.

Sandburg announces: Band Concert - Public Square - Nebraska City

Chorus (joined by Sandburg):
BG: Flowing and circling

AH: Dresses, summer white dresses
CS: Faces
AH: Flushed cheeks
BG: Flung like cherry blossoms
CS: And gigglers
BG: God knows gigglers
CS: Rivaling the pony whinnies of the livery stable blues.
BG: And there's cowboy rags, and there's river rags and boys on sorrel horses hurl cornfield laughter to the girls in dresses . . .
AH: Summer white dresses
CS: Amid the cornet staccato and the tuba umpa . . . Gigglers!
BG: God knows gigglers!
CS: Daffy with life's razzle-dazzle. Slow good-night melodies and home-sweet-home, and the snare drummer/bookkeeper in a hardware store nods "Hello!" to the daughter of a railroad conductor - a giggler. God knows a giggler!
AH: And the summer white dresses filter fan wise out of the public square.
CS: The crushed strawberries of the ice cream soda places; the night wind in the cottonwoods and willows; the lattice shadows on door steps and porches; these know more of the story.

Anne Hills sings (as Lillian):
Somebody's tall and handsome
Somebody's brave and true
Somebody's hand is very firm
And somebody's arms are blue

Somebody came to see me
Somebody came last night
Somebody asked me to marry him
Of course, I said, "All right."

Sandburg:
Dream girl. You will come one day in a waver of love, tender as dew, impetuous as rain. The tan of the sun will be on your skin, the purr of the breeze in your murmuring speech. You will pose with a hill flower grace. You will come with your slim expressive arms, a poise of the head, no sculptor has caught, and nuances spoken with shoulder and neck as many a skies in delicate change of cloud, blue and glimmering sun. Yet, you may not come, oh, girl of dream. We may, but pass, as the world goes by, and take from a look of eyes into eyes, a film of hope and a memoried day.

Chorus (Both):
We know he was a poet
And he was a dreamer, too
He lived his life the way he wrote his poems
A husband and a father
And a family man, you know
He loved his home
He loved his home

Carl Sandburg dreamed his poet's dreams
Tried a million jobs, it seems
But the most important thing he'd done
Was to meet sweet lady, Lillian.

Sandburg (on phone):
Hello, Ruben? Rube! (Laughing) Well hello, old boy! No, I'm up in Manitowoc, Wisconsin, working as an organizer for the Social Democrats. I'm rounding up the dilatory locals, trying to put some new spirit in them. Oh, no, there's just expenses, but I am learning a lot. Wisconsin socialists are different from most. Yeah, yeah. They have very little use for a theory of a social and industrial cataclysm. They don't think the proletariat are stepping in and organizing the cooperative commonwealth. They want to participate. It's wonderful!
Yourself, Rube? Oh, that's fine, that's fine. Actually, yes. I met a wonderful woman, Lillian Steichen. Her brother's a photographer. She's a teacher down in Princeton, Illinois. Oh, delightful! Good thinker, good thinking, good head on the woman. She sent me a marvelous letter. I had sent her my leaflet, *Labor and Politics.* Well, she liked it, but she wrote a very perceptive comment about my poem, *The Dream Girl.* Wait a moment, I'll read it for you. Now wait till you hear this first. She says, "My hope is that socialism will gradually create an environment favorable to the development of such a millennial dream girl, but meanwhile, under capitalism, your dream girl must be a leisure class product." (laughs) She's a winner! I'm writing to her.

Chorus (Both):
Tell me of your deepest heart
And I will tell you mine
That we might know each other here
Upon this page of time

Sandburg (writing a letter):
Dear Lillian,
Dear Miss Steichen,
Dear Lillian Steichen,

    It is a very good letter you sent me. It softens the intensity of this guerilla warfare I am carrying on up here. Never, until lately, in the work I do with the Social Democrats, have I felt the attitude and had the experience of being a teacher. For those outside the party I am an advocate, but those within the organization have so much to learn, and to show those who have intelligence what to do to get the hypercritical to constructive work and to give cheer to the desperate and arousal to the stolid, sometimes I, too, know just what it is to be a teacher. The Dream Girl in the poem is millennial form, formed in the mist of an impressionist reverie. Millennial and at the same time, impossible, but, my good girl, she is not of the leisure class, as we know the leisure class! She is a disreputable gypsy, *(banjo begins to play in the background)* and can walk, shoot, ride, row, hoe in the garden, wash dishes, grimace, haggle, live on half-rations and laugh at luck.

    I will, out of in-born generosity and largeness of nature, forgive you for writing such a long letter, provided, as hereinafter stated, that you repeat the offense.

Bob sings:
Ah who will shoe your pretty feet?
And who will glove your hand?
Who will kiss your ruby lips
When I'm in a foreign land?
When I'm in a foreign land?

Anne:
Father will shoe my pretty feet
Mother will glove my hand
But you will kiss my ruby lips
When you're home from a foreign land.
When you're home from a foreign land.

Bob:
You are like to me a turtle dove
Bob and Anne:
That flies from vine to vine
A-mourning for his own true love
As I will mourn for mine
As I will mourn for mine.

Anne:
You're like to me a sailing ship
That sails the raging Maine
Bob and Anne:
If ever I prove false to you
The raging sea will burn
The raging sea will burn

Sandburg (writing a letter):
Dear Lillian,
 Back from a long hike again. Sand and shore, night and stars and this restless inland sea, plunging white horses of surf in a forever coiling Pickett's charge at Gettysburg. On my left, a ridge of jaggedly outlined pines, their zig-zag jutting up into a steel grey sky. Under me and ahead a long brown swath of sand. To my right the expanse of dark. But overall, sweeping platoons of unguessable stars, stars everywhere, blinking, shy, hiding, gleams, blazing effulgent beacons. An infinite traveling caravansary going somewhere. "Hail!", I called. "Hail! Do you know, do you know, you veering cotillions of worlds beyond this world, you marching, imperturbable splendors, you serene, everlasting spectators, where we are going? Do you know?" And the answer came back, "No, we don't know. What's more, we don't care!" And I called, "You answer well, for you are time and space. You are tomb and cradle. Forever you renew your own origin; shattered today, reshaped tomorrow in a perpetual poem of transformations; knowing no goal, expecting no climax, looking forward to no end, indulging in no conception of a finale, content to move in the eternal drama on which no curtain will be wrung. You answer well. I salute you tonight. I believe you, oh stars, and I know you we have met before, met many times. We will meet again, and meet many times." All this time I was striding along at a fast pace and a steady ozone-laden wind led me on, and when I turned from the sea, there burst on my vision the garish arc lamps of the municipality of Two Rivers, Wisconsin. So I turned to the sky and said, "Good-bye, sweet stars, I have had a good companionship with you tonight, but I must leave starland and enter the corporation limits of Two Rivers town. Remember me, oh stars. And remember Lillian, down in Princeton, Illinois." And as I plodded along past the huddles of fishermen and the tenements of factory workers, I quoted from the barefooted immortal Athenian, "The gods are on high Olympus. Let them stay there." Yes, let the gods who are on high Olympus stay where they belong and let us turn to the business of rearing on earth a race of gods. There, it's out of me,

Lillian. It was a glorious hike. I shall sleep and sleep tonight, and you are near tonight; so near and so dear. A goodnight kiss to you, great heart, good lips, good eyes, my Lilian.
P.S. *(Laughs)* P.S.S. *(Laughs even harder)* I will never get this letter written and finished. It will always need postscripts. I end it - six minutes after I have to set more. All my life I must write at this letter, this letter of love to the great woman who came and knew and loved. *(The banjo starts to play the main theme in the background)* Lillian, you have letters and letters to come. And we will send, love birds, with love songs flying out over the world. We cannot live the sheltered life with any bars up. It's us for the open road. Loosing the birds, loosing the birds, twenty thousand beautiful vibrating, fleeting, indomitable happy love birds singing love songs, swelling the world's joy.

Chorus (Both):
Again and then again
With his paper and his pen
His letters fell like whispers
In her ear, soft as April,
Anne:
His letters fell like whispers
In her ear.

End of Act I

L-R: Tom Amandes, Anne Hills, Bob Gibson

PHOTO COURTESY ALLAN SHAW

THE COURTSHIP OF CARL SANDBURG

ACT II

A banjo begins quietly playing the main theme.
Bob Gibson and Anne Hills, the Chorus, begin to sing:

Both:
He said a fella needed to be
Rooted to the land.
With a wife to stand beside him
Why, a man could take a stand.
Then he wove together threads of life
Into a lovin' plan
While he wandered 'cross the country
Far and near
Again and then again
With his paper and his pen
His letters fell like whispers in her ear
Soft as April
His letters fell like whispers in her ear.

He wrote to her of dreams and the ambitions
That inspired him
Their letters murmured fantasies
The two of them conspired in
Then he settled in Milwaukee
At a dry goods store that hired him
And he gave the sal'ried worker's life a whirl
So from party organizin'
He went to writing advertisin'
But the best he ever wrote was to his girl

Sandburg (Reciting ad copy):
"Special Reductions - Great Sample Sale!" By God! "Low Prices - Terrific Selling!" Jesus wept! "Quality, God damn it, and Prices!" Oh hell, "Sacrifice Sale - Sacrifice! Great Offerings!" Holy Mother of God! "Buy from us! Purchase Here!" For Christ's sake!

Chorus (Both):
Oh, I had a girl
And her name was Daisy
When she sang the cat went crazy
With St. Vitas's and deliriums

And all kinds of cataleptics

(On this verse joined by Sandburg - all three)
One day she sang a song about
A man who turned himself inside out
Sandburg:
And he jumped
In the river
'Cause he was so very sleepy

Sandburg (Writing a letter):
Lillian,
    Yes, the permanent job is mine. They'll fire the other man in the morning and begin taking their chances with me. God love Kroger's Department Store! Yes, it's a long, long way from the Social Democrat Party, but it means we'll get married that much sooner, my love. I'll be getting 20 a week for now, as I understand it. I edit the store news for a bargain circular and make copy for three daily papers. Oh - also write the window show cards. Generally, whatever advertising goes into the paper, that will be my responsibility. I'm quite a cog in this machine if I make good. Old man Kroger says when I've demonstrated that fact, there'll be from 1,000 to 2,000 a year in it. I think that means they'll either raise my pay or fire me within a couple weeks. I can't see how I can fail to make good. No part of this store publicity machinery puzzles me. Beats newspaper work of most kinds.
    (Banjo begins to play in the background) I want you to come on - come out here to Milwaukee, my darling. If you don't hear from me Thursday night in the mail, then come on. I'll talk to you then. And Lillian, hurry!

Chorus (Both):
Eyes like the mornin' star
Cheeks like a rose
Laura was a pretty girl,
God, almighty, knows.
Weep, all ye little rains
Wail, winds, wail
All along, along, along
The Colorado trail

Sandburg (Reading a letter as he writes):
    It was a beautiful visit, Lillian. But now, about the essentials. I like your idea of the wedding doings at the farm. They will look at you

so when we go to Galesburg one day. Downtown and at the college they will look, and they will find you baffling and only sense something of the power in beauty, wisdom and love; something as far off and cross textured as my poetry; and warm and open as myself. They won't understand you any more than me, but they will love you. Yes, you will be good for them. I shall save Sturgeon Bay for the honeymoon. Inasmuch as we recognize some spectral validity in a wedding, we must also concede a period of time immediately following the wedding known as a honeymoon. Yes, we will call it a honeymoon, and then we will have done with concessions to society. We'll do our own christening and baptizing and, if it ever comes to funerals, we'll just read a few lines of Whitman, ourselves, let it go at that. Such an adventure it will be, dear love pal, mate, woman, sweetheart, proud, beautiful Lillian!

P.S. I'm sending a five with this. It leaves me broke, but I can't raise money when I have money. I'm going to try and have fifty dollars or more for our starting. We'll make a compact that all money from literature sales will go into the baby fund. Should range around 15 or 20 dollars a month, and increase at that. And I'll turn over to you, every once in awhile, if not twice, all there is to spare over our material needs. The baby fund! It will grow and such a baby - such a baby it will be! Such a reckless cub! Never to hear a "Don't!" Learning fire by getting burnt. Getting religion and ethics and love powers from our kiss-in; never knowing that he or she is being educated, just living and unfolding. Such a cub!

Chorus (Both):
Went to see my gal on Sunday
Ho-di-um-dum diddle-long day
Didn't get back till a week from Monday
Ho-di-um-dum diddle-long day
I've got a nickel, she's got a dime
Ho-di-um-dum diddle-long day
Went to Lynchburg, had a time
Ho-di-um-dum diddle-long day

Sandburg (on phone):
Ruben, Old chum! (laughs) Well, I wanted you to be the first to know. Lillian and I expect to have a little red, babbling heir-apparent arrive this summer - June. Oh, uh, he or she will probably constitute our vacation, so it'll be up to you and Laura to come up and visit us. Oh, Rube, I . . . .

Chorus (Both):
I got a gal on Sourwood Mountain
Ho-di-um-dum diddle-long day
So many pretty girls I can't count 'em
Ho-di-um-dum diddle-long day
Ducks in the pond, geese in the ocean
Ho-di-um-dum diddle-long day
Devil's in the women if they get the notion
Ho-di-um-dum diddle-long day
Ho-di-um-dum diddle-long day
Ho-di-um-dum diddle-long day
Devil's in the women if they get the notion
Ho-di-um-dum diddle-long day

Sandburg (on phone):
Another baby! Well, we're going to call this one Janet. No, she's fine. She's another lusty howler, like Margaret was. I love it, Ruben. Fatherhood is my natural calling. I think it suits me. My work? My work is mostly with the children now.

Chorus (Both):
In Frisco Bay there lives a whale
She eats pork chops by the bale
By the hogshead
By the schooner
And sometimes by the pillbox
(Sandburg joins in)
Her name is Luta, she's a peach
But don't leave food within her reach
Sandburg:
Or babies
Or nursemaids
Or chocolate ice cream sodas

Sandburg:
I've finally gotten the publishers to take my work seriously; seriously enough to send me financial advances. I'm working on a collection of short stories for children I'm calling "Rutabaga Tales"; really just a series of pieces I've written for little Margaret.
(clears his throat) "Poker Face, The Baboon, and Hot Dog, The Tiger"
BG: When the moon has a green rim, the red meat inside, with the black seeds on the red meat . . .
AH: Then in Rutabaga Country, they call it a "watermelon moon" And you can look for anything to happen!

BG: It was a night when a watermelon moon was shining
AH: Lizzie Lazarus went to the upstairs room of a potato-faced blond man.
BG: Poker Face, the baboon, and Hot Dog, the tiger, were with her.
AH: She was leading them on a pink string
Sandburg: And on and on, Ruben. I love to read to these two little wide-eyed girls who giggle. Yes, they giggle, Rube. It's a joy to gather the girls together and tell them stories, or read from something that I'm writing just for them.
(clears his throat) "THE FIVE MARVELOUS PRETZELS"
Five nights before Christmas, five pretzels sat looking out of a grocery window lighted by five candles. Outside . . .
AH: Snow falling!
BG: Big white snowflakes, soft and quiet.
CS: They see a man outside the window. He looks in while they look out.
BG: And they see him brushing snow off his left shoulder with his right hand, and brushing snow off his right shoulder with his left hand.
AH: And he's shaking snow off his hat, and putting his hat back on his head.
CS: But they don't hear the man say, "Well, well, well! Five pretzels! And how many children is it I have at home, running upstairs and downstairs, in and out of the corridors?
BG: One?
AH: Two?
BG: Three?
AH: Four?
BG: Five!
AH: One for each pretzel!
CS: Now early that afternoon, the five pretzels decide that they will go with a circus.
(Chorus sings Big Top music that goes on behind the next line)
CS: And be trapeze actors. On billboards everywhere:
All Three shout: THE FIVE MARVELOUS PRETZELS!
AH: In big letters!
CS: And they run out of their dressing rooms in pink tights, bow to the audience and throw kisses; one kiss with the right hand and the other kiss with the left hand.
AH: And the man with the big musical megaphone calls:
BG: THE FIVE MARVELOUS PRETZELS!
CS: Up in the air they go. Two of them hang by their knees and throw the other three pretzels back and forth in the air - in the empty and circumambient air. So far . . .

All three: So good!
CS: Then they argue.
BG: Fuss!
AH: Dispute!
CS: Wrangle!
AH: Which two will hang by their knees?
BG: And which three will be thrown back and forth in the empty and circumambient air?
CS: All five want to be the two that hang by their knees. None of them want to be thrown back and forth. So they say . . .
All three: "Let's forget it!"
CS: Now, they decide, instead . . .
BG: That they will ride on the heads of the elephants .. .
AH: In the vast . . .
BG: Mammoth . . .
CS: Stupendous . . .
All three: Parade of the elephants! *(Make elephant trumpeting noises)*
CS: On billboards everywhere, people will see on each elephant . . .
AH: One dazzling, glittering, little pretzel in pink tights . . .
BG: Bowing and throwing kisses . . .
CS: One kiss with the right hand, the other kiss with the left hand! Yes!
All three: So they decide.
CS: And just before the first elephant comes out leading the parade
AH: The man with the big musical megaphone calls . . .
BG: THE FIVE MARVELOUS PRETZELS!
CS: So far . . .
All three: So good!
CS: Then comes the argument.
BG: Who should ride on the head of the first elephant?
AH: And who should come out first, bowing and throwing kisses to the audience?
CS: They argue!
BG: Fuss!
AH: Dispute!
BG: Wrangle!
CS: Then at last, decide.
AH: Whoever rides the first elephant today . . .
BG: Rides the last elephant tomorrow.
CS: Ha, ha, ha, ha! Then they see the man outside the window.
BG: And they see him brushing snow off his left shoulder with his right hand, brushing snow off his right shoulder with his left hand.
AH: And shaking snow off his hat and putting it back on his head.

CS: And the man walks into the store, and comes out . . .
BG: With the five pretzels in a paper sack!
CS: And he walks along the street . . .
AH: In the falling snow; big white snowflakes on his shoulders . . .
BG: And on his hat.
CS: And does he know, as he walks along in the falling snow, what happened that afternoon and evening among the pretzels?
AH: No!
CS: Does he know that he has in his sack . . .
All three: (muffled) THE FIVE MARVELOUS PRETZELS!
CS: No!
AH: Does he know that afternoon they decided to join the circus and be trapeze actors, and then changed their minds?
BG: NO!
CS: Does he know that they decided, instead, that they will ride on the heads of elephants, bow and throw kisses, while thousands of people laugh, cheer and cry . . .
All three: LOOK! LOOK! THE FIVE MARVELOUS PRETZELS!
CS: No!
AH: Then what does the man know about what the pretzels want to be?
CS: Nothing. Absolutely nothing! Which shows how ignorant some people are.

Chorus (singing):
(Bob)
He's gone away
For to stay a little while

(both)
And he's comin' back
If he goes ten thousand miles
Look away over yonder
Look away

Sandburg (Reading a letter as he writes):
Lillian Dearest,
    I've just given another reading, the third reading, the first real quiet reading, to the letter you tucked into my pocket as a good-bye note. There were tears in it and a big gladness and a strong-hearted woman, my pal in it. I would not choose to report this war, but I am glad of the call to cover it. Whenever I see the young men in their coarse wool uniforms, going off to France to do battle, I know that ours is not a real separation - only a space between heartbeats. What

we are having is only a breath of the world's storm. We will hope that resolves and consecrations enough have been born out of the millions of separations, enough for the remaking of the world. What with your line about Janet waving and Margaret's dear note, it all tugs at me tonight. I got the warm kiss of your calling me "Buddy" at the finish. *(Banjo plays in the background)* What we know is that all the chances are in favor of our sitting under our own cherry tree someday and talking about the year that Carl went away. And when I say, "God keep you," I mean it in its oldest and deepest way. It is awhile again until we maintain our establishment, our really truly home, and unless some overparticular people rake up the leaves, it will be a fine yard for a homecoming celebration. It's been mystically wonderful lately, that back yard with a half moon through the poplars to the south and a haze and rustlings - always high or low rustlings - on the ground in the trees, a sort of grand "Hush, hush, child." And as the moon slanted in last night and the incessant rustlings went on softly, I thought that if we are restless, fail to love life big enough, it's because we've been away too much from the moon and the elemental rustlings. I like Walt Whitman, musing among the ashes of dead soldiers, talking as though he knows that there is a thing he calls love, which is a reality finer than death. I haven't got room here to work it out, but soon we should go hand in hand again.

Chorus (Both):
There's a man
Goin' round
Takin' names
There's a man
Goin' round
Takin' names

Chorus continues to hum the tune in the background
Sandburg:
With sweet little Janet and Margaret, I'm ready for anything all the time. Everyday I come home and I find them alive, I take as a day snatched from death. I think, too, about how they die every week. The Margaret that was learning to talk three years ago is dead and replaced with an endless chatterer. The little fluff of a Janet we had a year ago is gone. Every beautiful thing I know is ephemeral, a thing of the moment. Life is a series of things that vanish.

Chorus (Both):
There's a man
Goin' round

Takin' names
There's a man
Goin' round
Takin' names
And he took my brother's name
And he left my heart in pain
There's a man
Goin' round
Takin' names

Sandburg:
I had two brothers go with diphtheria when I was a boy. We had a double funeral on a bitter winter day. My family buried two children that had barely lived long enough to named, and whenever I think of those two, who emerged into so little of living and then faded off, my head gets into all the big overtones of life, that hazy illusion of time and clocks. We are all such little things. A day of life is a day snatched from death, and the only fool is the one who can prove that death is a blank nothing or something less than life.

Anne Hills (speaking):
Let a joy keep you. Reach out your hands and take it when it runs by, as the Apache dancer clutches his woman. I've seen 'em live long and laugh loud, set on singing, singing, smashed to the heart under the ribs with a terrible love. Joy always. Joy everywhere. Let joy kill you. Keep away from the little deaths.

Banjo begins to play
Sandburg:
Lillian and Janet and Margaret call me back to the white blossoms that were singing all by themselves, a wonderful soft piece this morning. This was their first real day for greetings of the season, a quiet summer opening, without advertising. All heavy with raindrops, sheer white and wild, the sun gleaming rainbows and prisms from them, a pathos of eager living in them, a pathos of eager living in them.

Chorus:
(Bob)
My dearest dear
The time draws near
(Anne joins)
When you and I must part
But little you know

Of the grief and woe
In my poor achin' heart
In my poor achin' heart

Oh, hushaby
Don't break my heart
Don't let me hear you cry
The best of friends
Must part sometime
So why not you and I
So why not you and I

Her lips were like
The roses fair
That bloom in the month of June
Her voice was like
A sweet instrument
That sang a mournful tune
That sang a mournful tune

Sandburg (Reading a letter as he writes):
    No, there's not much question about it, Ruben. She's very sick. Margaret's a very sick little girl. We've seen several doctors about it. It's not exactly fatal. Rube, she's got nocturnal epilepsy and could, if she had a seizure in the middle of the night if she were unattended and alone . . . *(choking)* It's not fatal in itself, but it's a life sentence for such a little girl. She doesn't understand. She's so confused. She doesn't know what she's done that this should happen to her. She tries very hard. She's very brave. She's a good soldier, real good. Lillian and I are learning to love her all the more because she is so brave. We just go on a day at a time. That's what we do. We just go on.
    Sometimes there's nothing left but the work. When the world is falling apart and the sadness presses on your chest with a terrible weight, and there is no sense to be made out of all the things that seemed in perfect order a little while ago, a man must turn to his work; throw himself at it with a fever, abandon all thought and feeling and go to work. I am bereft of answers, plans, dreams. I do not know today what I knew yesterday, but there must be a tomorrow. So I shall work.

Bob Gibson introducing: Ladies and gentlemen, the poet of the prairie, Mr. Carl Sandburg!

Sandburg:
I was born on the prairie, and the milk of its wheat, the red of its clover, the eyes of its women, gave me a song and a slogan. You came in wagons making streets and schools, singing, "Yankee Doodle," "Old Dan Tucker," "Turkey in the Straw"; you in the coon skin cap at a log house door hearing a lone wolf howl; you at a sod house door reading the blizzards and the chinooks. I am dust of your dust as I am brother and mother to the copper faces, the worker in flint and clay. I am here when the cities are gone. I am here before the cities come. I last while old wars are fought, while peace broods, mother-like, while new wars arise in the fresh killings of young men. I take peace or war. I say nothing and wait. Have you seen a red sunset drip over one of my cornfields; the wave lines of dawn up a wheat valley out of the prairie brown grass crossed with a streamer of wig-wam smoke? Here I saw a city rise and say to the peoples 'round the world, "Listen! I am strong. I know what I want. I am the prairie, mother of men. Wait. They are mine; the threshing crews eating beefsteak; the farm boys driving steers to the railroad cattle pens. They are mine; the crowds of people in a Fourth of July basket picnic listening to a lawyer read the Declaration of Independence, watching the pinwheels and Roman candles at night, the young men and women, two by two, hunting the bypaths of the kissing bridges. They are mine; the horses looking over a fence in the frost of a late October saying, 'Good Morning!'; to the horses hauling wagons of rutabaga to market. The cornhuskers wear leather on their hands. There is no let up to the wind. Look at six eggs in a mockingbird's nest. Listen to six mockingbirds flinging follies of 'Oh, Be Joyful,' over the marshes and uplands. Look at songs hidden in eggs." Oh, prairie mother, I am one of your boys. I have loved the prairie as a man with a heart shot full of pain over love. Here I know I will hanker after nothing so much as one more sunrise or a sky moon of fire doubled to a river moon of water. I speak of new cities and new people. I tell you the past is a bucket of ashes. I tell you yesterday is a wind gone down; a sun dropped in the west. I tell you there is nothing in the world; only an ocean of tomorrows; a sky of tomorrows. I am a brother of the cornhuskers who say at sundown, "Tomorrow is a day."

Chorus (Both):
So we leave our hero
With his children and his wife
You can read his poetry
To know more of his life
Anne:
We leave him with his daughters

And his love maid, Lillian
Both:
They just go on
They just go on
With faces toward tomorrow
They go on.

(Bob's banjo begins to play "Down In The Valley")
Sandburg (Reading a letter as he writes):
Dear Margaret,

    This is only a little letter from your daddy to say that he thinks about you hours and hours, and he knows that there never was a princess or a fairie with so much love. We are starting on a long journey and a hard fight; you and Mother and Daddy and Janet and Helga - all of us - and we are going to go on slowly, quietly, hand in hand, all of us, never giving up. And so we are going to win, slowly, quietly, never giving up. We are going to win!
    Daddy

Chorus (Both):
Down in the valley,
The valley so low,
Hang your head over,
Hear the wind blow.

Hear the wind blow, dear,
Hear the wind blow,
Hang your head over,
Hear the wind blow.

Sandburg:
Writing this letter,
Containing three lines,
Answer my question,
Will you be mine?

All three:
Will you be mine?
Will you be mine?
Answer my question
Will you be mine?

Roses love sunshine,
Violets love dew,

Angels in heaven
Know I love you.

Know I love you, dear,
Know I love you,
Angels in heaven
Know I love you.

(Sandburg finishes alone, unaccompanied:)
Know I love you, dear,
Know I love you,
Angels in heaven
Know I love you.

Chorus (Both):
Whether it's your child or friend,
Or very special lover,
If you find you're full of
Lovin' feelings for another,
Don't try to hide the light of love,
Or keep it under cover,
Don't wait for fate to pull you both apart.
I'll tell you what you oughta do,
Just tell them what they mean to you.
Tell them all the love that's in your heart.
Do it now.
Tell them all the love that's in your heart.

End of ACT II

(Courtship of Carl Sandburg, *as transcribed from the tape sold at performances in Chicago with the cast of Tom Amandes, Bob Gibson and Anne Hills)*

Courtship of Carl Sandburg ©1984 Courtship Productions, Inc.
All songs published by Robert Josiah Music, Inc.

Appendix

The Chicago Club Scene

A large part of the charm of folk music is its invitation to everyone to participate — the feeling an audience member gets, as Bob did from Pete Seeger, that "I could do this, too." Unfortunately, it is possibly also the reason that folk music is no longer the national sensation that it was briefly in the early '60s, because where it flourishes is in the intimate club setting. Chicago had the distinction of being the center for folk music, probably in large part because of Bob's long time residence there, but also because of its unique longstanding network of clubs that catered to folk music. Despite the fact that Bob came and went, spending time over the years in Colorado, New York, California, Texas and Oregon, he always returned to Chicago, and while he was a native New Yorker, Chicago always claimed him as her own. Bob explained what made Chicago so special in the world of folk music.

Credit has to go to Chicago, which remained good for folk when it died elsewhere. It all centers around the Old Town School of Folk Music. For a while I was director of special events there — events like putting together concerts where the performer gets everything above expenses. The school graduates over a thousand people a year, and when you think of all the years it's been in operation, that's a lot of people, and even that spreads like ripples on a pond.

I love playing for peer groups, and Chicago has the most qualified audiences I've ever seen. They appreciate a good lick when they hear it. Chicago also has that Second City thing going for it. New York City digs results, but Chicago digs the action. You can survive in Chicago by just being a character.

John Irons:
One of the things that I think is integral to telling the story of Bob is the migration of music from the Old Town area. Actually it was even further south than that at first — down around Chicago Avenue and around Michigan and State — places like the Fickle Pickle and Gate of Horn and a lot of folk clubs. I think what killed those places was there was no place to park. So it moved further north, and the center became the Earl of Old Town, but parking was a bad there, too. Then it went out to Lincoln. Parking wasn't much better, but at least you could park about three or four blocks away

and walk in, and it was accessible by public transportation, too. That ran for a bunch of years. I don't know where you go now to hear folk music as the common fair. Places like the Charleston do some folk music some nights and other nights they've got jazz and piano — different things. Another place is No Exit. They've been around forever. It's really a throwback to earlier times kind of place. You've got a lot of people there that don't realize we're going to bridge the century real soon, and they sit there and drink coffee and play chess during the day and read Karl Marx and grow goatees.

THE OFF-BEAT ROOM
Kenmore & Granville
1955

As Bob discussed earlier, what provided the spark to inspire the listening club movement was Ken Nordine's Off-Beat Room. Located on Granville and Kenmore, it was a place Nordine started so he could perform his word jazz. In this setting he established what had not existed before, the concept that if you came in, you had to pay attention or leave. He ran the club on his own terms of, "Anybody talks, gets out." While in existence only about six months, it was there long enough to give a young man named Albert Grossman the idea that there was a possibility out there for something other than a rowdy bar atmosphere. The result, while even it didn't last a very long time, was a club that became a national icon and the true center of the folk revival.

THE GATE OF HORN
Chicago & Dearborn
1956-1961

Ed Holstein comments on the impact the Gate had:
 The Gate of Horn just meant so much to so many people because it was the first alternative nightclub. Before that, nightclubs were like Chez Paris — fancy places. The Gate was a place that served char broiled hamburgers, which nobody was real familiar with, and dark beer. There was a hipness to it. Women wore turtleneck sweaters and skirts and the guys wore corduroy sport coats and thin ties and smoked pipes. It was really different then. People dressed up. Everybody had a show outfit. Gibson & Camp looked like Brooks Brothers salesmen. Regimental striped tie, herringbone sport coats with thin lapel. Even at Second City there was a dress code. You had to wear a tie.

As Bob said of the club:
 The Gate of Horn was the very first place where folk music as

such was the draw. It was in the basement of the Rice Hotel. It had a greater effect upon a number of people than did all the clubs put together in those days. People would come up to me and say, "We don't go to clubs usually, but we go to the Gate of Horn all the time."

The original Gate of Horn did not have an extremely long life, but its impact was so great that it shaped the club scene for decades, including another couple of incarnations of the Gate itself in much plusher surroundings. Bob Gibson's friend George Matson describes the difference in the new place on Rush Street:
I was at the new Gate of Horn, but it was rather sterile, I understand, compared to the old Gate. It was slick. It lasted a fairly long time — six or eight years.

George Carlin recalls the atmosphere surrounding this scene that was so important in shaping the folk movement in Chicago:
I was there at the scene — not at the first Gate of Horn, but at the second Gate of Horn. I was never a part of the first one. I would say that my time in Chicago really began when I went there with my partner in 1960 through 1964 probably, so just that little window, and it was most intensified probably from '62 to '64. I mostly hung around with the Gate of Horn manager, Bob Wettloffer, and I really didn't associate or socialize much with any of the artists who came in. Al Grossman was around there. I would see him occasionally. I never sat down and talked with him. He was kind of a distant figure who was highly revered or respected or feared or whatever. But mostly I hung out socially with Bob Wettloffer and a few people around him, so I wasn't part of that scene in the strictest sense of the word.

Really what it amounted to was that the second Gate of Horn was a coffee house with a liquor license. I went in and I worked there the first night of my solo career in 1962 the day after I broke up with my partner Jack Burns at the Living Room, which was a nightclub just down the street on Rush. I opened up the following night as a solo act at the Gate of Horn with Dave Guard and the Whiskey Hill Singers, which was a group with Judy Henski, Buckwheat and Dave Guard and I've forgotten the other person. I opened that show, and they were the headliners. I came back to the Gate of Horn probably six or eight months later still in 1962, and I was the opening on a three act bill with Miriam Makeba and Peter, Paul & Mary. I hung around a lot, we smoked a lot of pot and drank a lot of things, and it was kind of a fun thing, 'cause at that time I was in a kind of a weird position. I was still working the Playboy Clubs because of my contract that remained for my partner and me when we broke up, so I fulfilled those contracts as a solo. I was pretty much a mainstream comic who had not yet gotten significant television exposure, so I was walking a fine line. I was trying to be mainstream to get my career started with respect to TV, and at the same time, my heart and my sentiments and my philosophy were far more compatible with the people in the folk era, in the folk movement and the beat and the emerging hippies. It was the period in between beatniks and hippies. So I was working in the Playboy Club in a very straightforward mainstream act and then hanging around at night and doing this other stuff sometimes at Mother Blues or over at the Rising Moon. (I think it was called the Rising Moon before it was called Mother Blues.) It was over on Wells Street. I'd go and do guest sets there. I never worked it as an artist working there — I did guest sets coming over from the Playboy. But the Gate of Horn was really my introduction to that world of pot smoking, folk singing, anti-establishment people who eventually generated the hippie period. So I was just learning all that stuff, although I came out of Harlem and I was a pot smoker since I was 13. I mean I wasn't a newcomer to any of that stuff. I had never been a real enthusiastic supporter of mainstream ideas. I was a fuck-up and an outcast and I was a dropout and I left high school after one year and I got kicked out of the Air Force. I did all the things that I felt I had to do to retain my autonomy and my individuality, but still had this dream of being a comic in the movies or something, so I sort of had to walk both paths. And the Gate of Horn turned out to be a good outward manifestation for me of the kind of stuff I really felt inside, so I gravitated toward them.

EARL OF OLD TOWN
1615 Wells St.
1961-1982

Rick Neely remembers the Earl:
That Gate of Horn scene could never ever be duplicated again. There were some pretty wild kind of similar flavored times, I'm sure, at the Earl of Old Town because that place was pretty loose, too. Earl of Old Town came in after the fact. Folk music had pretty much died all around, and Earl said, "Yeah, I'm gonna have folk music, and everybody else told him he was crazy. They said, "Man, that's done and gone. You're nuts!" Somehow the Earl latched on. Earl's was wild and hip and it was a comfortable, cozy thing. They had a good hamburger. It was just right on the edge of being too strange for words and just the most "In" place. They had Christmas decorations up in the front window all year long. But the music was always very good. He always hired good music. Steve Goodman came up through there, John Prine came up through there, Bonnie Koloc — they all started at the Earl and got well known. He just had a knack for doing this. And, of course, Gibson came in there. Fred Holstein was a house act and played night after night. He was like the house musician and later went on to be at Somebody Else's Troubles

that his brother, Ed, and Steve Goodman had. They all ran that place.

On a Friday or Saturday they used to do three shows at the Earl. The first show would be kind of subdued and just kind of get through it, and then they'd turn the audience. They'd run the first group out and the next group, that had been standing out in the street for an hour by then, would come in and order their two drinks. The second show was a little bit wilder, but by the time the third show unfolded, it was off the scale. If you were there for the second show, you could stay for the third show. You had to pay again, but you could stay. That way they were pretty certain that there would be a full house for the late show. Other musicians from around town would drop in after their gigs, so you never knew who you might see. Steve Goodman might get up and play guitar; Gordon Lightfoot was there one night and got up and sang; John Denver was there one night. All these people were influenced by Bob in one way or another, and they would come in to kind of pay homage. It was very exciting. It would go late into the night because the Earl had a 4:00 license, and it would be 5:00 in the morning before that joint would break up. Those are some of the fondest kind of times.

We used to go to these things at the Earl and then go to Al & Jeff's Laugh In Restaurant which is now gone. It was at the Lincoln Hotel right where Wells Street comes to an end where it butts up into Lincoln Ave. We'd have breakfast and then at 7:00 in the morning drive down to Maxwell Street which was an open air market on the south side of the city where you could buy anything, legal or otherwise. I was 21 or 22 then, and that was a whole scene that I had never been exposed to, and it was just always an adventure — something new — the whole way. It was really great times.

George Carlin adds:

Places like the Earl of Old Town were stops along the way. As I say, I really had my other career path to follow, and it took me away a lot. I was only in Chicago at certain times during the year, because of either working in some place in Chicago or taking a little time in between jobs to spend a week there, so I wasn't based out of there. All of my hanging out was part of the "after it's dark, everybody goes out a gets high and tries to get laid scene," so the Earl of Old Town was just another stop on that — so was the Plugged Nickel — and there are others whose names I've probably forgotten that were just part of the rounds you made.

Earl J.J. Pionke was interviewed in the summer 1977 issue of Come For To Sing. *In that he commented on the club:*

In 1961 I started our pub, The Earl of Old Town. That was just when the folk boom of 1960 started. Before then I had been the bartender and manager of a large neighborhood package goods store. I started going around to see the good local folk musicians who were playing around town in those days — Fred Holstein, Ginni Clemmens, Willie Wright, etc. They were playing at places like Montmarte and the Blind Pig and the Fickle Pickle. Fred used to play at the Old Town Pump one or two nights a week. Then Mother Blues opened, and Wells Street really started coming alive. I used to follow Fred and Ginni wherever they were playing. I got into folk music right away, but then all of a sudden, everything started to change, and folk music was on its way out.

I almost bought the old Gate of Horn when they changed its location. It was funny — we had a deal struck, and Allan Ribback, the owner, had even given me a list of the folk performers I couldn't hire so we wouldn't give direct competition to the new Gate of Horn, but I didn't want any of his performers. I was going to do a blues thing. I figured nobody was playing blues on the North Side. This was 1964, and I had everybody lined up. We were going to sell hamburgers and beer. Then the landlord wouldn't accept us because neither my partner or I had ever owned a music club before. They didn't want to take a chance on us so it passed.

With the changes in folk music interest, pretty soon George Ramsey at the Yellow Unicorn was the only folk club left. So I went to George and said, "I can't imagine Wells Street without folk music. I'm going to put folk music in the Earl." He said, "Are you out of your mind? Folk music is dead. I'm about ready to toss in the towel here."

I decided to poll 15 people. As soon as 15 people said I was going to fail, I knew I had a winner. I went over to Poor Richard's, which was Richard Harding's place on Sedgweick, where Fred Holstein was tending bar and doing a little singing. I said, "Fred, I'm going to put folk music in the Earl. You're my number-one favorite Chicago singer and I want you to open for me. We started folk music on November 1, 1966. Fred opened up with Maxine Sellers. Ginni Clemmens followed next, and then Willie Wright came in. That's how we started the ball rolling.

Our business had fallen off some until we put the music in. It was amazing — within four or five weeks, we were doing real nice. We're talking about low dollars back then — no cover charge, 50 cents for a stein of beer, a buck for a mixed drink and the whole hamburger plate was only a buck. We didn't have a stage then. We had a beautiful red bar stool that was higher than anything else in the room. That lasted for about four months, and then one day I said, "Hey, you guys, I'm gonna give you all a raise." I built a stage six inches high, and gave them a six-inch raise!

We had people like Jim Post, Bonnie Koloc, Steve Goodman and John Prine all start here. Bonnie Koloc came in when she was working down the street at the original Quiet Knight that Richard Harding was running. She'd been working there a long time. It was funny, because Fred had been working for me for a long time, and he finally said, "Earl, I'm gonna go over there and work for Richard for a while." I said, "Fine, work there, but come back." Then Bonnie came over from there to work with us.

Jim Post and his wife Kathy were working as Friend and Lover back then, and they really made the Earl click. Steve Goodman came in about 1968 and John Prine came in two or three years after that.

At the Earl, we got to be a family, and that spirit sort of carried the whole thing. The best moments were always involved with our own kids — Ed Holstein writing *Jazzman;* Steve Goodman completed his *City of New*

Orleans in our "star-cave" dressing room in the back room; Bonnie Koloc, John Prine and Steve Goodman all got record contracts — and it all happened at once. It was still a shared feeling; we all felt that we'd gotten hit with a bombshell!

Earl had a habit of booking people and then forgetting about it. He said he had a lot going on and sometimes there was too much to keep up with.

Brian Bowers:

I came to Chicago because the Dillards told me about the Earl of Old Town and that I'd be perfect there, so I called and talked to Earl and set up a time to come and meet him and play for him. I told him the Dillards had told me about his club and how good it was and I wanted to come and audition for him. He said, "Oh, yeah, yeah!" I was on my way home to Seattle and spent a couple hundred dollars to fly into Chicago and play for him, and the son of a bitch didn't show up. I was mad I got hold of the guy that ran the bar for Earl — his name was Gus. He had a flat top, and he was a wild one. I garnered him and made him come in the back room and said, "Hey, man, I don't know what your boss thinks the deal is here, but I spent $200 to come over here and play three or four tunes for him, and he don't even show up! He's a jerk!" Gus said, "Well, play for me." So there we were in the back room and I played for him. He said, "Wow, you're really good! I'll tell him!"

A week later I was coming through again, and Earl came and listened to me this time. He said, "Gus told me you're really good, and you were mad at me that I didn't show up! You know, things happen!" I said, "Hey man, I spent $200 to come here and play for you and you didn't even show up. You may be rich, but $200 doesn't grow on trees for me!" I don't think anybody much talked to Earl like that because he was the big cheese in town — he had Prine and Goodman working for him — so he was amused at that point. The long and the short of it was that before I played, he said, "If you're any good, don't you worry about your $200. You'll make that and a lot more from me. So I played something for him and he said, "Hey, man, you ARE good!" He said, "I'll tell you what we'll do — I'm gonna book you for two weeks, and we'll figure the price and everything."

Then he said, "Come on, I want to take you around — I want you to meet some people." So he took me over to Richard Harding at the Quiet Knight. Well, he didn't take me. He told me to play for Richard and tell Richard that I was gonna play for Earl. I didn't know the politics, so I went storming into Richard Harding's and I said, "Somebody told me to come play for you." He said, "Oh, yeah? Well go ahead." I played for him, and he said, "I'll give you a job." I said, "I've already got a job with this guy who told me to come play for you." He said, "Well, who is it?!" I said, "This guy named Earl Pionke." Richard was furious.

Bonnie Koloc was one of those who played regularly through the years at the Earl and remembers it with great fondness:

When I first went to Chicago there was the old Quiet Knight owned by Richard Harding, which was down south on Wells Street, and I worked there for that summer of 1968. (Richard had had a very successful folk club called Poor Richard's before that which was just a few blocks west of where he was at Wells Street, and I think the neighborhood got, like, real bad.) Earl used to come down and hear me at the Quiet Knight. He wanted to hire me for a month. I'd heard it was a very noisy place, so I thought, "Oh, my God, what if I hate this place?" So I said, "Well, two weeks." We badgered around, and he said, "Two weeks and a two week option," which sounded better. I had learned to sing, not in quiet folk clubs, but I in Iowa at places like the Ramada Inn cocktail hour, so I learned how to handle an audience. The Earl turned out to be totally my cup of tea. I just knew how to get them quiet, and it was really successful the first two weeks so I stayed another two weeks, and then gradually I'd work a month and then I'd lay off a month. I never worked too long because I worried that people would get tired of me. I wanted to make it so people couldn't see me all the time, and that worked really well for me for a long period of time because then I could still draw.

The Earl was a real long narrow dark club, funkiest floors in the world, old brick walls. Earl had all this memorabilia, handmade signs and chairs. It had wooden bench chairs and funky tables and the windows in front were, like, these old windows, and at Christmas they'd hang up wreaths and these imitation candelabras. One time they put fake snow decorations on the window and they stayed up all year. When I was really packing them in there, they would just jam people in there. They would have eight people at a teeny little table. I don't know why the fire department didn't close them down, because it was just packed. They would keep people waiting outside while they'd clear all the tables. These poor people would be standing out there and they'd be freezing. I always was afraid they thought that it was me holding things up. Then when Earl got them in, he'd wait quite a while before I could go on. Again, I always thought that the people thought that it was me, but it was a bar and they wanted everyone to drink. I used to love to make my grand entrance from the front door. One night I could barely get in there. They had people stuffed around tables, and then they had standing room only in the back and I had to sort of like shove my way to get in. I couldn't get from the back room. One night it was so packed they had them sitting on the bar stools and on the bar.

All the people there were such characters. Antone the cook had been a cook in the circus —- or that's what I heard — and on your cheeseburgers he would make a face out of the cheese. They had candles that would drip up on the bar, and they'd turn into huge wax formations. The waitresses were always pretty interesting. A lot of them had degrees or they were just real different. There was Liz who was at the door, Pete the bartender who had been a cop at one time I think and Jimmy Johnson a round black guy at the bar that I thought was great and Gus the doorman who was a guy who had a flattop and white socks. They were all just wonderful to Earl. They all knew each other as kids. Jimmy and Pete and I'm pretty sure Gus knew each other when they were growing up. They were real west side Chicago kids. Earl had a hot dog stand to help support his family. It was a real Chicago kind of place. It was great. It was open 'til five in the morning. My natural time is to go to bed real early and get up early, and at that time I was working all night, so I painted my bedroom chocolate brown so it would be dark and covered the windows with quilts so I could sleep in the daytime.

Earl was Polish, and when I met him he was blonde. He always wore a white shirt, and later he let his hair grow real long and had a long goatee — I think he still does. He really knew how to have a good time. Sometimes he would serve us champagne at special times. I'd always joke with him about that, because within twenty minutes you had a headache. I always joked that he made his champagne in the basement. It could be pretty crazy, but was never afraid to work there. Here I was a young 23 year old girl in Chicago singing in a club at night, but they always watched out for me. I always felt safe there. Earl was always very good to me. If there was ever any kind of problem, I could just say, "Somebody's hassling me," and Earl would take care of it. And if Earl thought there were going to be bad people coming in he'd warn me. I remember once he said, "These guys are gonna come in and they want to hear you sing and they may want to talk to you, and you tell them I'm your manager and that you don't know nuttin'!" So I never had a problem – EVER! They were very protective of me. Earl and I had nose to nose arguments, but it was great. Actually he took me to see Peggy Lee because he knew that I liked her. He wasn't perfect, but he was a great guy to me.

The Earl was almost like out of a movie scene, and I have more people who come and hear me, come up and say, "I saw you at the Earl." I remember when I first started there, we had trouble getting the papers to write anything about what was happening at the Earl because it sort of held this attitude like everybody was at Mr. Kelly's and around the Gold Coast downtown. I mean everybody considered that a folk club in Old Town was not a great place to write about. That sort of changed. Basically while the Earl was open I never played anyplace else — except I went down to Mr. Kelly's which was, like, THE place. Nobody went from a folk club to Mr. Kelly's. That was like where Barbra Streisand played. And then I think Earl thought that I wouldn't come back — that he'd lost me — and I'm so loyal and I thought it was so cool to go from a folk club to Mr. Kelly's and back again. One of the things was that everybody came into the Earl. A lot of people who were in medical school, a lot of college kids. A lot of the best friends that I have and whose families I've watched grow up, I met because they just wandered in off the street. They are like family to me.

It was such a scene. There'd be hookers there and go-go girls. One night Bryan Bowers who played great autoharp was standing up there. He always wore these cut off shirts, and he had big beautiful muscles because he was very athletic, and he was playing this darling little autoharp. It was very late at night and this girl — I think she was a hooker — she was dancing right in front of him. There was a stage, but the stage was just a little platform and there were tables right up next to it. I always used to set my glass on the table, so I had people right at my feet. Gus went and grabbed the back of her skirt and pulled her out the door, and Bryan's singing, "Oh, Gus, you shoulda handled that better." Another night I thought this guy came in the door and he had something the size of a rifle wrapped up in a towel. I was right in the middle of a beautiful ballad and I'm singing and I'm singing, and I thought, "Oh no this guy's going to start shooting and fill the place with lead," but I just kept singing, and when I got done, Gus got him out the door. I went to Gus, and I asked him if he had a gun and he said, "No, no no!" But he wouldn't have told me. Periodically there would be a big fight and Earl and Gus would come leaping over the bar. When Antone died, he wanted his ashes put behind the bar at the Earl, so Earl brought the in, and Gus told him he'd quit if he put them up. They were in the basement of the Earl for a long time.

The back room was just incredible. There was a freezer in the back and Earl had a desk there and it was all just piled with junk and papers and posters stacked to the ceiling and falling all over the place. One night on Halloween, Gus came to me before the show and said, "Jane Russell is here!" And I said sarcastically, "Sure she is!" So I went in the back and there was a white ermine coat in the back that was crawling with cockroaches, and I thought, "Oh, God, Jane Russell's going to go home with a pocket full of cockroaches." So I got up and sang, and there she was sitting at a table right at my feet. She really was quite beautiful! She had to be in her fifties then. One night Bob Dylan came in. Another night Paul Simon got into town to do some research for his movie, *One Trick Pony*. Some cab driver told him about me, and he called me and said he'd like to go out to some clubs with me. I said, "Sure." Elvis Presley had just died, so he wanted to see all the things on TV about Elvis. I brought him over to my apartment, and we watched the coverage on television for awhile, and then we went out and I showed him around. I was working that weekend, and he was going to come see me. The whole place was packed that night, and you couldn't get in, so when Paul Simon got there, Gus wouldn't let him in. I could've killed Gus. I loved Paul Simon, but I don't think it would've mattered to Gus who it was.

When John Belushi was in town to do the *Blues Brothers* movie, they rented this place in the back. It was a little place called the Sneak Joint, an old tavern, and Earl owned that too - they wanted a private place where they could all go, so they kind of like rented it from Earl so they could hang out there. That was really wild.

I remember Steve Goodman coming in there when he was very young — just 19. Freddie Holstein worked there a lot, too. Actually Fred is one of my favorite folk singers. His pitch will wander. It's not perfect, but he tells a story, and he picks the best material and has beautiful phrasing. I always enjoy his work. But he worked a lot there. He's always so good to me.

There was a guy there who used to love Freddie Holstein and me, and he was a hit man! We knew that he was, and he'd say, "I don't care, I don't care, I love you guys! You guys are the greatest!" It was really scary to talk to him.

So that's the kind of place it was. It was just characters like out of a movie. I loved it. I truly loved it.

The Earl was open on Thanksgiving — they were open for everything — so we'd bring in a turkey or they'd cook one there or one of the agents would bring one in, and people would bring in food, and we'd just sit around and eat together. It was really like a home to a lot of people. It was family, and it was wonderful.

From Bob's medley of his songs called Sing Us Some of the Old Songs, *which became a regular feature in his later performances, comes this line:*
Three a.m. at the Earl of Old Town
Freddie's stackin' chairs
Gus is countin' up the take
And I'm stumblin' up the stairs...

What has become of these people? Bonnie offers this:
    I heard that actually Gus has done a lot of theatre, and he works as a doorman right now. The one stacking chairs was Freddie Turner, a very old black guy that Earl had known for a long time. He was like a guard dog. He would not let anybody through that door. I had a piano player come once, and we were going to rehearse — I even rehearsed at the Earl — and Freddie would not let the piano player in. He'd say, "I don't care, I don't care! Gus said..." I said, "It's OK Freddie." When I got there, then he'd let him in. As for Earl, I heard that he had bought a place down near Pullman — that's a section of Chicago.

    My friend said that the Earl is now a Fern bar. I thought that whoever had it would have just cleaned it up and then had all kinds of pictures and some of the memorabilia and had really good food and had it like "Memories of the Earl" or something like that. That would have made a great place. But they went in and just totally changed the place. The first owners after the Earl had it really high tech. It was just awful. Now at least it's a little warmer. It is so strange for me to go in there now. The stage was in the middle against the south wall. The place faces east/west. The stage was on the right as you went in. I think they might have booths there now, but there weren't any then. There were just tables. The bar actually was where the bar is now only it was longer, and then they had a kitchen. Where the pool table is now at the back was where the kitchen was.

    The place that I really worked the most and was a real scene was the Earl. I worked there from '68 to whenever he closed. I still came back and worked there periodically after I went to New York until '82, but it was depressing then. It had changed a lot. The real heyday when Steve and Fred and I and other people worked there was '68 to about '76. It was the center of a lot of people's lives for a while.

The Earl location in its 1998 incarnation.

QUIET KNIGHT
Belmont Ave. & Halsted

Bonnie Koloc

I never knew Richard Harding's first club, Poor Richard's. Richard then went up and took the Quiet Knight uptown on Belmont & Halsted. He had the second floor and it was quite a lot larger. He had two that were called the Quiet Knight. The first one was on Wells Street right beside Mother Blues on South Wells and that's where I first worked in Chicago. That was pretty exciting. That was in '68 and it was right in the middle of all the craziness of the summer — Bobby Kennedy was killed and all the cops and you had the national convention. Richard always had a big hunk of keys hanging on his pants and he had a huge German shepherd named Duke that he kept behind the bar. He also had a gun behind the bar, so if anybody came in and started any kind of trouble, he'd say, "Duke!" and he'd leap over the bar and the dog would take after them. This happened frequently during my songs.

SOMEBODY ELSE'S TROUBLES
Lincoln Avenue
1974-78

Troubles partners, Fred Holstein, Earl Pionke, Duke Nathaus, Ed Holstein. (1977-from CFTS)

This was a joint effort club owned by Earl Pionke, Duke Nathaus, Ed and Fred Holstein, Steve Goodman and Bill Redhed.

MOTHER BLUES

Bonnie Koloc:

Mother Blues was a blues club on S. Wells. There was a Dr. Scholls factory on the same street that would have been about three blocks south of the Earl, and it was right straight across from a school. Right beside it was the Quiet Knight. Mother Blues was a big long narrow hall — kind of a basement. I heard Paul Butterfield there one night. That was a very popular club. I never hung out in there. I just went in a couple of times. It closed shortly thereafter.

ORPHAN'S

Bonnie Koloc:
    I did play at Orphan's some, but that was after the Earl closed. It was a nice place, but it was never like my home. Basically while the Earl was open I never played anyplace else — except I went down to Mr. Kelly's. Orphans was kind of a folk club, but they had other stuff. They had a variety of stuff. They had jazz, all kinds of rock & roll. That was on Lincoln Ave. practically right across from the Biograph.

SADDLE CLUB

Bonnie Koloc:
    The Saddle Club was a bar that was on North Avenue when the Old Town School of Folk Music was on North Avenue. On Thursday night all the people from the school would go over there and they had an open mike. It was wonderful. It wasn't owned by the Old Town School. They just allowed them to use it for that night. When the school moved over to Armitage they used to go over to another place. I don't remember what that was called — but people who wanted to play in a club could go over on a certain night and get up and perform. It was truly a unique deal. That's where I first heard John Prine. He was taking guitar lessons. He was a postman at Melrose Park married to his first wife, and he had written all these incredible songs like *Sam Stone*. I couldn't believe it.

HOBSON'S CHOICE
5101 N. Clark St.
1984

    This was Bob's own venture in club management which he had in 1984. Located at 5101 N. Clark St. in Chicago, it had been a restaurant before Bob took it over, and Bonnie Koloc says that the previous owner was murdered back behind the building. Using what he had learned at the Gate of Horn, Bob offered good food, the staple being his own chili recipe, a bar and a separate listening room. He used it not only for bringing in big name folk stars, but also as a platform for showcasing new talent, one of his great passions in life. He brought the likes of Michael Smith, Josh White Jr., Anne Hills and many more.

    Bob defined his philosophy with Hobson's:
    I was trying to run a place with certain kinds of principles and goals. It was a wonderful place for people to perform with a very small intimate room and a real connection between performers and audience. Of course, I changed the nature of how they performed. Instead of doing one-nighters, I had them come in for longer periods of time, like two to four weeks.

PHOTO COURTESY ROD KENNEDY

Bob outside Hobson's
in 1984

The author on a Pilgrimage to the
Hobson's location in 1998, at that time
empty

PHOTO BY HEIDI WALTER

HOLSTEIN'S
2464 N. Lincoln Ave.
1981-1988

Ed Holstein talks about the club he ran with his brother Fred:

Holstein's sat about 175 people. We snuck in 200 when it was real crowded. It was very similar to the Gate of Horn in a lot of ways, I think — it had a separate room. It was at 2464 N. Lincoln Ave. Holstein's was open 1981 to 1988 but, we were also involved in a club called Somebody Else's Troubles '74-'78 and Bob and Hamid worked there, too. In fact we used to have these things called "Cook & Sings" where we would cook a meal and there would be a show and supposedly the performer would prepare the meal. I think Bob might have done his Texas chili or gave the recipe to the cook to do. I wasn't impressed with it and I told him, 'cause there were no beans in it. I was disappointed because I wanted more vegetables in it or something. But I guess that's what Texas chili is - just meat. But I missed the beans and green peppers. It was unreal. It was six bucks for a meal and them. We had John Prine one time and he had White Castle hamburgers. It was disgusting. Imagine 750 White Castle hamburgers in a room. They're steamed so the grease just sits there. They cook about 100 of them on a grill. They put them on frozen, they put onions on them and they put a pickle on it. They have a big hole pressed in the middle and they shrivel down. It's a great experience just to watch.

Ed Holstein - '98

We did everything at Holstein's. We did children's shows, we did Klezmer music, Irish music, Cajun. I was the first one to bring a Cajun Band to Chicago — Queen Ida. Nobody wanted to book her. I booked her based on her photograph. She was turned down by Fitzgerald's which is now known as

I COME FOR TO SING - 403

a Cajun place! I don't think they would ever admit to that, but the agent told me that. I'd never heard of Zydeco music. Nobody in Chicago had then. He sent me a picture of this woman, and I said, "Oh, I'm bookin' her!" She looked so great with that getup. I put her picture in the ad and it said "Queen of Zydeco!" She was a woman who drove a school bus, and she used to play for private parties. She played at a party Francis Ford Coppola had, and he said to her, "You oughta go on the road. You're great. You're done with the school bus gig." Well, I'd never heard a note that she played, but this just looked like the greatest thing. So I put an ad in the Reader - "QUEEN OF CAJUN ZYDECO MUSIC!" I didn't know what "Zydeco" meant, but the place was packed. It was on a Tuesday night and the place was just mobbed with people. And all of a sudden I'm like the authority, right?! Like, I know everything, so somebody said to me, "What does Zydeco mean?" I looked around the house, and I said, "It means a good Tuesday night!"

So we did stuff like that. A lot of Irish music. Tom Waits and Elvis Costello and Pogues played at Holstein's. Steppenwolf was having a show with them called *Frank's Wild Years*. A friend of mine called me up and said, "Tom Waits and Elvis Costello are looking to get together and just have a couple of quiet beers with some people from Steppenwolf. They don't want to be bothered. They're looking for a joint." And I said, "Well, we open at three and Bonnie Koloc's off at 12 so you got three hours. Come on down." As soon as I got off the phone, I went up and down the neighborhood telling people that Elvis Costello and Tom Waits were going to be at Holstein's. The place was mobbed! And naturally, we ran up $776 in two and a half hours, and then I kicked them off the stage. I got on stage and said, "You gotta go now! Sorry, thanks for coming." But we had a lot of fun.

Holstein's closed because the lease was up. It was that simple. They wanted more money to renew and we were tired. It's hard to keep booking. We booked 300 shows a year and ran a bar. The audience was getting older. It was getting harder to get down there. I was just getting lazy. I'd been there seven years working seven days a week. I left there and started bartending and producing some concerts, doing a little performing. Running a club was really all the time. I'd been involved in Somebody Else's Troubles that way, too. The only time we'd have long bookings was like Gibson & Camp would be four days, Best of Friends was there for ten days, but that was maybe twice a year. The rest of the time it was one night or two nights. The place is a college frat bar now — serves chicken wings. We got out of it at the right time because the neighborhood was changing.

1998 incarnation of Holstein's location

Bonnie Koloc:
Holstein's was beautiful. You'd walk in and one side was like a hippy dippy restaurant and on the other side it was a bar and all brick — very pretty. Then you went in a little room which was another all brick room, and they

had a little stage and chairs and elevated, kind of like a theatre. It was small and beautiful. I just loved it. Back in those days that neighborhood was all factories and neighborhoods. It's gotten much more polished up now.

HARRY HOPE'S
Cary, Illinois

George Matson:
　　Harry Hope's was an old ski chalet in Cary. Basically it was a barn on top of a hill that used to be an active ski area. It was a wonderful venue. It was big and roomy. It had an upstairs show lounge and it had pews and pews of wooden auditorium seats — that type of thing. I got the end cap from one or them. I was going to put Harry Hopes and the opening and closing date on it in a ceramic oval and give that to Bob when he got his place fixed up. He was always going to settle someplace, but that never happened, so I've still got that. I snuck in after it was condemned and closed and pulled one of those out of there. It was a great place with a really good room, and Bob played up there quite a bit. It later moved to Elgin, but it never really caught on there.

Bonnie Koloc:
　　Harry Hope's was run by a couple of guys out in Cary, way out from Chicago. It was an A-frame wooden kind of place, and I guess they just got people from all around there. I used to play there quite often. It was a little bar and performance place.

CHARLOTTE'S WEB
Rockford, Illinois

Bonnie Koloc:
　　Charlotte's Webb was an old synagogue. Karen and Bill Howard, who lived out in Rockford and were in construction, started the club as a hobby and brought out a lot of great people. It lasted for quite a long time. One night I was in the middle of *Amelia Erhardt's Last Flight,* and they had a big thunderstorm and all the lights went out. Another time there was this huge blizzard when I got there. I'm so compulsive about being at gigs that I drove and I got just right ahead of the storm, but it caught up with me. We got in to the motel, and Bill had to come get me in his four-wheel drive. There was so much snow that the whole town was totally shut down, but people started coming in on cross country skis and the show went on!

George Matson:
　　Charlotte's Web as a non profit organization still exists, but the building it was in, was condemned. They decided it was cheaper to rent spaces that were right for the few shows a month that they do than it was to fix the building up.

Bonnie Koloc:
I look back now on this whole scene, and I think it's like an incredible movie. Sometimes it seems like it never happened at all and that it was some kind of dream that I had. But you know what's funny is that when I sing, it has no time. When I'm playing guitar or if singing a song like *Roll Me on the Water,* which I used to begin with, I mean then, it just seems like no time has passed and when I'm singing it's like I'm at the Earl again.

There were other clubs that came and went that also were central to the folk scene. Some were mentioned briefly but there was no one to expand on them. Some weren't even mentioned, but they all played their part. Maybe in a future edition we'll hear more. There were places like the Fickle Pickle, the Centaur, Poor Richard's, The Rising Moon, Wise Fool, the Bull, Yellow Unicorn. Blind Pig, Old Town Pump and the Clearwater Saloon. All worked together to provide an atmosphere that made Chicago the center of the musical universe for folk music and influenced most other forms of popular music that followed the folk revival of the '60s.

Earl J.J. Pionke was quoted in Come For To Sing *in 1977:*
When the folk wave occurred in Chicago, with the Gate of Horn, then Mother Blues, and then the Earl of Old Town, it afforded the local musicians a chance to get work on a somewhat regular basis. As more clubs came into being, it became true that you could make a living here and do some writing while you worked as a musician. In Chicago, you can grow and work and write. There are a lot of clubs, and they don't pay a lot of money, but they pay enough for someone to get by.

There's a real togetherness here — the clubs, the Old Town School, WFMT, all those things. You can do your thing and you can share. There's a great hospitality here, and there's a community of writers. That's what makes Chicago such a haven — it's not the pot of gold, but it's a good place to grow.

The School, the guys at the Midnight Special on WFMT, Studs Terkel — all these things spell Chicago to me. We may not see each other all the time, but the hospitality is always there. I don't care what they say about the Coasts — let's stay backward here in Chicago. Let the crazy rockers stay out in L.A, smoking their mysticism or whatever...let the fast-paced New Yorkers be back there, knowing they're Number One. Let's just be what we are, and let them be what they are.

PERFORMERS INDEX

Bob Gibson photos, *i, 1, 5, 6, 7, 9, 12, 13, 14, 16, 18, 19, 20, 31, 32, 51, 52, 53, 64, 65, 71, 72, 87, 88, 97, 102, 112, 113, 123, 128, 135, 136, 137, 150, 159, 160, 173, 174, 178, 179, 180, 184, 186, 188, 190, 195, 198, 199, 200, 209, 210, 211, 221, 222, 226, 238, 245, 246, 247, 248, 271, 275, 302, 304, 376, 389, 403*

Algren, Nelson, 45
Allen, Woody, 75
Amandes, Tom, *136,* 140, 147-149
Baez, Joan, 32, 37, 38-40, 42, 44, 53, 54, 58, 69, *71,* 83, 193, 233, 241, 253-254, 255, 288, 303
Banducci, Enrico, 121
Bare, Bobby, 108
Basie, Count, 32
Bassette, John, 118, 119
Beatles, 58, 85, 102, 241, 254, 266, 269, 292
Belafonte, Harry, 25, 75
Belafonte Singers, 56
Berman, Shelley, 75
Bessie Smith & Gospel Pearls, 80
Best of Friends, 156-158, 271
Bikel, Theodore, 40
Bishop, Thom, 131, 133, 134, *135*
Blake, Brian, 24
Boguslav, Ray, 55
Bowers, Bryan, 118, 119, 130, 260-261, *260*
Brand, Oscar, 189, 202, *209*
Broonzy, Big Bill, 1, 28, 34, 44, 82
Brothers Four, 61
Brown, Fleming, 290
Brown, Herb, 47, 48, 49, *51,* 59, 267
Brown, John, 35, 45, 49, 202, *209,* 216, 218, 240, 242, 246
Brown, Lance, 120
Brown, Les, 33, 34, 43, 53, 69

Bruce, Lenny, 26, 44, 60, 110, 216
Buckley, Lord Richard, 110, 216
Buffalo Springfield, 84, 266
Burda, Jan, 155
Byrds, 84
Byrne, Jane, 133
Camp, Bob (Hamilton), 41, 42, 45, 46, 47, 48, 49, *51, 52,* 53, *53,* 54, 56, 59, 60, 61, 62, 63, *64, 72,* 75, 77, 83, 107, 109, 111, 120, 124, 125, 126, 127, 174, *174,* 175, 176, 177, *178, 179,* 188, 189, 215, 217, 218, 238, 240, 241, 255, 258-259, *258,* 261, 263, 271, 272, 274, 297, 303
Carlin, George, 44, 109, 263
Caselotti, Adriana (Snow White), 27
Cash, Johnny, 106, 108, 274
Chad Mitchell Trio, 78, 298
Charles, Ray, 61, 287
Child, Marilyn, 57, 76
Clancy Brothers, The, 46, 108, 157
Clark, Gene, 112
Clayton, Paul, 36, 263
Clemmens, Ginni, 109, 110, 131, 132, 133
Clooney, Rosemary, 32, 265
Close, Del, 48, 109
Cohen, Wolfie, 26, 27
Coleman, Cy, 59
Collins, Judy, 40, 43, 44, 46, 53, 69, 70, 83, 157, 259
Coltrane, John, 60

I COME FOR TO SING - 407

Cook, Sam, 61
Cosby, Bill, 75, 79
Court, John, 53
Craig, Cathryn, *209*
Crosby, Bing, 302
Crosby, David, 70, 79, 80, 105, 106, 112
Damron, Allen, *128,* 219
Darden, Severn, 110
Darling, Erik, 4, 131, 221, *221,* 227
David, Marv, 154
Davis, Mac, 273-274
de Cormier, Robert, 56
Denver, John, 61, 277
Dyer-Bennett, Richard, 23, 26
Dylan, Bob, 40, 44, 53, 54, 55, 56, 57, 58, 78, 79, 80, 87, 106, 254, 255, 277, 284, 292, 293
Ebert, Roger, 244
Eddy, Mary Olive, 20, 21, 23
Edelsten, Mark, 180
Ellington, Duke, 35
Elliott, Ramblin' Jack, 112, 117, 230
English, Logan, 55
Fariña, Mimi, 189-191, *190*
Farrell, Charlie, 27, 28, 59
Fred Kaz Trio, 30
Fromholz, Steven, 154
Gavin, Jimmy, 41, 54
Genevieve, 34
Gilbert, Ronnie, 55
Godfrey, Arthur, 32, 67, 68, 86, 228
Gooding, Cynthia, 36
Goodman, Steve, 111, 132, 230, 254
Gottlieb, Lou, 46, 53, 189, 256, 259
Green, Meridian, 92, 96, 176-177, *199, 221,* 223-224, 237, *238,* 239, 242-244, *243, 247, 248,* 249, 275, 291
Griffith, Nanci, 129, 154
Grossman, Albert, 32, 33, 34, 35, 36, 37, 38, 41, 42, 46, 53-63,*53,* 79, 80, 176, 303
Guard, Dave, 55, 189
Guth, John, 114
Guthrie, Woody, 2, 20, 35, 58, 82, 206, 252, 253, 263, 304

Guy Mitchell Show, 75
Hamilton, Frank, 4, 258
Harding, Richard, 102, 217
Harris, Emmylou, 202, *209,* 267
Hartford, John, 202, *209*
Hassilev, Alex, 53, 221, *221*
Havens, Richie, 79 , 261, 267
Hays, Lee, 55
Heffner, Hugh, 59
Hendrix, Jimi, 54
Henske, Judy, 56
Hellerman, Fred, 55
Hernandez, David, 131, 132, 133, 134, *135, 159*
Hester, Carolyn, 55
Hillman, Chris, 105, 106
Hills, Anne, *136,* 140-146, 148-149, 151, 153, 155-158, *159,* 197, 219, 240
Hinahosa, Tish, 129
Hirsch, Jim, 215, 216
Holstein, Ed, 59, 75, 83, 109, 111, 114, 131, 162, 188, 229, 265-266, *265, 292, 401, 403*
Holstein, Fred, 111, 174, 241, 264-265, *401*
Holzman, Jac, 77, 80
Hood, Sam, 86, 97
Hootenanny, 84, 86, 254
Horton, Johnny, 105
Hudson, 168
Hutchinson, Barbara Baily, *209*
Ian & Sylvia, 86, 292
Ingraham, Bob, 70
Irish Rovers, 108
Ives, Burl, 3, 68
Jagger, Mick, 302
Joplin, Janis, 53, 54, 58
Just Four, 70
Kennedy, Rod, 127, 129, 185, 196-197, 219
Kerrville Folk Festival, 127, 130, 153, 196, 219, 276, 283
Kerry, Bob, 44, 45
King, Carole, 102
King Jr., Martin Luther, 39
Kingston Trio, 42, 55, 73, 76, 85, 158, 269, 292, 298

Kristofferson, Kris, 117
Koloc, Bonnie, 111, 263-264, *263*, 397
Laine, Frankie, 32
Lamb, Antonia, 104, 112, *113, 248*
Laks, Lenny, *178*, 269-270
Lavin, Christine, 268
Leadbelly, (Huddie Ledbetter), 82, 303
Lee, Katie, 34
Lehning, Kyle, 201, 202, *209*
Lehrer, Tom, 37, 288
Lennon, John, 32, 61, 265, 266
Les Baxter's Balladeers, 70
Lightfoot, Gordon, 61, 102, 107, 176, 253, 254-255, *254*, 292-293
Limeliters, 55, 292, 298
Locorriere, Dennis, 202, *209*
Lomax, John, 21, 23, 82, 253
Loudermilk, John, 43
Lovett, Lyle, 129
Macarus, Julianne, 180
Mailer, Norman, 60
Mangson, Cindy, 156
Mapes, Jo, 56, 267
Marshall, E.G., 131
Martin, Dean, 292
Mathis, Johnny, 33
McCartney, Paul, 266
McCurdy, Ed, 26, 74, 100, 202, *209*, 260
McFarlane, Elaine (Spanky), 45, 105, 201, 202, *209*, 215, 216, 217, 218, 246
McGuinn, Roger (Jim), 46, 66, 84, 95, 104, 105, 106, 112, 123, 215, 216, 217, 218, 257-258, *257*, 297
Mellencamp, John, 70
Mike Douglas Show, 75
Milner, Martin, 76
Mitchell, Guy, 75, 76
Model, Roy (Lord Composer), 24
Monroe, Vaughn, 78
Moore, Mary Tyler, 131
Music, Lorenzo, 131
Muskrats, 300
Neff, Ricky, 69
Neil, Fred, 79, 80

Neiman, Leroy, 46
Nelson, Willie, 108
Nichols & May, 32, 230
Niles, John Jacob, 22
Nordine, Ken, 28, 33
North, Dave, 172
Ochs, Phil, 194, 216, 276-281, 292, 300
Odetta, 23, 36, 39, 40. 46, 53, 58, 69, 86, 176, 214, 233, 263, 284
Okun, Milt, 55, 56, 78
Old Town School of Folk Music, 130, 189, *195,* 215, 216, 254, 276, 284
Parsons, Gene, *199*
Parton, Dolly, 108
Paxton, Tom, 41, 102, 124, 125, *128,* 141, 151, 153, 155, 156, 157, 158, 172, 196, 197, 202, *209,* 216, 219, 233, 240, 255-256, *255,* 281, 282-283, 285
Peabody, Eddie, 68, 287, 288
Peter, Paul & Mary, 54, 56, 57, 58, 62, 78, 102, 110, 124, 131, 158, 196, 215, 216, 217, 218, 219, 292, 303
Petty, Tom, 218
Pionke, Earl, 109, 116, 120, 232, *394, 401*
Porco, Mike, 58, 74, 80
Presley, Elvis, 32, 54, 257
Prine, John, 107, 109
REM, 218
Reed, Susan, 23, 26
Reynolds, Nick, 55
Ribback, Allen, 34, 43, 47, 49, 53, 80
Rickles, Don, 33
Robeson, Paul, 1
Rogers, Gamble, 260
Rolling Stones, 266, 292
Romney, Hugh (Wavey Gravey), 255
Rose, Biff, 113, *113*
Rosmini, Dick, 125, 126, 127
Rowe, Helman, 28
Sandburg, Carl, 21, 136-149, *137*
Schmidt, Claudia, 118, 119, 130
Scott, Molly, 55
Scott, Mick, 266-267
Scott, Randolph, 43

I COME FOR TO SING - 409

Seeger, Pete, 1, *1,* 2, 3, 4, 19, 20, 35, 39, 55, 59, 69, 83, 85, 105, 206, 221, 227, 241, 253, 258, 263, 292, 303, 304
Seeger, Toshi, 2
Settle, Mike, 83
Shane, Bob, 55
Sharp, Cecil, 23
Shaw, Allan, 42, 65, 66, 69, 73, 78, 83, 86, 92, 189, 193, 201, 221, *221,* 269
Shelton, Robert, 55
Sills, Paul, 63
Silver, Roy, 79, 80, 107
Silverstein, Shel, 42, 45, 46-49, 79, 80, 83, 89, 106. 107. 109, 112, 113, 117, 118, 126, 130, 136, 172, 187, 188, 192, 197, *200,* 200-209, *209, 210,* 216, 222, 238, 241, 244, *244, 248,* 253, 257, *257,* 272-274, 284
Simon & Garfunkel, 59, 102, 218, 269
˙Simon, Carly, 265
Sinatra, Frank, 32, 33, 54, 75, 76
Skymonters, 62, 120
Smith, Michael, 70, 86, 120, 131, 132, 133, 134, 135, *135,* 156, 157-158, *159,* 176, 180-183, *180,* 191-192, 193, 200, 219, 222, 229, 233-234, 242, 261, *261,* 271, 277, 291-292, 297
Smith, Virginia, 164
Smothers Brothers, The, 46, 70, 86
Sneeky Pete, 106
Sorkin, Dan, 45
Spanier, Muggsy, 35
Starrs, John, 138

Stookey, Noel Paul, 46, 55, 57, 58, 216, 267
Tarriers, The, 25, 44
Tate, Ray, 114, 115, 138
Taylor, James, 102
Tedesco, Tommy, 80
Terkel, Studs, 34, 42, 81, *200,* 203-206, 241, *241,* 249, 259, *259,* 297
Thieme, Art, 268, 269, 288
Travers, Mary, 46, 55, 56, 216, 217, 267
Tull, Eric, 140-146
Tyson, Ian, 267
Van Ronk, Dave, 55, 227
Vega, Suzanne, 300
Warren, Rich, 56
Washington Squares, 300
Weavers, The, 26, 42, 55, 174, 269
Wein, George, 37, 53, 54
Weintraub, Fred, 73, 74
Weissberg, Dick, *221*
White, Josh, 23, 26, 44, 46, 74, 75, 265, 269, 278-279, 298, 304
White Jr., Josh, 125, 152, 153, *159,* 201, 202, *209,* 215, 216, 217, 218, 230, 240, 249, 262-263, *262,* 268, 284-285, 292-293, 298
Winters, Jonathan, 68
Yarbrough, Glenn, 36, 53, 76, 78, 201, 202, *210,* 242, 256-257, *256,* 278
Yarbrough, Holly, 209, 242, 249
Yarrow, Peter, 46, 53, 55, 56, 58, 129, 202, *210,* 214-215, 216, 218, 219, 267, 303-304, *303*

CAROLE BENDER is a writer and graphic artist based in Tulsa. As a folksinger while a student at Oklahoma State University in the early 1970's, her idols were Tom Paxton and Gordon Lightfoot, which eventually led to Bob Gibson and this book.

Printed in the United States
5308